TRI-S office

Access in London

Access in London

Essential for anyone who has difficulty getting around

Research and survey work carried out by
Pauline Hephaistos Survey Projects
with assistance from Artsline and Tripscope

written by
Gordon Couch, William Forrester and David McGaughey

BLOOMSBURY

The guide is based on survey work carried out in 2002 by members of the Pauline Hephaistos Survey Projects group. Over the years, the group has produced some twenty access guides, and this is the fourth edition of the London one.

The group of surveyors included a variety of people, some able-bodied, some wheelchair users and some disabled walkers. We come from several universities and colleges, from St Paul's School in London and from Lord Mayor Treloar College near Alton in Hampshire. A few of the group are 'post-student' age, and are working in a variety of jobs.

The name sounds a bit of a mouthful, but Pauline arises from St Paul, and some of us come from a Christian group attached to St Paul's School called the Pauline Meeting. The Hephaistos part of the name arises from the Greek god who was the smithy, and the equivalent of Vulcan in Roman mythology. He was a son of Zeus, who was foolish enough to defend his mother, Hera, during some major row. Zeus kicked Hephaistos off Mount Olympus and, after a long fall, he landed at the bottom and broke his leg. In frescoes he is shown with one leg facing one way, and the other turned through 90°. He has been adopted by some as the Greek god for disabled people, and gave his name to a school near Reading which a number of the group attended before its closure.

First published in 1996

This fourth edition published in 2003 by
Bloomsbury Publishing Plc
38 Soho Square
London W1D 3HB

www.bloomsbury.com

ISBN 0-7475-6933-9

Diagrams on pages 7, 86 and 88 by Graham Hiles
Other diagrams and maps by Helen Humphreys
Diagram on page 7 reproduced from *Designing for the Disabled* by Selwyn Goldsmith with the kind permission of the publishers RIBA Publications Ltd

Typeset by Hewer Text Ltd, Edinburgh
Printed and bound in Italy by Legoprint

Contents

List of useful addresses

Artsline
54 Chalton Street NW1 1HS
Tel/Textphone: 020 7388-2227, see page 15.

Centre for Accessible Environments (CAE)
Nutmeg House, 60 Gainsford Street SE1 2NY
Tel: 020 7357-8182, see page 16.

DaRT the **Accessible Transport Users Association**
Room 210, The Colourworks, 2 Abbot Street E8 3DP
Tel: 020 7241-2111.

DIAL (UK) National Association of Disablement Information and Advice Lines
For local centres, see page 16.

Forrester (William)
1 Belvedere Close, Guildford, Surrey GU2 6NP
Tel: 01483-575401, see page 18.

Greater London Action on Disability (GLAD)
336 Brixton Road SW9 7AA
Tel/Textphone: 020 7346-5800, see page 18.

Holiday Care
7th Floor, Sunley House, 4 Bedford Park, Croydon CR0 2AP
Tel: 0845-1249974, see page 19.

Pauline Hephaistos Survey Projects (PHSP)
39 Bradley Gardens, West Ealing W13 8HE
(the authors of this guide, also referred to as Access Project).

Royal Association for Disability and Rehabilitation (RADAR)
12 City Forum, 250 City Road EC1V 8AF
Tel: 020 7250-3222, see page 21.

Transport for London, Access and Mobility Unit
42-50 Victoria Street SW1H 0TL
Tel: 020 7222-1234 *Textphone:* 020 7918-3015, see page 23.

Tripscope
The Vassall Centre, Gill Avenue, Bristol BS16 2QQ
Tel/Textphone: 0845 758-5641, see page 24.

Wheelchair Travel
1 Johnston Green, Guildford, Surrey GU2 6XS
Tel: 01483-233640, see page 24.

Acknowledgements

This project has involved a large number of people, without whom the guide would never have been researched or written. The various activities have included:

- ensuring that the necessary financial basis was secure, for which we are particularly grateful to the trustees of the charitable trust, to past members and friends of the group who have contributed by gift aid and to various charitable trusts and companies who have sponsored or supported us;
- careful preparation and planning of what was to be visited and ensuring that the surveyors were well briefed about what to look for;
- undertaking the practical research, by visit;
- writing, proof reading, editing, preparing diagrams and symbols and the host of meticulous and time-consuming activities that are necessary in putting together the text of such a guide;
- publishing, distribution and publicity.

We would like to express our thanks to all of the following, in their different roles, some large, some small:

The surveyors who did the foot- and wheelwork in London and who contributed to various phases of the project:
Alex Armitage, Silke Bernhart, Jane Blacklock, Stephen Bovey, Hannah Brown, Charlie Cahill, Gordon Couch, Mark Crouch, Frances Denniss, Matthew Evans, William Forrester, Alex Frith, Shivani Gupta, Jonny Hall, Ellie Hawkins, Sam Hole, David McGaughey, Charlie Malston, Craig Newport, James Osborne, Rachel Pagnamenta, Emily Powell, James Ross, Vikas Sharma, Annika Stennert, James Thomas, Nick Tjaardstra, Zelah Vincent, Peter Wellby, Nick Windsor.

Those who commented on our draft text, such as John Olver at Tripscope, Ian Seabrook at the TfL Access and Mobility unit, and Peter Presland-Jones at DaRT. There are several members of the group who have spent hours and hours in proofing and commenting, especially Craig Newport, James Osborne, Alex Frith, James Ross and Emily Powell.

Past members and friends of the group who have contributed with donations and covenants and who gave us the confidence to commit ourselves to the project:
Roger Ayers, Dave Allport, Tim Atkinson, Dave Aubrey, James Clay, Ian and Rachel Copeland, Gordon Couch, Raymond Couch, Richard Donaldson, Alex Gordon-Brander, Harry Gostelow, Paul Haines, Alan Kerr, Tom Kiggell, Mayo and Thalia Marriott, Richard Marshall, Geoff Matthews, Emily Powell, Adrian Rates, Ben Roberts, Rob Stanier, Roger Stone, David Wallace, Nick Windsor, Mark Worledge.

The trustees of the charitable trust which finances the activities:
Dave Aubrey, Isabel Baggott, Gordon Couch and Mukesh Patel; and Peter Stevenson, who inspects and certifies our accounts.

Our sponsors, who provided essential supplementary finance:
The AB Charitable Trust
KMPG

We would also like to thank:
Ealing Community Transport for supplying two accessible minibuses to help with the survey work; and Bloomsbury Publishing for agreeing to publish the guide which will ensure that it is widely available through conventional bookshops as well as through disability organisations and the 'disability network'.

Abbreviations

ALG	Association of London Government
BB	blue badge for parking concessions. A Europe-wide scheme. Widened here in the guide to include any reserved parking for disabled people
BO	box office
NR	National Rail
CP	car park
D	door width (cm)
D, ST	the door width and side transfer distance in adapted loos, in cm
D,W,L	the door width, cabin width, and length of a lift, in cm
DAR	Dial-a-Ride
DaRT	Accessible Transport Users Association
DDA	Disability Discrimination Act
DisEnq	number for enquiries by disabled people
DLF	Disabled Living Foundation
DLR	Docklands Light Railway
ETC	English Tourist Council
Ext	extension
FC	Football Club
GF	ground floor
GFB	ground floor bedroom
GLA	Greater London Assembly
GLAD	The Greater London Action on Disability
H	height
HC	Holiday Care
HR	handrail
JLE	Jubilee Line Extension
L	length (cm)
LGF	lower ground floor
LTB	London Tourist Board
M	management or administration telephone number
M25	the orbital motorway going right round Greater London
Middx	Middlesex
MSCP	multi-storey car park
NCP	National Car Parks
NKS	RADAR National Key Scheme
NR	National Rail
OB	orange badge for parking concessions, now replaced by the blue badge (from April 2003)
PHSP	Pauline Hephaistos Survey Projects
RADAR	Royal Association for Disability and Rehabilitation

RecM   recorded message
RNIB   Royal National Institute for Blind People
RNID   Royal National Institute for Deaf People
SOLT   Society of London Theatre
ST   side transfer space (cm)
TfL   Transport for London
UGCP   underground car park
W   width (cm)
YHA   Youth Hostels Association
YMCA   Young Men's Christian Association
YWCA   Young Women's Christian Association

16thC, 19thC etc are used for 16th century, 19th century etc.

The other guides in the PHSP series are:

Access in Paris
Access in Israel
and the Palestinian Authority
Access to Football Grounds

These are available from:

39 Bradley Gardens
West Ealing
London W13 8HE, UK

www.accessproject-phsp.org

Introduction

This book sets out to give detailed information about travel, accommodation, leisure activities and tourist attractions for people with mobility problems. It contains a unique guide to London's accessible pubs that have a **wheelchair toilet**, and as always, we have included our '*good loo guide*'. Those who will find the guide useful include people who use a wheelchair, elderly persons, those who use a stick or crutches, and those with young children in buggies. They include London residents, day trippers, people visiting relatives in London, and, of course, visitors and tourists. We have included information where possible for people who are hearing or visually impaired. Some will be in need of the guide for only a short time if they are recovering from an accident.

The preparation, research, fundraising and organisation necessary to publish this book was carried out by the members of PHSP (Pauline Hephaistos Survey Projects), working in cooperation with Artsline and Tripscope. The information is firmly based on the experiences of disabled people, and virtually every entry has been wheeled into or walked into, and measured, by our survey teams. Most of the information gathering was carried out during 2002.

GLAD (Greater London Action on Disability) have estimated that there are tens of thousands of chair users in London, and over 400,000 people with disabilities. In addition, many disabled people come to London as visitors, and this is a guide for everyone. There are many other people for whom the step-free access described in this guide is useful, including families with children in buggies.

We assume that this book will be used in conjunction with other guides and information. In particular we recommend the *Eyewitness Travel Guide to London* published by Dorling Kindersley. This contains an area by area account and uses illustrations and cutaways which often clarify access. In addition a good street plan is essential, and if you're driving into central London, we recommend the *Blue Badge User Guide*. We appreciate the expense involved in buying other books and maps, but there's really no way round it. Some information can be found now on the internet, but its quality is variable, and it doesn't replace that which is available in guidebooks and maps.

In the guide, we have tried to be objective by describing what the barriers are, where they are, and how (if possible) to get around them.

This approach allows you to make up your own mind as to whether or not a visit is practicable, or on how much help you might need. We have included many places where a real effort has been made to overcome barriers. Do bear in mind, however, that inclusion in the guide doesn't imply accessibility, and what we're doing is to describe the places listed.

PHSP is a small voluntary Christian-based group which aims to educate its own members about what is possible, as well as to collect information. Some of our members get round on legs, some get round on wheels and others have crutches. We try to ensure that the people we meet when surveying understand the need for uncomplicated access to places for EVERYONE. **In particular, making special arrangements, like having to ask for separate entrances to be opened, asking for the key to the toilet, or having to ring first before coming, are much more of a pain than most people realise.**

The use of access guides can enable people with disabilities to affect the process of increasing awareness and bringing about change, simply by being there as part of the public. We have found that attitudes (and facilities) in London have changed quite dramatically since the earlier editions of the guide, and generally for the better. While there is a long way to go, particularly in connection with the vexed question of accessible transport, people seemed much more aware of disability issues and of people's rights to access than they were only a few years ago. The implementation of the Disability Discrimination Act (DDA) in 2004, and the preparation for meeting its requirements will encourage change.

Why travel?

If you already have travelitis (the travel bug), then you will know why so many people do it. However, if you're unsure about it, then perhaps we can encourage you by sharing our experiences. Since the 1970s, when some of our group first wanted to travel, we have been to various parts of France, to Jersey, Norway, Germany and Israel, normally writing guides as we went. Because the group consists of both disabled and able-bodied people, we ran into barriers and problems that would normally have been divisive. In practice, we tackled problems together, and found that, given the right information, and with a bit of determination, most things were possible. We gathered this information together on a systematic basis, and have made it available via these Access guides.

Our experiences have been fun, we've learned a lot, and done things that in the normal course of events we'd never have even thought of doing. We do think that 'travel broadens the mind', and in particular it has brought us into contact with many, many people. The majority have been interesting, interested and helpful, though occasionally we have met people with attitudes that were more obstructive than a spiral staircase!

Overall it has brought a series of memorable experiences. Each member of the group will have a different tale to tell. We have encountered new cultures, and seen some amazing sights. Even though there may have been a few problems and difficulties, they've been worth it.

If you are still not convinced, we recommend *Nothing Ventured* by Alison Walsh, published by Harup Columbus, London. This includes the stories of several people with disabilities going to all kinds of exotic places, as well as destinations in Britain and in Europe. Even though it is now out of print, you should be able to borrow one from your local library.

Why London?

There is an enormous amount to do, see and discover in London. The West End is up with Broadway in offering a variety of high class entertainment, and there are museums and restaurants which match those you'll find anywhere else. There are pageants, street markets, galleries and night clubs. Although accessibility varies, there are enough historical buildings, art galleries and museums with good access to fill any itinerary. You will find that there is a healthy mix of cultures and races, partly arising from emigration from countries of the old Empire, and partly from the importance of the city as a business centre. You will also find that things become somewhat frantic during the morning and evening 'rush hour' when people are getting to and from work on weekdays.

A brief history

There is no evidence that the ancient Britons settled on the site of what is now London. The Iron-Age inhabitants arrived in the southeast of England around 500 BC, and one of their settlement areas was in what is now Heathrow Airport. *Londinium* grew after the Roman invasion in 43 AD. After Roman rule, the Dark Ages saw London controlled by Saxon invaders, who were often in dispute with the Vikings for control of the country. This was until 1066 when William the Conqueror took over, changing Saxon England into Norman England.

London grew in both population and prestige, becoming England's most important city. The oldest parts of the Tower of London date from the late 11thC. There was a large palace and abbey at Westminster, where Chaucer and many other famous people are buried. Tudor London saw the reign of Henry VIII, which is best discovered at Hampton Court where he lived. The population increased rapidly. During the Stuart period the bubonic plague hit the city, reaching its peak in 1665 with the Great Plague. London then took another purging, with the Great Fire in 1666. This is said to have been started accidentally by a baker in Pudding Lane, and the site is commemorated by a huge Doric column, known as the Monument. As part of the reconstruction, St Paul's Cathedral and many other famous churches were built.

The effects of the industrial revolution can be seen clearly. There are old power stations in central London. There was extensive development, including the Docklands, towards the east and this area is now being rapidly redeveloped. Throughout the Georgian, Regency and Victorian eras, London grew enormously. There was a mixture of elegant housing for the wealthy, much of which remains, and of rat-infested tenements for the poor (well described by Dickens in his many novels). This reflected the success of both traders and industrialists and the human cost of that success. The less attractive parts have been, or are being, extensively rebuilt and redeveloped. The architecture of the times can be seen in many of the remaining buildings, with extensive Victorian development in outer suburban areas.

London became the capital of the British Empire, the world's largest city, and the world centre for banking and trade. Since then its relative importance has declined, but it remains one of the great capitals of the world. *We hope that you have an enjoyable visit, and that the information in this guide will be helpful.*

How the guide is arranged

The guide starts with general information, and a chapter on getting around which provides the basis for visiting. There are chapters on accommodation, on the sights and on entertainment. Where appropriate, we have grouped the write-ups into geographical areas. In particular, we have differentiated between places inside the North and South Circular roads, and those outside but within the M25. The M25 is the orbital motorway going right round Greater London with a radius of about 25 to 30km. The North and South Circular roads form an inner ring with a radius of very roughly 10km. There's a bigger area north of the river than there is to the south. The split is shown on the diagram which includes an indication of where central

London is, marked as the West End and the City. It also shows which out-of-town shopping centres we have described.

The write-ups on places of interest are grouped into geographical areas. Within sub-sections, write-ups are normally presented in alphabetical order.

We include information about watching sport, about shopping, and on places for a day out, a few of which are outside the M25 ring.

Ring Roads

also showing the Thames, Lee Valley
and out of town *Shopmobility* sites

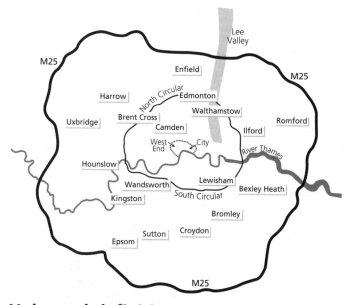

Units and definitions

We have given measurements in centimetres (cm), and metres (m). Although these are the units increasingly being used internationally, many British people still think in Imperial measures. To convert metric measurements to the more familiar Imperial units, use the following guidelines:

10 centimetres is about 4 inches (2.5 centimetres = 1 inch)
1 metre is about a yard
1 litre is about 2 pints
1 kilo is about 2 pounds

The diagram on the facing page gives the approximate dimensions of a standard wheelchair. Chairs vary considerably in size, so it's worth checking the exact dimensions of yours to relate to the measurements given in the guide. With powered chairs, it's also worth checking its weight as well as adding your own weight, as some platform stairlifts have weight and size restrictions.

Steps are listed by number, with $+$ indicating steps up and $-$ indicating down. Occasionally we list them as $\pm$, in that it depends on which direction you are coming from.

Movable chairs and tables

In cafés, restaurants and pubs we have not said each time that the chairs and tables are movable. It is assumed that they are movable, and therefore more convenient for chair users and for others. **Where they are not movable, or if the seats and tables are high up or might cause a problem, we have said so.**

Toilets

Our definition of a **wheelchair toilet** is one where the toilet is unisex; the door opens outward; the door width (D) is greater than 70cm and the side transfer (ST) space is greater than 70cm. If the toilet does not quite meet these criteria, but is adapted for a chair user, then we call it an **adapted toilet**, and we give the appropriate measurements and information. Where the cubicle is INSIDE the Ladies or Gents toilet area, we describe them as being **wheelchair** or **adapted cubicles**. Unless specified, the toilet seat is at the standard height of about 45cm. We are aware of the need for the provision of a higher pan for those with arthritis. As toilets with higher pans are not yet widespread, we have not made a separate category, but for information and specifications, see *Designing to Enable,* described on page 31.

We have described the roadside disabled person's toilets, which bear a certain resemblance to the telephone box used by Dr Who, as 'Tardis' toilets. These can be opened using a RADAR key and are available 24 hours a day.

Lifts

A **lift** is in a lift shaft, with doors, and a cabin which can be large or small. It goes up and down between the floors of a building.

An **open lift** is a small rectangular vertical lift, usually to take one

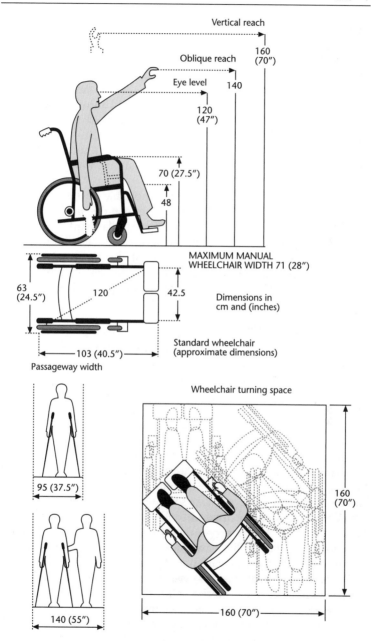

Vertical reach

160
(70")

Oblique reach

Eye level   140

120
(47")

70 (27.5")

48

MAXIMUM MANUAL
WHEELCHAIR WIDTH 71 (28")

63
(24.5")   120   42.5   Dimensions in
cm and (inches)

103 (40.5")   Standard wheelchair
(approximate dimensions)

Passageway width

Wheelchair turning space

95 (37.5")

160
(70")

140 (55")   160 (70")

Design considerations

chair user at a time and bypassing just a few steps – often added in a building as an afterthought.

A **platform stairlift** goes up stairs (attached to the wall) and has a platform which can take a wheelchair, and occupant.

A **'seated' stairlift** goes up the stairs (attached to the wall) and has a seat into which the passenger has to transfer. This is very useful for many disabled walkers, but for a wheelchair user, their chair has to be carried up or down the stairs by someone else.

For lift measurements, we quote: door width (D), cabin width (W) and cabin length (L). On this basis, you can decide whether the lift is large enough for you to use.

A **stairclimber** is a free-standing and portable device to which a wheelchair may be attached. The most common one used is a **Scala-mobile**, but there are also some with long caterpillar (tank-like) tracks. These devices usually need two people to operate them, but they can enable a chair user to be helped up or down stairs. We would comment that the only versions we've come across are not very comfortable to use, and that only a few people are willing to operate them.

Disability terms

Throughout the book we have used positive language about disability, and tried to take a positive attitude to obstacles. The barriers are there to be overcome, not simply accepted, and for a long time we have been part of the movement involved in breaking down barriers. Members of our group have a variety of disabilities and as a result, are handicapped by the world around them.

We talk about disabled people and not 'the disabled'. When people refer to a 'disabled toilet' they imply that the cistern doesn't work, and not that it is big enough for a chair user. We would encourage the use of the descriptor 'accessible toilet' in the future, although replacing the well-accepted 'disabled toilet' will take some time. We have used the terms **wheelchair toilet**, or **adapted cubicle**, with some specific criteria attached to the description. Amazingly (we think) we found places where parking, entrances and other facilities are still described as being for 'invalids'. Emphatically, we do not regard ourselves as being invalid or ill.

The use of language changes, and there is, of course, a danger in worrying too much about precise political correctness. Nonetheless a sensible use of language can help to change attitudes, and to increase understanding, especially if it causes people to ask, 'Why did you say it that way?' RADAR issue a briefing on the use of disability terms, and will send a copy if asked.

General information

Climate

Visitors must take into account the generally mild but unpredictable weather. There are hot spells in the summer and cold periods in the winter but the forecast of 'sunshine and showers' is all too common. When packing, you should allow for chilly winds in the winter (and even the possibility of snow and ice). It may rain at any time, but there are often good spells of several weeks when it will be dry and sunny. If you come in the summer, remember that relatively few buildings have air conditioning. The temperature can vary from 32°C/90°F right down to −11°C/10°F. Places to go if it's really wet or cold include the big museums, the Barbican and South Bank areas, or some of the very big shops or covered shopping areas. Covent Garden is a possibility, with both shelter and street entertainment. If it's fine, the parks and riverside are particularly attractive.

Electrical supply

Note that if you are travelling from the USA, and possibly from some other parts of the world, your electrical equipment (battery chargers, for example) may not work in the UK. This is because the supply is at 240 volts and 50 cycles, whereas the American supply is at 110 volts and 60 cycles, and not all equipment will operate on both systems. Make sure that you check on where to get hold of equipment that works before setting off.

Emergencies

In the event of accident or emergency, the standard procedure is to telephone the Police, Fire or Ambulance Service by dialling **999**. That way you'll get the right help or advice. The first person you'll speak to is the operator who will ask, *'Which service do you require?'* When you then get through, you can explain what is needed.

Normally both doctors and dentists are available only during working hours. If you need to collect a prescription, your nearest police station keeps a list of local pharmacies and their opening times. Two chemists open late are:

Bliss 54 Willesden Lane NW6 *Tel:* 020 7624-8000 *Open 09.00-22.00 Mon-Sun.*
Boots Piccadilly Circus W1 *Tel:* 020 7734-6126 *Open 08.30-20.00 Mon-Sat, 12.00-18.00 Sun.*

The Medic Alert Foundation, 12 Bridge Wharf, 156 Caledonian Road N1 9UU
Tel: 020 7833-3034 *Fax:* 020 7278-0647
website: www.medicalert.org.uk *e-mail:* info@medicalert.org.uk
Medic Alert provides a useful service for those with medical problems that could be compounded by treatment after an accident. It is of special importance to those who have epilepsy, haemophilia, diabetes or allergies, and to those who need regular doses of a particular drug. Life membership is available for a nominal fee. Members wear a metal emblem engraved with the telephone number of the Emergency Service and a note of the immediate medical problems of the wearer. Additional medical information is filed at the Emergency Headquarters, where the telephone is staffed 24 hours a day.

SOS Talisman Co, 21 Gray's Corner, Ley Street, Ilford, Essex IG2 7RQ
Tel: 020 8554-5579 *Fax:* 020 8554-1090
Talisman operate a similar service to Medic Alert, which works on the basis of including information in a small locket which is worn permanently.

Maps and guides

The street plans of London come in a huge variety of sizes. Some cover the whole of greater London, almost out to the M25, others cover just the central areas. They come in ring bindings, in soft covers, and in hardback. There are four principal publishers: the AA for Street-by-Street guides, Collins, Ordnance Survey and Geographers (for the AtoZ series). They're all good, and much depends on your choice of style. You can get a good ring-bound, large-scale street plan for central London and the Docklands area for less than £5, and the one we recommend is the one published by Collins. It is called the *Superscale London Atlas*.

Website sources which can be helpful in locating places include:

www.multimap.com;
www.streetmap.co.uk;
www.upyourstreet.com.

These can all provide you with a local map based on a postcode or, possibly, on a street name together with the area name.

There are numerous listings about what is happening in London, including pamphlets from the LTB and other tourist offices. The *Evening Standard*, which is London's evening paper, has listings, as do some of the national dailies. It has a searchable website, www.thisislondon.com. On Thursday, the *Evening Standard* includes a magazine called *MetroLife*. The most extensive listing of events is in *Time Out* which comes out weekly. This tells you about theatres, restaurants, sporting, musical and special events, and exhibitions. If you want to get a copy before you leave, their website is: www.timeout.com, *e-mail*: net@timeout.co.uk or *Tel:* 020 7813-6060.

Note also *The Big Issue*, which is a weekly magazine which provides both an income and hope to some of London's homeless people. It includes interesting articles on London issues, and information about what's going on.

There are literally dozens of guidebooks to London, all with slightly different angles and presentation. A listing here does not imply that their advice for disabled visitors or residents is particularly good and that's why you need *Access in London*!

When choosing a guide, check the date of publication, as things change, particularly prices and opening times. There are many specialist guides to particular aspects of London and its history and life. Where relevant, we have detailed these in each chapter.

For general guides to interesting and historic places, we recommend the *Eyewitness Guide to London* published by Dorling Kindersley. It includes good area maps and building cutaways which are relevant to access. The other one with particularly good building cutaways is the Michelin *Green Guide*. Other guides that we have found useful include: the Lonely Planet *London*, *The Rough Guide to London* and *Time Out London*. Fodor's *London Companion* gives a comprehensive and readable background to many interesting places and events.

In addition to those already mentioned, there are:

- the *Blue Guide to London*;
- the *Everyman Guide to London*;
- the London Transport *Capital Guide*;
- the *AA Essential Explorer Guide to London*;
- Fodor's *London*;
- Frommer's *London*;
- the *Insight Guide to London*;

- *Let's Go, London*;
- the *London Handbook*, a new guide from the Footprint collection, first published in 2001;
- Thomas Cook's *Travellers' London*;
- the *Unofficial Guide to London*;
- the *Virgin Guide to London*.

If you are on a tight budget, *London for Free,* published by Harden's Guides, gives hundreds of ideas for activities and visits for which there is no charge. If you are looking for something to do with the children, try *Days Out With Kids* from Two Heads Publishing, or *Take the Kids, London*, published by Cadogan Guides.

Big books that include a great deal of background information or look at the city from a different angle, include *The London Encyclopaedia* edited by Ben Weinreb and Christopher Hibbert and published by Macmillan; *London The Biography* by Peter Ackroyd and published by Vintage; *Terence Conran on London*, which has some superb illustrations and is published by Conran Octopus; and finally *London from the Air* by Jason Hawkes and published by Ebury Press.

Telephones

The code for London is 020 with phone numberss in the inner area being followed by a 7 and those further out by an 8. The inner area covers central London and Docklands numbers while the outer area covers most subscribers more than 4 miles from Charing Cross. You need an eight-digit number when dialling between the zones. If in doubt consult a phone book. Outside London, different codes apply. If in doubt, ask the operator for advice (dial 100). For emergency services dial 999.

For directory enquiries use 192 for UK numbers (valid until August 2003) or 153 for international numbers. Note that this operation is currently being opened up to competition, so new services are being provided, with different charges applying. The search for numbers can be carried out online, and two sites are www.bt.com/directory-enquiries and www.192directory.co.uk. One of the new numbers for directory enquiries is *Tel:* 118118.

If you are ringing the UK from abroad, there will be a local code, probably 00, followed by 44 for the UK, and this REPLACES the first 0 in the London code, so to dial 020 7785-6399 from abroad, you would dial 00-44-20-7785-6399.

Unfortunately, an increasing number of organisations are using automated reply systems on their phones, so it becomes increasingly difficult to actually speak to a person. Additionally, many queries are dealt with in call centres, which can be hundreds of km away from London, so the person answering may have no local knowledge.

The use of the phone has changed dramatically during the past five or ten years, with spectacular growth in the use of mobile phones. If you know the right number, using a mobile can enable you to call for assistance when directly outside a building, and it can enable you to ring for a cab.

For people who only want a mobile phone for a short period, rental is an option, which should be compared with buying a pay-as-you-go one. It very much depends on what you want it for, and how much you are prepared to spend. One advantage is that you can call ahead quite easily, and you can even call from outside a building saying that you need some assistance.

If the phone is just for emergencies, and to make a small number of brief calls, hiring need not cost an arm and a leg. One company offering phones for hire is **Adam Phones** at www.adamphones.com *Tel:* 0800 123-000 from within the UK. Hire conditions involve a £200 deposit, and a £7 fee for both delivery and collection of the phone. Call charges are 40p/minute for most of the day. If you spend an average of £5/day, there is no daily rental charge, and if you spend less than this, the rental charge is a flat rate £1/day. Adam Phones offer the alternative of simply hiring a SIM card to insert in your own phone, if it is compatible with GSM 900MHz networks.

For temporary use, the hire option should be compared with the use of a pay-as-you-go phone, especially as you might be able to sell this on to someone else when you have finished with it. There will be an upfront phone purchase fee of something like £70 to £80, and you probably need to purchase some air time, so the total will be in the £80-100 range, depending on what offers are around at the time. Daytime call charges will be quite high, but you will be easily contactable at no charge, and sending text messages is relatively cheap. There are numerous suppliers, and one of the big ones is the Carphone Warehouse at www.carphonewarehouse.com, *Tel:* 0808 100-9250.

Useful organisations and contact points

There are many sources of information and who you go to depends on what you want to know. If you need advice or help, you often have to be persistent and try different contacts if your first or second enquiry does not produce a satisfactory answer. We list here some general sources and the major organisations of and for disabled people. Remember that much depends on whom you speak to. They may be new in the organisation; they may be in a hurry to do something else. On the other hand, you'll often come across people who will go to a great deal of trouble to help.

Many organisations use multiple-choice questioning when you ring up. Often are held in a queue with no indication of how far back you are. There is also much greater use of voicemail – which doesn't always produce a response. The only advice we can give is that if the query is important, be persistent, and/or try some other way of getting an answer.

Note that more and more organisations post information posted on their websites. Some of these sites are comprehensive and easy to use. Others, inevitably, are less user-friendly. If you're looking for more contact points or information, most sites have a links page, and you may find somewhere else that has what you need.

If a telephone number or address listed here has changed, you will almost certainly be able to get the new one from one of the other agencies listed, or via directory enquiries.

Action for Blind People, 14 Verney Road SE16 3DZ
Tel: 020 7635-4800 *Fax:* 020 7635-4900
website: www.afbp.org *e-mail:* central@afbp.org
Offers information and advice. Publications include a regular newsletter, and *Ability not Disability* which is a detailed brochure describing their services.

Age Concern, Astral House, 1268 London Road, Norbury SW16 4ER
Tel: 020 8679-8000 *Fax:* 020 8765-7211
website: www.ace.org.uk *e-mail:* ace@ace.org.uk
Age Concern is the focal point for all voluntary groups concerned with information and services for older people. **Extensive information and advice service.**

Artsline, 54 Chalton Street NW1 1HS
Tel/Textphone: 020 7388-2227 *Fax:* 020 7383-2653
website: www.artsline.co.uk *e-mail:* artsline@dircom.co.uk
Artsline provide an up-to-date telephone information and advice service about all aspects of access to arts and entertainment activities. **They have a great deal of experience and knowledge of what is possible and practicable, and an extensive and well-researched database about access to theatres, cinemas, music venues, galleries and museums.** Apart from suggestions about where to go, they may be able to tell you something about the attitudes of management. They can advise about which events are free. **Artsline are concerned to promote participation in the arts by disabled people as well as informing about the possibilities of spectating.** The telephone service currently operates Mon to Fri from 09.30 to 17.30. They are involved in the publication of a monthly magazine DAIL *(Disability Arts in London)* which has up-to-the minute listings and reviews.

British Council of Organisations of Disabled People (BCODP), Litchurch Plaza, Litchurch Lane, Derby DE24 8AA
Tel: 01332-295551 *Fax:* 01332-295580 *Textphone:* 01332-295581
website: www.bcodp.org.uk *e-mail:* bcodp@bcodp.org.uk
The BCODP is an umbrella organisation working to ensure that disabled people have the major say in policy issues and decisions which affect them.

British Tourist Authority (BTA), Thames Tower, Blacks Road, Hammersmith W6 9EL *Tel:* 020 8846-9000 (administrative offices only)
The BTA operates the **British Visitor Centre**, 1 Lower Regent Street SW1Y 4XT with mainly step-free access. It provides a wide range of information and services of a general nature about travelling in and through Britain. Only limited information for disabled visitors is available.

Can Be Done, 7 Kensington High Street W8 5NP
Tel: 020 8907-2400 *Fax:* 020 8909-1854
website: www.canbedone.co.uk *e-mail:* cbdtravel@aol.com
Can be Done is a small tour operator that organises tailor-made holidays and tours in London and elsewhere in the UK, for both groups and individuals. All are 'accessible'. Its director, Jackie Scott, is herself a chair user, and aware of the travel requirements of disabled people.

Centre for Accessible Environments (CAE), Nutmeg House, 60 Gainsford Street SE1 2NY
Tel: 020 7357-8182 *Fax:* 020 7357-8183
website: www.cae.org.uk *e-mail:* info@cae.org.uk
The CAE aims to improve access to buildings and the environment generally, working with and through architects and others. It offers information and training on the accessibility of the built environment for disabled people. It has a useful range of publications including design sheets and reading lists. Expert information can be provided on all technical and design issues relating to access provision. CAE promotes an excellent series of seminars on a wide range of topics, training workshops and an access audit service.

DIAL (UK) (National Association of Disablement Information and Advice Lines), St Catherine's, Tickhill Road, Balby, Doncaster DN4 8QN
Tel: 01302-310123 *Fax:* 01302-310404 *e-mail:* DialUK@aol.com
DIAL coordinates local groups offering free advice and information on all aspects of disability. Each centre is run by a group of local people with direct experience. The groups operating in the London area are:

- **Barking and Dagenham DIAL**, St George's Day Centre, St George's Road, Dagenham, Essex RM9 5JB *Tel:* 020 8595-8181;
- **Hackney DIAL**, 16 Dalston Lane, Hackney E8 3AZ *Tel:* 020 8275-8485;
- **Islington ARCH**, 90 Upper Street, Islington N1 0NP *Tel:* 020 7226-0137;
- **Lewisham Association of People with Disabilities**, 67 Engleheart Road; Catford SE6 2HN *Tel:* 020 8698-3775;
- **Richmond RAID**, The Avenue Day Centre, Fortescue House, Stanley Road, Twickenham TW2 5PZ *Tel:* 020 8898-4225;
- **Romford and Havering DIAL**, 1 Angel Way, Romford RM1 1JH *Tel:* 01708-730226
- **Waltham Forest DIAL**, 1a Warner Road, Walthamstow E17 7DY *Tel:* 020 8520-4111;
- **Wandsworth DIAL**, Atheldene Centre, 305 Garratt Lane, Wandsworth SW18 4DU *Tel:* 020 8870-7437.

Disability Alliance (DA), Universal House, 88 Wentworth Street E1 7SA
Tel: 020 7247-8776 *(11.00-15.00) Fax:* 020 7247-8765
website: www.disabilityalliance.org

The DA consists of many of the major voluntary groups and produces *The Disability Rights Handbook*. This is updated every year, and outlines the various benefits to which disabled people are entitled in straightforward language. This handbook also contains a comprehensive list of the organisations of and for disabled people. Telephone advice is given but the office is not open for personal callers. The *Rights Advice Line* is *Tel:* 020 7247-8763, currently open Mon and Wed 14.00-16.00. For advice at other times, you can try the DSS's Benefits Enquiry Line on 0800-882200.

Disabled Drivers Association (DDA), National HQ Ashwellthorpe, Norwich NR16 1EX
Tel: 01508-489449 *Fax:* 01508-488173
website: www.dda.org.uk *e-mail:* ddahq@aol.com
The DDA aims to encourage and help disabled people to achieve greater mobility. It has branches all over the country. They publish a quarterly journal *The Magic Carpet*.

Disabled Drivers Motor Club (DDMC), Cottingham Way, Thrapston, Northants NN14 4PL *Tel:* 01832-734724 *Fax:* 01832-733816
website: www.webdot.ukonline.co.uk.ddmc
The DDMC also aims to encourage and help disabled people to achieve greater mobility. Information is available from the office, and via a bi-monthly journal *The Disabled Driver*.

Disabled Living Foundation (DLF), 380 Harrow Road W9 2HU
Tel: 020 7289-6111 *Textphone:* 020 7432-8009 *Fax:* 020 7266-2922
website: www.dlf.org.uk *e-mail:* dlfinfo@dlf.org.uk
The DLF works to help disabled people in aspects of ordinary life which present difficulty. It has a large showroom and has a comprehensive information service on specialised equipment of all kinds. Advice is given on visual impairment, incontinence, music, sport, clothing and skincare. A publication list is available on application. *An appointment is necessary as you usually get shown round by an expert.* Their showroom is completely accessible and has **a wheelchair toilet**. Parking is possible if you book. The display includes a special kitchen for visually impaired people. Their website is useful, and they have an excellent list of factsheets.

Disabled Persons Transport Advisory Committee (DPTAC), Zone 1/14, Great Minster House, 76 Marsham Street SW1P 4DR
Tel: 020 7944-8011 *Textphone:* 020 7944-3277 *Fax:* 020 7944-6998
website: www.dptac.gov.uk *e-mail:* dptac@dft.gsi.gov.uk

DPTAC was set up as an independent body to advise government on the transport needs of disabled people throughout the UK. It produces a wide range of reports and advice, and consults extensively with the aim of advising government about appropriate policies to meet people's needs. Because of its wide brief, it can also be a useful source of information.

Disablement Income Group (DIG), POB 5743, Sinchingfield CM7 4PW
Tel: 01371-811621
DIG promotes the financial welfare of disabled people through a programme of advice, advocacy, research, information and training. It publishes *The Journal* quarterly.

Forrester (William), 1 Belvedere Close, Guildford, Surrey GU2 6NP
Tel: 01483-575401
William is a London Registered Guide, and a round-Britain tour escort. He is a chair user himself, and has extensive experience of organising and leading trips and visits, both for disabled individuals and groups. For London visitors, he offers a tailor-made day tour, travelling together by accessible taxi. Specialist tours are available of Westminster Abbey, the British Museum and Houses of Parliament, and an itinerary planning service is offered. Early booking is necessary.

Greater London Action on Disability (GLAD), 336 Brixton Road SW9 7AA
Tel: 020 7346-5800 *Fax:* 020 7346-8844 *Textphone:* 020 7326-4554
Information line: 020 7346-5819
website: www.glad.org.uk *e-mail:* info@glad.org.uk
GLAD provides advice and information to disabled residents, and helps organisations of disabled Londoners to work more effectively. It campaigns for full civil rights legislation for disabled people and represents the interests of disabled people when decisions are being made. It produces a number of useful publications, including a *Directory of Greater London Borough Disability Organisations*, a regular newsletter *London Disability News* together with *Boadicea* which is primarily for disabled women. It has recently published an *Accessible Tourist Attractions Factsheet* on its website, which includes much useful information supplementing some of that which we include in our guide, but which in common with most 'access' literature, does not address the question of the distances involved.

Hearing Concern, 7/11, Armstrong Road, Acton, London W3 7JL
Tel: 020 8743-1110 *Textphone:* 020 8742-9151 *Fax:* 020 8742-9043
National helpline: 0845-0744600
website: www.hearing.concern.org.uk
e-mail: hearing.concern@ukonline.co.uk
Everyone with a degree of hearing loss is at a disadvantage. It's a
disability which attracts little attention but can be difficult and
embarrassing. Hearing Concern is a leading provider of advice
and support for deaf and hard-of-hearing people.

Holiday Care, 7th Floor, Sunley House, 4 Bedford Park, Croydon
CR0 2AP, Surrey RH6 7PZ
Tel: 0845-1249973 (information); 0845-1249974 (administration);
Textphone: 0845-1249976 *Fax:* 0845-1249972
website: www.holidaycare.org.uk *e-mail:* holiday.care@virgin.net
The UK's central source of travel and holiday information for
disabled or disadvantaged people, Holiday Care produces the *Holiday Care Guide to Accessible Accommodation* which gives details of
accessible facilities and attractions across the UK and an information sheet on *Accessible Accommodation in London* inspected against
the National Accessible Standard. They have been instrumental in
improving some of the attitudes concerning disability and disabled
travellers within the tourist industry.

London Tourist Board (LTB), 6th Floor, Glen House, Stag Place
SW1W 5AG (address for administrative purposes only).
Tel: 020 7932-2000 *Fax:* 020 7932-0222
website: www.londontouristboard.com
LTB and borough tourist office desks are the main source of tourist
information in London. They can tell you whether places will be
open and give information about costs and concessions. The amount
of specialised information they have for disabled visitors is extremely
limited, and the most likely thing to happen is that you will be offered
a copy of *Access in London*!

In inner London there are *Tourist Information Centres* as follows:

Britain Visitor Centre, 1 Regent Street, Piccadilly Circus, SW1Y
4XT.
Open: Mon 09.30-18.30, Tue-Fri 09.00-18.30, Sat and Sun 10.00-
16.00; Jun-Oct, Sat 09.00-17.00.

London Visitor Centre, Arrivals Hall, Waterloo International Terminal, SE1 7LT.
Open: Daily 08.30-22.30.

Outer London *Tourist Information Centres* are at:

- **Bexley Hall Place**, Bourne Road, Bexley, Kent, DA5 1PQ. *Tel:* 01322-558676 *Fax*: 01322-522921.
  Open: Mon-Sat 10.00-16.30, Sun 14.00-17.30.
- **Croydon**, Katharine Street, Croydon, CR9 1ET. *Tel:* 020 8253-1009 *Fax:* 020 8253-1008.
  Open: Mon, Tues, Wed and Fri 09.00-18.00, Thu 09.30-18.00, Sat 09.00-17.00, Sun 14.00-17.00.
- **Greenwich**, Pepys House, 2 Cutty Sark Gardens, Greenwich SE10 9LW. *Tel:* 0870 608-2000 *Fax:* 020 8853-4607.
  Open: Daily 10.00-17.00.
- **Harrow**, Civic Centre, Station Road, Harrow, HA1 2XF. *Tel:* 020 8424-1103 *Fax:* 020 8424-1134
  Open: Mon-Fri 09.00-17.00, Sat and Sun closed.
- **Hillingdon**, Central Library, 14-15 High Street, Uxbridge, UB8 1HD. *Tel:* 01895-250706 *Fax:* 01895-239794.
  Open: Mon, Tue and Thur 09.30-20.00, Wed 09.30-17.30, Fri 10.00-17.30, Sat 09.30-16.00, Sun closed.
- **Hounslow**, The Treaty Centre, High Street, Hounslow, TW3 1ES. *Tel:* 0845 456-2929 *Fax:* 0845 456-2904.
  Open: Mon, Wed, Fri and Sat 09.30-17.30, Tue and Thur 09.30-20.00, Sun closed.
- **Kingston**, Market House, Market Place, Kingston upon Thames, KT1 1JS. *Tel:* 020 8547-5592 *Fax:* 020 8547-5594.
  Open: Mon-Sat 10.00-17.00, Sun closed.
- **Lewisham**, Lewisham Library, 199-201 Lewisham High Street, SE13 6LG. *Tel:* 020 8297-8317 *Fax:* 020 8297-9241.
  Open: Mon 10.00-17.00, Tue-Fri 09.00-17.00, Sat 10.00-16.00, Sun closed.
- **Richmond**, Old Town Hall, Whittaker Avenue, Richmond, TW9 1TP. *Tel:* 020 8940-9125 *Fax:* 020 8332-0802.
  Open: Mon-Sat 10.00-17.00 Easter Sunday-end Sep, Sun 10.30-13.30.
- **Swanley,** London Road, BR8 7AE. *Tel:* 01322-614660 *Fax:* 01322-666154.
  Open: Mon-Thur 09.30-17.30, Fri 09.30-18.00, Sat 09.00-16.00, Sun closed.

- **Twickenham**, The Atrium, Civic Centre, York Street, Twickenham, Middlesex, TW1 3BZ. *Tel:* 020 8891-7272 *Fax:* 020 8891-
  7738.
  Open: Mon-Thur 09.00-17.15, Fri 09.00-17.00, Sat and Sun
  closed.

The LTB operates a comprehensive range of recorded information
services called *Visitorcall*. They cover events, shows, where to take
the children, river trips and the weather. There are as many as 35
different numbers. The principal ones are listed in the London
Business and Services Telephone Directory. The information is
regularly updated, but will include nothing about access.

Royal Association for Disability and Rehabilitation (RADAR), 12
City Forum, 250 City Road EC1V 8AF
Tel: 020 7250-3222 *Textphone:* 020 7250-4119 *Fax:* 020 7250-0212
website: www.radar.org.uk *e-mail:* radar@radar.org.uk
RADAR is the central coordinating and campaigning body working
with all the voluntary groups concerned with disabled people. It
supports over five hundred local and national disability organisations, and campaigns for improvements in disabled people's lives.
RADAR provides advice and information on a wide variety of
subjects to support independence and equality for disabled people,
including access, housing, specialised equipment, benefits available
and local authority responsibilities. It produces an extensive publications list: an annual guide for disabled people, *Holidays in the
British Isles*; the monthly *RADAR Bulletin*; and the *National Key
Scheme Guide* to accessible toilets using the RADAR key.

Royal National Institute for Blind People (RNIB), 224 Great Portland
Street W1W 5AA
Tel: 020 7388-1266 *Textphone:* 0845-758691 *Fax:* 020 7388-2034
website: www.rnib.org.uk
The RNIB promotes facilities for the rehabilitation, training and
employment of blind people and provides a range of braille publications. It advises on a wide range of problems and needs. RNIB
publishes a monthly magazine, *New Beacon*. Their publication
European Cities Within Reach – London is promoted as an access
guide to London, and usefully mentions a few places which provide
audio guides. RNIB publications come from Customer Services, PO
Box 173, Peterborough PE2 6WS *Tel:* 0845-7023153 *Textphone:*
0845-585691 *Fax:* 01733-371555.

Royal National Institute for Deaf People (RNID), 19-23 Featherstone Street EC1Y 8SL
Tel: 020 7296-8000 *Textphone:* 020 7296-8001 *Fax:* 020 7296-8199
Free information line: 0808-8080123 *Free textphone:* 0808-8089000.
website: www.rnid.org.uk *e-mail:* helpline@rnid.org.uk
The RNID aims to promote and encourage both the alleviation and prevention of deafness. It is mainly a service organisation, and offers information and training. RNID Typetalk is the national telephone relay service which enables deaf and hard-of-hearing people to communicate. The RNID has a library, a medical research unit and the Tinnitus Helpline. If you're looking for advice and information about equipment, visit the **Sensory Services Centre**, Ground Floor, Connaught House, Broom Hill Road, Woodford Green, Essex IG8 0XR *Tel:* 020 8498-9911 *Textphone:* 020 8498-9922 *e-mail:* redbridge@rnid.org.uk.

SCOPE
6 Market Road, Barnsbury N7 9PW
Tel: 0808 800-3333
website: www.scope.org.uk *e-mail:* cphelpline@scope.org.uk
Scope's services for people with cerebal palsy focus on four areas:
• support and information for parents and carers;
• education;
• daily living;
• work.
It has branches all over the country, and publishes the widely read magazine *Disability Now*.

SHAPE (London),
LVS Resource Centre, 356 Holloway Road N7 6PA
Tel: 020 7619-6160 *Textphone:* 020 7619-6161 *Fax:* 020 7619-6162
website: www.shapearts.org.uk *e-mail:* info@shapearts.org.uk
SHAPE is a major provider for disabled people of training in the arts and is an enabler of access in the widest sense. In addition it runs the **Shape Ticket Scheme** to enable disabled and elderly people to enjoy a wide range of arts events. Membership of the scheme costs less than £10 a year. Under certain circumstances, they may be able to provide a volunteer to go with you, and provide transport. The number of West End performances at which these facilities can be provided is quite limited, and you need to be well organised at least two to three weeks before the event.

Shopmobility
12 City Forum, 250 City Road EC1V 8AF
Tel: 020 7689-1040
website: www.justmobility.co.uk/shop *e-mail:* nfsuk@lineone.net
Shopmobility provides invaluable services and resources in a number
of outer London shopping centres (and in many other parts of the
country). It tries to ensure that disabled people have equal opportunity of access to both shops and services. Most commonly schemes
are sited in the centre of shopping areas with adjacent BB spaces.
Shopmobility offers scooters and both manual and powered chairs
for use, and will have valuable local knowledge.

The Shopmobility website is excellent, and includes a wealth of
information about all the schemes, including when they are open,
how many parking places there are, and what they offer in the way
of help. There is also a listing on www.disabilityuk.com/mobility/
01shopmo.

The London Shopmobility schemes are currently at:

Bexley Heath *Tel:* 020 8301-5237;
Brent Cross *Tel:* 020 8202-1702;
Bromley *Tel:* 020 8313-0031;
Camden *Tel:* 020 7482-5503;
Croydon *Tel:* 020 8688-7336;
Edmonton *Tel:* 020 8379-2551;
Enfield *Tel:* 020 8366-8081;
Epsom *Tel:* 01372-727086;
Harrow *Tel:* 020 8427-1200;
Hounslow *Tel:* 020 8570-3343;
Ilford *Tel:* 020 8478-6864;
Kingston *Tel:* 020 8547-1255;
Lewisham *Tel:* 020 8297-2735;
Romford *Tel:* 01708-739431;
Sutton *Tel:* 020 8770-0691;
Uxbridge *Tel:* 01895-271510;
Walthamstow *Tel:* 020 8520-3366;
Wandsworth *Tel:* 020 8875-9585.

Transport for London (TfL), 42-50 Victoria Street, SW1H 0TL
TfL Call Centre *Tel:* 020 7222-1234 *Textphone:* 020 7918-3015.
Advice is available 24 hours a day
website: www.tfl.gov.uk
Only limited parts of the Underground are accessible, see the map

and description in this book, or the excellent *Tube Access Guide*, a map/guide published by TfL. An increasing number of low-floor and wheelchair-accessible buses are coming into use. There is detailed information in the chapter on *Travelling and getting around.*

Tripscope, The Vassall Centre, Gill Avenue, Bristol BS16 2QQ
Tel/Textphone: 0845 758-5641 (with a local call rate from anywhere in the UK) *Fax:* 0117 939-7736
website: www.tripscope.org.uk *e-mail:* enquiries@tripscope.org.uk
Tripscope offers a wealth of practical information on travelling both in the UK and abroad. They are experienced and friendly, and are knowledgeable about travel to and within London. Advice is free, and is available during normal working hours.

Wheelchair Travel, 1 Johnston Green, Guildford, Surrey GU2 6XS
Tel: 01483-233640 *Fax:* 01483-237772
website: www.wheelchair-travel.co.uk
e-mail: trevor@wheelchair-travel.co.uk
Probably the best (and almost the only) source of converted vehicles for hire. Trevor Pollitt who has established and built up this service over a number of years is well known to us. Wheelchair Travel has a number of adapted minibuses with either tail-lifts or ramped access available for hire with or without a driver. In addition they have cars with hand controls, and 'Chairman' cars.

Equipment repair and hire

There are a number of places where it is possible to hire special equipment, including wheelchairs, and others where you can buy equipment. We list here some of the principal sources. For local advice, the nearest Shopmobility might be a good source, or the local borough disability association. Alternatively, you might try the Disabled Living Foundation and look at its factsheets.

It is possible to hire wheelchairs from the local branch of the **Red Cross.** Contact the **National Headquarters, West Tower, 10th Floor, 3 Albert Embankment SE1 7SX** *Tel:* 020 7793-3360 *Fax:* 020 7793-3361. They will have details of the local centres throughout London.

All Handling (Movability)
492 Kingston Road, Raynes Park SW20 8DX
Tel: 020 8542-2217 *Fax:* 020 8395-4410
website: www.movability.com

A long-established family-run firm which addresses mobility needs including wheelchairs, scooters, stairlifts and various specialised equipment. Powered and manual chairs are available on hire.

Direct Mobility Hire (DMH)
8 Cheapside, North Circular Road, Palmers Green N13 5EP
Tel: 020 8807-9830 *Fax:* 020 8807-4213
website: www.directmobility.co.uk
DMH have a wide range of homecare products available either for hire or purchase, including wheelchairs.

GBL Wheelchair Warehouse
Units 1-3 Shield Drive, West Cross Centre, Brentford, Middx TW8 9EX
Tel: 020 8569-8955 *Fax:* 020 8560-5380.
Ramped access and **a wheelchair toilet** on-site. Small CP. GBL is a firm run by chair users. They offer a wide range of chairs, new, ex-demo or secondhand, and have an excellent hire or repair service. If you have a problem, give them a ring. The units are on an industrial estate near the Gillette tower on the A4, and are built where the old Firestone factory used to be.

Independent Living Company
11 Hale Hill, Mill Hill NW7 3NN
Tel: 020 8931-6000
website: www.independent-living.co.uk
There are +2 steps at the entrance but a portable ramp is available. Has a wide range of homecare equipment available for hire or purchase, including wheelchairs and scooters.

Keep Able
Tel: 08705 202-122 (mail order)
website: www.keepable.co.uk
Keep Able stock a range of specialist equipment and gadgets for disabled people.
   There are two stores in the London area:

- 11–17 Kingston Road, Staines Middx TW18 4QX *Tel:* 01784 440044 *Fax:* 01784 449900. Just outside the M25, and near the junction with Staines High Street;
- 615–619 Watford Way, Apex Corner, Mill Hill NW7 3JN *Tel:* 020 8201-0810. *Fax:* 020 8201-0840. By the junction of the A1 and the A41.

Medi World
436 Streatham High Road, Streatham SW16 1DA
Tel: 020 8679-2489
Ramped entrance. A wide range of homecare equipment available for hire or purchase, including wheelchairs.

Repairs to NHS equipment

We made some enquiries about what to do if you are visiting London and you have trouble with any equipment that may have been supplied by your local NHS Trust. An obvious question is, 'What do I do if my wheelchair breaks down?'

Unfortunately we didn't get any straight answers. The problem is that each NHS Trust has its own contracts for things like repairs, and each Trust may have different conditions. If it is something fairly straightforward like a puncture, and you can get it repaired at modest cost, then the thing to do is to get it fixed. Take the bill back to your own NHS Trust Supplies office/depot, and they'll probably pay up. One thing you need to bear in mind is that if you have to 'call out' one of the private suppliers listed here, there may be a significant charge over and above the cost of the repair. Possibly the best thing we can suggest is that you take with you the phone number of your own NHS Supplies office and then, if you have a problem, at least you can ring up and say, 'Help! What should I do?' Alternatively, go through the NHS Trust Supplies office nearest to where you are staying. Organisations that have been helpful to us on various occasions are the AA and RAC. If you are a member or are staying with a member, there may be some simple repairs that they can help with.

Escalators

Escalators are a common way of providing for an easy change of level in a building. In the guide, we have concentrated on giving information about lifts, because they are the most convenient and safest way of getting step-free access for most of our readers. Many families with children in buggies find that escalators are a convenient way of changing level, provided that a few sensible precautions are taken, such as avoiding having things hanging off the buggy which can touch any of the moving parts.

Elderly people and some disabled walkers find escalators difficult and they're obviously a problem for most solo chair users. Our own experience, however, is that they are a safe and easy way of changing levels for a chair user with one or two sensible **and strong** able-bodied friends, and most of our survey teams have learned how to cope. The pusher must be strong enough to control the chair safely and smoothly over a kerb. On an escalator the trick is simply to balance the wheelchair on the back wheels at the point of balance. The person behind pulls or pushes the chair on to the escalator, placing the wheels in the middle of a step as it opens up. The person in front pushes gently and horizontally against the chair and is only there to steady the chair if necessary. **It's much easier than it sounds, but don't try it unless your able-bodied friends are strong enough**.

Facilities for those with hearing impairment

An increasing number of venues and auditoria are now making provisions for people with reduced hearing. Two systems are commonly used. Induction loops consist of a loop of wire right round the area, carrying an electronic signal which can be picked up on a conventional hearing aid. In practice, there are sometimes technical problems. There may be a good signal in one part of an auditorium and not in another. There have been cinemas with two or three loops where you can see a film in one, and tune in to the soundtrack of another! If you need to use the loop signal, it is usually worth ringing in advance to ensure that it's switched on and working. They can probably advise about the best place to sit, and it is possible to 'tune' the system while you are there, if it is unsatisfactory. If you're lucky, this can be done while the adverts are showing before the main film. A variation on the loop system which is available in some places is that you can get a 'personal' necklace loop which you simply wear around your neck while switching your hearing aid to the T position.

The other system is called Sennheiser, based on an infrared signal with special earphones to pick up the sound. You will sometimes be asked for a nominal deposit to ensure the return of the earphones. Infrared systems can be highly directional, and you may have to sit in designated seats. Most new systems being installed in theatres and auditoria use infrared signals, as the sound quality is generally better.

A number of telephones now have an induction coupler, and a few ticket offices use a mike behind the glass with a coupler outside, but their use is not yet widespread. A number of arts centres listed have special activities for people with hearing impairment, and there are occasional 'signed' performances at theatres. For the latest information ask **Artsline**, **RNID** or **Hearing Concern**.

Typetalk/Minicom/Textphones

Typetalk is a communication system for those who find conventional phones difficult because of hearing or speech loss. For easy communication with someone who is hard of hearing, or for communication between deaf people, Typetalk provides a simple and convenient method. The most common equipment supplier has been Minicom, and so the provision is often called by that name, just as vacuum cleaners are commonly called Hoovers. We have referred to them as **Textphones**. The equipment consists of an add-on to a conventional phone which has a keyboard, and a display panel. Alternatively, it is possible to hook up a computer and screen to provide the 'text' part of the signal, although you need the right software to make it all work. It's a way of avoiding the need to buy another piece of equipment, if you can utilise what you already have. The RNID offer a Uniphone, where all the necessary equipment is incorporated into one terminal. With developing technology, an increasing number of 'one piece' terminals will no doubt become available. Consult either British Telecom (BT) or the RNID.

For a conversation, a Textphone terminal is needed at both ends. If you speak, the phone will work conventionally. If you use the keyboard, then the display at the other end will show your message. Thus a hearing person can talk to a deaf person, or two deaf people can type messages to each other.

For communications with or from someone who has hearing or speech loss, the Typetalk service can be invaluable. One end of the conversation can then be on a conventional phone. The other needs to be a Textphone. A deaf person can use it to communicate with someone on an ordinary phone and vice versa. The conversation goes via a Typetalk operator who provides a friendly and entirely confidential service. If you speak, the phone works conventionally. If you are hard of hearing, the Typetalk operator types in the message from the hearing person which is then displayed on your small panel. If you type in your conversation, rather than speak it, the operator will read the message out to the person you're ringing. Any reply will then be typed back to you. The service is funded by BT and run by the RNID. It is available throughout the country, and can be used for international calls. You pay the same charge as you would for a conventional call, and if your calls take longer as a result of using Typetalk, there is a rebate available.

For information on Typetalk, contact:
RNID **Typetalk**, PO Box 284, Liverpool L69 3UZ,
Tel: 0800 7311 888 (voice) or 0800 500 888 (text)
e-mail: helpline@rnid-typetalk.org.uk
Braille terminals are available for deaf-blind people. They are more complex than the simple Typetalk phone, and if this facility might be of use, contact the organisation below:

Deafblind UK, 100 Bridge Street, Peterborough PE1 1DY
Tel: 01733 358 100 *website:* www.deafblind.org.uk.
If you're deaf or hard of hearing, or have loss of speech, it's a brilliant service, although naturally it takes a bit of getting used to. Textphone terminals are becoming more widely used, and this allows those who are hard of hearing both to get and to provide information by phone.

Facilities for those with visual impairment

It is difficult to describe the special facilities for people who are visually impaired, as only one of our surveyors really understands what is involved. What she says is that much of the information in the guide is useful, including that about surfaces, distances and steps. The first edition of the guide was made into a Talking Book, and we hope that this may be done again.

A good number of major museums and a few theatres now provide a range of items/exhibits which can be felt and handled, and some lay on special exhibitions from time to time for visually impaired people. If you have a particular area of interest, it's best to contact the museum direct. **Artsline** may also be able to help.

Price concessions

A number of places offer price reductions for chair users, or blind people, and/or, sometimes, for a friend or escort. Sometimes the concession is for those who are 'registered' disabled, although documentary evidence is rarely demanded.

Reductions are sometimes available for others such as pensioners or those on benefit. The problem is that concessions are highly variable and can depend as much on who's on the door as on official policy. The offer of price concessions for entrance is a well-intended gesture, particularly in view of regulations which say that chair users may not enter some places without a friend or escort. We have always taken the view that the right of access is even more important, even if you have to pay for it. This essentially comes from our experiences over past years when people's rights to access have not been so widely recognised, and people have told us that 'you cannot come in'.

Because of their variability, and because they may apply to some disabled people and not to others, we have tended not to detail price concessions. The whole subject is confused, and the rules sometimes change. **Artsline** (020 7388-2227) will be able to advise about the up-to-date situation at particular venues. Places where there are well-established concessions for chair users include most major museums; Legoland and Thorpe Park; many historical buildings; the South Bank (National Theatre and Festival Hall complex); the Barbican; the Coliseum; Fairfield Arts Complex in Croydon; the Royal Opera House; the Tower Bridge Walkway and the Tower of London. There are many others.

There are nearly always reductions in ticket prices for children, and it is becoming increasingly common for places to offer 'family tickets', sometimes for two adults and up to three children.

Stairlifts and portable stairclimbers

While the provision of a ramp is always preferable, several venues and museums have installed stairlifts to help overcome the access barriers inside buildings. If the height difference is too great, a ramp may be impractical. There are several types, the most common being the platform stairlift which goes up an inclined stairway and the open (vertical) lifts which do not need massive foundations. There are also the 'portable' stairclimbers of the Gimpson or Scalamobile variety.

While such lifts are much needed, our experience in going round surveying is that a significant number of the platform stairlifts are not working. Vertical open lifts to bypass a few stairs are simpler, and are probably less likely to go wrong, but they too need regular testing and maintenance. There are several problems and, too often, finding the operator who has the key and who knows how to work it can take an age. Minimising the cost means that they can be of somewhat lightweight construction. Maintenance and testing isn't always as thorough as it should be and some are not built to carry electric chairs. When used for this they break down as a result of the load.

Portable stairclimbers are promoted by some as being the 'answer' to access problems where making modifications to an old building is perceived as being difficult and expensive. In practice, they are only of use when there is absolutely no alternative, and in most cases they are not used much, because of the problems involved.

There are two basic types. One is based on something that looks like a tank track, and at least one manufacturer of these is Gimpson. The other, called a Scalamobile, has a smaller footprint, and relies on a stairclimbing mechanism on the end of a pole.

Both can only accommodate some chairs, and both can be quite uncomfortable to use. Clamping the chair on can be really difficult. Some providers clamp a manual chair to the device and insist that you transfer into that. Back in the mid-1990s, a Scalamobile was used to get up the 13 steps to the ground floor (GF) of Buckingham Palace when it was open in the summer. It has been replaced by a proper platform stairlift, which is much more satisfactory.

Apart from the limitations of the equipment, they have batteries that need to be kept charged up, and when something is only used occasionally, this is commonly not the case. Another disadvantage is that people operating them need to be well-trained, and quite strong. Thus you have to have the right people around as well, as most people would not be confident enough to operate it. With a lift, even with a platform stairlift, only a minimal amount of training is needed to operate it safely, and most people would be able to do it.

If it's really important, telephone first to check that the lift you need to use is working. The best practice for such stairlifts is to install robust well-engineered equipment which is strong enough to carry electric chairs, and to test the lifts every day so that repairs and maintenance can be carried out as soon as there is a problem.

Specialist books and publications

There are a large number of these, and listings can be obtained from the CAE, DLF, GLAD, RADAR, RNIB, RNID, SCOPE and other major disability organisations. Several have already been mentioned in the descriptions of the various specialist organisations.

One valuable resource is the book *Designing to Enable* published by the **Gateshead Access Panel**, Unit J30, The Avenues, 11th Avenue North, Team Valley, Gateshead NE11 0NJ *Tel:* 0191 443-0058 *website:* www.gatesaccess.dial.pipex.com. It includes design advice relating to parking, pavements, doorways, accessible toilets, baby changing and feeding facilities, workplaces, hotel rooms, signs and notices and a whole range of other things. An important feature of the book is that it doesn't only present designs and specifications, but also attempts to explain the reasons for various provisions, thus increasing people's understanding.

For example, in discussing baby-changing and feeding facilities, they say 'Some designers are incorporating these facilities inside the accessible toilet compartment. We would not recommend this, due to the time taken to change and feed a small child whilst a disabled person may have an urgent need to use the toilet.

'The baby-changing facilities needed by both non-disabled and disabled people should be sited in a different area. The changing shelf should be wheelchair accessible, and a compromise height of 80cm is recommended. Other features include providing a sink near the changing shelf so that attention can be kept focused on the baby whilst reaching for the water, and ensuring that nappy disposal bins do not impede access for wheelchair users.'

Although the book is quite expensive (at £35), in our view it's good value – and its content is continually being upgraded with regular new editions.

Toilets/loos

Finding suitable toilets is a serious problem for many people, and particularly for disabled people whose needs are more exacting. While American readers will be used to referring to the john or the bathroom, in Britain the bathroom is the room with a bath, and not necessarily with a toilet. The informal word for toilet is 'loo'.

There are far more adapted toilets around now than there were when the guide was first published. Quite a few *McDonald's*, *Burger King* and *Pizza Hut* restaurants have one, as do new shopping precincts, and a small, but increasing, number of pubs. We include a chapter entitled the *Good Loo Guide*, which covers much of central London.

You would be well advised to get hold of one of the special NKS (National Key Scheme) keys available from RADAR which will open approximately half the adapted toilets including most of those provided by local authorities and those on rail stations. They ask for prepayment for keys, which cost less than £5 including postage. If you're wanting to send money from abroad, note that small cheques, even ones made out in sterling, are of little value as the bank may charge well over £5 for processing a cheque drawn on a foreign bank. RADAR will send a key to your UK address, and will help if they can.

For the distinction we have made between a **wheelchair toilet**, an

adapted toilet (both unisex) and those in the Ladies or Gents areas, see page 6.

Useful websites

Since the last edition of the guide, the amount of information available on the internet has increased enormously. In addition, searching for specific data has become much easier, with search engines provided by most ISPs, and with ones like www.google.com.

Having said that, a great deal of the information about access, and some of it about the services provided for disabled people is incomplete, and sometimes inaccurate. This is largely because most of the people providing the information don't understand what is needed.

Throughout the text, we have referred to people's websites as a contact point through which to get further information. Some of the sites are well laid out and informative, with appropriate information available for people with special needs. Some have downloadable maps and diagrams.

Overall the quality of the information on websites is highly variable; sometimes the most useful section on a site is the links to other places, where you may be able to find what you want.

In this section we just highlight a few sites that may be of particular use, and this is something that we will aim to update (in due course) on our own website, which is www.accessproject-phsp.org.

Key London sites include:
- www.londontouristboard.com for the LTB;
- www.timeout.com for events listings;
- www.thisislondon.com, which is the *Evening Standard* site;
- www.tfl.gov.uk, which is the site for Transport for London.

Important disability sites include:
- www.disability.gov.uk, the official government information site;
- www.disabilitynow.org.uk, related to the magazine published by SCOPE;
- www.dlf.org.uk for information about equipment for disabled people;
- www.glad.org.uk, the site of the Greater London Action on Disability;
- www.youreable.com.

For both watching and joining in arts events, the **Artsline** site is the one to look at first, www.artsline.co.uk, and they are planning to have online access to their databases on the accessibility of entertainments venues fairly soon. If you want to take part in **sporting activities**, there's www.londonsportsforum.org.uk.

There are many **international sites** which will provide a broader perspective, and we list just a few. These will all have useful links taking you to a very wide range of sources:

- there is www.access-able.com the site of the **Access-Able Travel Source** which has gathered a huge amount of information and advice. We have been in touch for many years with Carol Randall who set it up. A little while back, the site combined with **Travellin' Talk** to provide a discussion forum and the opportunity for people with disabilities to exchange information and to offer emergency assistance to each other;
- **Access for Disabled Americans** www.accessfordisabled.com publish a regular newsletter and produce an *Around the World Resource Guide*;
- **Global Access** at www.geocities.com/Paris/1502 have some pages titled *Disabled Travel Network*, where (among other things) they list our guides. They also publish a free internet magazine every month to which you can subscribe;
- **Mobility International** www.miusa.org is a non-profit organisation that promotes international educational exchange and travel. They maintain information sheets on many places in the world, and have some sixty regional offices.

With the widespread use of computer technology, there have been many developments which have been of particular value to people with disabilities. These include the use of software which enables visually impaired users to use their computers together with a wide range of other applications. The leading supplier of information in this area is **AbilityNet** www.abilitynet.org.uk, who have a freephone helpline *Tel:* 0800 269-545 (in the UK) or *Tel:* 01926 407-425.

Travelling and getting around

This chapter is written initially from the point of view of someone arriving in London, possibly for the first time. It can readily be used, however, by residents, and there is a section on facilities that are only available to people who live in London boroughs.

There is a brief section for those arriving by air, and one detailing National Rail (NR) services. We describe the main rail termini together with stations that have step-free access within a roughly 50km radius. There is advice and information for car and minibus users, and then sections on using underground trains and buses. The car section includes details of central London car parks. These are equally applicable to residents and visitors. There is also advice and information about using taxis and minicabs.

London is big, and much of its public transport system was designed a century ago. There has been limited investment in improving the facilities and, until quite recently, the needs of disabled passengers have not really been considered. While that is changing, it will take many years before the system will meet the aspirations of the majority of disabled travellers.

Travelling around in London is one of the biggest problems for the disabled person who wants to be both independent and mobile. Since the last edition of the guide in 1996, there has been some progress, but it's still difficult. It's also very much 'two steps forward, one step back'. For example, the Jubilee Line Extension (JLE) has opened, providing a potentially invaluable section of the tube with step-free access, but there have been serious operational and reliability problems with some of the lifts installed. Many more wheelchair-accessible buses have appeared, and according to Transport for London (TfL) about three-quarters of London buses are accessible. However, the reliability of the ramps being used is not good. Our experience during the summer of 2002 was that only around 50% of the bus journeys attempted by our chair users on supposedly accessible buses were actually successful.

The Docklands Light Railway (DLR) and the Croydon Tramway are the only significant parts of the system to have step-free access. All black taxis are now, in principle, wheelchair accessible, but attitudes on the part of drivers are variable. Also, some of the older taxis are quite cramped inside. For car users, there are some BB spaces in London, including a limited number at major sights/sites – see the individual write-ups in the guide. Traffic is very congested, and driving in London isn't everyone's idea of fun. For London residents, Dial-a-Ride (DAR) and Taxicard services provide limited door-to-door services.

Insofar as disabled people remain concerned and upset about the lack of progress towards a fairer society where everyone can take part on an equal basis, the slow progress with developing an accessible transport system is probably the issue where they have most justification in calling for rapid change. Unfortunately while the future funding of the Tube is a matter of political controversy, many investment decisions have been delayed. The fragmentation of the railways has been unhelpful, and the disappearance of printed material and its substitution with information from call centres and from the internet is a great loss. Investment in lifts at a good number of the Circle, District and Hammersmith and City Line stations could make an enormous difference to the accessibility of the Underground. The costs involved would be relatively small com-pared with providing lifts down to the deep sections of the Tube, because the stations are all near the surface. In addition the funding of a few people at call centres who 'know their stations' would be an enormous help. In this respect, TfL is now pretty good, but some of the rail companies leave a lot to be desired.

In spite of all that slightly negative commentary, **with the right information and with a little determination and planning, you should be able to get to most of the places you want**, although you may have to use some taxis or bring your own transport.

If you need advice and/or up-to-date information about particular journeys, try:

- the **TfL Call Centre** *Tel:* 020 7222-1234 *Textphone:* 020 7918-3015 *website:* www.tfl.gov.uk. Advice is available 24 hours a day for disabled travellers;
- **Tripscope**, The Vassall Centre, Gill Avenue, Bristol BS16 2QQ *Tel/Textphone:* 0845 758-5641 (with a local call rate from any-where in the UK during normal office hours) *Fax:* 0117 939-773;
- **DaRT**, the **Accessible Transport Users Association**, Room 210, The Colourworks, 2 Abbot Street E8 3DP *Tel:* 020 7241-2111. DaRT membership is open to anyone who uses Dial-a-Ride (DAR) or Taxicard services and, among other things, they cam-

paign for adequate funding for the services. A specific goal is to ensure that all transport becomes accessible for disabled people.

Note that visitors can now get temporary membership of some of the DAR schemes, currently those in Camden, Hammersmith/Fulham, Kensington/Chelsea and in Westminster. This scheme doesn't yet cover Lambeth and Southwark, but contact DaRT for the latest details.

In the guide, we are looking at things largely from the point of view of someone making their own plans and bookings. If you are arranging your trip through a tour company, it is essential to make your needs clear, and to make sure that the person you are dealing with has really understood, and that the information is passed on. Too often people think that 'goodwill' is a substitute for knowledgeable action.

It is important for you to understand the probable limitations of the 'system' and also to check that things can be (and are) organised to your satisfaction. There can be a difference between what the friendly-sounding booking clerk says, and what actually happens when you turn up. You'll sometimes meet someone at your destination who'll say, 'I didn't know anything about that . . .'

Arriving

You may arrive in London by plane, train, coach or in your own transport, and each is discussed.

By air

If you fly into London, you will have needed to find out from the airline about access problems en route, and their policies regarding disabled passengers. All the airlines seem to have slightly different rules and approaches.

Excellent general advice about flying is given in a free booklet called *Flying High*, published by the **Disabled Living Foundation**. It was produced in conjunction with British Airways, and includes sections on planning your journey, things to be aware of at the airport, and availability of a personal toilet on board the aircraft (particularly useful if you are unable to get to the toilet). In addition **DPTAC** have just published a guide called *Advice for Disabled Flyers* which includes a lot of helpful comments on aspects of air travel for disabled people. For contact details see page 17.

Airports were amongst the first places to provide facilities for disabled passengers, and on a relative basis, they have been quite good for a considerable time. If you use the biggest airports, there should be step-free access through the terminal to the aircraft door, but occasionally this may not be so, either because of a breakdown, or possibly for security reasons. Chair users quite often have to transfer to an alternative 'loading' chair in order to get to a seat on the plane.

At certain times airports can become extremely congested. For example, it is wise to avoid Friday evenings and bank holiday weekends if you possibly can. Besides this, at both Heathrow and Gatwick, long distances are involved. A big problem for most travellers tends to be handling their luggage, getting to the airline desk, and simply finding out where it is for a start! For passengers arriving, luggage handling on to whatever transport is used to reach the hotel or other accommodation is a potential hassle. At smaller airports (like London City), access to the aircraft will almost certainly be via a flight of steps.

If you make prior arrangements it is normally possible to ease your passage through the system, and to get onto and off the plane using an ambulance-type carrying chair. Both Heathrow and Gatwick have little buggies to take elderly and/or disabled walkers through the terminal to the departure lounge.

Virtually all airports have adapted toilets on both sides of the security desks. However, there are only a limited number of them, and if you want to use a toilet you would almost certainly be wise to do so before the departure gate. Don't let 'the system' whisk you through too quickly without giving you the chance of going to the loo. There are usually adapted toilets in the arrival areas where you are waiting for luggage, but they're not always well signed, and you may have to ask. Not all are unisex, although these days, most are.

Transport links to and from the airports

There are accessible transport links to and from the four major airports we've covered. Much depends on how much luggage you have, as handling it on and off trains and buses can create a hassle. While you may be able to use a luggage trolley at the airport, there may not be anything similar at your destination to help with luggage.

At Heathrow the accessible links are:

- by A2 bus to and from central London, Euston and King's Cross, which involves a minimum amount of hassle. In addition, all the TfL bus services serving each of the terminals use wheelchair-accessible buses. Those for Terminals 1, 2 and 3 go from a central bus station reached via underground tunnels, involving, inevitably, quite long distances;

- by the Heathrow Express train direct to and from Paddington. The trains are frequent and fast. For a single traveller, it's much cheaper than using a taxi, and you may be able to make a much shorter taxi journey from Paddington;
- on the Underground. The Piccadilly Line platforms on both Heathrow tube stations have step-free access using lifts, but you can only go directly to three more central step-free stations: Hammersmith, Earl's Court and Caledonian Road; see the section on the Underground on page 71.

When Terminal 5 is built at Heathrow it will almost certainly be accompanied by greatly improved public transport links, including, hopefully, a train link to Waterloo.

To and from Gatwick, the accessible link is the Gatwick Express in and out of Victoria. For Stansted it is the Stansted Express from Liverpool Street.

There are plans to extend the DLR to London City airport, and in the meantime there's a wheelchair-accessible Airport Bus service from Liverpool Street Station.

If you do not have too far to go, getting to or from the airport by car, taxi or minicab may be much the easiest way.

Gatwick

Gatwick Airport, Gatwick, West Sussex RH6 0NP
Tel: 0870 000-2468 *Textphone*: 01293-513179 *website* www.baa.com
There are two terminals with a short train link between them, which has step-free access. Overall, the site is large, so be prepared for long distances, and at busy times for congestion and crowds of people. If you have walking difficulties, make sure that your airline knows about it, and use the buggies provided to make things easier. **Travelcare** offer advice and information to anyone who has a problem connected with special needs. Contact details *Tel:* 01293-504283 *Fax:* 01293-503317 *e-mail:* gatwick.travel-care@ukgateway.net. There is also some limited information on the BAA website under 'special needs'.

Heathrow

Heathrow Airport, 234 Bath Road, Harlington, Hayes UB3 5AP
Tel: 0870 000-0123 *Textphone:* 020 8745-7950 for general enquiries
website: www.baa.com (look at the pages on 'special needs')
There are four terminals, three (1, 2 and 3) of which are linked by underground passages with step-free access, although there are several hundred metres between them. Terminal 4 is on a separate site. It can be reached by the Underground with only single steps involved (getting on and off the trains). In one direction you have to go via Hatton Cross and change trains. If you have difficulty in going between terminals, there is a *Help Bus* available (*Tel:* 020 8745-5185) which has a lift and wheelchair spaces. Note that there are only a few of these, so you will need to allow extra time for transfers. Textphones should be available at all the information desks.

Parking details for BB holders are given on the BAA website, but the badge scheme does not operate on any of Heathrow's roads. There are some BB spaces in CPs, but note that most have a height limit of 2m. **Travel-care** at Heathrow can provide information and assistance for passengers with special needs in making connections of one kind or another. Contact details *Tel:* 020 8745-7495 *Textphone:* 020 8745-7565 *Fax:* 020 8745-4161 *e-mail:* heathrow_travel_care@baa.com.

London City

London City Airport, Royal Docks, E16 2PB
Tel: 020 7646-0088 *website:* www.londoncityairport.com
London City is a small airport, so boarding the aircraft involves steps. Assistance with boarding can be arranged, but it is inherently less accessible than the other London airports.

Stansted

Stansted Airport, Stansted, Essex CM24 1QW
Tel: 0870 000-0303 *Textphone:* 01279-663725 *website:* www.baa.com
A modern and relatively small terminal. There are some 'air bridges' to facilitate step-free transfer into the aircraft, but not all flights use these, so sometimes there are steps involved. There is some limited information on the BAA website under 'special needs'. Note that some of the cut-price airfare companies are charging passengers for the use of a chair, if you need one to help you to board. Your own

chair goes off to be loaded in the hold, and you may have to pay £15 for the privilege of using an airline/airport chair for loading/transfer.

By coach

Coach travel offers good value, if you can manage the steps involved getting on and off. Things have certainly got easier during the last few years as more disabled people have made use of the network. The most important thing is to inform the coach company of your needs when booking. So long as they, and you, are happy, the only general advice is to arrive in good time and make your needs known to staff. Note that there is a useful coach station at Heathrow Airport, although car parking is some 300m away. The main coach station is at Victoria, although some coaches arrive and depart at a 'drop-off' point in Pancras Road, opposite King's Cross Station. A Senior Coachcard is available for discounted travel on National Express for those aged 55 or over.

National Express are operating an experimental service from Bath, Chippenham and Swindon to Heathrow and London using new vehicles fitted with a lift for wheelchairs. From early in 2003 there will be five trips a day using these coaches, which are intended to pave the way for the introduction of new services and vehicles from January 2005 onwards when all new coaches will have to be fully accessible. Their additional needs helpline is *Tel:* 0121 423-8479 or you can *e-mail:* additionalneeds@nationalexpress.co.uk.

Victoria Coach Station, 164 Buckingham Palace Road SW1W 9TP *Tel:* 020 7730-3466 *DisEnq:* 020 7824-0000 *Fax:* 020 7824-0016 *e-mail:* terry.barnes@tfl-vcs.co.uk. London's central coach station and the arrival and departure point for most coach services to places all over Britain and the continent. It is some 500m from Victoria Rail Station, and has been extensively modernised. It is possible to drop passengers off at the coach station itself, or there is an NCP in Semley Place. The coach station is served by a number of wheelchair-accessible bus routes.

The main entrance is on the corner of Elizabeth Street. There is step-free access throughout with good signposting.

On arrival at Victoria, there are signs leading to the Help Point which provides information and assistance to disabled travellers. It is opposite Gate 21 Lane B, and if you are coming by taxi you can ask to be set down by the office. There are two **wheelchair toilets (D90 ST80 NKS)** nearby.

If you need assistance, contact the Help Point. Given notice, it is possible to help passengers on and off, but the operator needs to be aware of your needs at both ends of your journey. On-board toilets in coaches, where provided, are tiny, and for all practical purposes should be regarded as 'inaccessible'.

By rail

There is a huge network of rail lines through the London suburbs. It is more dense south of the river, where there are fewer Tube lines. You can pick up an excellent map of the system called *London Connections* from a number of information points, or by ringing National Rail Enquiries *Tel:* 0845 7484-950 *Textphone:* 0845 6050-600 *website:* www.nationalrail.co.uk.

As there are so few journeys 'inside' London that it is possible to make by train without major access problems, we will describe the network in detail in this section.

A booklet called *Rail Travel for Disabled Passengers* is available. This includes practical advice and contact phone numbers. It also contains details of concessionary fares, and of the Disabled Persons Railcard. This offers reduced fares for you and an adult companion. It is valid for a year, and at the time of writing cost £14. Cards are available from **The Disabled Persons Railcard Office**, PO Box 1YT, Newcastle-on-Tyne NE99 1YT. The booklet and other leaflets are available at main stations and it can be downloaded from www.nationalrail.co.uk after using the Disabled Assistance button.

Remember that there is a step up into the carriage on virtually all trains, but if you can manage this, you can take the train to central London. Some older carriages have two steps. The larger stations now have movable ramps to help get on or off the train. The ramps can be a solid piece of engineering, and may be quite heavy to handle. Staff need training in their use. There are some newer and lighter ramps made of aluminium coming into use. These are slightly narrower, making it easier to fit into the doors. There are even some fibreglass ramps available which can fold up like a suitcase, and these are used on First Great Western. Hopefully, good practice over the provision of ramps will be shared around among the different operators.

If you are using a smaller station, possibly one that isn't always staffed, most operators ask for 24 hours' notice of your travelling plans, so that they can provide any assistance which is needed. If you are travelling with friends, so that assistance isn't needed, make sure that you don't bump into a staff-operated lift at a place with no staff!

The map shows the main peripheral stations with step-free access.

Links to and from Accessible Rail Stations

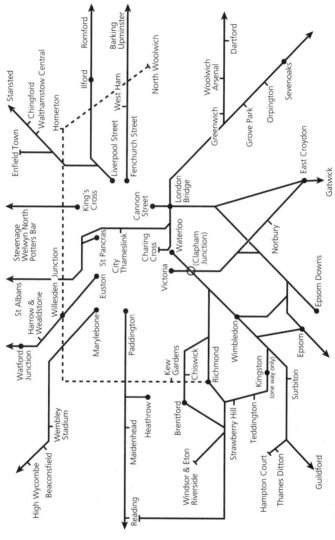

See text for station details (especially Clapham Junction)

The range of options, although limited, is growing. City Thameslink Station has step-free access and is potentially of great use as a central destination. It is not open after 9pm or at weekends which considerably reduces its value. Charing Cross can be a really useful central destination. In addition, London Bridge now has lifts to both the Northern Line and the JLE. Unfortunately the JLE lift there has been one of the more unreliable ones.

If you don't want to drive in London you can park, or stay, near a station with step-free access to the platform. From a central London station, you can then use a taxi; an accessible tube station (if you're near one); a bus; or you may be able to walk or wheel. Charing Cross, London Bridge and Waterloo, for example, are all near major sights.

There was a problem with updating this section, since there are now as many as a dozen train-operating companies. We contacted all of them on what was supposedly the contact number for passengers with special needs. A few companies did have a 'dedicated' line for this purpose, but with most we simply got through to someone in the customer service call centre. In terms of access information at the stations, the people we spoke to tried to be helpful, but several were unknowledgeable. In all the calls, we only spoke to two people who had immediate and in-depth knowledge. In connection with some of the companies, we found that we knew a great deal more than they did, resulting from the visits we made to stations in 1995 for the previous edition of this guide.

The information in this section is based on those 1995 visits, together with additional information gathered by ringing the train-operating companies. We made many additional visits in 2002 but not quite everything was reinspected. If something is vitally important for you, then the ways to crosscheck it are to contact Tripscope, or to use the numbers listed below where appropriate.

Virtually all the central main line stations in London, being termini, have step-free access everywhere. In addition, most have portable ramps for easing the transfer of chair users into and out of the trains. Most, though not all, have taxi pickup points just outside, or inside the station. Nearly all of them have a disabled person's toilet, usually with an NKS lock.

Stations in and around London with step-free access, some via service lifts, include:
(a * indicates that there is some reservation, either about the whole of the station having step-free access, or about the hours of opera-

tion, or that the station is not staffed. **If the station is listed without comment, there should be step-free access throughout the day**.)

This section is best used in conjunction with the *London Connections* map.

• Thames Trains
Paddington
access to platforms 13 and 14 for suburban services is via a ramp which is halfway up platform 12. Most of the trains that go to and from Reading start on the main line platforms. **Wheelchair toilet (D80 ST75)** inside the first aid room on platform 1.
Heathrow Airport
Maidenhead
* step-free access to platforms 4 and 5. New lifts are being installed to make the station fully accessible.
Reading

• Chiltern Railways
Marylebone
wheelchair toilet (D100 ST85 NKS) just inside the door to the Ladies.
Wembley Stadium
* long (50m +) and steep ramp up to road level. The station is not generally staffed.
Beaconsfield
* ramped access from both sides. The station is not always staffed.
High Wycombe
flat access to platforms 1 and 2. Platform 3, the platform for trains to Marylebone, reached by ramped underpass from the end of platform 2.

• Silverlink County
Euston
both side entrances to the station have steps (+ 4 from Melton Street, + 14 from Eversholt Street). Ramped entrances from Euston Road and the bus station. **Two wheelchair toilets (D75 ST80 NKS)** off the concourse near the end of platform 1.
Willesden Junction
* new lifts to all platforms were installed in 2002.
Harrow & Wealdstone
* new lifts have been installed.
Watford Junction
main CP over 100m away. Two BB spaces just outside. **Wheelchair toilet (D95 ST75 NKS)** by the ticket office.

- **Silverlink Metro (Richmond to North Woolwich via north London)**
Richmond
see write-up under South West Trains.
Kew Gardens
ramped access in both directions, although southbound there is a locked gate.
Homerton
via ramps in both directions.
North Woolwich

- **Thameslink**
St Pancras
Wheelchair toilet (D70 ST70 NKS) near the end of platform 7. Note that the station was being extensively renovated when we visited.
St Albans
* flat access to platform 1, and platform 4 at peak times. At other times, and for platforms 2 and 3, staff assistance is required to cross the track.
City Thameslink
* closes early on weekdays, and is closed at weekends. **Wheelchair toilet (D80 ST75 NKS)** in a corner of the concourse, past the ticket barrier and the lifts, on the right.
Blackfriars
* ramped access from about 100m to the east next to Puddle Dock, but not well marked. It's about 300m long. Platforms 1, 2, 3 and 4 have step-free access, but platform 5 for northbound Thameslink trains can only be reached via a stepped subway.
East Croydon
steepish ramp leading to and from all platforms. **Wheelchair toilet (D95 ST90 NKS)** on platform 4. The Croydon Tramway stops nearby.
Gatwick Airport

- **WAGN Railway** (from King's Cross)
King's Cross
* wheelchair toilet **(D90 ST130 NKS)** on platform 8. Note that due to extensive construction works associated with the new Channel Tunnel rail link, the station will be seriously disrupted for much of the time up until 2007, when the work is due to be completed. Part of the programme is to make all the Tube lines accessible via lifts.
Potters Bar
Welwyn North
both platforms have flat access via separate entrances.

Stevenage
* needs an NKS key for the lift 'out of hours'. It was out of service when we surveyed.

• **WAGN Railway** (from Liverpool Street)
Liverpool Street
On two levels, with lift (D90 W145 L210) access. **Wheelchair toilet (D85 ST75 NKS)** off the ticket office at platform level.
Enfield Town
Walthamstow Central
has flat access from street level on either side, Priory Avenue or Selbourne Road.
Chingford
Stansted Airport

• **First Great Eastern**
Liverpool Street (see above)
Ilford
* some platforms with flat access, others via a platform stair lift (W67 L80) which is not very reliable. **Wheelchair toilet (D85 ST110 NKS)** through the foyer on the left.
Romford
* steep bumpy ramp to the left of the main station bypasses + 11 + 12 steps. The ramp is closed in the early evening, and you may have to get a staff member to open it. All platforms have ramped access.

• **c2c (London to Southend)**
Fenchurch Street
lift (D125 W150 L190) to platforms. **Wheelchair toilet (D90 ST120 + NKS)** at platform level.
West Ham
* via a service lift, but note that the station is only staffed during busy periods.
Barking
* all eight platforms can be reached using a service lift (D180 W180 L200) to platform 1, and then steepish ramps, although long distances are involved.
Upminster
* level access to platform 1 via a new ticket office by the Station Approach CP. Service lift (D200 W200 L200) to platforms 2, 3, 4 and 5 so that interchange between Fenchurch Street trains and the District Line is possible. **Wheelchair toilet** on platform 1.

- **Connex**

Victoria
wheelchair toilet (D70+ ST70+ NKS) by the main toilets on the right side of the station, looking towards the platforms.
Charing Cross
wheelchair toilet (D70+ST80+ NKS) off a corridor linking to the street.
Cannon Street
* lift access to all platforms, but the station is closed at weekends.
London Bridge
wheelchair toilet (Tardis type) immediately outside by the taxi drop-off point. There's a second one on platform 5. Lifts go to both the JLE and Northern lines.
Greenwich
with a step-free link to the DLR.
Dartford
platforms accessible via lifts. **Wheelchair toilet (D140 ST95 NKS)** just inside the Ladies – unisex cubicle.
Orpington
* the Crofton Road entrance gives flat access to platforms 1 and 2. The Station Approach gives flat access to platforms 5, 6, 7 and 8. Platforms 3 and 4 can only be reached via ±26 steps. The trick for avoiding the steps is to choose a train that terminates at Orpington.
Grove Park
* ramped access to all platforms except platform 1, which is a branch line to Sudbridge Park and Bromley North only (with ±29 steps).
Sevenoaks
lift access to all platforms. **Wheelchair toilet (ST70)**. Need to get a key from the staff.
Woolwich Arsenal
* ramped access to both sides of the station through gates which can be opened by NKS key. **Adapted toilets (ST60 NKS)** on platform 1 and opposite the station entrance.

- **South Central**

Victoria (see above)
London Bridge (see above)
Richmond (see below under South West Trains)
Wimbledon (see below under South West Trains)
Epsom
* large service lifts, although one was out of action when we surveyed.

Epsom Downs
Norbury
* steepish ramps to both platforms
East Croydon (see page 46)

- **South West Trains**
Waterloo
step-free access everywhere, including Waterloo East via lift and
ramps. **Wheelchair toilet (D70+ ST70+ NKS)** in the foyer by the
Ladies, off the main concourse. There's another **wheelchair toilet** on
Station Approach Road just outside, where the 211 buses pull in, and
by the First Aid post. Step-free station exit through the arch by the
big central clock and there's a lift down to the JLE near the end of
platform 4. Note the link to Bank Station (which is step free, but
involves steepish slopes and an inclined Travelator at Bank), and to
the JLE (with its slightly dodgy lift).
Clapham Junction
* a huge station whose platforms are linked by either an underground tunnel or an overhead footbridge. **It cannot be described as
accessible**. There is, however, a portable stairclimber, and a chair
user can be strapped to it to get up and down the stairs. Allow plenty
of time, and if possible, give them some warning. It's a fairly
alarming device, but it works, and we've used it when changing
trains.
Chiswick
*flat/ramped access to both sides, and there are portable ramps on
both platforms. Not always staffed.
Brentford
* unstaffed station with step-free access on either side, and a road
bridge linking the two platforms. The angle of the track means that
the step getting on and off trains is particularly big on both sides.
Richmond
* a key station on the District Line tube, South London lines, and at
the end of the line to North Woolwich. The platforms are reached via
−22 steps, but there are service lifts (D160 W190 L290) to all
platforms. There is alternative step-free access from the CP. **Wheelchair toilet (D90 ST200 NKS)** at platform level near the end of
platform 6.
Wimbledon
lift access to all platforms, and link between NR trains, the District
Line and Tramlink. **Adapted toilet (NKS)** on platforms 7/8 was
temporarily closed when we surveyed.

Kingston
* only platform 3 has step-free access, but trains run from this platform on a loop to and from Waterloo. Platforms 1/2 can be reached using a platform stairlift.

Teddington
* level access from both sides to the platforms, but narrow door D57 to get into the ticket office.

Strawberry Hill
* level access to both platforms.

Surbiton
Flat or lift access to all platforms. Disabled persons' toilet on platform 2/4 (NKS).

Guildford
step-free access to all platforms via a steeply ramped underpass with no handrails. **Adapted toilet (D80 ST35 NKS)**, large cubicle, on platform 2.

Windsor & Eton Riverside
wheelchair toilet (D85 ST75 NKS) off the concourse.

Thames Ditton
* steepish ramp to both platforms.

Hampton Court
* has +2 steps at the entrance which can be bypassed by a ramp at the side towards the back of the station.

Enquiry numbers for disabled people wanting to make rail journeys and either to get information, or to request assistance when travelling, are:

Anglia Railways	01473 693 333 (*Textphone:* 01603 630748)
c2c	01702 357640 (*Textphone:* 01702 357640)
Central Trains	08457 056027 (*Textphone:* 08457 078051)
Chiltern Railways	01296 332114 (*Textphone:* 08456 050600)
Connex	08706 030405 (*Textphone*: 01233 617621)
	08450 002211 (local call rate)
First Great Western	08457 413775 (*Textphone:* 08456 050600)
Gatwick Express	08705 301530 (*Textphone:* available)
GNER	08457 225444 (*Textphone:* 0191 2213016)
Heathrow Express	08456 001515
Midland Mainline	0114 2537654 (*Textphone:* 08457 078051)
Silverlink Train Services	(*Textphone:* 08457 125988)
	(Metro) 08456 014867
	(County) 08456 014868

South Central	08451 237770 (*Textphone:* 01233 617621)
South West Trains	08456 050440 (*Textphone:* 08456 050441)
Thames Trains	0118 9083607
Virgin Trains	08457 443366 (*Textphone:* 08457 443367)
WAGN Railway	08457 818919 (*Textphone:* 08457 125988)
	DisEnq line only available Mon-Fri
	during normal working hours
Wales and Borders	
Trains	08453 003005 (*Textphone:* 08457 585469)
Wessex Trains	08453 000517 (*Textphone:* 08457 585469)

These numbers were taken off the National Rail website www.nationalrail.co.uk. Most of the numbers listed take you through to customer services. Some only operate their 'help' line during normal working hours. Some companies have specialist staff who are well informed about access issues and about the facilities on their network. In our experience, by far the best service is that provided by the staff at the Virgin Trains call centre (*Tel:* 08457-443366 for Journey Care) who were helpful and knowledgeable both about their own stations, and about those used by other operators. Virgin probably have the largest network, although much of it is for cross-country journeys rather than those in and out of London. They have trains operating in and out of both Euston and Paddington. Their website is particularly useful relating to stations outside London as they publish details about the accessibility of most of the stations on their network.

Since the disappearance of British Rail, and the privatisation of the railways, the system has become fragmented. This has had the result that it is more difficult to get reliable information (relating to access in particular), and journeys involving changing trains have become more difficult. Many of the staff will try to be as helpful as possible, but they cannot speak for the personnel working for other operators.

Most of the London termini are well described by Railtrack on www.railtrack.co.uk under major stations.

By train or ferry from the continent

Using the Channel Tunnel provides the possibility for an easy transport link across the channel. In particular, for car drivers, *Le Shuttle* service for carrying cars from Calais to Folkestone allows people to stay in their cars during the journey, thus greatly simplifying (and speeding up) getting across.

The *Eurostar* trains from Paris and Brussels all have two desig-nated chair spaces, with an adapted toilet nearby, and these bring you directly into Waterloo International Station, in the heart of London. Waterloo International has step-free access through to the main station concourse using ramps and lifts. There are **wheelchair toilets** on both sides of customs control. The downside of the service is that only two people can travel together at a discount price, which can easily break up a family, as a third or fourth passenger has to pay a first-class fare. Also wheelchair passengers are not able to take advantage of other cheap offers and discounts.

If you are going to another destination in London, there is a taxi rank outside the International Station, though with a low kerb, it can be more difficult to get into the taxi. There is a link to the JLE tube station. There are (accessible) buses, numbers 205 and 705, which link with the other mainline rail stations; see the listing under *Buses* later in the chapter. To get to Euston, it's probably easier to use the 59, 68 or 168 from near the roundabout outside the station. The Waterloo and City Line provides a (slightly difficult) step-free link through to the DLR; see the separate write-up. The pedestrian exits from Waterloo Station are quite long with significant slopes. These are generally down to get out, but up if you're trying to reach the station.

The large modern ferries on the Calais to Dover run all have lift access from the car deck to upper parts of the ship, and also have well-adapted **wheelchair toilets** on board.

Getting around

As undoubtedly the most flexible and convenient method of trans-port for many is the car (in spite of traffic jams and parking problems), we will consider this first, followed by taxis and minicabs. Then we will describe the facilities on TfL tubes and buses. The rail network has been described already in terms of getting into the centre from the suburbs. Even Londoners find the variety of possible routes confusing, and may be largely unaware of the range of facilities.

By car or minibus

For many disabled people, getting around by car or adapted minibus is the only practical way, since much of the public transport system is inaccessible. Drivers have to face a fairly aggressive driving style and congestion, especially during rush hours. There can also be parking problems. Having said that, driving in London is certainly more disciplined than it is in other large European cities like Paris or Rome.

Your reaction to driving in London will depend very much on experience as well as on driving skills and temperament. Londoners tend to be very positive and to go quite fast. Driving speeds have dropped over the years due to congestion. Major junctions are all controlled by traffic lights, and most lanes are now clearly marked. This makes it easier for visitors. Problems include the one-way streets and no-right-turns (and sometimes even no-left-turns), which seem to crop up everywhere. The secret is not to panic and just press on. Make sure that you've got a good map. If you have a navigator, so much the better, but if you have a map you can at least stop and sort yourself out, working out another route if necessary.

One way of making constructive use of your car or minibus, and also of the accessible transport facilities, is to drive into the Docklands, park near a station there and use the DLR for some of your sightseeing/visiting. Equally you could park at Richmond and use the train in to Waterloo (for the South Bank) or at East Croydon and go to City Thameslink, Charing Cross or Victoria. With the opening of the JLE, the possibilities for parking just outside the centre, and coming in to stations such as Westminster, London Bridge or even Caledonian Road (via Green Park), have been greatly increased.

During 2003, as an experiment to reduce congestion, the central London **congestion charge** was introduced in the area bounded by Park Lane in the west, Euston Road and Pentonville Road in the north, Commercial Street and Tower Bridge in the east and New Kent Road, Kennington Lane and Vauxhall Bridge in the south. The initial charge was £5 per vehicle, either payable in advance or by 22.00 on the day of travel. Details about the charge and how it works can be obtained on *Tel:* 0845 900-1234, on www.cclondon.com or by writing to Congestion Charging, PO Box 2985, Coventry CV7 8ZR. Vehicles used by disabled drivers that are exempt from Vehicle Excise Duty are not charged. For blue badge holders, you need to register with TfL, which will cost £10. You will then have to inform them when you going into the congestion charge area, as the vehicle you are travelling in will then be exempt from the charge.

It remains to be seen how successful this policy will be, and obviously the charge may vary with time, but it could provide the basis for reducing congestion and for more investment into the public transport system. Both should benefit disabled residents and visitors. It is not quite clear how it will work for a disabled visitor who uses a hire car, but doubtless the hire company will be able to advise. For visitors to London from European countries, their local **BB** should be valid. For visitors from other countries, contact DaRT for advice.

Parking at or near your destination isn't always as difficult as people make out. If you can plan in advance, it is possible to reserve a space at some major sites and sights in London, and details are given in the guide. Bear in mind that there are only a small number of such spaces.

Parking for Blue Badge holders

There's a comprehensive map entitled the *Blue Badge User Guide* showing the location of the BB spaces throughout central London. It doesn't, however, say how many spaces there are at each location. The map is available from the **Association of London Government (ALG) Mobility Unit**, New Zealand House, 80 Haymarket SW1Y 4TZ *Tel:* 020 7747-4777. If you want a copy, just ring up, and they'll send it. Many of the spaces have a maximum time limit, commonly of three or four hours although some, particularly between Charing Cross Road and Kingsway, have a limit of one hour. The map also shows where there are public wheelchair accessible toilets (most of which use the RADAR key). It doesn't show the ones in the main line stations.

Note that the BB scheme does not apply in parts of Camden, nor in the whole of the City, Kensington and Chelsea or Westminster. This means, among other things, that there is no free parking on meters or in Pay and Display areas. What is worse is that the regulations are different in each borough, although efforts are being made to harmonise the rules. The BB does apply in Lambeth and Southwark, which are both south of the river.

The central boroughs listed also have special schemes for disabled people who either live or work in the area, and some of the special bays provided can only be used by those holding appropriate badges (green for Camden, red for the City, purple for Kensington and Chelsea and white for Westminster).

If you display your BB, you should not be clamped or towed away, even if you are parking illegally. You may incur a fine, and/or if the vehicle is causing an obstruction it may be moved to somewhere nearby.

One snag with trying to park in London is that the meter and Pay and Display signs often give no information for BB holders, AND if you ask, you're quite likely to be given wrong information, because people around don't always know what the regulations are. It's all a bit of a lottery. We are advised that if you do get a ticket, and you are not causing an unacceptable obstruction, that you should contest it. While you may, eventually, have to pay, a good number of **BB** holders appeal successfully against the charge.

There are two kinds of penalty: Penalty Charge Notices are issued by councils while Fixed Penalty Notices are issued by the police. If your vehicle is missing when you return, call the TRACE service (*Tel:* 020 7747-4747, 24 hours) and someone should be able to tell you what has happened to it.

Other useful contacts for queries about parking include:

Camden Parking Solutions, PO Box 20219, NW1 1WS *Tel:* 020 7681-4646
City of London Parking Services, 2 White Lyon Court EC2Y 8PS *Tel:* 020 7332-1548
Kensington and Chelsea Parking Shop, 19-27 Young Street W8 5EH *Tel:* 020 7361-4216
Parking and Traffic Appeals Service, PO Box 1010, Sutton, Surrey SM1 4SW *Tel:* 020 7747-4700
website: www.parkingandtrafficappeals.gov.uk
Westminster City Council Parking, PO Box 4053, SW1E 6XB *Tel:* 020 7823-4567.

Central car parks

Most 'pay' CPs, run by groups like NCP, do not offer concessions or free parking for **BB** holders. Nonetheless if there are three or four people using a car, pay parking can be worth it, as it may enable you to do many more things more easily. Note, for example, useful CPs at Whiteleys, at Selfridges, and under the National Theatre. There are reduced rates for parking in the evenings.

There are a good number of public CPs in central London. Although often full during the day, they are commonly readily available in the evenings and at weekends. Note that most MSCPs have a vehicle height limit that would exclude most minibuses.

Descriptions of many of the West End car parks are included below. The two main operators are:

- **NCP (National Car Parks)** 19-27 Young Street W8 5EH *Tel:* 0870 606-7050 *website:* www.ncp.co.uk;
- **Masterpark** *website:* www.masterpark.org.uk.

NCP publish a listing and a map, and if you would find this useful, you can write in and ask for a copy. In theory all such car parks are accessible to a chair user, as it is possible to enter and exit by the car ramp. This can be difficult and/or somewhat dangerous, and is not very practicable if you are parked several storeys up or down! In such car parks a lift is essential, unless there is a valet parking service in operation.

We have listed the CPs in alphabetical order. There are no designated BB spaces in the NCPs, unless specifically stated. Many of the Masterparks claim to have 'disabled parking bays', but do not say how many. If you wish to reserve a BB space ring the Masterpark Customer Care Officer on *Tel:* 020 7641-2629.

Adeline Place YMCA (NCP), W1P 3AD
Tel: 020 7637-0964
140 spaces, UG, 24 hrs, 188cm clearance. The main entrance and exit are on Adeline Place. There are two levels. There is a lift (D80 W85 L155), which takes you out step free to Great Russell Street. To the lift on level two there are +1+1 steps. To the lift on level one is +1. There are two BB spaces on level one, but the main entrance takes you down to level two, and you then must go up a level. Many spaces have large side transfer room.

Arlington House (NCP), SW1A 1RL
Tel: 020 7499-3312
90 spaces, UG, 24 hrs, 190cm clearance. Enter and exit at the end of Arlington Street, near the junction with Bennet Street. The CP is on one level underground. Pedestrians enter and exit via the car ramp, which is steep.

Audley Square (Masterpark), W1Y 5DR
Tel: 020 7499-3265
293 spaces, MS/UG, 24 hours, 193cm clearance. On Audley Square, just off South Audley Street and across from Tilney Street. Main entrance on South Audley Street and exit via Audley Square. Seven levels. The lift (D80 W160 L95) is on the left as you walk in, with step-free access from Audley Square. Three floors are above ground, three below, and all floors are step free from the lift. There are sixteen steps between levels.

Berners Street (NCP), W1P 3AD
Tel: 020 7637-9333

96 spaces, MS, 198cm clearance. Mon-Fri 7:00-19:00. Located near Oxford Street. Four levels. The main entrance and exit are on Berners Street. You leave your keys with an attendant who parks your car.

Bilton Towers (NCP), W1H 7LB
Tel: 020 7723-8840
153 spaces, UG, 24 hrs, 198cm clearance. Entrance and exit on Great Cumberland Place, by junction with Seymour Street.

Brewer Street (NCP), W1R 3HS
Tel: 020 7734-9497
426 spaces, MS, 24 hrs, 198cm clearance. On Brewer Street, near the intersection of Great Windmill Street and Lexington Street. Main entrance and exit on Brewer Street leading to four levels. There are no steps to the large lift (D85 W105 L135) which provides access to street level via $-1-1$.

Britannia Hotel (NCP), W1K 2LA
Tel: 020 7493-1400
165 spaces, UG, 24 hrs, 182cm clearance. Underneath Britannia Hotel, main entrance and exit on Adam's Row. On two levels, and you drive into the lower one. There is a lift (D95 W140 L95), and flat access from the lift on all floors and to Adam's Row.

Brunswick Square (NCP), WC1N 1AF
Tel: 020 7278-9792
272 spaces, UG, 24 hrs, 190cm clearance. Entrance on Marchmont Street, exit on Hunter Street. Entrance via steep ramp. No lift.

Bryanston Street (NCP), W1H 7AB
Tel: 020 7499-0313
300 spaces, MS, 24 hrs, 198cm clearance. Entrance and exit on Bryanston Street, just north of Oxford Street.

Carrington Street (NCP), W1J 7AF
Tel: 020 7629-9606
175 spaces, UG/MS, 24 hrs. Clearance 183cm. On Carrington Street, by the junction with Shepherd Street. Cars enter and exit on Carrington Street. On four floors, and without a lift. From the UG floor there are $+10+6$ steps. From the first floor there are $-7-10$, and from the second/roof level there are an additional $-3-16$.

Cavendish Square (Masterpark), W1M 9HA

Tel: 020 7499-8165/020 7629-6968

558 spaces, UG, 195cm clearance, Mon-Sat 6:00-24:00. Located under the Cavendish Square roundabout. You can drive there from Oxford Street by taking Holles Street, or go directly from Wigmore Street. Main entrance and exit on Cavendish Square. The ticket booth, where you must pay before getting your car, is + 1 step. The pavement leading to it is 68cm at its narrowest. The CP is a gentle corkscrew shape going down into the ground. No lift, and there are three levels below ground from where there are + 25 to surface.

Chesterfield House (NCP), W1Y 5TB

Tel: 020 7629-6706

50 spaces, UG, 198cm clearance, Mon-Fri 8:00-19:00. At end of Chesterfield Gardens, which is a cul-de-sac off of Curzon Street. Cars enter and exit on Chesterfield Gardens. No lift or stairs, and the CP is on one level. Pedestrian access is via the car ramp. Keys are left in car only if no bays are available. If necessary, car park attendants can park vehicle for you.

Cleveland Street (NCP), W1T 4JX

Tel: 020 7580-6254

84 spaces, UG, 244cm clearance. Entrance and exit on Cleveland Street, by the junction with Foley Street.

Cramer Street (Masterpark), W1H 3HF

Tel: 020 7935-5966

200 spaces, surface. No height limit, as this is an outdoor CP with a rough paved surface. Mon-Fri 7:00-18:30. The entrance and exit are on Moxon Street, and the CP itself is located between Aysbrook and Cramer Streets. There are + 5 steps to St Vincent Street, but it is not necessary to take these as you can easily leave via the car entrance on Moxon Street.

Denman Street (NCP), W1D 7HG

Tel: 020 7734-5760

120 spaces, UG 24 hrs, 195cm clearance. Between Shaftesbury Avenue and Sherwood Street, and about 30m from Piccadilly Theatre. The entrance is on Denman Street and the exit on Great Windmill Street. The CP is small and all on one level. Pedestrian access is by the car ramp. This can be difficult, because the space between the barrier and the raised pavement is narrow.

Drury Lane (NCP), WC2B 5PH
Tel: 020 7242-8611
330 spaces, UG, 24 hrs, 188cm clearance. Entrance in Parker Mews, about 40m from the junction with Parker Street. Four levels. There are two BB spaces on level A, about 50m from the lift (D90 W120 L135) which gives step-free access to the surface in Drury Lane and to all levels. 14 steps between levels and to the exit on Macklin Street. A small +1 step to the ticket booth on level A.

Grosvenor Hill (NCP), W1K 3PX
Tel: 020 7499-4331
200 spaces, UG, 188cm clearance. Entrance at the back on Grosvenor Hill, exit on Bourdon Street.

Holborn (NCP), WC1A 1JP
Tel: 020 7836-2039
240 spaces, MS, 24 hrs, 183cm clearance. Entrance and exit on Museum Street, between High Holborn and West Central Street. There are three floors, all above ground. There is a lift (D90 W110 L140), and step-free access to all floors via this lift. There are two BB spaces on the ground floor near the exit, but no discount for blue badge holders.

Holiday Inn (NCP), W1W 5AJ
Tel: 020 7387-7587
65 spaces, UG, 24 hrs, 183cm clearance. Near Great Portland Street tube station, with the entrance on Bolsover Street and exit on Great Titchfield Street.

London Marriott (NCP), W1K 5EL
Tel: 020 7491-8038
85 spaces, UG, 188cm clearance. Mon-Sun 7:00-20:00. At corner of George Yard and Balderton Street. You leave your keys with attendants, who park all vehicles.

Marylebone Road (NCP), NW1 5AR
Tel: 020 7935-6078
150 spaces, UG, 24 hrs, 213cm clearance. Entrance on Marylebone Road near junction with Gloucester Place, exit on Glentworth Street.

Minories, E1 8LP
Tel: 020 7702-9160
400 spaces, MSCP, 24 hrs, 426cm clearance. Located between

Minories and Mansell Street, just north of Tower Bridge. Car entrance is on Mansell Street; pedestrian entrance is on Shorter Street. Four BB spaces on the GF, by the pedestrian entrance. **Wheelchair toilet (D75 ST70 NKS)** also by this entrance. Four other levels (NB height clearance only 202cm) of parking are served by two pedestrian lifts (D80 W110 L140).

Newport Place (Masterpark), WC2H 7PU
Tel: 020 7641-7320
320 spaces, UG, 24 hrs, 198cm clearance. At the end of Gerrard Street, on the corner of Newport Place. Enter and exit via Gerrard Place. Three levels (eight split levels). Pedestrian entry is step free via two lifts (D85 W105 L152); on each floor there are small split levels (+8 − 1 steps or − 1), but these can be bypassed using the car ramps.

Park Lane (Masterpark), W1Y 3TJ
Tel: 020 7262-1814
679 spaces, UG, 24 hrs, 208cm clearance. At the Marble Arch end of Park Lane, by Cumberland Gate. Enter and exit from Park Lane, just outside the congestion charge zone.

Portman Square (NCP), W1H 9FJ
Tel: 020 7935-5310
439 spaces, UG, 24 hrs, 193cm clearance. Entrance and exit on Gloucester Place, just off Portman Square.

Sanderson Hotel (NCP), W1T 3NG
Tel: 020 7300-1407
50 spaces, UG, 183cm clearance. Mon-Fri 7:30-19:00. Located on Berners Street, near Oxford Street. The main entrance and exits are on Berners Street. There is one floor, and no lift. There are + 22 steps to street level. Keys are left in the car if the CP is full.

Selfridges see write up in the *Shops* chapter.

Sherwood Court (NCP), W1H 5HD
Tel: 020 7723-1506
70 spaces, UG, 198cm clearance. Entrance and exit on the corner of Bryanston Place and Shouldham Street.

Swiss Centre (NCP), WC2H 7BL
Tel: 020 7734-1032

87 spaces, UG, 193cm clearance, Mon-Sat 8:00-4:00. On Leicester Street, which is where the cars enter and exit. You leave your car at the entrance for the attendant to park. Pedestrians enter via car ramp. One floor.

Trafalgar Square (Masterpark), SW1A 2BN
Tel: 020 7930-1565
213 spaces, UG, 24 hrs, 195cm clearance. On Spring Gardens, just off Cockspur Street. Entrance and exit on Spring Gardens, with a fairly narrow pavement meaning wheelchairs will mostly have to use the road. Eight levels. A lift (D80 W90 L170) to the right of the car ramp links the odd-numbered levels. There are two BB spaces on Level Three. There are − 7 steps from the odd- to the even-numbered levels, which can be bypassed by the ramps: however, most spaces near the surface are reserved for offices.

Upper St Martin's Lane (NCP), WC2H 9DL
Tel: 020 7836-7451
140 spaces, MS, 24 hrs, 188cm clearance. Opposite West Street. Cars enter via corner of Monmouth Street and Shelton Street, and exit via Shelton Street. You leave your car at the entrance and hand over your keys at the ticket booth, which has + 1 step. The raised pavement into the CP is very narrow, and was blocked with cars when we surveyed. Four floors.

Water Gardens (NCP), W2 2DG
Tel: 020 7723-4940
350 places, UG, 24 hrs, 188cm clearance. Entrance and exit just off Edgware Road, just off Norfolk Crescent.

Welbeck Street (NCP), W1M 7HA
Tel: 020 7487-4376
360 spaces, MS, 193cm clearance. Mon-Fri 7:00-22:00, Sat 8:00-20:00. On Welbeck Street, near Wigmore Street and across from Debenhams. Entrance on Marylebone Lane and exit on Welbeck Street. Ten levels. Two lifts (D90 W130 L110), and all floors have step-free access to and from lift. There are + 7 between all floors, and flat access from the lifts to street level. It may be difficult exiting via car ramp because of narrow space between the pavement and car barrier.

Whitcomb Street (Masterpark), WC2H 7DT
Tel: 020 7839-5858

296 spaces, UG/MS, 24 hrs, 175cm clearance. At the junction with Orange Street. Entrance and exit on Whitcomb Street. Sloped area. This CP is on 16 levels, and there are two BB spaces on street level. Levels 1-8 are below ground, and 9-16 are above. The doors to levels 1 and 2, below street level, are 72cm wide. Those to all other levels are 66cm. Level 16 is not served by the lift and there are + 7 steps to it. Exit/entry from the street involves ± 1 step and there's a lift (D90 W70 L170). You have to pay before getting back into the vehicle, and the booth has + 2 large steps.

Car/van rental

Probably the best (and almost the only) source of converted vehicles for hire, including minibuses with tail-lifts, is **Wheelchair Travel**, 1 Johnston Green, Guildford, Surrey GU2 6XS *Tel:* 01483-233640 *Fax:* 01483-237772. See page 24.

It is possible to hire vehicles with the 'Chairman' conversion from **Gowerings Mobility**, Bone Lane, Newbury, Berks RG14 5UE *Tel:* 0845 608-8820 *Fax:* 01635-529400 *website:* www.goweringsmobility.co.uk. These can take a chair user in the car. You have to collect the vehicle from Newbury.

By taxi and minicab

Taxis and minicabs are widely available. London taxis are of unique design, adapted from the old-fashioned hackney (horse-drawn) carriage of Victorian times. Black cabs are licensed by the police, and every vehicle carries its licence number. They operate a meter on which the fare is recorded. Although cabs are relatively expensive as a way of getting around, they offer great convenience, reasonable accessibility, and if the fare is shared between several people, the cost per person comes down.

Taxis can be hailed (stopped) in the street, but while they are legally obliged to take a fare, not all will stop for wheelchair users. There are drivers who seem to become temporarily blind when they don't want to stop, because they can't be bothered with the ramps. TfL will start to provide Disability Equality training to all drivers of black cabs in 2003, so it is hoped that the situation will improve progressively.

All black taxicabs are wheelchair accessible in principle, as it is a legal requirement. The largest cabs, and by far the best for accessibility are the TX1 and the Metrocab. The TX1 has additional headroom and a very neat fold-out ramp which is built into the taxi floor, and is easy to use. There is a newer TX11 model coming into use which is even better than the TX1, and the TX111 is being planned. The TX11 has a longer ramp, and includes belts and restraints for a chair user. This, however, is a slightly mixed blessing, because it can take several minutes to fix all the necessary straps, and that's time when the meter is ticking.

In some of the older cabs such as the FX4 models, a chair user can be quite restricted, and may have to sit 'sideways on' with his head bent over at a funny angle. In addition the black cab design is particularly difficult for people with arthritis as the main seat is back some distance away from the door, and you have to bend down to get in. One American who wrote to us said that it was undignified for an elderly gentleman to have to crawl on his knees to get to the seat, as he couldn't easily bend down.

The newer vehicles have a fold-out dickie seat on a hinge, which means that it can be unfolded, and will swing right outside the cab over the pavement. You can then sit down outside, and swing in while sitting on the seat. This may well help some, but cab drivers aren't necessarily quick to spot when you might need this facility.

If you want to take a wheelchair-accessible cab, the story is still a bit of a lottery. At a main cab rank, you can simply wait until a TX1, TX11 or a Metrocab turns up, and there are increasing numbers of these vehicles. If you want a cab to go to the theatre, a museum or to the shops, there are three main companies:

- **Computercab**   020 7286-6070 (cash bookings); 020 7286-0286 (credit card bookings)
- **Dial-a-Cab**   020 7253-5000 (cash bookings); 020 7426-3420 (credit card bookings)
- **Radio Taxicabs** 020 7272-0272 (for either cash or credit card bookings)

There are a few details to be aware of. If you're unlucky, the phone line to the cab company will be busy. One of us recently spent thirty minutes hanging on the phone to a cab company being assured that 'we will answer as quickly as possible' (true) and that 'we'll be with you very soon' (a downright lie). The use of mobile phones can make all this easier, and if there are two or three people in the party, you can each phone a different company, and simply use the first call to get through. If it's raining, it'll be much, much longer before you'll be able to get a cab, and you may have to be very patient. It might even be worth going to a restaurant!

Even a 'booked' cab may not turn up. It is not guaranteed. One of our surveyors booked a ComCab to pick him up after a concert at the Barbican. None came and he was told that 'no cab was available'. As a result, he finished up pushing all the way to Waterloo.

As a casual user, there are limits to pre-booking. Houses, hotels and business premises are generally OK as a pick-up point, and restaurants are pretty much acceptable. When it comes to museums, theatres, cinemas and other places where you may need a cab, you will have to negotiate carefully. From the cab company's viewpoint, it is infuriating if you book a vehicle which isn't necessarily right outside the theatre door when you come out, and you take the nearest empty cab instead – ignoring the one you've booked. The different companies have slightly different approaches to all this. You are more likely to be able to pre-book if you pay by credit card, and you may well get through more quickly to an operator.

Radio Taxicabs offer an Account Service which might be of interest to London residents wanting to make use of taxi services several times a year. It is slightly more expensive, but does offer pre-booking facilities. If you order a cab by phone, there will be an initial charge to enable the cab to reach you, but this should not exceed £4 or £5. In addition, credit card bookings tend to pick up a compulsory 10% surcharge.

There's a useful service provided by **Black Taxi Tours of London** (*Tel:* 020 7935-9363 *e-mail:* info@blacktaxitours.co.uk *website:* www.blacktaxitours.co.uk) who offer a two-hour tour for £75 if started before 18.00 or £85 if started later than this (2003 prices). They have accessible taxis, and the great advantage of such a tour is that you can get into the squares, mews and back streets where no tour bus would be able to take you.

Minicabs are conventional cars, and because you can transfer sideways into a seat, they may be easier for some people to use than a London taxi. They can only be ordered by phone, or by prior arrangement, but cannot pick you up in the street. You can go to a minicab office and order one. Minicabs have offered a variable level of service in the past, and there are still some unlicensed operators out there, some of whom may hang around outside stations or nightclubs.

Minicabs are now in the middle of a three-stage procedure of licensing. This involves:

- the drivers;
- the companies;
- individual vehicles.

The first two stages of this process have been completed, and in due course, the vehicles will be licensed as well, thus making standards much more uniform. The TfL website has a searchable database of licensed minicab operators.

The general advice given is to always pre-book through a licensed operator. Check that the driver knows your destination before getting in, and that there is an agreed fare. People should normally sit in the back, and it's sensible to carry a mobile phone.

If you cannot use the public transport system, and do not wish to drive around, taxis and minicabs are almost your only other option.

Transport for London (TfL)

Transport for London
Windsor House, 42-50 Victoria Street SW1W 0TL
Tel: travel information 020 7222-1234 (24 hours) *Textphone:* 020 7918-3015 *website:* www.tfl.gov.uk
TfL runs both the buses and Underground. Its principal function is to provide a fast mass transport system which best meets the needs of Londoners and visitors. It is only relatively recently that the requirements of disabled passengers have been seriously addressed, and the provisions that have been made are restricted because in many cases they are seen as being too costly. When new facilities are built, it is accepted that accessibility is important, but the necessary modifications to older underground stations, for example, have only been made in a few places.

A GLAD survey a few years ago showed that over 400,000 Londoners could not use the normal public transport system because of their disability. There will be tens of thousands of visitors who will have problems, and probably many more who will be deterred from coming altogether.

Special provisions, particularly for passengers who need step-free access, are still quite minimal, and most are shown on our Accessible Tube Stations diagram. The DLR reaches Tower Gateway and the Bank, and is being extended with a new line past London City Airport. The new JLE opens up more possibilities as all the stations from Westminster to Stratford are accessible. There are a handful of other accessible stations, and we include in our list (and on the diagram) those which are due to become step free during the next five years. If the current political dispute about funding is sorted, more may have lifts installed before 2010. In a recent London Underground policy statement '*Unlocking London For All*' it was announced that there are plans to install lifts at seventy additional stations over the next 10-15 years and we very much hope that this will be the case. Funding such a programme will be a major issue.

TfL produces various free maps, guides and leaflets, including a comprehensive *Tube Access Guide* which is both a map and listing of all the stations which people can use without stairs and escalators. The map was developed in conjunction with SCOPE during 2001, and is an extension of the map in our 1996 edition. TfL also produces a range of literature, including a useful *Large Print Central London Area Bus Guide* with a listing of services which are (or should be) wheelchair accessible.

One thing that we do have to warn people about is that during the rush hour peaks, it's difficult enough for anyone to get on some of the central tube trains or the buses, and it's probably not practical for most disabled people to battle with the crowded system. It's not easy to design a system that copes with the levels of overcrowding commonly experienced.

Buses

London has an extensive network of bus routes, and an increasing number of bus lanes. There is an excellent TfL listing in the *Large Print Central London Area Bus Guide*. Buses tend to take longer than the Underground, although you will see much more of London if you use them. Note that modern buses can accelerate and brake quite sharply, and it is therefore important to find a seat quite quickly. For a disabled walker, if you're uncertain, it's worth asking the driver to wait briefly until you are seated, *and* to say when you are getting off.

One very constructive change that is well under way is the introduction of low-floor buses. These have only small steps at the entrance or exit and, using a simple extending ramp, can enable chair users to travel relatively easily. These buses are much easier for parents with buggies and baby carriages, people with heavy luggage and for elderly people with shopping trolleys. For a chair user, the entrance is usually through the doors in the middle of the bus, and there's a 'reserved' place where you can back your chair against a tall padded support, so that you don't slide around if the bus brakes sharply. This idea is excellent, as it gets over the need for any complicated system of clamping.

At the time of writing, something approaching three-quarters of London's buses have this facility. Details of all the wheelchair-accessible routes are given in the index to TfL's area bus guides which can be obtained by phoning the Call Centre line *Tel:* 020 7222-1234.

There are, however, some teething problems, and using the buses can still be a bit of a challenge for a chair user. During our survey visits, chair users from within our team made more than fifty trips on wheelchair-accessible buses. About half the journeys were unsuccessful, mainly because the ramp did not work, and in several instances we 'disabled a bus' because the ramp came out, and wouldn't go back again! Everyone had to get off and wait for the next bus! The usual reason for ramp problems is that the driver needs to pull in tight to the kerb as the ramp is less than 1m long. The kerb also needs to be of an adequate height. If the ramp is not supported on the kerb it can flop down, and be difficult to get back in again.

The necessary manoeuvre for the bus is sometimes quite difficult, especially when cars are parked at the bus stop.

In two or three instances, the attitude of the driver was not helpful and sometimes we ran into the problem that the allocated space was already taken up by baby buggies. Parents were surprisingly unwilling to pick up their baby and fold their buggy, to facilitate the use of the space by a wheelchair user. Having only one staff member on a bus (the driver) means that it can be more difficult to sort out problems like this.

In addition, it is hard for a solo chair user to make any contact with the driver. The system has taken this on board, and there's a blue button by the wheelchair space to alert the driver that the ramp is needed at the next stop. All too often, this separate bell is disconnected, either because it makes too loud a noise, or because there are too many false alarms from other passengers using it.

If possible, it's a good idea to let the driver know where you want to get off when you get aboard, even though this may entail some loud shouting.

Clearly, in time, the engineering and maintenance problems with the ramps should get sorted and staff training will be more thorough. As part of the bus company contracts, TfL has started to provide Disability Equality training for both bus drivers and their managers.

When most buses are accessible, and the ramps can be relied upon, usage will increase, and the whole business of getting on and off will hopefully become more routine. Some hassles, particularly on busy routes, are likely to remain. You should be able to follow the story as it develops in the *Transport For All* magazine published by DaRT. By 2008, TfL anticipates that all the buses will be low floor and wheelchair accessible. Also, there's a concerted effort via the bus operator contracts to improve the reliability of the ramps. Since some fierce monitoring, the proportion of ramps that don't work is reported to have dropped to around 10%. This does not, however, address the other problem with their use, where the bus does not line up correctly alongside the pavement, and the ramp flops down due to the weight of the chair.

Currently, if it's possible, we would advise only using the buses where there are several accessible routes going your way, as this maximises the chance of finding an accessible bus with a working ramp.

Key accessible bus routes in the centre

Some of the (potentially) accessible bus services and routes which run from accessible tube and NR stations to and through central London, passing close to places of interest described in the guide, are listed below. The list is inevitably selective, but London's bus map looks a bit like a pile of unruly spaghetti and the routes are difficult to disentangle. Finding the right route is difficult, particularly for a visitor. In the list, the accessible station en route (marked NR or DLR where appropriate) is put in **bold**, and the accessible tube stations are described more fully in the next section. They are marked on the map on pages 72 and 73.

We list first two routes linking the main NR stations, and a central riverside route (RV1) linking many central sights. Note that the buses do not all stop at a single spot outside some of the larger places. Most bus stops have a local map indicating where the different routes stop, and usually it is clear on the TfL *Large Print Central London Area Bus Guide* which is regularly updated. The * indicates a station that is due to become accessible before 2005.

- *Route number*
205 Whitechapel, **Liverpool Street NR**, **King's Cross NR**, **Euston NR**, **Marylebone NR**, **Paddington NR**. This links main line NR stations and has taken over half the previous *Stationlink* route
705 **Paddington NR**, **Victoria Coach Station**, **Victoria NR**, **Waterloo**, **London Bridge NR**, **Fenchurch Street NR**, **Liverpool Street NR**. This route has taken over the other half of the *Stationlink*

service, but it is time-restricted, and doesn't operate after about 20.00

RV1 The riverside service on a circular route from **Tower Gateway (DLR)**, Tower Bridge, **London Bridge**, Tate Modern, Gabriel's Wharf, National Theatre, Festival Hall, London Eye, **Waterloo** (York Road), Westminster Bridge, Aldwych (Somerset House), Covent Garden

- *From Westminster*: District Line and JLE
3 Crystal Palace, **Brixton***, Lambeth (Imperial War Museum), **Westminster**, Trafalgar Square, Oxford Circus
24 Pimlico, Victoria, **Westminster**, Trafalgar Square, Camden
77A Aldwych, Trafalgar Square, **Westminster**, Tate Britain, Wandsworth
88 Clapham Common, Tate Britain, **Westminster**, Trafalgar Square, Oxford Circus, Camden
148 Camberwell, **Westminster**, Victoria, Marble Arch, Shepherd's Bush

- *From Waterloo*: NR and JLE (note that only the 211, 507 and 705 go from Station Approach reached via the main exit by the clock. Most other services go from Waterloo Road at a lower level, reached via the lift going down to the JLE station ticket hall. The RV1 goes from York Road)
1 see Canada Water (below)
26 **Waterloo**, Aldwych, St Paul's, **Bank (DLR)**, Liverpool Street station, Hackney
59 Streatham Hill, **Brixton***, **Waterloo**, Russell Square (British Museum), Euston
68 West Norwood, Camberwell, **Waterloo**, Russell Square (British Museum), Euston
76 **Waterloo** (Baylis Road), Aldwych, **Bank (DLR)**, Tottenham
77 **Waterloo**, Vauxhall, Tooting
139 **Waterloo**, Aldwych, Trafalgar Square, Oxford Circus, West Hampstead
168 **Waterloo**, Russell Square (British Museum), Euston, Hampstead Heath NR station (not going near Kenwood House)
171 Holborn, Aldwych, **Waterloo**, Elephant & Castle, Catford
172 Brockley Rise, **New Cross**, Elephant & Castle, **Waterloo**, Aldwych, St Paul's
176 Penge, **Waterloo**, Trafalgar Square, Leicester Square, Oxford Circus

188   see North Greenwich (below)
211   **Waterloo**, Victoria, Chelsea, **Hammersmith**
507   **Waterloo**, Victoria (Mon-Fri only until 20.00)
521   see London Bridge (below)

- *From London Bridge*: NR, JLE and Northern Line (note that a number of the routes go along Tooley Street, others come up Southwark High Street. Some go across London Bridge and others go down Southwark Street. Routes 17, 43, 48, 149, 521 and 705 all stop in Station Approach)

17   **London Bridge**, Mansion House, King's Cross, **Caledonian Road**, Archway, and for Kenwood House, transfer at Archway to route **210**
35   **Brixton***, **London Bridge**, Liverpool Street
40   Dulwich (library), **London Bridge**, Aldgate
43   **London Bridge**, **Bank**, Islington, Friern Barnet
47   see Canada Water (below)
48   **London Bridge**, Liverpool Street station via Monument, Hackney, Walthamstow
133   Liverpool Street, **Bank (DLR)**, **London Bridge**, Kennington, **Brixton***, Streatham
149   **London Bridge**, Liverpool Street, Edmonton, Ponders End
521   **London Bridge**, St Paul's, **Waterloo** (Mon-Fri only until 19.00)

- *From Bank*: DLR
see 25, 26, 43, 76, 133

- *From Canada Water*: JLE and East London Line
1   **Canada Water**, **Waterloo**, Aldwych, Tottenham Court Road (see also 188 below)
47   Liverpool Street, **London Bridge**, **Canada Water**, Lewisham, Catford
188   see North Greenwich (below)

- *From North Greenwich*: JLE
188   **North Greenwich**, Surrey Quays, **Canada Water**, **Waterloo**, Aldwych, Russell Square (for British Museum)

- *From Stratford*: DLR, JLE, NR
25   Aldgate, **Bank** (on Mon-Fri), **Tower** (Sat and Sun), Holborn, Oxford Circus

- *From Caledonian Road*: Piccadilly Line
274   Islington (Angel), **Caledonian Road**, Camden, Zoo, Baker Street, Marble Arch
17   see London Bridge (above)

- *From Earl's Court*: District and Piccadilly lines
74   Putney, **Earl's Court**, South Kensington (museums), Hyde Park Corner, Baker Street
328   Chelsea, **Earl's Court**, Kensington High Street, Golders Green

- *From Hammersmith*: District, Piccadilly and Hammersmith & City lines:
10   **Hammersmith**, Kensington (Albert Hall), Oxford Street, Euston, King's Cross
27   Camden, Paddington, Kensington High Street, **Hammersmith**, Turnham Green
211   see Waterloo (above)

- *From Lewisham*: DLR
436   **Lewisham**, **New Cross**, Victoria, Marble Arch, Paddington

The Underground (Tube)

Because the system is old, and very deep in many places, there are steps and escalators at the vast majority of stations. However, things are gradually getting better, and there's now a detailed map and listing called the *Tube Access Guide* which was developed by TfL in conjunction with SCOPE which is an extension of the map we made for the 1996 edition of *Access in London*. This TfL guide includes a listing of all the accessible stations, and of cross-platform links. Note that **there's a step in and out of nearly all the trains**, and that the step height is highly variable, and it may be a step up, or it may be down. It can be as much as 30cm, and in the *Tube Access Guide* mentioned above, there is a colour coded indication of how big the step is. In addition, a few of the platforms underground are curved, so that occasionally quite a gap opens up between the train and the platform edge. This is not the case (we think) at any of the accessible stations.

We include a simplified version of the map entitled *Accessible Tube Stations* on pages 72 and 73. Contact the TfL Call Centre for more detailed and up-to-date information and in particular to find out if the lifts are working. There is also a TfL book called *Access to the Underground*. This is a detailed description of *all* the stations, but it's quite difficult to understand unless you know the station already.

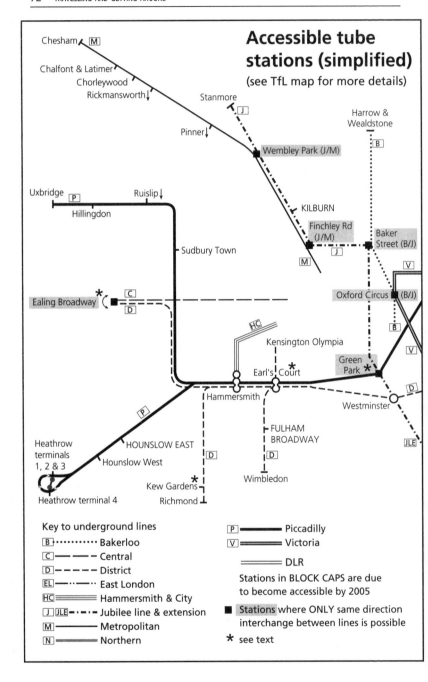

Accessible tube stations (simplified)

(see TfL map for more details)

Chesham M

Chalfont & Latimer

Chorleywood

Rickmansworth↓

Stanmore J

Harrow & Wealdstone B

Pinner↓

Wembley Park (J/M)

Uxbridge P

Ruislip↓

Hillingdon

KILBURN

Finchley Rd (J/M) J

Baker Street (B/J)

Sudbury Town

M

V

Ealing Broadway ✱ C D

Oxford Circus (B/J)

B

V

HC

Kensington Olympia

Green Park ✱

Earl's Court ✱

Hammersmith

Westminster

D

FULHAM BROADWAY

Heathrow terminals 1, 2 & 3 P

HOUNSLOW EAST

Hounslow West

D

Wimbledon

JLE

Heathrow terminal 4

Kew Gardens ✱

Richmond

Key to underground lines

B ·········· Bakerloo

C — — — Central

D – – – – District

EL —··—··· East London

HC ══════ Hammersmith & City

J JLE —·—·— Jubilee line & extension

M ———— Metropolitan

N ══════ Northern

P ━━━━ Piccadilly

V ══════ Victoria

══════ DLR

Stations in BLOCK CAPS are due to become accessible by 2005

■ Stations where ONLY same direction interchange between lines is possible

✱ see text

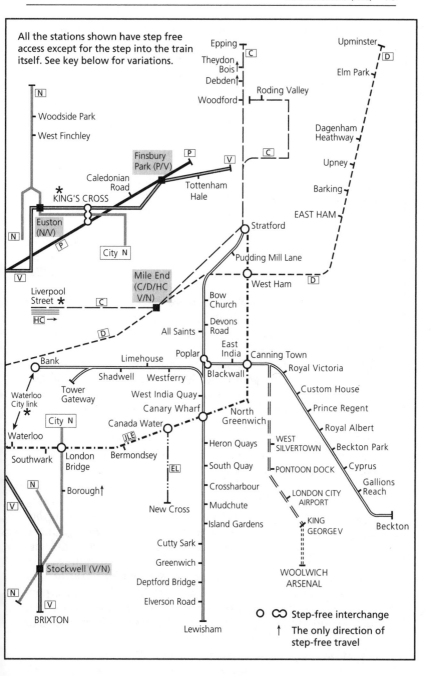

All the stations shown have step free access except for the step into the train itself. See key below for variations.

○ ∞ Step-free interchange
↑ The only direction of step-free travel

In our diagram, we have included nearly all the accessible stations, including those that will become accessible by 2005. As it was necessary to simplify the standard tube map, the following commentary may help to illustrate what is possible. On the map, all the named stations are accessible step free apart from the step into the train. Those due to open soon are shown in BLOCK CAPITALS and those with platform-to-platform interchange are also shown, although these do not have step-free access to the surface.

We have included only the northern part of the **Bakerloo** Line as the single accessible station is Harrow & Wealdstone. Using it does, however, offer the possibility of same-direction transfers onto the Jubilee Line at Baker Street (hence linking with the JLE stations) or onto the Victoria Line at Oxford Circus. After that, none of the Bakerloo stations offer step-free transfer or access.

The **Central** Line is accessible only to the east/northeast of London, although there is the possibility of same-direction transfers at Mile End, and of changing lines at Ealing Broadway, at the other end of the line.

We have omitted the **Circle** Line, whose main 'access' function is to take passengers eastwards (initially) around from Liverpool Street to Westminster, and can take passengers back to Liverpool Street by going all the way around the circle.

The **District** Line has accessible stations both in the east and the west. You can come in from either Richmond or Wimbledon, and both Hammersmith and Earl's Court are fully accessible, as is Westminster (with its link to the JLE). To the east, there's same-direction transfer at Mile End, and a second link to the JLE at West Ham. Five more stations are fully accessible en route to Upminster. There's also the link to Kensington Olympia, and several more stations are due to become accessible during 2003/4.

The **DLR** is accessible throughout (always dependent on the appropriate lifts being operational), and a new extension is being built via London City Airport to King George V (Dock). A further extension to go south of the river to Woolwich Arsenal is planned.

Only the southern bit of the **East London** Line is shown as the only accessible link is the one to and from New Cross and Canada Water. We have only included the **Hammersmith & City** Line in the briefest detail. The line has accessible stations at Hammersmith, Liverpool Street (going east only), West Ham and Barking, with same-direction transfer possible to the Central Line at Mile End. This then links to Stratford and to the DLR and JLE.

The **Jubilee** Line is accessible at Stanmore, and will be so at

Kilburn, and there are same-side transfers possible to and from the Metropolitan Line. At Green Park, there's a possible lift transfer to the Piccadilly Line, and that's an 'either-way' transfer, as it doesn't just depend on crossing the platform. The line continues to what we have called the JLE (Jubilee Line Extension) where all the stations between Westminster and Stratford are fully accessible. This opens up huge possibilities for both wheelchair users, and other people with disabilities.

We have only included the western end of the **Metropolitan** Line, which links with same-side transfer to the Jubilee Line. It later goes through the unidirectional Liverpool Street Station, but terminates at the next stop, Aldgate (which is not accessible).

The **Piccadilly** Line is accessible at Heathrow in the west, and then through Hammersmith and Earl's Court. At Green Park there's the possibility of transfer to the JLE. After that, only Caledonian Road is accessible, but there's the possibility of same-side transfer at Finsbury Park, enabling you to get to Tottenham Hale on the Victoria Line.

The **Victoria** Line will soon be accessible at Brixton. There is the possibility of same-direction transfer at Stockwell onto the Northern Line. Plus there's the possibility of same-direction transfer at Oxford Circus to the Bakerloo Line (to get to Harrow & Wealdstone), and at Euston to the Northern Line. Finally, Caledonian Road, which is just north of King's Cross, is fully accessible.

The stations on the Underground that have step-free access (but with a step into the train) are:
Barking (using a railway lift and ramps)
Bermondsey (JLE, via one lift)
Brixton (lifts are under construction for commissioning in 2004)
Caledonian Road (one lift)
Canada Water (JLE, via two lifts)
Canary Wharf (JLE, via two lifts)
Canning Town (JLE, one lift)
Chalfont & Latimer
Chesham
Chorleywood
Dagenham Heathway
Earl's Court (Piccadilly Line, via a lift and the Warwick Road entrance; a lift from the District Line platforms is under construction for commissioning in 2003, also linking to the Warwick Road entrance)

East Ham (lifts are planned for 2003)
Elm Park
Epping
Fulham Broadway (lifts planned for 2003)
Hammersmith (both stations and all platforms; the Piccadilly and District Line station is accessed by lifts; Hammersmith & City Line station has step-free access)
Heathrow terminals 1, 2 and 3
Heathrow terminal 4
Hillingdon (via lifts)
Hounslow East (lifts are planned for 2004)
Hounslow West (platform stairlift)
Kensington Olympia
Kew Gardens (one side only; on the other, you have to get a gate unlocked; you could stay on the train to Richmond, and then come back again to get to the other side)
Kilburn (lifts are planned for 2003)
King's Cross (lifts to the Circle/Hammersmith Lines are planned for 2005, and to the deep platforms by 2007)
London Bridge (JLE and Northern Line both have lifts, with separate entrances some 400m apart. The step-free JLE entrance is from Duke Street Hill)
New Cross
North Greenwich (JLE, two lifts)
Richmond (lift)
Roding Valley
Southwark (JLE, two lifts)
Sudbury Town
Stanmore
Stratford (Central, DLR, JLE with lifts to all platforms)
Tottenham Hale (lift)
Upminster (NR lift on request to get to the District line)
Upney
Uxbridge
Waterloo (JLE, one lift. The step-free JLE entrance is from Waterloo Road, and there's a lift down from the NR station near platform 4)
West Finchley
West Ham (JLE with lift; lift for the District Line under construction for 2003; also c2c)
Wimbledon (lift)
Woodford
Woodside Park

On the map showing accessible tube links, we have included a few stations with step-free access in one direction only. For example, at **Liverpool Street** the eastbound Metropolitan/Circle Line platform can be accessed by lift. You can then go round to Westminster (and use this as a base for getting to other places). To return, you would simply have to take the Circle Line the 'long way round' to get back to the accessible platform.

In addition there are a few cross-platform links that are of particular value. Generally you can only get a train on another line going in the same direction, but some of these make useful journeys possible. Key stations with cross-platform links between lines are:

Baker Street (Bakerloo/Jubilee)
Ealing Broadway (Central/District)
Earl's Court (District/Piccadilly on completion of lift work)
Euston (Northern, City Branch/Victoria)
Finchley Road (Metropolitan/Jubilee)
Finsbury Park (Piccadilly/Victoria)
Green Park (Piccadilly/Jubilee only, by lift) with transfer in either direction
Mile End (Central/District/Hammersmith & City)
Oxford Circus (Bakerloo/Victoria)
Stockwell (Northern/Victoria)
Wembley Park (Metropolitan/Jubilee)

A few stations such as Hyde Park Corner have step-free access if you can use the escalators. Note that escalators and lifts aren't always operational, and although London Underground have been undertaking an extensive replacement programme, some are still really old.

Waterloo to City link

There is an important link between Waterloo International station and the Waterloo-City Line. This means that you can get from the main concourse on Waterloo to and from the DLR network. Consequently you can come in from suburban stations to Waterloo or Waterloo East, and go to Bank, Canary Wharf and to Tower Gateway, using a step-free route.

The route involves taking the lifts from the Waterloo concourse down to the level under the main station where the International ticket office is and where arrivals come in. Go down the ramp alongside the road, and turn left past the Underground ticket office.

Go through the bypass gate (operated by NKS key) where the trolley barriers are and out through the double doors, turn right and take the ramp down to the Waterloo-City platform.

At Bank there is a gently inclined Travelator (a moving walkway) followed by a steepish slope, to take you up to the ticket office ring. From this level there are staff-operated lifts either down to the DLR platform using two lifts, or up to King William Street using a third lift, but you need staff help throughout.

Going the other way involves a little extra time at Waterloo. There is lift/ramped access at Bank Station via the Travelators to the Waterloo-City train, but note that the ramps are really quite steep. At Waterloo, the arrivals platform only has stepped access to get out (about +30). However, what happens is that the trains go into a siding for a few minutes before returning to Bank via the ramped departure platform. Consequently, if you cannot manage the stairs, you should tell the driver when leaving Bank (he has to walk the length of the train to change ends) that you need to go via the sidings. The London Underground tell us that this procedure is currently being 'formally clarified'. The route from the departures platform is up the ramp, through the gate bypass into the International station and then up in the lifts to the main Waterloo concourse.

Docklands Light Railway (DLR)

The DLR is London's only major fully accessible transport system. It links Lewisham and Greenwich, to Stratford, Tower Gateway or Bank. An extension goes through the northern docklands to Beckton. There's a planned addition which will go through the southern docklands via London City Airport to the King George V Dock, which may then go across the river to Woolwich Arsenal in due course. **All the stations have step-free access with a lift or ramp from street to platform. The coaches have special spaces for a chair user.** The railway is built with some quite tight curves in places, and with some steepish gradients. As a result, the 'ride' can be a bit rough on certain sections, and our advice is simply to 'hang on tight' and you'll be OK, but it's best to be prepared.

During the early years of operation, there were some problems with the serviceability of lifts, but the situation seems to have improved considerably. As the line runs at a high level over much of its length, the lifts are essential as you might otherwise have to manage anything up to 60 or 80 steps. At Bank there is lift access in three stages. From street level the lift at Bank is tucked away out of sight a short distance along King William Street. There is an intercom to access it. At a lower level there are two further lifts down to the DLR platform. You need staff assistance to use the route as the lifts to the Northern Line are only used by passengers during rush hours, and the final lift needs a staff member with a key. If you want to make enquiries about the serviceability of lifts at DLR stations you want to use on a particular day, ring 020 7363-9700.

Tramlink

This is a relatively new service in south London, using modern fully-accessible trams. It operates on a route which goes from Wimbledon via Mitcham and Croydon, on to either New Addington, Elmers End or Beckenham. The trams provide virtually step-free access, and are much easier for a wheelchair user or disabled walker to get on and off than a bus. There is no need for a supplementary ramp for example. There is a reasonably generous wheelchair space in each car, which can also be used by people travelling with young children in buggies, although chair users have priority. The trams also tend to accelerate and brake more smoothly than buses which makes for a more comfortable ride.

The main places of interest en route are Croydon and Wimbledon, and much of the route goes through suburban south London, making it of considerable value to local residents. Croydon has extensive shopping facilities, the Fairfield Halls and the Clocktower Arts Centre. Both East Croydon NR Station, and Wimbledon NR and tube stations are fully accessible, providing a quick way of getting into central London.

For information about Tramlink use the central TfL call centre *Tel:* 020 7222-1234 *Textphone:* 020 7918-3015 *website:* www.tfl.gov.uk. There are maps on the website which can be downloaded. Ring TfL and they'll send you a map and details, and the route is shown in the NR map *London Connections.*

There are proposals for extending the existing network to places like Sutton, Purley, Streatham, and possibly even Lewisham and Bromley. Studies and consultation are underway for a cross-river tramway, and for one in west London, but all these schemes will take many years before they reach completion.

Services for London residents

There is an excellent magazine called, *Transport For All* published by DaRT, the Accessible Transport Users Association, and supported by TfL. It includes updated information about the provisions which are discussed in this section.

The principal improvement in the transport system for disabled residents in London has been the provision of Dial-a-Ride services, and the use of the Taxicard. Both have gone through changes, in particular due to cuts in funding (and threatened cuts). Recently, the Mayor of London has allocated additional funds for these services, but not all boroughs have accepted the funding. Taxicard is funded by borough councils, and Dial-a-Ride by ring-fenced money from central Government. In recent years, the provisions have varied from borough to borough, and from year to year – all of which is most unsatisfactory. **Most schemes have tight limitations on the number of journeys any individual can make**. Dial-a-Ride is currently administered by TfL, who undertook an extensive review of the provisions during 2001. The principal recommendation from this was that Dial-a-Ride should be operated by a single company, and this was implemented in 2002.

Dial-a-Ride (DAR)

DAR use wheelchair-accessible minibuses, and provide a door-to-door service for those unable to use ordinary buses or trains. The idea is excellent. You can ring up and they will organise a driver to take you shopping, to visit friends or to go to church, either alone or with companions. DAR can be used by people living in sheltered housing, where several people may want to go to the same destination, either on a regular basis or one-off outings. The concept is good, although it requires a little organisation to make use of the service. With the establishment of one central controlling company, the provisions made by DAR should improve and should become more uniform – but this will take time.

For applications and general enquiries, your first contact depends on which borough you live in. For:

Camden, Hammersmith and Fulham, Kensington and Chelsea, Westminster
Tel/Textphone: 020 7266-6100
Barnet, City of London, Enfield, Hackney, Haringey, Islington
Tel/Textphone: 020 8829-1200
Barking and Dagenham, Havering, Newham, Redbridge, Tower Hamlets, Waltham Forest
Tel/Textphone: 020 8498-8200

Bexley, Bromley, Greenwich, Lewisham, Southwark
Tel/Textphone: 01689 896-333
Croydon, Lambeth, Kingston, Merton, Richmond, Sutton, Wandsworth
Tel/Textphone: 020 8879-5023
Brent, Ealing, Harrow, Hillingdon, Hounslow
Tel/Textphone: 020 8970-0090

The central enquiry point if you have problems or queries is DAR at Ash Grove Garage, Mare Street, E8 4RH *Tel:* 020 7241-7456 *e-mail:* joyce.mamode@tfl-buses.co.uk. If you feel that the reply you get is unsatisfactory, or if you want more information, contact **DaRT**, the **Accessible Transport Users Association**, Room 210, The Colourworks, 2 Abbot Street E8 3DP *Tel:* 020 7241-2111. DaRT membership is open to anyone who uses Dial-a-Ride or Taxicard services and, among other things, they campaign for adequate funding for the services. A specific goal is to ensure that all transport becomes accessible for disabled people.

Taxicard

This provides a complementary service to Dial-a-Ride, and is also for those who cannot use public transport. The card gives a reduced price taxi ride but, like all schemes, it has its limitations. Basically you pay a flat fee of £1.50 if the taxi meter shows anything up to £10.30 on weekdays, £11.30 at weekends and £12.80 at night. The scheme will pay for any extras such as evening, night or weekend journeys, but not for additional passengers. If the cost is over £10.30, you pay £1.50 plus the extra. With recent changes, the Mayor of London has boosted the funding for the scheme, and tried to ensure uniformity of provision in different boroughs. DaRT will have the latest information about the conditions in the schemes in the different boroughs. They also have application forms.

The scheme is administered by ALG Taxicard, part of the Association of London Government. For more information, you can contact: **ALG Taxicard**, New Zealand House, 80 Haymarket SW1Y 4TZ *Tel:* 020 7484-2929 *e-mail:* taxicard@tcfl.gov.uk, or look at www.taxicard.co.uk. It provides door-to-door transport on a flexible basis. Several people can travel together (thereby reducing the cost per head), and the journey is subsidised.

The snags are that when you make a phone booking, the driver will start the meter wherever he is when he receives the radio message.

Additionally he is technically charging waiting time if you are a little bit slow in getting out of the house, although this running time should never cost more than £1.50. When you try to make a booking, if there are no taxis immediately available (particularly if you require a wheelchair-accessible cab), the taxi company may not be able to let you know until the last minute that it hasn't got a cab for you.

The limitations on the permissible number of journeys vary from borough to borough and some have withdrawn from the scheme. Because of the somewhat bureaucratic procedures for the driver who needs to reclaim his money from the Taxicard scheme, there are some taxi drivers who refuse to accept payment by Taxicard. If you use a taxi, you must make sure first whether your Taxicard will be accepted.

The companies currently involved are Computer Cabs (ComCab) *Tel:* 020 7474-6545 and in some boroughs, DialaCab *Tel:* 020 7426-3421. When a ComCab is not available, a DataCab may be sent instead. Cabs which display the ComCab logo can now be hailed on the street, or picked up at a taxi rank. There are currently about 2,500 of these cabs, but this only represents about 15% of the total. There have been problems recently, associated with the move of the ComCab call centre to Aberdeen and Edinburgh, and these are common to many distant call centres. Hopefully things will settle down, and the staff there will become familiar with the London atlas and the satellite tracking of the position of the cabs to find the nearest vehicle. It's quite a tall order for people who have no local knowledge.

Freedom Pass travel permits

These can be used on the buses, tube, DLR, Tramlink, on rail services within the Greater London area and on some River Thames boat services. They are available to pensioners, disabled and/or blind people, resident in London. Who is entitled to a permit can vary from borough to borough, and the first point of contact in order to find out is your local Social Services Department.

The permits offer free travel at any time for disabled people, but only after 09.00 Monday to Friday, and at any time over the weekend and on public holidays, and for pensioners (both men and women aged over 60). These are extremely valuable to a lot of people but as the public transport system presents major access problems, they will not be applicable to many users of this guide. A detailed leaflet is available from the **ALG Mobility Unit**, New Zealand House, 80 Haymarket SW1Y 4TZ *Tel:* 020 7747-4777.

Accommodation

Accommodation in London tends to be expensive. However, with the arrival of hotels like Express by Holiday Inn, Ibis, Premier Lodge, Travel Inns, Travelodge and most recently ETAP, the provisions have become a great deal better for the disabled visitor wanting reasonably-priced accommodation. Provisions in the more expensive hotels have improved as well, but not much in most cases, and some have even got worse.

Choosing where you stay is likely to depend on a combination of location, cost and accessibility.
There is a 'trade-off' between spending more money in the centre of London, and maybe being able to walk or wheel to many of the places you want to visit, or staying further out and travelling in – by whatever means. Whatever you decide, it will be a compromise. It might even be worth considering using two or three different hotels to make it easier, overall, to get around and visit the places you want to get to.

Be aware that some of the 'chain' hotels such as the Comfort Inns and Best Western are in old converted buildings. While you might expect that they would have accessible rooms because of their American roots, most of them don't, because of the difficulties and cost of modifying old buildings.

We include hotels in various price ranges, as well as campsites, and youth hostels. We have concentrated on lower-cost accommodation, and virtually all have step-free access and adapted rooms. Some have parking for BB holders. Some are quite close to accessible tube/DLR stations and others are in very central locations. Our visits showed that there are an increasing number of hotels in London which provide disabled visitors with step-free access to adapted rooms, and to the other main facilities.

Indicated price information in the listing is based on the cost of a double/twin bedded room and includes the cost of TWO people staying, including breakfast and VAT.

The indicators below should only be used as a rough guide for comparison purposes.

£	up to £50
££	£50-£80
£££	£80-£120
££££	£120+

If a hotel is on the borderline, we have used a dual indicator. For example, the Travel Inns, which cost about £50 a night outside the centre, are listed as **£/££**. If a hotel is on the £80 borderline ($\pm$£10) it is rated as **££/£££**.

A number of hotels have weekend reductions, which are not taken into account here, and it generally costs less to stay in London during the winter months, compared with the summer. To find out about special deals and reductions, contact the hotel directly. It's generally less easy for disabled visitors to be able to take advantage of 'cheap offers' of accommodation, through agencies and websites, as the conditions attached don't usually allow a choice of room, and sometimes not even of the hotel itself.

It is quite difficult getting useful and accurate information. The web, of course, is overloaded with information, but our experience is that a great deal of it is both inaccurate and incomplete. We looked at a considerable number of sites and listings and found that they had no common criteria for defining 'accessible'.

We tried a website 'crawl' to find out how to get discounted rates at some of the hotels we have listed. There are a large number of sites, including www.london-hotel-bookings.co.uk; www.YourStay.com; www.hotel-assist.com; www.totalstay.com and www.DiscountCityHotels.com. You can get an updated list by using Google, and searching London Hotels. One of the sites (hotel-assist) had a live chat facility which we used. Out of a huge portfolio of hotels, they could only offer one with adapted rooms for a disabled guest. When we looked through their list we immediately found half a dozen others that had adapted rooms which the website operator had no knowledge of. When we challenged our chat 'partner' he very honestly told us that 'in many cases the web write-ups are delegated by hotel managements to a junior staff member who doesn't understand the implications of what they are including or excluding'. This certainly makes it much more difficult for disabled people to take advantage of discounts – but if you do a web search in conjunction with the information in this guide it may at the very least give you a bargaining lever which might help you negotiate a competitive rate.

We found one site, www.wotif.com, which offered very substantial discounts (like 30-50%) including discounts at the Regent Palace Hotel, and at several others with accessible rooms listed here in the guide. Wotif seemed to have no mechanism for booking the adapted rooms. In discussing it with the reservations department at the Regent Palace, we could get no clear picture about the discount which would be offered on an adapted room, though there was a strong suggestion that it *would* be discounted substantially, equivalent to the price quoted by Wotif.

A source that IS accurate, and where the information is well researched, is the English Tourism Council (ETC) whose information is used by Holiday Care. The ETC have recently introduced a new series of classifications relating to accessibility, but are finding that hoteliers are quite reluctant to seek a rating. It seems to us that the 'standards' that have been adopted are more intended to improve the design and build of new premises than they are to provide helpful information to disabled visitors. The standards themselves seem to be unnecessarily demanding. Most of the hotels we list, and would regard as being pretty good, do not qualify for level 3 or 4 ratings (the ones that indicate a wheelchair user can use them because there is step-free access together with a number of other provisions). Thus, while the ratings are reliable, the classification system misses out on a lot of accommodation that is perfectly practical and usable by many disabled people. Encouraging hotels to describe their facilities accurately would be of much more use than applying blanket 'standards' and at the very least the two approaches should run in parallel.

One slightly bizarre and obtuse issue we discovered when visiting hotels this time is that nearly all of them which offer adapted rooms provide *only* a double bed in those rooms. Some can offer an additional folding bed, but in some of the rooms there is insufficient space for this. As a double bed would not be the choice of all travellers, it is to be hoped that hotel chains will, in the future, modify this policy. Most offer their able-bodied guests the choice of double beds, single/twin beds and family rooms, and this choice should be extended to their disabled guests as well. Several of the managers at Express by Holiday Inn Hotels said that because of the provision of double beds, the interconnecting room would normally be made available for a carer without extra charge, although this might not be possible if the hotel is fully booked.

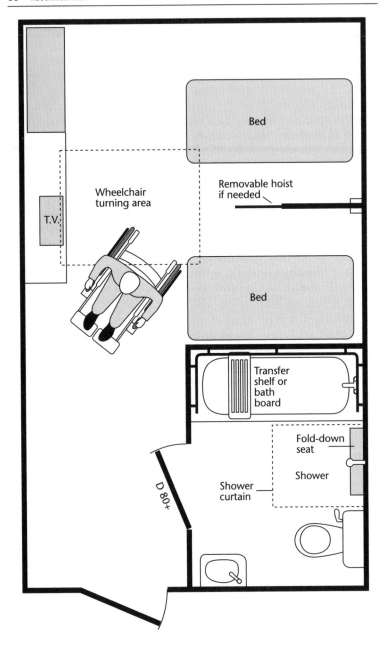

Bed

Removable hoist
if needed

Wheelchair
turning area

T.V.

Bed

Transfer
shelf or
bath
board

Fold-down
seat

Shower

D 80+

Shower
curtain

Room design for disabled guests

The hotel chains have adopted different policies with regard to the adapted bathrooms provided. For example, Travel Inns, Premier Lodges and most Travelodges provide a bath with a shower over it and appropriate grab rails. **Express by Holiday Inn, and some Ibis Hotels provide an excellent wheel-in shower facility**. We hope that as understanding of people's practical needs becomes more widespread, the provisions will continue to improve and, at the very least, people will be able to choose between having a wheel-in shower and a bath with grab rails. The management at Premier Lodge hotels say that they are looking at the issues, and that some new premises will include bedrooms with a wheel-in shower and offer the choice of twin beds. The Travel Inn chain is also considering the provision of wheel-in showers, but it will be many years before they become the norm. A basic specification for a wheel-in shower is illustrated in the diagram on page 88.

In the meantime, **it would be of enormous help to some if hotels would provide a 'bath board'**. This is a simple and inexpensive way of enabling many disabled people to use a movable shower head safely, without having to get properly 'into' the bath. The board consists simply of a slatted board which fits across the bath with two 'fixers' braced against the inside of the bath to hold it in place (see diagram on page 88). It is a piece of equipment which is readily available from most of the companies listed under *Equipment repair and hire*. Alongside this provision, the shower controls must be reachable from a sitting position on the board, and room-service staff must be encouraged to leave the shower head within reach.

In our view, hotels and other venues need to produce a brief descriptive 'access' leaflet (perhaps building on what is here in the guide). This would clarify the issues as well as being helpful to both staff and visitors. The descriptions could easily be included in website information, and would probably be more useful than the ETC ratings system.

Amongst the **best facilities for value and low cost from an access viewpoint** are the two ETAP hotels and the Rotherhithe Youth Hostel; **for value and location**, there are the Travel Inns at County Hall and Tower Bridge, the Premier Lodge and Express by Holiday Inn at Southwark, and the Regent Palace. Finally **for five-star ambience and good accessible rooms** there are the Copthorne Tara and Thistle Marble Arch, with the Tara offering excellent value if booked through Holiday Care.

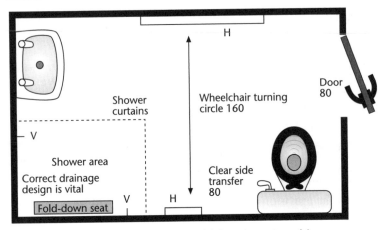

Overall dimensions 250 x 180 (150cm min) (not drawn to scale)

H = horizontal grab bar
V = vertical grab bar
Dimensions in cm

Arrangement for a wheel-in shower

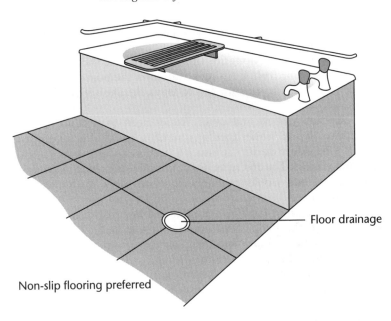

Using a bathboard

Hotels where you can find a wheel-in shower include:

- the Formule 1 and ETAP hotels at Barking and London City Airport;
- Sleeping Beauty Motel, Leyton;
- the Rotherhithe Youth Hostel;
- Hotel Ibis, at Greenwich and Stratford;
- the Shalimar Hotel, Hounslow;
- the Oak Lodge Hotel, Enfield;
- Comfort Inn, Vauxhall;
- Days Inn, Lambeth;
- the Holiday Inn Express Hotels, in the City, Hammersmith, and Southwark;
- the Copthorne Tara Hotel, Kensington;
- Thistle Hotel, Charing Cross;
- the Thistle Hotel, Marble Arch.

In the write-ups we have concentrated on accommodation that is fairly central, or which is near an accessible public transport route. We have included a few places because they have parking. Most of the 'chains' make fairly standard provisions, so if it's a Travel Inn or a Travelodge, you'll know that they provide only a double bed, and that the bathroom will have a low-level bath with handrails. Some hotels can fit in a small single bed as well if requested, and most Travelodges provide a sofa in the room which doubles up as a single bed. If it's an Express by Holiday Inn, it will have rooms with a wheel-in shower. The Ibis chain has changed its specifications, so older ones may have a bath with rails in the bathroom while newer ones have wheel-in showers. We *hope* that Travel Inns and Travelodge will also start providing wheel-in showers, and that *all* of them will start offering the choice of twin or double beds in their adapted rooms.

If you are happy to stay a little way out, there are many more options, and we suggest that you use the relevant websites to establish what is on offer. These include:

- www.accorhotels.com (for Formule 1)
- www.daysinn.com
- www.etaphotel.com
- www.grangehotels.com
- www.hiexpress.co.uk
- www.holidayinnlondon.co.uk
- www.ibishotel.com
- www.millenniumhotels.com

- www.premierlodge.co.uk
- www.thistlehotels.com
- www.travelinn.co.uk
- www.travelodge.co.uk

Alternatively, you can ring one of the hotels listed in the guide, and get them to send you an up-to-date listing of all their premises, which will tell you where they are in the suburbs – and also about any new ones in central London. However, some of the brochures do *not* list places with accessible rooms, for example Bass Hotels (for Express by Holiday Inn) and Days Inn/Howard Johnson. This is, in our view, a surprising omission.

'Automated' hotels

We have called the ETAP and Formule 1 hotels 'automated', because they are not run in the conventional way, and there are times of the day when they are not staffed. Around check-out time in the morning, generally from 07.00 to 11.00, and when most people check in, between 17.00 and 20.00, there should be someone at reception. At other times, you can check in to the hotel using a credit card in the slot/screen outside which is rather like a bank cash machine.

What you do is insert your card, and say how long you want to stay. **If you want one of the adapted rooms, you must book this in advance**, at which stage you will give a credit card number. When you put the credit card in, it should recognise your booking and allocate you an adapted room. **You cannot do this directly on the screen outside**. When your booking has been recognised and accepted, you will be given two keypad codes, one to open the main door, and a different one to enable you to get into your room. Remember to write these down, and make sure that everyone staying there has a copy!

In Formule 1, the adapted shower and toilet is situated off the corridor, while in the ETAP hotels, they are en suite. Because the hotels can be run by a small number of staff, they offer extremely good value. For two or three people travelling together they can provide clean and comfortable accommodation for only about £15 or £20 per night each, which for London is very reasonable. Hopefully more of these will be built.

Hotels

Hotels are listed by postal area, with the most central areas first, i.e. W1, W2, WC1, WC2, NW1, SE1, E1, EC1 and EC3. These are all shown on the hotels map, with the exception of the Langland, which does not offer easy wheelchair access, but is a good-value hotel for a disabled walker. We have listed the information within the various sections by price so that the cheapest places appear first, and the most expensive ones last.

In describing the bedrooms we have usually quoted the width of the bedroom door first (eg D75), then the bathroom door width, and then the side transfer space alongside the toilet.

The numbers in the listing correspond to those shown on the hotels location maps (see pages 92–5).

W1

① Regent Palace
Piccadilly Circus W1B 5DN
Tel: 0870 400-8703 *Fax:* 020 7287-0238
website: www.travelodge.co.uk
Situated at the junction of Glasshouse Street and Sherwood Street, with a nearby NCP on Brewer Street. The hotel is very central, and just off Piccadilly Circus. Flat entrance to dining room, pub (+ 1 step at the entrance, 15% step free) and three lifts (D90 W105 L110) which go to all eight floors. **Two adapted rooms** with twin beds, of which room 3022 was seen; D75, bathroom D75 ST95 with wheel-in shower. Room 3022 is about 40m from the lift while room 1113 is right by the lift. Note the comments above about discounted rates.
£££

② Thistle Marble Arch
Bryanston Street, Marble Arch W1H 8AE
Tel: 020 7629-8040 *Fax:* 0870 333-9216
e-mail: marblearch@thistle.co.uk
By the junction with Portman Street. NCP 50m away with concessionary rates for hotel guests. Main entrance + 4 steps and then an escalator to first-floor reception. A separate entrance to the right has a push button to open the door, and takes you through to a lift (D110 W150 L120) to go up to reception. Flat access to dining room, bar and a **wheelchair toilet (D85 ST350).** Main lifts (D85 W130 L130) to the left of reception give step-free access to **ten adapted rooms**. Six connect with another room. Room 368 seen: D85 with a remote control to open the door, bathroom D90 to a wheel-in shower with a folding seat and ST85. You can have the choice of either twin beds or a double.
££££

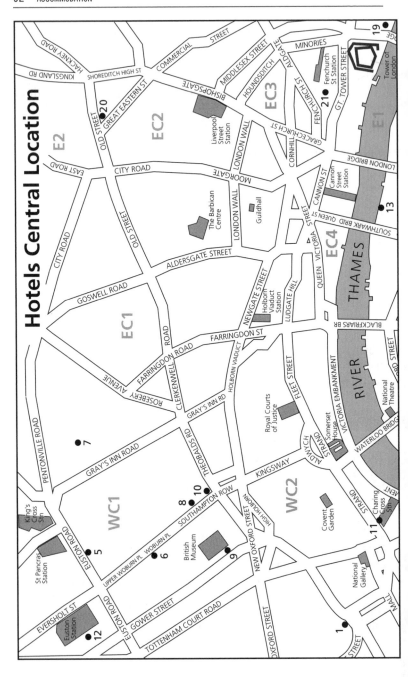

Hotels Central Location

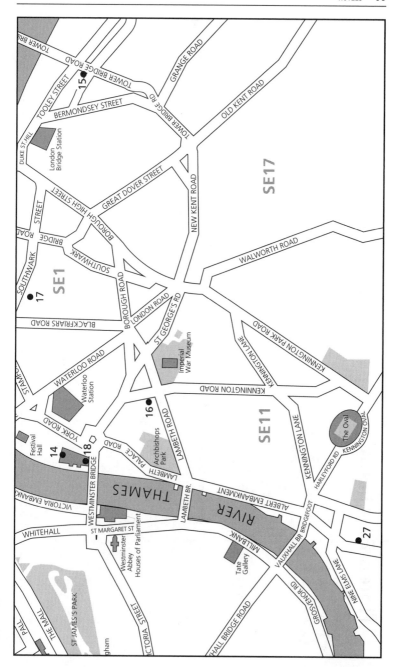

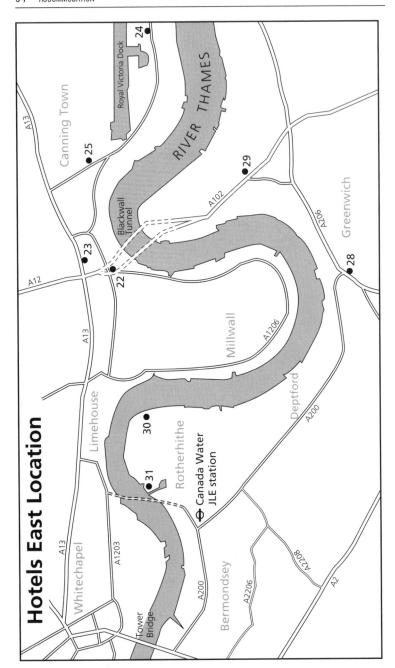

Hotels East Location

Hotels West Location

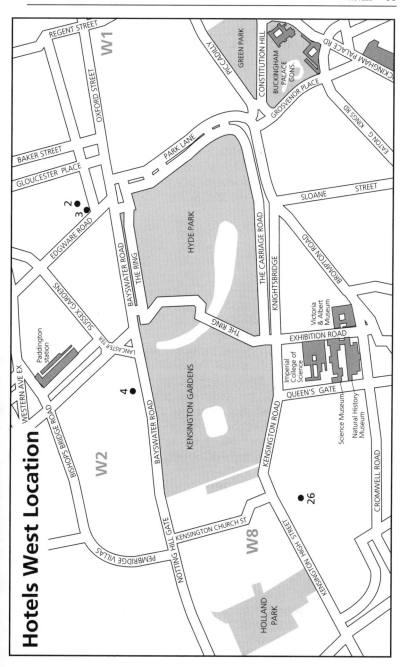

③ **Marriott Marble Arch**
134 George Street W1H 6DN
Tel: 020 7723-1277 *Fax:* 020 7402-0666
By the junction with Forest Street. UGCP on two floors with step-free lift access. Main entrance on Forest Street with revolving door which can easily be bypassed. Step-free access to reception and restaurant. Bar is +3 steps with an open lift (D90 W100) to bypass them. Lifts (D100 W120 L200) go to **one adapted room** on the first floor. Not seen. We were told that it has a double bed, a bath with rails and that there is an interconnecting room. **Wheelchair toilet (D80 ST100)** on the GF opposite the bar. On entering the hotel go to the right of reception, past the lifts, and it's a little further along, on your left.
££££

W2

④ **Columbia**
95-99 Lancaster Gate W2 3NS
Tel: 020 7402-0021 *Fax:* 7706-4691
e-mail: columbiahotel@btconnect.com
Situated off the Bayswater Road about half way between Queensway and Lancaster Gate tube stations. Parking for up to six cars. There's an NCP at Queensway. Entrance +2 steps, ramped, and then step-free to reception, lounge, bar and restaurant. Lift (D80 W120 L135) to all four floors. **One adapted room**, no. 212, seen: D80, bathroom D80 ST70, with a low-level bath with rails and a seat at the back. **Wheelchair toilet (D80 ST100+)** on the GF past the bar and restaurant on the left. Normally locked, but ask at reception for the key.
££/£££ (ETC access category 2).

WC1

⑤ **Travel Inn Euston Road**
1 Duke's Road WC1H 9PJ
Tel: 0870 238-3301 *Fax:* 020 7554-3419
A large blue building on the junction with Euston Road. Three BB spaces in CP under the hotel, accessed off Duke's Road. The main entrance is step free. Accessible restaurant, bar and **wheelchair toilet (D70+ ST70+)** on the GF. Three lifts (D85 W140 L140) give access to all other floors. **Fifteen adapted rooms** all with low-level bath and

grab rails. All have double beds, but a single bed can be added if requested. Room 103 seen: D80, bathroom D80 ST120. It contained the extra single bed, which made the room somewhat cramped. The hotel is located within 500m of Euston, St Pancras and King's Cross stations.
££/£££

⑥ **Royal National**
Bedford Way WC1H 0DG
Tel: 020 7637-2488 *Fax:* 020 7837-4653
e-mail: info@imperialhotels.co.uk
Vast hotel with over 1600 rooms spread over two wings, situated in the courtyard between Bedford Way and Woburn Place, north of Russell Square Gardens. Contains a number of restaurants, bars, and shops. There is an UGCP run by NCP with lift access to the hotel and a flat entrance to the foyer and lifts. All GF facilities are step free except −1 in North Breakfast room. Eighteen numbered lifts (D90 W160 L100) give access to the seven floors. **Ten adapted rooms**, all twins, but of two different types. We saw room 3057 with bathroom D90 but no ST space. The bath has handrails and a seat. Room 1224 has D80, bathroom D80 ST80 with a pole alongside the bath to assist getting in and out, but no handrails. Wheelchair cubicles (not seen) in the Gents and Ladies by the confectionery shop near south reception. **Wheelchair toilet (D85 ST80)** which is kept locked, 30m to the right of north reception. Because of the sheer size of the hotel, you may have to go up to 200m between facilities.
££/£££

⑦ **Holiday Inn King's Cross**
1 King's Cross Road WC1X 9HX
Tel: 020 7833-3900 *Fax:* 020 7917-6163
e-mail: reservations@holidayinnlondon.com
Situated at the junction with Calthorpe Street, with covered CP in front including two BB spaces. A ramp bypasses the +5 steps to reception. On the GF there is a ramped bypass for +6 to the restaurants and bar. From reception, three lifts (D90 W115 L135) go to all floors. There are **two adapted rooms** on the first floor. Room 143 seen: D80, bathroom D80 ST115 and a low bath with grab rails. There was a double bed, and a sofa bed. **Wheelchair toilet (D90 ST100)** in the basement, 20m to the left of the lifts, through some double doors and opposite the Bloomsbury Suite.
£££/££££

⑧ Bonnington
92 Southampton Row WC1B 4BH
Tel: 020 7242-2828 *Fax:* 020 7831-9170
e-mail: sales@bonnington.com
This seven-floor hotel opposite Bloomsbury Place has recently been extensively renovated. There is an UGCP run by NCP at the Imperial Hotel 100m north towards Russell Square Gardens. As well as a bar and restaurant (+ 2 steps to an upper level) on the GF, there are two lifts, one (D80 W85 L215) opposite the reception desk, the other (D80 W110 L140) to the right beyond reception and bar, by a **wheelchair toilet (D85 ST100). Eighteen adapted rooms**, rooms 701 to 706 on the GF and two on each subsequent floor. All rooms are within 50m of reception via a lift, have a toilet with ST75 + and handrails around the bath.
££££

⑨ Radisson Edwardian Marlborough
9-13 Bloomsbury Street WC1B 3QD
Tel: 020 7636-5601 *Fax:* 020 7636-0532
e-mail: resmar1@radisson.com
On the corner with Great Russell Street, 200m from British Museum. Valet parking available for nearby NCP. Ramped entrance and step-free access to two lifts (D75 W105 L135), dining room and bar. **Four adapted rooms**. Room 118 seen: D85, bathroom D75 ST70. **Wheelchair cubicles (D90 ST100)** in the Ladies and Gents toilets, to the left past reception, through the double doors labelled Glass Bar, then right.
££££

⑩ Grange Holborn
50-60 Southampton Row WC1B 4AR
Tel: 020 7242-1800 *Fax:* 020 7404-1641
e-mail: holborn@grangehotels.co.uk
Located on the corner of Southampton Row and Vernon Place, opposite the Cochrane Theatre. No parking on site but NCP nearby. Step-free entrance with lifts (D90 W130 L130) to all floors. The restaurant on the first floor is step free, with a **wheelchair toilet (D85 ST85)** on the left before the restaurant entrance. **Four adapted rooms** with double bed, D80, bathroom D85 ST75. The bath has grab rails, and staff can fit a chair/seat to the bath on request. The basement pool area can be reached step free by asking staff, but there are still −4 steps to the poolside.
££££

WC2

⑪ **Thistle Charing Cross**
Strand WC2N 5HX
Tel: 0870 333-9105 *Fax:* 0870 333-9205
e-mail: reservations.charingX@thistle.co.uk
Just on the right as you come out of Charing Cross station, there is
one BB space by the entrance for short-term parking; two longer-
term spaces may be booked in advance. There are unavoidable
cobbles outside the entrance and a large revolving door. Alternatively you can go through a door to the right, opened from inside
with a bell (H130) to attract attention. The GF has the reception and
a small public bar (D82) with 1cm lip, as well as two lifts (D85 W125
L160) to all floors. The restaurant and lounge bar are on the first
floor, to right and left of lifts respectively and are step free. **Wheelchair toilet (D75 ST110)** to the left from the lounge bar. **Two adapted
rooms**, of which we saw room 210: D85 with a double bed and an
adjoining room. Bathroom D85 ST100 and wheel-in shower.
££££

NW1

⑫ **Ibis Euston**
3 Cardington Street, Euston NW1 2LW
Tel: 020 7388-7777 *Fax:* 020 7388-0001
e-mail: 80921@accor-hotels.com
Right by Euston Station on the corner of Drummond Street. Four
BB spaces on ground level in the staff CP can be made available on
request. Flat main entrance. Step free to reception, bar and restaurant. Two lifts (D100 W140 L140). **Eight adapted rooms**. Rooms 135
and 235 seen: D75, bathroom D74 ST100. They have four rooms
with twin beds, and four with a double. Some have a connecting
room. All have a low-level bath with grab rails. **Adapted toilet (D61
ST70)** on the GF. Note the somewhat narrow door. Key from
reception. Go straight on through the bar area, and the toilet is
on the far side on the right, and immediately right down to the end of
the corridor. Then on the right.
££/£££

SE1

⑬ Premier Lodge Bankside
Anchor Inn, Bankside SE1 9EF
Tel: 0870 700-1456 *Fax:* 0870 700-1457
e-mail: southwark@premierlodge.co.uk
The hotel is attached to the Anchor Inn, and its entrance is in Bank
End, opposite Vinopolis. Go through the arch over slightly rough
paving to find reception on your left. One BB space in the CP
outside. There are **three adapted rooms**, all on the GF. Room 4 seen:
D75, bathroom D75 ST70 with a bath with grab rails. All have
double beds, and there's just enough room for a folding bed. Breakfast is served in the Chart Room on an upper floor of the Anchor
pub. This is reached from the hotel via a lift (D75 W95 L130) and an
open lift (D80 L120). There is a **wheelchair toilet (D85 ST70)** in the
hotel level with the Chart Room. Access to the main parts of the pub
is from the riverside (see under Anchor Inn in the chapter on *Pubs
and bars*).
££/£££

⑭ Travel Inn County Hall
County Hall, Belvedere Road SE1 7PB
Tel: 0870 238-3300 *Fax:* 020 7902 1619
Located in County Hall with the main entrance some 25m from the
junction with Chicheley Street. Two BB spaces available, there are
other BB spaces up to 500m away on Belvedere Road and also in
nearby public CPs. Main entrance + 15 steps (with HR). The
alternative step-free route involves going through the big black
security gates by the junction with Chicheley Street. There are always
security staff on duty by the gates and this route also leads to the BB
spaces. Unfortunately the staff are in a small hut inside the gates and
it is not always easy to attract their attention. Having a mobile phone
so that you can contact Reception is a sensible precaution. This
partially sloped route is about 60m long and gives access to the
basement. Three lifts (D85 W160 L150) give access to all five floors.
Step-free restaurant/bar and **wheelchair toilet (D70+ ST 70+)** are
all on the GF. There are **thirteen adapted bedrooms** all with low-level
bath and double beds. A single bed can be added if requested. Room
205 seen, which was easily big enough to take an extra bed. D80,
bathroom D75 (sliding) ST75. We were told that most of the
accessible rooms were large enough to accommodate an extra bed
comfortably, and are larger than the rooms in most other Travel

Inns. The hotel is very centrally located on the south bank, which compensates for the hassle getting in and out.
££/£££

⑮ **Travel Inn Tower Bridge**
159 Tower Bridge Road SE1 3LP
Tel: 0870 238-3303 *Fax:* 020 7940-3719
On the west side of Tower Bridge Road, at the junction with Tanner Street. Parking with twelve BB spaces is accessed from Tanner Street. Flat to reception. The restaurant and bar on the GF is about 50% step free. Some high bar tables. Three lifts (D75 W90 L125). **Twelve adapted rooms**, two on each floor, including the GF. All have double beds and low-level bath with rails. Room 2 seen: D85, bathroom D80 ST80. **Wheelchair toilet (D85 ST70)** on the GF opened by using a guest card.
££/£££

⑯ **Days Inn**
54 Kennington Road SE1 7BJ
Tel: 020 7922-1331 *Fax:* 020 7922-1441
e-mail: waterloo@daysinn.com
Located very near the Imperial War Museum by the junction between Kennington Road and Cosser Street, near the Lambeth Road. It is nearly 1km from Waterloo Station. CP with two BB spaces. Step-free entrance. Inside the bar and restaurant are both on the GF. Two lifts (D80 W110 L140) go to all five floors. There are **two adapted GFBs**, and **one adapted room on each floor (six in total)**. Room seen with D85 and wheel-in shower D85 ST150. **Adapted toilet (D85 ST65)** to the left of reception. Go through the double doors to the left of the lifts and follow the corridor.
££/£££

⑰ **Express by Holiday Inn Southwark**
103 Southwark Street SE1 1EA
Tel: 020 7401-2525 *Fax:* 020 7401-3322
e-mail: stay@expresssouthwark.co.uk
Located at the junction with Bear Lane. No on-site parking. Main entrance +3 steps, but there's a step-free route about 30m away. Go round the hotel to the right and use the 'deliveries' entrance at the back. On the GF the reception, bar and restaurant are all step free. **Five adapted rooms** reached via the lift (D80 W120 L85). All have double beds, wheel-in showers, and interconnect with another room.

Room 103 seen: D85, bathroom D75 ST100. **Wheelchair toilet (D85 ST80)** on the GF, to the left of reception and through a door. It is near the step-free entrance.
£££

⑱ **Marriott County Hall**
Westminster Bridge Road SE1
Tel: 020 7928-5200 *Fax:* 020 7928-5300
Located on the south side of Westminster Bridge in the old County Hall. Main entrance +9 (no HR) +7 steps. This can be bypassed by going right to the other end of County Hall (about 250m) where there is another way in through the big black gates by the junction with Chicheley Street. There are always security staff on duty and this route also leads to the BB spaces. This partially sloped route gives access to the basement, but it's about 250m back to the hotel. The restaurant, bar and reception are all on the GF, and are step free. **Five adapted rooms**, not seen. We were told that they all had double beds. **Wheelchair toilet (D95 ST80)** to the right of the main entrance under the 'Gents' sign.
££££

E1

⑲ **Thistle Tower**
St Katharine's Way E1 9LD
Tel: 0870 333-9106/9206 *Fax:* 020 7481-3799
e-mail: tower.businesscentre@thistle.co.uk
By the northern end of Tower Bridge by the river. Relatively expensive, but well located. On-site CP with one BB space at ground level and one in UGCP with valet parking. Step-free access from the east. Ramp bypasses +2 at entrance. Lift (D100 W170 L140) to dining room, bar and **wheelchair cubicles (D70 ST90)** in Ladies and Gents on upper foyer level. **Two adapted rooms** with double beds and no adjoining room, on first floor reached by four lifts. Room 105 seen: D85, bathroom D85 ST125 with wheel-in shower.
££££

EC1

⑳ **Express by Holiday Inn London City**
275 Old Street EC1V 9LN
Tel: 020 7300-4444 *Fax:* 020 7300-4555

Situated at the junction with Pitfield Street. Parking at the back for five cars including one BB space. Step-free entrance, and flat to the restaurant and bar. Two lifts (D75 W110 L180). **Six adapted rooms**. We were told that they all had a wheel-in shower and all had double beds. There would be insufficient space for an extra bed. **Wheelchair toilet (D75 ST75)** on the GF; turn to the right by reception, and down the corridor. It's 15m away on the left.

EC3

㉑ Novotel Tower Bridge
10 Pepys Street EC3N 2NR
Tel: 020 7265-6026 *Fax:* 020 7265-6060
On the corner of Cooper's Row, and some 250m north of the Tower of London. No parking, but NCP in Minories about 300m away. Step free to reception, bar and restaurant. Three lifts (D80 W115 L135). **Twelve adapted rooms**. We were told that six have wheel-in showers and six have baths with handrails. All have queen-size beds, and six connect to an adjacent room. GF contains a **wheelchair toilet (D85 ST75)**. The hotel is about 400m from Tower Gateway DLR station.
££££

E6

Beckton Travel Inn
1 Woolwich Manor Way, Beckton E6 4NT
Tel: 020 7511-3853 *Fax:* 020 7511-4214
On the corner of Winsor Terrace and next to Beckton DLR station. The DLR gives step-free access into Tower Gateway and Bank stations, among other places. On-site CP with BB spaces. Flat entrance. Forty GFBs, **two adapted**, both with a double bed. One seen: D75, bathroom D85 ST85. Low-level bath with rails.
£/££

E14

㉒ Ibis Docklands
1 Baffin Way E14 9PE
Tel: 020 7517-1100 *Fax:* 020 7987-5916
Situated at the junction with Prestons Road south of the A1261 flyover and interchange. The area is rapidly developing and chan-

ging. The step-free way to get to the main door is an opening in the wall opposite Gaselee Street. CP outside with two BB spaces. Between the CP and the hotel is a gate which is locked at night but with an intercom H140. Step free to reception, bar and restaurant. The hotel is about 400m from the Blackwall DLR Station. This is reached by going across Prestons Road towards the DLR sign. Then go down the 50m slope and under the flyover. Turn right and up the slope to the station. There's a shorter way at road level but it involves several kerbs.

££

㉓   **Travelodge Docklands**
Coriander Avenue E14 2AA
Tel: 0870 191-1691 *Fax:* 020 7515-9170
Situated on the A13 East India Dock Road, near the north end of the Blackwall Tunnel. Approached only from the A13 westwards. CP outside with seven BB spaces. Step free to reception, bar and restaurant. **Fifteen adapted rooms** on the GF, all with double beds (and no room for a second bed) and low-level bath/shower. Room 004 seen, D70, bathroom D85 ST90. **Wheelchair toilet (D85 ST85)** on the GF near the bedrooms.

££/£££

E15

Ibis Stratford
1A Romford Road, Stratford E15 4LJ
Tel: 020 8536-3700 *Fax:* 020 8519-5161
Well located about 500m from Stratford Station which has accessible transport links to Liverpool Street, and via the JLE and DLR. It is also near Stratford Circus with opportunities for theatre, shopping and eating out. Parking for disabled guests may be possible by prior arrangement. Step free everywhere using lift (D80 W100 L140). Note that all the rooms have king-size double beds, and there are no twin-bedded rooms. **Six adapted rooms** with wheel-in showers (D80+ ST 80+). Room 205 seen, with one of the best adapted bathrooms we've seen anywhere. We were told that the others were the same, and that Ibis policy was to provide this design everywhere. It had a fold-down seat, an internal curtain so that you can keep your chair dry, and very adequate space and support bars etc. GF restaurant/bar with **wheelchair toilet (D70+ ST70+)**.

££/£££

E16

㉔ **ETAP London City Airport**
North Woolwich Road, Silvertown E16 2EE
Tel: 020 7474-9106 *Fax:* 020 7474-9347
e-mail: E5840@accor-hotels.com
Competitively priced, the hotel is located on the right of North
Woolwich Road, coming from the City, just after the Esso Petrol
Station roundabout, and opposite Oriental Road. On-site CP has
four BB spaces. Flat entrance with automatic reception, which is
80cm high. This takes Visa or MasterCard, confirms your reservation and takes payment for first night only (see the write-up on
automated hotels earlier in the chapter). Flat access to GF which has
reception desk, breakfast room and lift (D90 W105 L140) to all
floors. **Four adapted rooms**, two each on first and second floors.
Room 201 seen: D80, bathroom D75 ST160 with handrails for
wheel-in shower. The adapted rooms have a double bed and an
upper bunk for a third person. **Adapted toilet (D75 ST95 inward door)**
on corridor to the right past reception (staff have the key). The
adapted rooms need to be booked in advance. When the DLR is
extended, it should be reasonably near a station.
£

A new **Travel Inn** is due to open late in 2003 at London Docklands
(ExCel), Royal Victoria Docks E16 *Tel:* 0870 242 8000.

㉕ **Express by Holiday Inn Royal Docks**
1 Silvertown Way, Silvertown E16 1EA
Tel: 020 7540-4040 *Fax:* 020 7540-4050
e-mail: info@exhi-royaldocks.co.uk
Located between Brunel Street and Shirley Street. On-site CP
entered from Brunel Street and three BB spaces by the main
entrance. It is about 150m from Canning Town station on the
JLE and DLR. Step free to reception, bar and restaurant. **Four
adapted bedrooms** reached via the lift (D80 W105 L140). All have
double beds, wheel-in showers and interconnect with another room.
Room 202 seen: D85, bathroom D75 ST115. **Wheelchair toilet (D85
ST70)** on the GF to the left of reception.
£££

W6

Express by Holiday Inn Hammersmith
124 King Street, Hammersmith W6 0QU
Tel: 020 8746-5100 *Fax:* 020 8746-5199
e-mail: hammersmith@expressbyholidayinn.net
The hotel is just over 500m from Hammersmith Station. Go down
King Street, past the King's Mall. It is on the right in a new mews
(possibly not marked on the A-Z map), and just past Cambridge
Grove and Argyle Place. Four BB spaces. Entrance −5 steps,
bypassed by a ramp. Step free to reception, bar and restaurant on
the GF. Two lifts (D95 W100 L150) lead to **eight adapted rooms**, all
double bedded and with interconnecting rooms. All have wheel-in
showers. Room 101 seen: D80, bathroom D95 ST80+. The management said that the adjoining room would be free for a carer.
Wheelchair toilet (D80 ST70+) opposite reception.
££/£££

Novotel Hammersmith
1 Shortlands, Hammersmith W6 8DR
Tel: 020 8741-1555 *Fax:* 020 8741-2120
e-mail: H0737@accor-hotels.com
Turn into Chalk Hill Road from Shortlands, about 300m from Hammersmith Broadway off the Hammersmith Road. It is built on an upper
level terrace. Three BB spaces at ground level. Flat to CP lift (D85 W105
L150) to first-floor reception. There are also lifts (D110 W190 L120)
from the main entrance on Chalk Hill Road leading to the first-floor
reception. There are two bars, a shop and restaurants on the first floor
with step-free access. **Seven adapted rooms**, one on each floor 3-9. Room
3037 seen: D75, bathroom D90 ST70 with a wheel-in shower. Double
bed, but a single can be added. **Wheelchair cubicles (D85 ST85)** in
Ladies and Gents toilets on the first floor. Go to the right of reception,
30m down the corridor, on the right.
££££

W8

㉖ **Copthorne Tara**
Scarsdale Place, Kensington W8 5SR
Tel: 020 7937-7211 *Fax:* 020 7872-2509
Off Wright's Lane, about 250m from Kensington High Street.
UGCP without lift access, but valet parking is available. Flat

entrance. Five lifts (D115 W190 L135). Step-free access to all facilities. **Ten well-adapted rooms**, catering for people with a wide range of disabilities, and eight now have a wheel-in shower. **Wheelchair toilets (D70 + ST70 +)** on the GF and the mezzanine. Big hotel with long distances inside. Book through Holiday Care (*Tel:* 01293-774535) for a significant discount. HC membership costs about £20 a year.
££/£££ (with discount)

SW5

There's a **Travel Inn** in Kensington, 11 Knaresborough Place SW5 0YJ *Tel:* 0870 238-3304, which we have not visited, but which we are told has **four adapted rooms**, modified in the standard Travel Inn way. This means that the rooms have a double bed, and the bathroom has a bath with grab rails.

SW8

㉗ Comfort Inn Vauxhall
87 South Lambeth Road SW8 1RN
Tel: 020 7735-9494 *Fax:* 020 7735-1011
Situated on the corner with Old South Lambeth Road, about 800m south of Vauxhall Bridge. Small CP on site with three BB spaces. The + 3 steps at the entrance are bypassed by a ramp. Reception, lounge, bar and restaurant all on the GF, together with **five adapted rooms**. Room seen: D80 + , bathroom D75 and a wheel-in shower. We were told that all the rooms had a double bed and wheel-in shower. The hotel has no portable single beds to put in a room. There is a lift to the upper floors with non-adapted bedrooms. **Wheelchair toilet (D70 + ST70 +)** off the GF corridor.
££/£££

SW11

Travelodge Battersea
200 York Road, Battersea SW11 3SA
Tel: 0870 1911-688 (central reservations) 0870 0850-950
Large blue and white building on corner with Gartons Way. There are four BB spaces in CP off Gartons Way, opposite Homebase, from which there is a ramped entrance with an intercom. From York Road, there is a step-free entrance but it is through a revolving door

so the CP entrance may be better. No bar or restaurant. Two telephones (one lowered) and a freephone for taxi hire. **Four adapted bedrooms**, all with double beds, are on the GF. The one we saw has D75 and wheelchair bathroom (D85 ST90) with handrails all around the bath. Two lifts (D75 W130 L110) go to all other floors.
££/£££

SW18

Express by Holiday Inn Wandsworth
Smugglers Way, Wandsworth SW18 1EG
Tel: 020 8877-5950 *Fax:* 020 8877-0631
e-mail: wandsworth@oriel-leisure.co.uk
Located in an industrial area behind a BP petrol station, and near the Thames, about 700m west of Wandsworth Bridge. Smugglers Way is off Swandon Way. CP with 35 spaces including two for BB holders. Step free to reception, bar and breakfast room. Two lifts (D90 W100 L130). **Eight adapted bedrooms**, seven of them on the GF. All are double-bedded, with an interconnecting room. All have a wheel-in shower. Room 100 seen: D75, bathroom D80 ST100+. **Wheelchair toilet (D85 ST70)** on the GF.
£££

SE10

㉘ **Ibis Greenwich**
30 Stockwell Street, Greenwich SE10 9JN
Tel: 020 8305-1177 *Fax:* 020 8858-7139
On the corner of Greenwich High Street. Large pay-and-display CP at back. Entrance +4 bypassed by a ramp. Flat to dining room and lift (D80 W105 L135). **Two adapted rooms**: D80, bathroom D85 ST85 with wheel-in shower. **Wheelchair toilet (D75 ST70)** to left of reception. Located close to the new DLR station.
££/£££

㉙ **Express by Holiday Inn London-Greenwich**
Bugsby's Way, Greenwich SE10 0GD
Tel: 020 8269-5000 *Fax:* 020 8269-5069
Located about 1km from North Greenwich Tube Station, near the junction with John Harrison Way. Eight BB spaces by front entrance, which is step free. From the GF, two lifts (D90 W95 L125) provide step-free access to all seven floors. Reception, breakfast/tea

and coffee area, and **wheelchair toilet (D90 ST 150)** are all on the first floor. **Ten adapted bedrooms**, two on each floor 2-6. Four are for smokers. Room 203 seen: D75, bathroom D75 ST100 with a wheel-in shower.
£££

SE16

③ **Hilton London Docklands**
265 Rotherhithe Street, Rotherhithe SE16 5HW
Tel: 020 7231-1001 *Fax:* 020 7231-0599
70m north of the junction with Silver Walk, by the Thames. On-site CP. Entrance + 1 step with a ramp, to a central reception and two separate buildings. **One adapted room** on the GF of Wharf building reached via an open lift (W100 L160) bypassing + 8 steps. Room 1111 seen: D73, bathroom D73 no ST and a bath with rails. Twin-bedded. Twelve GFBs in the Wharf building which contains the dining room and bar with step-free access. **Adapted cubicles (D85 ST48)** in both Ladies and Gents. Eighteen more GFBs in Block A.
£££/££££

Near Gatwick Airport

Premier Lodge Gatwick Airport
London Road, Lowfield Heath, Crawley, West Sussex RH10 9ST
Tel: 0870 700-1388 *Fax:* 0870 700-1389
From Junction 9A of M23 follow signs to Gatwick Airport North Terminal roundabout, then for A23 Crawley. The hotel is next to Gatwick Manor House Pub. Large CP with five BB spaces. Step free to reception, lift (D80 W90 L130) to all floors and sloped corridor to the breakfast room (only 30% is flat). **Adapted toilet (D85 ST105)** where the door opened inward, and was blocked by a table, on right of corridor to Tythe Barn. **Four adapted rooms** on GF, all double-bedded and non-smoking. Room 110 seen: D75, bathroom D85 ST70 has low bath with grab rail but no seat. We were told other rooms were identical. Restaurant and bar in Gatwick Manor House pub to the left of hotel entrance. Entrance + 1 step, but inside the whole area is step free, apart from ± 1 up a ramp which bypasses + 2 and reaches 20% of GF and **adapted toilet (D85 ST65)**. Beer Garden + 2.
££

Premier Lodge Gatwick (South)

Crawley Avenue, Gossops Green, Crawley, West Sussex RH10 8NF
Tel: 0870 700-1392 *Fax:* 0870 700-1393
Just under five miles from Gatwick Airport, this hotel is located adjacent to the petrol station on Crawley Avenue. Five BB spaces in CP just next to step-free entrance leading to flat GF with reception desk, 100% flat bar and restaurant, and lift (D80 W100 L140) to all three floors. **Four adapted rooms** on GF are double-bedded and non-smoking. Room 3 seen: D75, bathroom D70 ST70. **Wheelchair toilet (D85 ST75)** on GF past the bar desk.
££

Travel Inn Gatwick

North Terminal, Longbridge Way, Gatwick Airport, Horley, Surrey RH6 0NX
Tel: 0870-2383305 *Fax:* 01293-568278
500m north of the North Terminal, by the Texaco garage. On-site CP with BB spaces. Flat to dining room, bar and **adapted toilet (D85 ST50)**. **Six adapted GFBs**, all with double beds. Room 10 seen: D85, bathroom D82 (sliding) ST88 with a low-level bath and grab rails. Another twenty GFBs. Other rooms step free from the lift (D79 W105 L125).
£/££

Travelodge Crawley

Church Road, Lowfield Heath, Crawley, West Sussex RH11 0PQ
Tel: 08700-850950 *Fax:* 01293-535369
150m off the A23 just south of Gatwick Airport. On-site CP. Separate BB spaces near entrance. Flat to dining room and bar. **Six adapted GFBs**, three with twin beds, three with doubles. Room 1 seen: D78, bathroom D80 ST93 with low-level bath and rails. Lift gives step-free access to other bedrooms.
£/££

Near Heathrow Airport

Ibis Heathrow

112/114 Bath Road, Hayes, Middx UB3 5AL
Tel: 020 8759-4888 *Fax:* 020 8564-7894
On the A4 about 300m from Harlington High Street, past the Holiday Inn. There are two BB spaces and a ramped kerb to an otherwise flat entrance. On the GF are a bar which is 90% step free

and a restaurant which is 100% step free. There are six lifts (D75 W125 L130) and **six adapted rooms**, all double-bedded. The one we saw had D70, bathroom D70 ST100 but no rails for bath and no wheel-in shower.
££/£££

Marriott Hotel Hayes
Bath Road, Hayes, Middx UB3 5AN
Tel: 020 8990-1100 *Fax:* 020 8990-1110
Five-storey white building on the left as you come up Bath Road from Heathrow, just past the junction with Sipson Road (A408). Twenty BB spaces, ten on each side of the building. Flat entrance through revolving doors leads to high reception desk and flat access to bars, restaurants and **two wheelchair toilets (D85 ST75)** by the lifts to far left of entrance. Four lifts (D110 W185 L125) go to all floors. **Twenty adapted rooms** on the first floor with either wheel-in shower or bath. Room 1005 seen: bathroom has D90 ST100 with wheel-in shower and fold-down seat, and room 1006 has D90 ST75 with bath and handrails.
£££

Le Meridien Heathrow
Bath Road, West Drayton, Middx UB7 0DU
Tel: 0870 400-8899 *Fax:* 020 8759-3421
Located on Bath Road by the junction with Sipson Road (A408). CP with four BB spaces, from which the main entrance is flat. Bars, restaurant and shop on GF all have step-free access. Six lifts (D90 W130 L155) serve five floors, with over a thousand rooms. **Ten adapted rooms**. Room 1927 seen: D75, bathroom D75 ST blocked by basin; bath with handrails. **Adapted toilet (D80 ST60)** on the GF to the right of main entrance.
£££/££££

Sheraton Skyline Heathrow
Bath Road, Hayes, Middx UB3 5BP
Tel: 020 8759-2535 *Fax:* 020 8750-9150
Big hotel on the A4 near the airport. On-site CP. Entrance + 2 steps with ramped bypass, automatic doors. Two lifts (D100 W160 L170). Flat to dining room. **One adapted bedroom** with card operated lock: D80, bathroom D80 with ST. Wheel-in shower. Long distances between facilities.
££££

Outer London

We have only included a few of the hotels in outer London, as there is much more choice anyway, and location is less important for most visitors, who will presumably have a car. It is worth looking at the websites and listings of ETAP, Express by Holiday Inn, Ibis, Premier Lodge, Travelodge and Travel Inns for other places. We have not attempted to visit all of them, and new ones are likely to be opened.

Hotels that we know about, which should all have adapted rooms, are:

- the new **Ibis** Hotel at Southway, **Wembley** HA9 6BA
  Tel: 0870 609-0963

Premier Lodge Hotels at:
- 435 Burnt Oak Broadway, **Edgware** HA8 5AQ *Tel:* 0870 700-1454
- Ferry Lane, **Brentford**, *Tel:* 0870 700-1450 (opening Sept 2003)
- Chertsey Road, Whitton, **Twickenham** TW2 6LS
  Tel: 0870 700-1440

Travel Inn Hotels at:
- Kenton Road, **Kenton**, Middlesex HA3 8AT *Tel:* 020 8907-4069
- Hayes (for Heathrow), 362 Uxbridge Road, **Hayes** UB4 0HF
  Tel: 020 8573-7479

Travelodge Hotels at:
- Ilford Central, Clements Road, **Ilford** RM10 9YO
  Tel: 0870 191-1693
- Ilford North, The Beehive, Beehive Lane, Gants Hill, **Ilford** IG4 5DR *Tel:* 0870 191-1692
- Kew Bridge, North Road, High Street, **Brentford** TW8 0BO
  Tel: 0870 191-1540
- 21 London Road, **Kingston** KT2 6ND *Tel:* 0870 191-1741
- Wimbledon, A24 Epsom Road, **Morden** SM4 5PH
  Tel: 0870 191-1695

Northwest (outer)

Hendon Hall
Ashley Lane, Hendon NW4 1HF
Tel: 020 8203-3341 *Fax:* 020 8203 9709
South off Great North Way (A1) into Parson Street, right on the junction with Ashley Lane, the hotel has two BB spaces 30m from reception. Step-free entrance leads to bar and restaurant (+1 to 50%) and lift (D85 W105 L150) to four other floors. **One adapted**

room (306) was not seen but we were told that it has a wheel-in shower and twin beds. **Wheelchair toilet (D80 ST95)** along corridor to left of reception. As the hotel was given a high rating in an ETB inspection, it is probably very well adapted, but a major snag is that it is on the third floor, and there is only one lift. Not an issue addressed within the 'National Accessible Standard'.
££££

West (outer)

Travel Inn Greenford
Western Avenue, Perivale, Greenford UB6 8TR
Tel: 020 8998-8820 *Fax:* 020 8998-8823
Located on the south (westbound) side of the A40 almost opposite the Hoover Factory and alongside the Myllet Arms restaurant/pub. CP accessed off the A40 or from Perivale Lane. Two BB spaces in the CP and step free to reception. **Two adapted rooms** on the GF about 20m away. Both have a double bed and adapted bathroom with sliding door D70+ ST75 and a low-level bath. A camp bed can be provided. There are many more GFBs. Meals are available in the Myllet Arms next door some 50m away. There is step-free access to 50% of the pub while the restaurant is all step free. Well signed **adapted toilet (D80 ST60** blocked by a bin) off the restaurant.
£/££

Shalimar
215 Staines Road, Hounslow, Middx TW3 3JJ
Tel: 0181 577-7070 *Fax:* 020 8569-6789
On-site CP. Ramped entrance. No lift. Flat to dining room and bar, and −1 step to patio. Eight GFBs. **One adapted room**: D85, bathroom D72 ST and a wheel-in shower.
££

Master Brewer Motel
Freezeland Way, Hillingdon UB10 9NX
Tel: 01895-251199 *Fax:* 01895-810330
By the junction with Long Lane. 250m from Hillingdon Tube Station which has step-free access, although there are some slopes en route. On-site CP. The Motel has two main blocks. Entrance to the main building is flat with revolving doors. A side door can be opened on request. Flat to reception, bar, and part of the dining room. **Wheelchair toilet (D70 ST150)** to the right of reception. **Two adapted rooms**

in the new block 150m from reception, which can be reached step free. You can park nearby. Room 302 seen: D72, bathroom D76 ST75 with a bath with grab rails. Over fifty GFBs.
££/£££

The Bridge
Western Avenue, Greenford, Middx UB6 8ST
Tel: 020 8566-6246 *Fax:* 020 8566-6140
Corner of Greenford Road. CP with two BB spaces. Ramped entrance, then flat to dining room, bar and lounge. **Two adapted GFBs**: D75, bathroom D80 (sliding) with ST70 + . Connecting rooms available. **Wheelchair toilet (D70 + ST70 +)** past reception.
£££

Holiday Inn Ealing
Western Avenue, Hangar Lane Gyratory System, Ealing W5 1HG
Tel: 020 8233-3200 *Fax:* 020 8233-3201
Located on the south side of the Gyratory System on the slip road leading to the A40 for Oxford. Four BB spaces and other parking along a sloped roadway outside the hotel. Step-free entrance, and the revolving doors can be bypassed by a door on the left. **Ten adapted GFBs** with D74, bathroom D80 + ST70. All have double beds and a low-level bath with grab rails. Two lifts (D75 W110 L140) go to all five floors, including the lower GF with the restaurant and bar. **Adapted toilet (D80 ST60)** through the door just to the right of the main entrance and 10m down the corridor.
££££

Northeast (outer)

F1 Formule 1 Barking
Highbridge Road, Barking, Essex IG11 7BA
Tel: 020 8507-0789 *Fax:* 020 8394-0750
Road access from North Circular (A406) southbound. There are two BB spaces in the CP by Highbridge Road next to Tesco CP. Automated hotel with reception only open Monday to Saturday 6.30-10am and 5-10pm and Sunday 7-10am (see the write-up earlier in the chapter). At other times it is necessary to use a keyboard and screen rather like a bank cash machine to check in. This is 140-150cm in height and set back 40cm from the wall. Step-free breakfast room on GF. **Four adapted rooms** on GF with D80 and sink. These need to be pre-booked by phone, as the automated system does not give you

the option of booking one of these rooms. You need a credit card to validate your booking on arrival. In the adapted rooms, the double bed has been turned round to provide space for a chair user, but one side of the bed is then against the wall. Shared wheel-in shower-room and **wheelchair toilet** on the GF with **D80 ST80**. The hotel is functional, and provides good value.
£

ETAP Barking
Highbridge Road, Barking, Essex IG11 7BA
Tel: 020 8507-8500 *Fax:* 020 8591-8700
Reached from A406 southbound. CP with two BB spaces by Highbridge Road, after Tesco CP entrance. Entrance +1 from CP with automated reception (see the write-up on automated hotels earlier in the chapter). Breakfast area and lift (D80 W95 L125) to all floors on GF. **Four adapted rooms**, two on GF, one each on first and second floors, with D85, double bed with single bunk above, bathroom D85 ST90 with wheel-in shower (seat height 45cm). **Wheelchair toilet (D90 ST95** with basin behind toilet) on the GF. The adapted rooms need to be booked in advance.
£

Sleeping Beauty Motel
543 Lea Bridge Road, Leyton E10 7EB
Tel/Fax: 020 8556-8080
By the junction with Russell Road. On-site CP. Ramped entrance. Step-free access throughout using lift (D75 L135 W90). GF has reception, dining room, bar and **four adapted rooms**, two with a bath (102/104) and two with a wheel-in shower (105/106). All have D75, bathroom D75 ST125, and both a double and single bed.
£/££

Travel Inn Ilford
Redbridge Lane East, Ilford, Essex IG4 5BG
Tel: 020 8550-7909 *Fax:* 020 8550-6214
By the junction with Roding Lane South. On-site CP. Flat entrance and step free to the fifteen GFBs. **Three adapted rooms** near reception. Room 1 seen: double bed, D85, bathroom D79 ST80. Low-level bath with rails. Ramp to breakfast room. Flat to adjacent *Beefeater* restaurant and bar. Staff said *Beefeater* building has a lift up to dining room level (not seen).
£/££

Travelodge Ilford
The Beehive, Beehive Lane, Gants Hill, Ilford, Essex IG4 5DR
Tel: 0181 550-4248 *Fax:* 020 8551-1712
Opposite the junction with Ethelbert Gardens by the Gants Hill roundabout on the A12. CP with four BB spaces. Flat to reception and all fifteen GFBs. **One adapted GFB** with double bed and rails around the bath (not seen). Restaurant and bar in Harvester building 40m away with flat access via pub entrance on the left.
£/££

Premier Lodge Barking
Highfield Road, Barking, Essex IG11 7BA
Tel: 0870 700-1444 *Fax:* 0870 700-1445
Situated just off the A406 North Circular Road, about 1km north of the junction with the A13. The hotel is one of a group of four (the others are Formule 1, Etap and Ibis) on a slip road to the A406. It is just over 1km from Barking Station which is accessible. Five BB spaces. Step free to reception, bar and restaurant. **Five adapted rooms**, all on the GF. All have a double bed, but there's room to put in an extra bed if requested. Room seen with D80, bathroom D85 ST85 and a conventional height bath.
££

Ibis East Barking
Highbridge Road, Barking, Essex IG 11 7BA
Tel: 020 8477-4100 *Fax:* 020 8477-4101
Situated just off the A406 North Circular Road, about 1km north of the junction with the A13. The hotel is one of a group of four (Formule 1, Etap and Premier Lodge) on a slip road to the A406. It is just over 1km from Barking Station which is accessible. CP outside with four BB spaces. Step free to reception, bar and restaurant. Two lifts (D70 W90 L120). **Four adapted rooms**. All are on the first floor, with double beds and wheel-in shower. Room seen: D75, and a tightish W70 gap between the door and bed. Bathroom with a wheel-in shower. Bathroom D80 ST80.
££

North (outer)

Oak Lodge
80 Village Road, Bush Hill Park, Enfield EN1 2EU
Tel: 020 8360-7082

A small privately owned hotel in a residential district. On-site CP. Flat entrance. Lounge and dining room on the GF, and **one GFB** with a wheel-in shower and toilet.
£££

Southwest (outer)

Travel Inn Chessington
Leatherhead Road, Chessington, Surrey KT9 2NE
Tel: 01372-744060 *Fax:* 01372-720889
Located near Chessington World of Adventures, next to the *Monkey Puzzle* pub, see write-up on page 361. CP. Ramp to reception. Twenty-one GFBs, including **two adapted**. Room 9 seen: double bed, D77, bathroom D75 (sliding) no ST. Low-level bath with rails. The pub next door has a **wheelchair toilet (D90 ST70)** to the right as you enter.
£

Travelodge Morden
Epsom Road, Morden, Surrey SM4 5PH
Tel/fax: 020 8640-8227
100m south of junction with Central Road. CP with two BB spaces. Flat to reception and all fifteen GFBs. **One adapted GFB**, room 1: double bed, with room for a folding bed, D85, bathroom D80 ST110 (slightly obstructed by the sink). Bath with rails. Restaurant and bar in *Harvester* building 60m away, and we are told that there is a disabled persons' toilet there.
££

Windmill on the Common
Clapham Common Southside SW4 9DE
Tel: 020 8673-4578 *Fax:* 020 8675-1486
Opposite the junction with St Gerard's Close. On-site CP. The building contains a pub, a hotel and a restaurant. Hotel has two entrances, reached from the CP by a 15m shallow ramp. The main hotel entrance has $+2$ steps, then flat to reception but $-3-1$ to the **adapted GFB**, restaurant and pub. An alternative way in (flat with bellpush to summon staff) is 20m to the left and gives step-free access to the adapted GFB, restaurant and pub. Equally, you can approach the room step free via the pub. Room 107 seen: D80, bathroom D75 ST90 and connecting door to room 106. **Wheelchair toilet (D70 ST90)** off the pub conservatory.
£££

Southeast (outer)

Travel Inn Croydon
104 Coombe Road, Croydon CR0 5RB
Tel: 020 8686-2030 *Fax:* 020 8686-6435
100m west of the junction with Conduit Lane. On-site CP. Slope up
to flat entrance. Nineteen GFBs, **two adapted**, Room 4 seen: D80,
bathroom D78 (sliding) ST100, with bath with grab rails and double
bed. Restaurant in the *Out and Out* about 100m away, with ramp
bypassing + 1 step at the entrance, then + 1 inside, and flat to part of
the restaurant and bar. **Adapted toilet (D80 ST62)** off the restaurant.
£/££

A new **Travel Inn** is due to open in 2003 in South Croydon, 1
Parkway, New Addington CR0 0JA *Tel:* 0870 238-3333.

Travel Inn M25 Westerham
Clacket Lane, M25 Motorway Service Area, Westerham, Kent TN16
2ER
Tel: 01959-565789 (booking 0870-2428000) *Fax:* 01959-561311
Located between junctions five and six. CP with BB spaces. Flat access
to twenty-eight GFBs with **three adapted**: D88, bathroom D85 ST140.
Main services building 50m away, step free throughout, and a Road-
chef and Wimpy restaurant nearby, both of which are step free.
££

Croydon Park
7 Altyre Road, Croydon, Surrey CR9 5AA
Tel: 020 8680-9200 *Fax:* 020 8760-0426
Less than 200m from the fully-accessible East Croydon Station.
UGCP, no lift access. Entrance flat. Two lifts (D105 W180 L135).
Flat to dining room. **One adapted GFB**: D64, bathroom D74 ST70.
Wheelchair toilet (D70+ ST70+) by the lifts.
£££

Camping and caravan sites

Perhaps a tent is not the most obvious accommodation for someone
visiting London. However, many disabled people go camping, and
the relatively low cost can make it an attractive proposition. At peak
times it is sensible to book in advance. In our view the London
campsites are reasonably well adapted. Note that the sites have

provision for only one wheelchair toilet and/or bathroom, which could be a problem if your visit coincided with that of several other chair users or other disabled people.

Approximate opening times are given here but they may vary from year to year. **Most of the sites cost less than £7 per person per night.**

Crystal Palace Camping and Caravan Site
Crystal Palace Parade SE19 1UF
Tel: 020 8778-7155
Near the Crystal Palace National Sports Centre. Terraced site with sloped tarmac paths and gravel chip/grass pitches. Ramped office. **Wheelchair toilet and shower** with fold-down seat replaces facilities which were separately in the Ladies and Gents areas. Open all year round.
£

Lee Valley Camping and Caravan Park (Dobbs Weir)
Charlton Meadows, Essex Road, Dobbs Weir, Hoddesdon, Herts EN11 0AS
Tel: 01992-462090
Take the Hoddesdon exit from the A10 and follow signs to Dobbs Weir. A 16-acre site with beautiful riverside surroundings and some on-site fishing spots with step-free access. Reasonably flat with tarmac paths and grass pitches. A new **combined wheelchair toilet and shower** (with a pull-down seat), has been built, which is step free. Open April-October.
£

Lee Valley Camping and Caravan Park (Edmonton)
Meridian Way, Edmonton N9 0AS
Tel: 020 8803-6900
Situated behind the (ex-)leisure centre, with flat access, tarmac paths and grass pitches. Ramp to **two wheelchair toilets** and showers **(D90 ST70)**. The shower is wheel-in, with a seat. Open all the year round. Shop with step-free access via a very small lip.
£

Lee Valley Camping and Caravan Park (Chingford)
Sewardstone Road, Chingford, E4 7RA
Tel: 020 8529-5689
On A112 between Chingford and Waltham Abbey about 4km south of junction 26 on the M25. Gently sloping site with tarmac paths and

grass pitches. Reception and shop have ramped access. Combined **wheelchair toilet/shower (D75 ST160)** with ramped access, grab bars and a movable plastic chair. Open March to October.
£

Self-catering

If you're thinking of a longish stay in London, and/or you're in a small group, self-catering offers particular attractions. Facilities are extremely limited and tend to be heavily booked. Costs per head vary depending on how many people are staying. We didn't manage to find any in central London that claimed to be 'accessible'. The one place we did find was near the M25 to the north.

Lee Valley Boat Centre
Old Nazeing Road, Broxbourne, Herts EN10 7AX
Tel: 01992-462085
At the Old Mill and Meadows site about 400m from the centre, there are four riverside chalets for hire. One is adapted for chair users with a shallow ramp at the front. It can sleep three to five people and there are two orthopaedic beds. The bathroom has D75 and there is ST75 for the toilet. The bath has a cradle. Weekly rates are offered, and also weekend and mid-week rates. Good value.

Hostels

Youth hostels

There are six Youth Hostels in the London area with varying degrees of accessibility. It is really only the Rotherhithe one that is of interest to people with disabilities. The hostels provide inexpensive accommodation for both individuals and groups. Accommodation is mainly in small dormitories or family rooms. They are only open to members but membership is available on arrival. Opening times and charges are detailed in a booklet from the Youth Hostel Association (YHA) Trevelyan House, 8 St Stephen's Hill, St Albans, Herts AL1 2DY *Tel:* 01727-855215. Hostels are mainly for young people but there is no age limit, and people of all ages use them. Booking is essential especially if you have specific requirements. The Rotherhithe YH has good adapted rooms. The provision was made under the auspices of the London Hotel for Disabled People Project who also sponsored the adapted rooms in the Copthorne Tara Hotel.

Please note that for comparison purposes, the indicated prices relate to the cost of TWO people staying. Prices were around £25 to £30 per person in 2002. The YH at St Pancras has lift/step-free access, and an adapted toilet on the GF. None of the facilities such as dormitories and bathrooms are adapted in any way, but it might be a good place for a disabled walker to stay.

③ **Rotherhithe YH**
Island Yard, Salter Road SE16 1PP
Tel: 020 7232-2114 *Fax*: 020 7237-2919
e-mail: rotherhithe@yha.org.uk
It's about 600m from Canada Water Underground Station (see map, page 94). No on-site CP but plenty of parking on the roads nearby. Flat to reception, restaurant and lounge/bar and a low-level payphone. There are **six adapted bedrooms**, two on each floor. Step-free access throughout via two lifts (D80 W105 L150). The adapted rooms have two normal beds and one bunk bed. Bathroom and toilet en suite, with a sliding door. Flat access shower with hand rails and ST80 + to the padded seat with an adjustable back. **Toilet with ST70 +**. There is an **adapted toilet (D85 ST65)** on the left as you enter the hostel. They have a policy of keeping the adapted rooms available for disabled visitors for as long as possible. However, since the facilities are such good value they are liable to get booked up, especially at peak times. About 100m away on the riverside is an excellent and accessible pub, the *Spice Island*.
£/££

YMCA/YWCAs

London City YMCA
8 Errol Street EC1Y 8SE
Tel: 020 7628-8832 *Fax*: 020 7628-4080
website: www.ymca.england.org.uk
e-mail: housing@london.city.ymca.org.uk
By the junction with Lamb's Buildings. Flat entrance. Lift (D85 W110 L130). Flat to dining room. **Five adapted rooms** on the first floor, one twin, four single. Two wheel-in showers and **two wheelchair toilets (D75 ST110)** off the corridor. There are three other slightly larger rooms on other floors with en suite bathrooms which are less spacious than the off-corridor facilities on the first floor. **Wheelchair toilet (D70 ST100)** on the GF to the right of reception and turn left.
£/££

YMCA Kingston
49 Victoria Road, Surbiton, Surrey KT6 4NG
Tel: 020 8390-0148 *Fax:* 020 8390-066
On the corner of Brighton Road. Ramped entrance bypasses +2 steps. Flat to dining room and bar. Lift (D80 W120 L130) gives step-free access to bedrooms on the second, third and fourth floors. **Three adapted rooms**. Room 201 seen: D70, bathroom D70 but no ST. **Wheelchair toilet (D75 ST95)** past the dining room entrance on the left.
££

London University halls of residence

London University has a number of halls of residence. During the vacations some are opened as hostels and conference centres. The facilities range from the basic to the pretty comfortable, but as a relatively cheap way of staying in central London it is hard to beat, especially if you want a single room (which is proportionately more expensive in a hotel). Halls will generally be available from March–April, July–September and possibly December–January, but exact dates will vary. Most of the main colleges have a website giving details, and some colleges have a special department looking after such bookings.

The principal groups with some accessible accommodation are:

- **Goldsmiths' Residences Services**, Loring Management Centre, St James's, New Cross SE14 6AD *Tel:* 020 7919-7133 (main no. 020 7919-7171) *e-mail:* c.andrews@gold.ac.uk
  website: www.goldsmiths.ac.uk
- **King's College Conference and Vacation Bureau**, 138 Strand WC2R 1HH *Tel:* 020 7848-1700 *Fax:* 020 7848-1717
  e-mail: accommodation.at.kings@kcl.ac.uk
- **London School of Economics Halls** *Tel:* 020 7955-7370 *Fax:* 020 7955-7676 *website:* www.lse.ac.uk/vacations

Nearly all the halls we visited said that they get large conference bookings months in advance, and this is their main 'market'. They will sometimes have room for some casual visitors but early booking is essential, if you want an adapted room. Many only provide bed and breakfast. Some are in central locations, and the best one we found was Bankside House.

Bankside House
26 Sumner Street SE1 9JA
Tel: 020 7633-9877 *Fax:* 020 7955-7676
e-mail: bankside-reservation@lse.ac.uk
Situated just behind Tate Modern and within 200m of the riverfront, it is well placed for visiting many of the sights/sites on the south bank, and some in the city. It is about 600m to Southwark Station which is accessible and on the JLE. It may be possible to negotiate about parking for disabled visitors. Ramped bypass to the + 6 steps to reception. There are **several adapted rooms** with wheel-in showers on each floor, making a total of 32. Lifts (D90 W130 L120) to all floors. We saw room 640: bathroom D75 + ST75 with a wheel-in shower including a fold-down seat. Breakfast room with step-free access. It is only open in the summer, but has good facilities.
£/££

King's College (details on previous page)
Great Dover Street Apartments
165 Great Dover Street SE1 4XA *Tel:* 020 7407-0068
Stamford Street Apartments
127 Stamford Street SE1 9NQ *Tel:* 020 7848-2960
Both are large blocks housing several hundred students. Each has three adapted rooms with step-free access and a wheel-in shower. We visited Great Dover Street (GDS), and were told that Stamford Street was virtually the same. At GDS there were + 4 steps to reception which could, of course, be bypassed, but only by activating a security gate. A lift (D75 W100 L120) bypassed the steps down to the main courtyard – which is huge. We saw room 52C with a wheel-in shower and **wheelchair toilet (D70 + ST70 +)**, although no grab rails or shower seat, which means that you might need to use a plastic chair. The Stamford Street location is very handy for visiting the South Bank facilities near Waterloo. There is no parking.
£/££

Places of interest

This chapter covers many of London's main historical buildings and attractions. **Entries are divided into inner and outer London and further split into small geographical areas. They are then listed alphabetically**. Where there are groups of sights quite close to each other, like the Guildhall, the Clock Museum and the Guildhall Art Gallery, they will be listed and described together. Some places, including museums and churches, may be cross-referenced to other appropriate chapters in the guide.

An increasing number of sights are accessible without much hassle, and a great variety of things can be seen with minimal difficulty. In addition, both staff attitudes and understanding have improved. There are, of course, problems in some places. These are usually because the buildings are old, because there are long distances involved and, of course, because disability awareness is by no means universal or uniform.

The number of places for getting good views of and over London is limited. Perhaps the best are the London Eye and the Tower Bridge Walkway. In addition, there are good views from Waterloo Bridge, the Oxo Tower, the Royal Festival Hall level 5 and Westminster Cathedral tower. Good vantage points are also to be found further out at Primrose Hill, Greenwich Park (up by the observatory), and Alexandra Palace. All of these can be reached step free, and several are described in more detail in this chapter.

There are plenty of opportunities for seeing famous buildings and getting a feel for important aspects of London's life and history without actually going inside the buildings. Some major sights do not have an 'inside' which you can visit, such as Admiralty Arch, the Albert Memorial, Big Ben, Cleopatra's Needle, Marble Arch, and Trafalgar Square. In each case some sense of the history comes from the architecture, the façade and the location.

There are statues all over the place. The *Eyewitness* guide we recommend describes some of these. There are more extensive descriptions in other books, and you can pick up an enormous amount of interesting information about London and its history from a study of the statues – most of which, by their very nature, can easily be seen. There's a particularly good description by Margaret

Baker in *London Statues and Monuments* published by Shire Publications, Princes Risborough, Bucks HP17 9AJ.

As elsewhere, our write-ups are descriptive and a listing does not mean that a site is fully accessible.

Inner London

City area

This comprises the City itself, together with the area just to the north and east. It includes the Tower, which is not strictly in the City, Tower Bridge and St Katharine's Dock. The write-up covers two areas in the *Eyewitness* guide: the City and Smithfield/Spitalfields. The so-called 'Square Mile' is an area with a high concentration of commercial buildings where millions of pounds change hands every hour. Parking is particularly difficult so it's a good idea to use a taxi or minicab if you can, or the DLR (to Bank or Tower Gateway). Note the possibility of using the Waterloo-City Line discussed in the chapter on *Travelling*, and that City Thameslink Station has step-free access, although it is not open at weekends. There are CPs at Minories, West Smithfield and the Barbican where you will probably find space. For a leaflet on parking facilities contact the City Parking Office, 1 Guildhall Yard EC2P 2EJ *Tel:* 020 7332-1022, otherwise see the *Blue Badge User Guide* described on page 54.

The pavements are narrow, and can be crowded during the week. However, it's a fascinating area and there are many old and famous buildings. If you need specific information, for example about opening times, the **City Information Centre** just south of St Paul's Cathedral (*Tel:* 020 7332-1456) is helpful, but we found that they knew little or nothing about access. The **City Access Group** publish a leaflet with a map showing the location of wheelchair toilets, and giving other details (c/o Access Officer, Department of Community Services, Corporation of London, PO Box 270, Guildhall, London EC2P 2EJ *Tel:* 020 7332-1995/1933 *Textphone:* 020 7332-3929 *website:* www.cityoflondon.gov.uk/accessoffice.)

All-Hallows-by-the-Tower
Byward Street EC3R 5BJ
Tel: 020 7381-2928
An interesting old and atmospheric church, offering the opportunity of doing some brass rubbing. Pepys watched the Great Fire from its tower. Recently built annexes mean there are now three step-free

entrances. Probably the easiest is via a shallow 20m-ramp into 'The Vestry' restaurant, on the east (Tower) side of the church. From here ramps bypass $-2-2$ en route through the Queen Mother's Building into the south side of the church. The entrance, via the main doors on the north side, has a steepish ramp to bypass -3 steps. Finally, if you go past both these entrances, along Byward Street to the west end of the church and follow the path around to the south side, automatic doors lead into the Queen Mother's Building.

The Brass Rubbing Centre is a friendly spot inside, at the west end of the church, with tables at a suitable height for most chair users and some brasses mounted on mobile plinths which you can put on your knees. By the font there are -2 and on the other side are two small crypt chapels down -18 or -12. **Wheelchair toilet (D80 ST80)** near the Vestry restaurant.

Bank of England Museum see chapter on *Museums and galleries*.

The Barbican is a sizeable area which has been redeveloped on two levels. It is bounded by London Wall, Moorgate and Aldersgate Street. There are historic sites, high-rise blocks of flats, offices, pubs and shops, both at ground level and on the high-level walkway which covers much of the development. The most interesting places are the Barbican Centre (see section on *Arts centres*), St Giles's Church, restored after extensive bomb damage, and the Museum of London (see chapter on *Museums and galleries*). Signposting around the area has been greatly improved.

Broadgate is a developing complex, built around Liverpool Street Station. It consists mainly of office blocks, but there are shops, markets, bars and restaurants. Broadgate Arena is a skating rink in winter and an entertainment venue in the summer. When we visited, there were some radio-controlled car races taking place. Access is pretty good with ramped/lift routes to most places, although a lack of signposting makes it confusing to a stranger, and there is only stepped access to the arena. There's a **wheelchair toilet** in Liverpool Street Station, and several others in and around the development.

Guildhall
Guildhall Yard (PO Box 270) EC2P 2EJ
Tel: 020 7606-3030
This has been the administrative centre of the City of London for nearly 900 years. The current building dates from the 15thC. Guild-

hall Yard outside has been pedestrianised, with some bumpy surfaces. You can visit and wander around in the famous Great Hall and Livery Hall, unless there's a council meeting. As council meetings are open to the public, you can still go in and listen, but without the freedom to wander. Flat entrance, and + 3 steps into the Hall can be bypassed by a signposted ramped route. To go to the Old Library (where there are occasional events) a platform stairlift bypasses + 10, then the split levels in the chamber are bypassed by temporary ramps. The crypt is about − 30 (steepish), bypassed by a platform stairlift, and there's a further stairlift to bypass 3 steps there. **Two wheelchair toilets (both D90 ST100)**, one on the GF near the Great Hall and the other in the office area past reception on the second floor. You will be escorted to both, for security reasons.

Just around the corner in Aldermanbury (with two BB spaces opposite) is the **Guildhall Library, Clock Museum and Bookshop**. All are reached via + 5 with a ramped bypass. The museum has been rehoused, and is flat inside. The bookshop is quite small. In the library there is a reading room, and a platform stairlift to the catalogue area, bypassing + 12. The staff can get the books which you have found on the microfiche. This building is likely to be redeveloped in the near future, and this should result in improved access. *Red Herring* is a nearby pub, see page 333.

Guildhall Art Gallery
Guildhall Yard EC2P
Tel: 020 7332-3700 *Fax:* 020 7332-3342
e-mail: guildhall.artgallery@corpoflondon.gov.uk
website: www.guildhall-art-gallery.org.uk
Built over a Roman amphitheatre, it houses the paintings and sculptures belonging to the Corporation of London. Admission is charged at some times of the day. It is located 50m from the Guildhall, across Guildhall Yard which is step free but bumpy. The entrance is step free and two lifts (D90 W140 L160) connect the four levels. There are three floors of galleries, as well as the remains of a Roman amphitheatre in the basement. One gallery floor is above ground level, and other galleries are below ground, with the amphitheatre remains at the lowest level. Throughout the gallery access is step free, though thick carpet may hinder movement. **One wheelchair toilet (D80 ST85)** on Level A1 opposite lifts and **two wheelchair cubicles** by the Gents **(D80 ST85)** and the Ladies **(D70 ST75)** on cloakroom level.

Leadenhall Market
Leadenhall Place EC3

A small but attractive Victorian market located near the Lloyd's building, with a variety of clothes and food shops. It's generally flat and compact but the main roadway is cobbled and there are kerbs. The *New Moon* pub has flat access to the bar and to the Gents toilet which has an **adapted cubicle (D75 ST60** inward opening door). The nearest wheelchair toilet is in Fenchurch Street station.

Lloyd's of London
1 Lime Street EC3

This is an interesting modern 'inside-out' building with the piping, ducting and the lifts built on the outside. Lloyd's is the centre of the world's insurance market. The public gallery closed some years ago.

Monument
Monument Street EC3 8AH
Tel: 020 7626-2717

A giant Doric column commemorating the Great Fire of London. It is 62m high and lies the same distance from the supposed site of the outbreak of the fire in Pudding Lane. There are + 311 spiralled steps, so it can hardly be described as accessible!

Museum of London see chapter on *Museums and galleries.*

Old Bailey (Central Criminal Court)
Old Bailey EC4M 7EH
Tel: 020 7248-3277

On the corner with Newgate Street, this is *the* central court complex where many famous cases are tried. All the courts have a public gallery. Courts 1 to 4 are entered from Newgate Street, with + 60 or so steps. Court 18 is a further + 17. From the entrance in Warwick Passage, Courts 13 to 16 are + 30; Courts 5 to 8 + 30 + 40, and Courts 9 to 12 are + 30 + 40 + 40! Although it is not one of London's more accessible places, we have been told that, on the 'other side' of the facility, for the court officials, lawyers, witnesses and those charged, there are changes being made to make some of the courts accessible. In addition, the public gallery of Court 17 is now said to be accessible.

The **Royal Exchange** is on the corner of Threadneedle Street and Cornhill, opposite the Bank of England. It was opened in 1844 to replace an earlier trading centre. In 2002 the central courtyard was reopened, surrounded by some very high-class shops. There are +8 to 10 steps at entrances on three sides, but there's a step-free route from the back, opposite the statue of Reuter. There's a wooden ramp en route, getting up +1 step. The façades in the courtyard are magnificent, even if you can't afford to go shopping! There's a lift (D80 W100 L110) in the far right corner (from the step-free entrance). This goes to a viewing gallery on the first floor, and a **wheelchair toilet (D70+ ST70+)** in the basement.

St Katharine's Dock
E1W 1TW
website: www.stkaths.co.uk
A busy and attractive area by Tower Bridge, forming one of the earlier stages of the Docklands Development. It is located alongside Tower Bridge between St Katharine's Way, East Smithfield and Thomas More Street. It can be accessed by many different routes, all step free, including the riverside walk by the Tower of London. The area is generally flat but there are cobbled sections. There is pay-and-display parking on St Katharine's Way and a UGCP 70m from the junction with Mews Street (going away from Tower Bridge). The area includes docks, shops, restaurants, cafés, bars and offices and the website includes a good map showing what is where. *Dickens' Inn* (see page 331) has a **wheelchair toilet** accessed by a lift. There is also a Tardis-style **wheelchair toilet (NKS)** very near a corner of the Thistle Hotel and on Cloister Walk 100m from St Katharine's Way.

St Paul's Cathedral see chapter on *Places of worship*.

St Bartholomew-the-Great see chapter on *Places of worship*.

Tower Bridge (Walkway and Museum)
SE1 2UP
Tel: 020 7403-3761 RecM 020 7940-3985 *Fax:* 020 7357-7935 *website:* www.towerbridge.org.uk
One of London's landmarks, completed in 1894. It houses a museum with an imaginative presentation of the history of the bridge, and there are superb views from the walkways joining the towers.

Entrance in the north-west tower, nearest the Tower of London. To avoid steps, approach it along the main Tower Bridge Road. Step-free access throughout the five floors via lifts (D120 W350 L150) at each end. These bypass some 200 steps. The walkways include good viewing points for children (with two steps, and handrails) and a ramped platform for chair users, so that all visitors can get good views and photographs. Visiting the engine room and the shop at the end of the visit involves either a step-free route southwards of about 400m, or −21−11 and 50m. The step-free route involves going along the bridge and doubling back along Horsleydown Lane. **Adapted toilet (D90 ST65)** on the second floor of the south-east tower by the lift, and a **wheelchair toilet (D90 ST75)** by the engine room.

Tower of London
Tower Hill EC3N 4AB
Tel: 020 7709-0765 *visitor services:* 020 7488-5694 *DisEnq:* 020 7488-5658
website: www.hrp.org.uk
One of London's prime tourist attractions. It is both a fortress and a royal palace, and its history goes back some 900 years. There are CPs at the Tower Thistle Hotel and Minories. Tower Gateway DLR station has step-free access. BB holders may be able to negotiate parking on the riverfront – but ring first. *There may be long queues to get in on popular days such as bank holidays and summer weekends.* Chair users and other disabled visitors should make their presence known at the Groups booking office (on the right, coming down the hill). **They have a really detailed 'Access' leaflet** which (unusually) adopts the same kind of descriptive approach as we do. If you want to explore as much as possible, try and get a copy. *It's good.* There is a **wheelchair toilet (D85 ST85)** outside the Tower ticket office on the right-hand side as you go down Tower Hill. Inside there are wheelchair toilets at only one location (see diagram).

The Tower consists of a group of buildings with two surrounding walls. The area is roughly 200m square and many of the paths and courtyards are cobbled and sloping. Since the buildings are several hundred years old, access to many of them is difficult, but it's possible to see a lot from outside. Chair users can get in to see the Crown Jewels, and go down to the basement of the White Tower.

The flat/sloped route round takes you through the Middle and Byward Towers and along Water Lane parallel to the river. On the left is the Gallery shop with step-free access. Turning left through the arch you go up the hill past the White Tower, turn left again, and the entrance to the Crown Jewels is in the middle of the courtyard at the top. Ahead is Tower Green where executions used to take place, and you'll probably see some of the famous ravens. You have to go back by the same route, and the whole distance is about 600/700m, partly cobbled.

Tower of London

Recommended Route
---- Level but sometimes bumpy
>>>> Slope
🔓 Wheelchair toilet

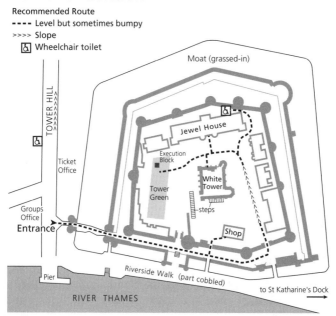

The **Crown Jewels** now have step-free access. Visitors pass through three halls, walking past large video presentations. You see the Jewels from a horizontal moving walkway. There are +3 steps to the viewing platform if you want to take a more leisurely look. The **White Tower** has +12+20+10 steps, but only +24 if you use the exit (D76) on the far (north) side. The basement is −15 from the north exit side. **There is a new lift** (D75 W75 L130) **which gives access to the basement exhibition**. You need to ask one of the Yeoman Warders to be able to use it. A complete visit to the Tower involves over 200 steps, some irregular and steep. The **New Armories** have been moved, and are +48. There is a café at the entrance to the New Armories building with step-free access. The only **wheelchair toilets** **(D85 ST70)** on the site are behind the Jewel House (by its exit). Go straight ahead past the White Tower, instead of turning left towards Tower Green. The attendant in either the Ladies or Gents has the key.

The **Ceremony of the Keys** is the ritual of locking up the Tower, which takes place every evening between *21.30 and 22.05* and has done so for some 700 years. Apparently, it was a little late one night in 1941 when a bomb blew the escort off their feet. Admission by ticket only from the Keys Clerk at the Tower and, although there are no steps, disabled visitors should mention their disability when applying. Book well in advance, and give alternative dates if possible.

Wesley's House and Chapel
49 City Road EC1Y 1AU
Tel: 020 7253-2262
About 150m from Old Street tube station. A space in the small CP outside the chapel can be reserved. Via the back entrance to the House, there are -15 steps to the basement, then $+1-1$, and $+15$ to the GF, $+21$ to the first floor and $+21$ to the second. The front door gives flat access to the GF, which has two rooms. Audio guide available describing the rest of the house. The Chapel is flat with lift (D80 W105 L140) access to the basement, containing a small museum with uneven but step-free access, and a **wheelchair toilet (D85 ST75)**.

The South Bank and Southwark

Listed in the *Eyewitness* guide as the South Bank, together with Southwark and Bankside. The south bank of the river opposite Westminster and the City has developed rapidly during the last few years. There is a pleasant riverside walk along much of it, going from near Westminster Bridge by the old County Hall, right the way along to Tower Bridge. There is a longer description of the route in the chapter entitled *Recommended itineraries*. There are accessible tube stations relatively near this part of the riverside, and the RV1 bus route as well. There are wheelchair toilets in the Festival Hall, National Theatre, Oxo Tower, Tate Modern, Shakespeare's Globe, Southwark Cathedral, London Bridge Station and Hays Galleria. There are also wheelchair toilets in several pubs en route, notably the Founders Arms and the Anchor.

Some of the sights are grouped around the Jubilee Gardens, notably the London Eye, London Aquarium, Dali Exhibition and the Festival Hall complex.

The Anchor see chapter on *Pubs and bars*, under SE1.

Bankside Gallery see chapter on *Museums and galleries*.

Bramah Tea and Coffee Museum see chapter on *Museums and galleries*.

Britain at War Experience
64 Tooley Street SE1 2TF
Tel: 020 7403-3171
This attempts to recreate the fury of the London Blitz. You can sit in an Anderson shelter and hear the raids overhead. Ramped entrance. There is a route without steps, but you need staff help. There's a door to bypass the $+1-1$ steps into the simulated lift (to the Underground). The Rainbow room has $+3$, but you can see in, while the Blitz area which otherwise involves $-11+11$ can be accessed via a 'fire exit'.

City Hall
Queen's Walk SE1 2AA
Tel: 020 7983-4000 *Textphone:* 020 7983-4458 *Fax:* 020 7983-4057
website: www.london.gov.uk/approot/gla/city_hall
The newly constructed offices of the mayor, often described as a glass onion. Located on the south bank of the Thames, halfway between Tower Bridge and HMS Belfast. There are four BB spaces, which must be reserved in advance with the GLA's Facilities Management (*Tel:* 020 7983-4750).

The main entrance is a revolving door on the riverside, with an alternative step-free entrance for wheelchair users 10m away. The building has ten floors, but the public only has access to the GF, lower GF, and floors two and nine. The GF is merely a reception area. A curved ramp in the centre of the building leads down to the lower GF; at the back of the GF are two public lifts (D100 W110 L180) which go to all the floors named above. The lower GF is entirely step free; it houses ten public meeting rooms and a universal prayer room. There is also a cafeteria and an impressive scale model of central London, best viewed from the ramp.

Floors one and two house the Assembly Chamber and the public viewing gallery, where council meetings take place. Next to the lift on floor two, at the back of the viewing gallery, there are spaces for wheelchair users. There are also some spaces at the front, which must be arranged in advance; you will be escorted to the first floor via separate lifts, which are identical, and immediately next to the public lifts, but behind a security barrier.

Floor nine is taken up by London's Living Room, which has spectacular views across London. It is open on alternate weekends, on Saturday morning and Sunday afternoon. From here, there is a dramatic spiral staircase that winds down to the Assembly Chamber. Frustratingly for our surveyor, this is not wheelchair accessible, engendering a sense of exclusion. The lift provides an alternative, less interesting way down.

All the meeting rooms have an induction loop. The only public toilets are on the lower GF, behind the information booth at the bottom of the ramp. There is **one wheelchair toilet (D90 ST100)** here. We were told that improvements to signposting and internal access are due over the next few months.

Design Museum see chapter on *Museums and galleries*.

Dali Universe
County Hall, South Bank SE1 7PB
Tel: 020 7620-2720 *website:* www.daliuniverse.com
An exhibition of paintings and sculpture illustrating the work of Salvador Dali. Admission charge. Situated between Westminster Bridge and Jubilee Gardens, the entrance on the riverside has +6 steps which can be bypassed by an alternative ramped entrance through the London Aquarium. You need to be accompanied by a member of staff for whom you'll have to ask inside. On the GF there is flat access to the exhibition. The shop is −6−1−5 by the exit onto Belvedere Road. There are −27 to another exhibit which can be bypassed by an open lift which is staff operated. **Wheelchair cubicle (D85 ST80)** in Ladies toilet on the GF near the end of the Dali exhibit. Some of the displays are dimly lit and the captions can be difficult to read.

Hay's Galleria
Tooley Street SE1
Situated just opposite the London Dungeon, this is an attractive development on the riverside on the site of an old tea wharf. The centrepiece is an arched courtyard with a remarkable working sculpture of a fantasy ship in the middle. There are good views of HMS *Belfast* and Tower Bridge from the river frontage, and a few pubs and restaurants. Most of the shops have flat access and there are some stalls. What is disappointing, is that the new *Horniman* pub and *Wall Street* restaurant have split levels. The planning permission regulations don't seem to work somewhere along the line.

On the approach to the Galleria there are some cobbled roads (presumably left to retain some of the original character of the place). There is an overhead walkway from London Bridge station with a lift D75 at the end to bypass the escalator and steps. The lift is called via an intercom system. Around the Galleria there are ramped bypasses to all the steps, though they're not always obvious. There's one eating place (*Café Rouge*) with flat access, and the upper, rather cramped parts of the *Horniman* pub, are step free. There are −5 steps to the bar, or −2 through a side entrance.

The situation over toilets would be laughable if it wasn't so infuriating. There are **three wheelchair toilets** on site, one inside, off the reception area of Counting House (near Tooley Street), one off the reception of Shackleton House (to the right of the four curved steps in the centre) and one ostensibly public one, with a green door, to the left of the four curved steps and close to the *Café Rouge*. The problem is that you'd never know they're there and the public **wheelchair toilet (D75+ ST75+)** is kept locked, with the key at Shackleton House. It is not signed or indicated – and it's 'not used' (quote from staff on site). **To use a toilet, ask one of the security staff or go to Shackleton House**.

HMS Belfast
Morgan's Lane, Tooley Street SE1 2JH
Tel: 020 7940-6300 *Fax:* 020 7403-0719
website: www.iwm.org.uk/belfast
This cruiser saw service during the Second World War, and supported the Normandy landings. She was active until 1965 and served in Korea. Now permanently moored on the riverside just upstream of Tower Bridge and run by the Imperial War Museum. Admission charge. CP on the corner of Tooley Street by Tower Bridge. The shop and ticket sales point are somewhat congested, and accessed via a threshold and D75. Entrance flat, with an open lift down to the level of the quarterdeck bypassing −4 steps. Note that the lift can only be reached along the right side of the gangway, which is normally the exit route. There is a steepish ramp to the boatdeck on an upper level.

They have gone to considerable lengths to make parts of the ship accessible, but it's difficult, as there are narrow gaps and doors to gun turrets, and high thresholds/bulkheads (which were designed to keep water out during rough weather). The decks are quite rough with various ridges and protrusions. Chair users will find that help is vital especially to get inside, as some of the ramps put over the bulkheads are very steep. You can get close to some of the smaller guns on the boatdeck. Towards the bow, where the anchors are laid out, there is a barrier 25cm high to get over.

Going up inside to see the bridge and wireless room, and down to the engine room and living quarters, involves steep ladders and well over 100 steps, and is only possible for the relatively agile. In spite of this, there's enough to see in the accessible parts of the ship, including all of the quarterdeck, to make it an interesting visit. There's a **wheelchair toilet (D90 ST100+)** on the quarterdeck level with portable ramps to help you negotiate the bulkhead threshold (which is 35cm high) to get to the loo. You need to ask, and the ramps involved are pretty steep.

George Inn
77 Borough High Street SE1 1NH
Tel: 020 7407-2056
A National Trust property which is the only traditional galleried coaching inn left in London. Cobbled approach with pub tables outside. Entrance to the Southwark Bar via −1 step, and there's an awkward turn because of a staircase just 120cm in front. Most chair users could probably manage with just a little help. The bar to the left is flat, but has a small step further in. It is very atmospheric.

London Aquarium
County Hall, Riverside Building, Westminster Bridge Road SE1 7PB
Tel: 020 7967-8000 (recorded info, and you eventually get through to a person!) *Fax:* 020 7967-8029 *website:* www.londonaquarium.co.uk
In the basement of the former Greater London Council headquarters, huge tanks have been installed containing fish and sea creatures, from all areas of the world. Admission charge. The entrance is from the riverside close to the London Eye. From Westminster Bridge Road there are 40+ steps, but there is step-free access from Belvedere Road and Chicheley Street through the Jubilee Gardens. The route is clearly marked but is some 600m from the steps by the bridge. Step-free entrance and accessible throughout, without steps, using the lifts. There are −16 steps to the first tanks on Level 1, bypassed by a lift (D130 W155 L190). On this level you can see the large Indian Ocean, Pacific Ocean and Atlantic Ocean tanks, along with freshwater fish and the Exhibition Room and Classroom. The same lift bypasses −19 steps to Level 2 which has further windows on the large tanks, where you can see invertebrates and fish from temperate and tropical waters and coral reefs. It is all step free. The rays are accessed via a slight ramp and you are invited to touch them! Owing to the height of the tank, this might be tricky for some chair users, but seeing them is not a problem. All displays are easily seen by a chair user, but the corridors are a bit dark. Exit is by escalators or a lift (D120 W120 L200) to the shop, half of which is −7−13, not bypassed. There are **wheelchair toilets** on Level 1 between the rivers/ponds section and the Pacific tank **(D90 ST110)** and also on Level 2 near the exit **(D90 ST80)**.

London Dungeon
28 Tooley Street SE1 2SZ
Tel: 020 7403-7221 *website:* www.thedungeon.com
A series of dark vaults under the London Bridge railway arches with gruesome waxworks representing some of the grimmer aspects of British history. Admission charge. Flat/ramped entrance for chair users to the left of the ticket office. Flat but slightly rough access throughout. There are some steps, but helpful staff will show you flat routes to bypass these. It's also dark inside, with eerie sound effects. If you visit at a busy time, there are unavoidable bottlenecks on the route which make things quite slow. **Wheelchair toilet (D80 ST85)** immediately on the left inside the door marked 'Ladies' just past the ticket office. Not signed outside.

London Eye
Jubilee Gardens SE1
Tel: credit card bookings 0870 5000-600 *DisEnq/bookings:* 0870 990-8885 *website:* www.ba-londoneye.com
The British Airways London Eye is a huge ferris wheel near West-minster Bridge. Erected to mark the Millennium, it is some 135m high and dominates the London skyline. Admission charge. It closes for a month in the New Year for essential maintenance. The ticket office is in the corner of County Hall, and there is a badly signed ramp to bypass the +6 steps at the front. You have to go south towards Chicheley Street alongside the County Hall building. At busy times, most people pre-book a timed slot for their 'flight'. This can be done either by phone or on-line. From the riverside walk, the approach to the Eye is up a ramp about 40m long. For chair users the staff will stop the wheel and slot in a little cover plate to make getting in easier. Each capsule takes up to thirty people. There's a central seat, but most people stand up and move around during the flight to see the views on different sides. There's adequate room for a chair user.

There are **two wheelchair toilets (D80 ST90)** inside the ticket office, to the left as you come in from the ramped entrance, opposite *Costa Coffee*.

Oxo Tower
Barge House Street SE1
Tel: 020 7803-3888
The tower was built in 1928 to advertise a meat extract. It now houses some shops (at riverside level) and bars and restaurants on higher floors. The Riverside Walk entrance is flat and there are three

large lifts at the back. On the second floor is a restaurant and upmarket brasserie both with **wheelchair toilets (D70+ ST70+)**. On the eighth floor is the Oxo Tower bar, brasserie and restaurant which is step free and has good views over the river. The viewing area is in fact 'public', even though it looks as though it's part of the bar, so you don't have to buy an expensive drink! **Wheelchair cubicles (D70 ST70+)** in both the Ladies and Gents on the eighth floor. Another **wheelchair toilet** on the GF was locked at the time of our visit.

Old St Thomas's Operating Theatre
9A St Thomas Street SE1 9RY
Tel: 020 7955-4791
West of Guy's Hospital and about 60m from Borough High Street. The museum is in the loft of a church, used in the 19thC as an operating theatre. Admission charge. The standard route is difficult even for the fit and able. It involves $+1+2$ and then $+34$ up a spiral staircase with a door 55cm wide en route and only a rope handrail. This leads to the ticket desk. Then there is $+17$, through D73, then -2. Access to the operating table is $+1+2-2$, *or* $+1+10-6$ via the balcony. There is an easier route, using a lift in the adjacent post office, although there are still some steps involved. As it involves post office staff, it is normally only available for pre-arranged groups.

Shakespeare's Globe Museum see chapter on *Museums and galleries*.

Southwark Cathedral see chapter on *Places of worship*.

Vinopolis
1 Bank End SE1 9BU
Tel: 0870 4444-777 *website:* www.vinopolis.co.uk
Situated at the junction with Clink Street, right by the Anchor pub and under the railway arches coming from Cannon Street Station. Vinopolis offers wine tastings and an audio tour of an exhibition covering 'the world of wine'. It is step free throughout, though a few of the surfaces are slightly rough. A full tour will take you some 400m, and might last a couple of hours if you linger over your wine tasting. **Adapted toilet (D75 ST65)** near the main entrance/exit, and to the left of the ticket desk. On the way round you will go past the Wine Wharf Restaurant where an open lift (W80 L110) bypasses $+3$ steps, and there's a **wheelchair toilet (D70 ST70)**.

Docklands

An extensive area to the east of London where there has been
massive redevelopment, mainly of business and commercial premises. It is served by the **only** fully step-free-access transport system
in London, the DLR. This runs mostly at a high level from the Bank
or Tower Gateway to Lewisham, Beckton and/or Stratford. It goes
to Greenwich, and near the new Museum in Docklands, and a trip is
recommended in itself, as it provides good views of the redeveloped
area. The main part of Docklands is north of the river. Some of the
area starts at London Bridge and is described under Southwark. St
Katharine's Dock is described in the City section. A booklet called
Visiting Docklands and Greenwich published by the DLR, Serco
Docklands Ltd, Castor Lane, Poplar E14 0DS, provides a well-
written and interesting account of what you can see in the area, and
its history.

The dominating landmark is the Canary Wharf office development which includes the tallest building in Britain. There's the
London Arena, a major museum, an interesting little farm and
the City Airport, and an increasing number of budget-priced hotels
with adapted rooms.

DLR see chapter on *Transport*.

London Arena see section on *Music venues*.

Mudchute Farm
Pier Street, Isle of Dogs E14 3HP
Tel: 020 7515-5901 *website:* www.tower-bridge.org.uk/mud1
The mudchute was formed from silt out of the Millwall Docks
together with waste clinker from local industries. The area is now
wonderfully quiet, and there's a delightful (and totally unexpected)
urban farm with sheep, cattle, pigs, goats, chickens, rabbits and
riding stables. There's even a llama. Local groups organise riding for
disabled people. On-site CP with flat access to the main building and
yard. Rough slightly hilly paths around parts of the farm. To see it all
you need to go some 300/400m. **Wheelchair toilet (D75 ST100)** in the
main building. Step-free access to the café.

Museum in Docklands
No. 1 Warehouse, Hertsmere Road, Docklands E14 4AL
Tel: 020 7001-9800 *website:* www.museumindocklands.org.uk

Housed in an old warehouse, the museum celebrates the impact of the port activity on the social and economic life of the area from Roman times to the present day. Part of the exhibition covers wartime experiences in docklands. Displays illustrate working methods and equipment in different eras, with interactive exhibits and a children's area. It all makes for a fascinating experience.

The entrance is about 300m from the West India Quay DLR station. It is on the quayside, past the *Ledger Buildings* pub if you approach from the other way. It is intended to provide several BB spaces on the dockside, bookable in advance, but negotiations about these are in progress, so ring to ask. There is an MSCP a little over 500m away, on Hertsmere Road, just past the UGC cinema.

Step-free entrance, with an information desk, café, a children's interactive exhibition area and a hall for special exhibitions on the GF. The exhibition is organised to take you through a series of exhibits in sequence, starting at the top of the building. Everything can be reached via lifts or ramps. The two lifts (D85 W120 L240) take you to the third floor at the top of the building. The route around the exhibition is around 100m long on each floor, with exhibitions on the third, second and first floors. Getting from the third to the second and from the second to the first involves the use of one of two open lifts (D90 L120). To leave the exhibition by a step-free route, you have to take the open lift back to the second floor and find the two main lifts in order to get back to the GF. There is an induction loop and wheelchair spaces in the lecture theatre which is on the top/third floor.

There are **two wheelchair toilets (D70 + ST70 +)** on the GF, one on the top/third floor, and one in the archives area on the first floor.

Holborn and the Strand areas

This comprises four areas in the *Eyewitness* guide, with important sites and sights like the British Library, British Museum, the Royal Opera House, the Strand and Soho. It includes Bloomsbury, Covent Garden and Trafalgar Square and extends as far north as the Euston Road.

British Library see chapter on *Museums and galleries*.

British Museum see chapter on *Museums and galleries*.

Chinatown is centred around Gerrard Street just north of Leicester Square. It has brightly coloured Chinese gates at each end, and is pedestrianised with smooth surfaces throughout. Most restaurants have at least one step at the entrance, but a few are step free or have only a tiny lip. A really good place to go for the Chinese New Year celebrations.

Covent Garden is the area behind the Royal Opera House and just north of the Strand. It is a development on the site of the old Covent Garden fruit and vegetable market. It's a pleasant place on a sunny day and is often crowded, especially in the evening. There are plenty of small shops and stalls and there is frequently open-air entertainment from buskers, small music groups and Punch and Judy shows. Note that parts of the Opera House are open during the day.

There are NCPs at the southern end of Monmouth Street, and in Parker Street on the corner of Drury Lane. Access by Underground from the Piccadilly Line involves less hassle than most stations. Getting off the train there are +19 steps, a lift and then −1.

Little thought has been given to the needs of disabled visitors except in the provision of toilets. Surfaces are rough and consist of cobbles or rough paving. The shops are mostly small, and up 1 or 2 steps. However, there are a good number of market stalls and much of the area is under cover, so it's a good place to go if the weather is uncertain. There's an open-air crafts market (that is, open at the ends but roofed over) on the south side.

Wheelchair cubicles (D85 ST85 NKS) in both Ladies and Gents toilets on Tavistock Court, on the south side between the Jubilee Hall Sports Centre and the LT Museum.

The **Punch and Judy** is the main pub and must rate as the most inaccessible in London, with bars involving either +30 or −30 steps (mind you, this didn't deter one of our more intrepid survey teams!).

Henry's on Henrietta Street is listed in the *Pubs and bars* chapter.

St Paul's Church, Henrietta Street WC2 (*Tel:* 020 7836-5221) is London's chief church for the theatrical profession. It backs on to Covent Garden, with the entrance on the other side. Outside there is a quiet garden with several seats, some shaded, which provides a nice spot for a rest or a picnic. Step-free access from either Henrietta Street or Bedford Street (via Inigo Place). Access to the church is via +4 steps, bypassed by a very steep ramp. Inside it is flat.

The **Royal Opera House** is described on page 291
From 10.00 to 15.00 you can access the Floral Hall and the Amphitheatre bars unless there's a matinee performance. From the box office area, the Floral Hall is reached using the first set of lifts. The Amphitheatre bar and the outside terrace are accessed step free using the second set of lifts at the far end of the foyer. There's a deli for snacks as well as a restaurant. **Wheelchair toilet** off the Amphitheatre bar. From the Covent Garden piazza entrance, the distance to the terrace is about 300m.

London Transport Museum see chapter on *Museums and galleries*.

Theatre Museum see chapter on *Museums and galleries*.

Dickens' House
48 Doughty Street WC1N 2LX
Tel: 020 7405-2127
Doughty Street is parallel to Gray's Inn Road. Entrance +1 step, then two rooms of memorabilia with flat access and −1 to shop. The rest of the house has steps: −14 to the basement and wine cellar, +19 to the first floor and a further +20 to the second floor. From the GF there are two small lips into the garden.

Fitzroy Tavern
16 Charlotte Street W1P 1HJ
Tel: 020 7580-3714
On the junction with Windmill Street. A traditional pub which was a meeting place for artists and writers between the wars, who gave the area the name *Fitzrovia*. Two entrances have flat access.

Leicester Square is now pedestrianised, with a small park and seats in the middle. There are some cobbles around the statue in the centre making it quite rough. Buskers and portrait sketchers can often be found in the northwest corner. It is surrounded by several major cinemas, and the new Warner West End a short distance away has flat/lift access throughout. There's a **wheelchair toilet** in the *Moon Under Water* pub (entrance +2 steps, but a portable ramp is available). There's also one in *McDonald's* **(step free D80 ST120)** at the junction of Swiss Corner and Panton Street.

Photographers' Gallery see chapter on *Museums and galleries*.

Piccadilly Circus is small but crowded, with its famous lights and the statue of Eros. It has been partly pedestrianised. Leicester Square is nearby, and en route is the Trocadero entertainment and shopping centre. There are **wheelchair toilets** in the Trocadero, and in *Burger King* **(D70+ ST70+)** on the north side by the junction with Glasshouse Street. There is also a Tardis public toilet **(NKS 24 hrs)** on the corner of Shaftesbury Avenue opposite Great Windmill Street.

Pollock Toy Museum see chapter on *Museums and galleries.*

Royal Courts of Justice
Strand WC2A 2LL
Tel: 020 7947-6000 *Textphone:* 020 7947-7593
For information, both for disabled visitors and those who have business with the courts, phone the accommodation office on 020 7947-6506. Helpful and knowledgeable staff will give information about both parking and access.

   The courts are situated at the junction between the Strand and Aldwych, just outside the City. The buildings have a magnificent Gothic façade. The large complex of courts is spread over five buildings (see diagram). These are the Main, West Green, Queen's, East Block and Thomas More buildings. Courts 1 to 28 are in the

Royal Courts of Justice

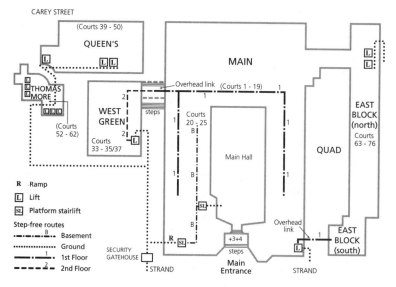

Main Building, 31 to 37 in the West Green, 39 to 50 in the Queen's Building, 51 to 62 and 77 to 79 in the Thomas More Building, and 63 to 76 as well as rooms E100 and E101 in the East Block. A map is available which shows the easiest routes for disabled people to get to various parts of the complex, and the authorities have gone to considerable lengths to make the site more accessible.

The principal entrance to the Main Building from the Strand has +3+4 steps. This leads straight through to the Great Hall which is the main place of interest to the casual visitor. Security personnel can be alerted by pressing the intercom button, located to the left of the main gates. An alternative route provides step-free access to the Thomas More, Queen's, West Green and Main buildings. It starts 50m west of the main entrance where there is a security checkpoint. We are using this in the write-up as a point of reference.

For people who wish to see the **Main Hall**, the accessible route is as follows: taking the security checkpoint as your start, enter the Main Building via a steepish ramp, which bypasses −6 steps. There are two further platform stairlifts (bypassing −5 and +16 respectively) giving access to the Main Hall, which is large and impressive.

For people coming on court business or those listening to a case, the following description outlines access to all the courts. We describe the situation according to our most recent visit but there will be ongoing changes, and the accommodation office will be able to advise.

From the security checkpoint, courts 52 to 62 and 77 to 79 in the **Thomas More Building** can be reached via the route shown on the diagram. There is a ramp bypassing the steps at the entrance and from here two sets of lifts (D90 W135+ L110+) give access to all floors. Court 51 can only be reached up a flight of steps from the GF. **Two wheelchair toilets (D85 ST70)** with a choice of low or high pedestals are located by the second set of lifts around the corner from the entrance.

The Queen's Building, which houses courts 39 to 50, can be approached step free from the Thomas More Building. Three lifts inside give step-free access to all the courts. Two are by the main entrance (D100 W200 L110) and one by the side entrance (D85 W120 L150).

Access to the **West Green Building** from the security checkpoint is shown on the diagram. Going up the ramp into the Main Building gives access to courts 37 (GF) and 33 to 35 via the lift (D75 W125 L100) to the left of the entrance. The West Green Building also houses the interim and preliminary application sections.

The second floor of the West Green Building links to the first floor of the **Main Building**. This is important as it is **the only step-free link** to the courts in the Main Building. Courts 1 to 19 are on the first floor of the Main Building. There are **wheelchair toilets (D70+ ST70+)** on the right side of the corridor towards the end.

Courts 63 to 76 in the **East Block (north)** are reached from the other side of the side on Bell Yard. A lift (D90 W155 L140) gives access to the courts. There are two **wheelchair toilets (D70+ ST70+)** on the third floor. **East Block (south)** is reached from a separate entrance off the Strand into the Main Building, shown on the diagram. Just inside is a lift (D85 W125 L110) which takes you to the first floor, from which there is a step-free route into the other building.

Two wheelchair toilets (D70+ ST70+) are at the southern end of the East Block; access depends on the use of platform stairlifts, which were not operational when we visited.

Sir John Soane's Museum see chapter on *Museums and galleries*.

Somerset House
Strand WC2R 1LA
Tel: 020 7845-4600 *website:* www.somerset-house.org.uk
e-mail: info@somerset-house.org.uk
Somerset House is one of the most important buildings of the 18thC. This grand building alongside Waterloo Bridge now houses three interesting collections and has a lovely terrace overlooking the river. The central courtyard has a magnificent fountain in the centre which becomes an attractive multicoloured display at night. In the winter it's an ice rink. There is one BB parking space which can be booked in advance. There is a good diagram of the layout in the *Your Site Plan and Brief History* leaflet. The site is huge and measures about 130m by 160m. There are several accessible refreshment facilities including the upmarket **Admiralty Bar and Restaurant** at courtyard level. What is open depends partly on the time of year.

There are three entrances from different levels:
• From the **Strand**, you come immediately to the Courtauld Galleries in and over the archway. Going about 100m directly across the courtyard, which is cobbled in places, there are two ramped entrances to the main exhibitions building, one to the left, and one to the right. The ramped entrance into the Hermitage Rooms is towards the left-hand corner under the sign saying Stamp Office. Inside, a lift (D80 W100 L130) takes you down to the Gilbert Collection at the Embankment level. The ramp to the right takes you to the Admiralty Bar.

- From **Waterloo Bridge** there's a ramp down on to the Riverside Terrace. To get into the building from here you have to go about 400m (turning left under the second arch, and then left and left again) to bypass the +8 steps up to the Seamen's Hall in the centre of the building.
- The third entrance is off the **Embankment**, under the big arch, about 80m from Waterloo Bridge. There are −2 steps, bypassed by a ramp to the left. To get into the building (at the level of the Gilbert Collection) there are +2, bypassed by an open lift (D90 L130). Just what that mini-lift is doing there is difficult to imagine as a ramp would have been simpler, cheaper and better.

The **Courtauld Gallery** (*Tel:* 020 7848-2526 *Fax:* 020 7848-2589 *e-mail:* galleryinfo@courtauld.ac.uk.) is housed in the rooms over the main entrance archway off the Strand. The paintings include some by famous Impressionist and Post-Impressionist artists. Access from the Strand is via +2 steps on the right side of the arch, or along the cobbled roadway, moving the temporary ropes. There is a rather poor ramped kerb onto the pavement. At the main entrance (on your right) there are +2 to the ticket office, then +5 to the lift. There's an alternative entrance for chair users further on giving step-free access to the lift (D150 W250 L150) which goes to all three floors. However, there is no bell outside with which to make contact with the staff, and once you have, there's a steep ramp en route on which most chair users would require assistance. The lift has quite an awkward ridge by the door when getting out, and the chairs available to be borrowed have small wheels. We saw an inexperienced user having quite a lot of trouble getting over it, as the front wheels got stuck and the occupant's ankles were jabbed by the footplates. Using the lift bypasses +59+34 spiralled steps to the upper galleries, or −24+2 to the basement. On the top floor, room 12 has +1, but a temporary ramp is available. The café and the **wheelchair toilet (D80 ST80+**, but with a high pedestal) are in the basement. The shop is on the other side of the arch with +2 at the entrance, but again, a portable ramp is available.

Going across the courtyard past the fountains, the **Hermitage Rooms** are step free from the ticket office in the Stamp Office at courtyard level. The ramps lead into this building from both corners of the courtyard. The ticket office is on the left side. They bypass +4 into the building. Inside the Hermitage Rooms exhibition there's an **adapted toilet (D80 ST60)**. Wheelchairs with large wheels can be borrowed.

A lift (D80 W100 L130) links the courtyard level **G** with the Embankment level **L2**, and the alternative entrance/exit. There is a shop (just outside) and a café. There is also a **wheelchair toilet (D80 ST80)**, and although the door opens in, the cubicle is deep enough for most chair users. Admission to the **Gilbert Collection** is from this level (**L2**). It is step free throughout, using a second lift (D80 W100 L130). Using the Gilbert Collection lift, you can go down to **L1** which is the King's Barge House under the shop,

The **Riverside Terrace** at courtyard level has seats overlooking the river and a ramp at one end of the wooden plinth with café tables and chairs. The easiest access to this is via the ramp from Waterloo Bridge. Near the ramps and under the first arch, there's a **wheelchair toilet (D80 ST80)**. The outer door is split, and if one half is bolted (as it was when we visited) it'd be a slight job to open. With only one door open the gap is D60.

Trafalgar Square is the home of Nelson's Column with its famous lions, and of a thousand pigeons. It was conceived by Nash, and mainly built in the 1830s. It is one of London's best-known landmarks, and around it are some major sights. The square is gently sloping and quite small. The only step-free access is via various road crossings, and there are ramped kerbs at some of them. The north side outside the National Gallery is becoming a pedestrianised area, and a new more central entrance to the Gallery is being built. There are **wheelchair toilets** in the nearby galleries, and in Charing Cross Station (NKS).

Around the square are:

- the **National Gallery** and the **National Portrait Gallery**, see chapter on *Museums and galleries;*
- **St Martin-in-the-Fields Church**, see chapter on *Places of worship*.

Trocadero
Coventry Street W1D 7DH
Tel: 020 7439-1791 *Fax:* 020 7734-3983 *e-mail:* trocad@globalnet.-co.uk *website:* www.troc.co.uk
A cavernous shopping and entertainment complex undergoing seemingly constant refurbishment, encompassing buildings between Piccadilly Circus and Rupert Street. The main entrance gives flat access from Coventry Street to some step-free shops. An open lift (D75 W100 L130) to the right of the main escalators bypasses +9 steps to the upper GF where there are more shops and access to the

staff lift (D80 W100 L140), operated by security guards. This goes to all other floors, including the basement. Various mezzanines can be reached by three user-operated open lifts. Rock Circus, which once filled a large area on the Piccadilly Circus side, has closed. Funland, a vast games complex (on levels 2 to 6) will soon move. Further developments are awaited, and there is considerable uncertainty.

Wheelchair toilet (D95 ST100) in the basement. The most accessible entrance to the UGC cinema (see chapter on *Entertainment*) is from Great Windmill Street.

Westminster and St James's

This is covered in two sections of the *Eyewitness* guide. The area includes some of London's most important sights, in particular the Houses of Parliament, Westminster Abbey and Buckingham Palace. Behind the Whitehall government offices there is St James's Park, an attractive area with a lake, fountains and a bandstand.

Buckingham Palace
The Mall SW1A 1AA
Tel: 020 7839-1377 for the Royal Collection Enterprises office which covers several royal sites.
For tickets contact **Ticket Sales and Information Office**, Buckingham Palace SW1A 1AA. *Tel:* 020 7321-2233 or on-line at *website:* www.royal.gov.uk

The palace is the Queen's London home and lived in by members of the royal family, and their staff. When the Queen is in residence, the Royal Standard is flown. The State Rooms in the palace are currently open to the public for about two months each summer. It is an interesting visit, and there are some impressive works of art on display.

Chair users are only admitted by prior arrangement. Contact and make bookings through the information office. While some 4500 people visit every day, only about 25 chair users are allowed, because of perceived problems of evacuation. These places seem to be heavily oversubscribed, and we know of people who have tried several times, and failed to get a 'slot'.

There are two routes for the tour:

- **a main route** which involves around 120 steps, and a distance of more than 1km, as it takes you out through the gardens and up to Grosvenor Place. Note that seating en route is quite limited, although there's a video presentation halfway around the State

Rooms visit, and there are benches in the garden outside;
* **an access-friendly route**, which is step free. You may have the opportunity of parking in the Quadrangle, inside the gates. Taxis are allowed inside to drop people off, but bear in mind that ALL vehicles are thoroughly security-checked. Note that both disabled walkers and wheelchair users can use the access route. The access route involves a distance of about 500m.

Tickets are picked up or purchased from an office in Green Park (if they haven't been posted to you before), and the public entrance is then about 300m away in Buckingham Palace Road, through the Ambassadors' Entrance (near the Queen's Gallery). Note that a strict 'timed ticket' system is used.

If you are using the access-friendly route, there is a ramp into the building from the Quadrangle, and then a platform stairlift (W79 L89) which can carry loads up to 225kg. This bypasses +13 steps, and can carry standard-size electric chairs.

Access is step free throughout, and the distance involved is less than 500m. There is a lift (D80 W105 L175) to the main rooms on the first floor (bypassing about ±50). **Wheelchair toilet (D115 ST115)** in Lady Barrington's Corridor, off the Marble Hall at the lower level. Because of your starting point, you follow a slightly different route to everyone else, as you have to go to and from the lift. They have organised a special shop for buying souvenirs, as the main one is out in the garden −3−10.

On special occasions and for distinguished foreign visitors, there are processions going to the palace, often starting at Victoria Station. **The Changing of the Guard** both at Buckingham Palace and at Horse Guards Parade, Whitehall, is a regular attraction for visitors. Mounted Life Guards pass the palace regularly at 10.50 and return at about 11.35, *except on Sunday when they're an hour earlier*. The Changing of the Guard takes place between 11.10 and 12.30 in the palace forecourt, *every day in summer and alternate days in winter*. **It is possible for disabled people to get permission to watch from inside the railings** since there is often a considerable crowd outside. If you are inside, remember that you're there for well over an hour, with no toilet. To get permission you should write to Comptroller's Office, Lord Chamberlain's Office, Buckingham Palace SW1A 1AA (*Tel:* 020 7930-4830). For other information, eg about the times of the events, contact the Army's administrative offices (*Tel:* 020 7930-4830).

Cabinet War Rooms see chapter on *Museums and galleries*.

Christie's
King Street SW1Y 6QT
Tel: 020 7839-9060
Famous auction house located on the corner with Bury Street. Well
worth a visit to exhibitions and auctions. Be careful not to nod or
sneeze as you might be buying something expensive. Entrance
$+3+1$ steps to reception and collections, then -2 to valuations.
The mezzanine floor where auctions take place is $+14+10$, bypassed
by the service lift (D110 L90 W200). For valuations of objects, the
valuers will come to you.

Houses of Parliament and Westminster Hall
Margaret Street SW1A 0AA
Tel: 020 7219-3000 *Textphone:* 0800 959-598
website: www.parliament.uk
The Palace of Westminster has been the home to the two Houses of
Parliament since the 16thC. The present mock-Gothic building was
built in Victorian times, although Westminster Hall dates back to the
11thC. When either House is sitting, you can get into the public
galleries via step-free routes. For obvious reasons, there is high
security, with airport-style searches, and you may have to leave
your bag in a cloakroom. Tours are possible at the invitation of a
Member of Parliament, or in the summer recess by phoning First
Call on 0870 906 3773, or using www.firstcalltickets.com. Please tell
First Call if step-free (wheelchair) access is needed, when buying your
ticket.

A braille guidebook and an access leaflet are available. Note that
the arrangements with First Call are under review.

**Normal access for members of the public is through St Stephen's
Entrance to the Central Lobby and involves about 30 steps**. There
are alternative entrances shown on the plan (*Tel:* 020 7219-3070
for visiting the Commons or 020 7219-3100 if visiting the House of
Lords). Parking for disabled visitors or dropping off in New
Palace Yard can be arranged if you give sufficient notice, and
there are a number of BB spaces. The police or staff on duty will
escort you everywhere because of security. There are two wheelchair spaces behind the Bar in the House of Lords (so you are
actually sitting in the chamber, rather than in the inaccessible
Strangers' Gallery). The Bar in this instance has nothing to do
with the serving of drinks!

The Palace of Westminster

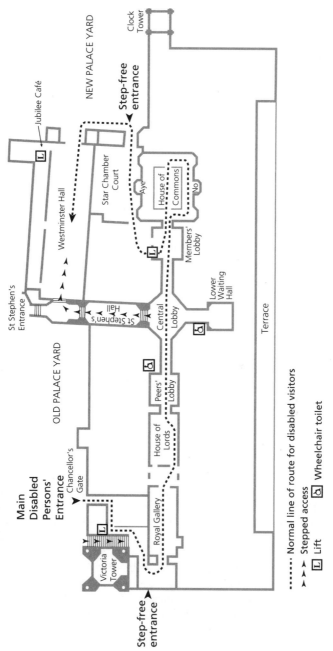

INNER LONDON

Clock Tower

NEW PALACE YARD

Step-free entrance

Jubilee Café

L

Westminster Hall

Star Chamber Court

Aye

House of Commons

No

Members' Lobby

Lower Waiting Hall

L

St Stephen's Entrance

St Stephen's Hall

Central Lobby

OLD PALACE YARD

Peers' Lobby

House of Lords

Terrace

Main Disabled Persons' Entrance

Chancellor's Gate

Royal Gallery

Victoria Tower

L

Step-free entrance

...... Normal line of route for disabled visitors

➤ Stepped access

L Lift

♿ Wheelchair toilet

In the Commons there are **four chair spaces** at the back of Strangers' Gallery. All can be reached step free via lifts and ramps. The view from the Strangers' Gallery is somewhat restricted, and our surveyor could only see about half of the chamber, but you can't see much more from the main seats.

One of our surveyors who uses a wheelchair visited both chambers (on a quiet day, probably) by simply asking at the gate. We were escorted everywhere by friendly staff.

If you go on a tour of the Commons and Lords by invitation, you will find that there is flat access throughout the main floor, and through the Commons lobbies (where they vote). The main route for members of the public visiting the building when the Houses are not sitting is shown on the plan, together with the location of the principal lifts. There are some fifteen lifts in different parts of the building, but only the two of relevance to visitors are shown on the plan. The flat area is shaded. There are **wheelchair toilets (D70 + ST70 +)** off the Peers' Lobby and off the Lower Waiting Hall, both on the main floor level of the lobbies. Towards the end of the tour, able-bodied visitors walk down the 5 steps to St Stephen's Hall and then the −36 into Westminster Hall. Those unable to do this can ask to get down to New Palace Yard via the lift, and from there, Westminster Hall is reached via shallow ramps.

At the end of the tour, off Westminster Hall, is the Jubilee Café. This is a new café for visitors, with a nearby **wheelchair toilet (D70 + ST70 +)**, both accessed by a lift bypassing −4 steps.

To get to the Committee Rooms, there is a lift from the corridor beyond the Lower Waiting Hall to the main committee corridors, upstairs. The Education Unit runs a special visits' programme for schools and would be pleased to discuss arrangements for disabled students (*Tel:* 020 7219 4750).

In a comment a few years ago from an MP, who was temporarily disabled, the Palace of Westminster was described as being extremely 'wheelchair-unfriendly'. He was looking at the building from the point of view of working in it, not just visiting. He described struggling with lifts that were too small and corridor doors which were too heavy to open without help. However, there are ongoing discussions about improving access and the new lift by the café has provided flat access to some meeting rooms, where there is another **wheelchair toilet (D70 + ST70 +)**. The only place without flat access is now the crypt, which is not open to visitors.

Parliament Square and Westminster Bridge

The square features statues of famous statesmen such as Disraeli and Churchill. It was Britain's first official roundabout (an oddity, given that it's square!). From the bridge you can get fine views up and down the Thames. Westminster Pier is a starting point for river trips to the Tower or Greenwich. **Wheelchair toilet (D80 ST80 NKS)**, just outside the QE II Conference Centre. The entrance is slightly cobbled at the junction of Broad Sanctuary and Storey's Gate. There's another **wheelchair toilet** to be built in 2003 by the pier for river trips. To reach the pier from the bridge and bypass the steps, you need to go nearly 100m east along the Embankment, and then come back towards the bridge.

The **Parliamentary Bookshop** is on the corner of Parliament Street and Bridge Street. Step-free access into the small shop which has some interesting publications and reports produced by Parliament and its committees.

Royal Mews

Buckingham Palace Road SW1 1AA
Tel: 020 7321-2233; for groups 020 7799-2331
website: www.royal.gov.uk
The entrance is between Palace Street and Bressenden Place on the other side of the road. The stables and coach houses were designed by Nash in 1825. You can see all the royal coaches used on different occasions. Admission charge, and limited opening times. The mews are basically flat and the route is step free. You'll find a few cobbles. The whole tour is about 400m. **Wheelchair toilet (D80 ST70)** in the corner of the courtyard, just past the state coach display, about 150m from the entrance.

St James's Park and Green Park

Park Office, The Store Yard, Horse Guards Approach, St James's Park SW1A 2BJ
Tel: 020 7930-1793 *website:* www.royalparks.gov.uk
The two parks are attractive, well shaded and centrally located around Buckingham Palace. They are flat or gently sloping and have tarmac paths throughout. Both have good maps at key entry points. There are refreshment facilities in St James's Park towards Horse Guards Parade at the end of the lake. There's also a bandstand with occasional performances. From the nearby bridge over the lake in St James's there's a unique view of the Whitehall offices, and by taking a judiciously framed photograph, you can persuade your

friends that you've been to Istanbul. **Wheelchair cubicles (D85 ST75)** inside both the Ladies and Gents, on the north side of the St James's Park at the junction with Marlborough Road.

St Margaret's Church see chapter on *Places of worship.*

Sotheby's
34-35 New Bond Street W1A 2AA
Tel: 020 7293-5000
Located between Maddox Street and Conduit Street. When we looked up the postcode on multimap.com, it lied, and placed it nearly a mile away! Famous auction house with up to three sales a day. Items are put on show three days before. Flat entrance to reception, then $+8+8$ steps to the first floor and $+7$ to the main gallery. Our survey team was told that all stairs can be bypassed by a service lift. We were told that you should phone at least a day in advance to use it. Hmmm.

Spencer House
27 St James's Place SW1A 1NR
Tel: 020 7514-1964 *RecM:* 020 7499-8620 *website:* www.spencerhouse.co.uk
The 18thC townhouse of the Spencer family, restored and refurbished at great expense by Lord Rothschild. It contains a fine collection of paintings and furniture. Most of the year, it is only open on Sundays, and tickets cannot be pre-booked. Situated just to the east of Green Park, parking is difficult, with three metered spaces but no BB spaces by the house. Temporary ramps can bypass the $+2+1$ steps at the entrance, though there is no bell to alert staff. From here the GF is step free, including the ticket office, shop and **wheelchair toilet (D85)**, though there is an awkward dog-leg out of the Palm Room into the Servants' Corridor.

A somewhat cramped lift (D80 W90 L135) takes you to the first floor, which is flat. The garden is open during the summer, with $+2$ from the GF to the terrace overlooking Green Park, bypassed by a portable ramp.

Wellington Arch
Hyde Park Corner W1J 7JZ
Tel: 020 7222-1234
Admission charge. Situated in the centre of Hyde Park Corner roundabout, it was built to commemorate various victories in the Napoleonic wars. There are step-free road crossings from most sides

of the roundabout. Car drop-off can be arranged, but there is no parking because of security considerations. The entrance on the inside of the arch is flat to the ticket office and lift (D75 W110 L130). This goes to the other three floors, each with small exhibitions and videos. All are step free. From the third floor, which is over the arch itself, there is an open lift (D90 W100 L135) to two outside viewing galleries on opposite sides. These have +2 steps on one side and a ramp on the other. There is a solid stone parapet of height 100cm in each case, but there are some fine views if you can see over the top.

Westminster Abbey see chapter on *Places of worship*.

Westminster Cathedral see chapter on *Places of worship*.

Whitehall runs from Westminster to Trafalgar Square and is a wide street flanked by government offices. There are several important statues of military leaders, including Monty (Field Marshal Lord Montgomery) from WWII and Earl Haig from WW1. Part-way along is the Cenotaph, which is the national memorial to those who have died in war. The annual ceremony of remembrance is held there in early November. Horse Guards Parade, with its daily Changing of the Guard ceremony (see entry on Buckingham Palace), is just beyond the Cenotaph towards Trafalgar Square.

Downing Street SW1 is halfway up Whitehall, and has a well-known resident at No. 10 (and another at No. 11). It is no longer possible to go down it, and you have to view the houses from behind the railings at the end of the road.

Banqueting House, Whitehall SW1A 2ER *Tel:* 020 7930-4179. Opposite Horse Guards Parade. It is the only remaining publicly accessible part of the Palace of Whitehall, as Wolsey's wine cellar is under the Ministry of Defence. Charles I was beheaded just outside in 1649. It contains the Banqueting Hall on the first floor, with magnificent Rubens paintings on the ceiling. There is +1 step at the entrance, then +17+6 inside. A route to bypass the steps through an adjacent office building can be made available given notice. It is available Mon-Fri if requested 24 hours in advance. In the Hall, there are seats around the walls. An area called the Undercroft is −3 from the entrance, but there is a ramped bypass behind the door to the left of the steps. Visitors are shown a video there about the building and its history. **Wheelchair toilet (D80 ST80+)** at the bottom of the ramp, which could be accessed even if you are not visiting the Hall upstairs.

Kensington and Chelsea

This includes three of the areas in the *Eyewitness* guide. Some of the important sights, such as the major museums, Kensington Gardens and Hyde Park, and the famous Harrods department store, are described elsewhere in the guide.

Chelsea Physic Garden
66 Royal Hospital Road SW3 4HS
Tel: 020 7352-5646
Located in the triangle formed by Royal Hospital Road, Chelsea Embankment and Swan Walk. It was established in 1673 by the Society of Apothecaries to study plants used for medicinal purposes. The entrance in Swan Walk has −3 steps, but there's a ramped alternative from Royal Hospital Road. Gravel paths throughout. Size: about 200m by 200m. Shop with step-free access, and **wheelchair toilet (D85 ST80)** near the flat entrance.

Chelsea Royal Hospital
Royal Hospital Road SW3
Tel: 020 7730-0161
A unique retirement home for soldiers; there are always Chelsea Pensioners around in their distinctive uniforms who are happy to chat. It is possible to visit the gardens and some of the Wren buildings, including the Great Hall and the Chapel. Three BB spaces by the Chelsea Gate. From either gate the grounds are flat, and it's about 150m to the main courtyard and hall. There are +10 steps to the chapel, and the same number to the Great Hall. Museum +2 steps. We were told that a **wheelchair toilet** has been installed.

Kensington Palace
Kensington Gardens W8 4PX
Tel: 0870 751-5170 BO: 0870 751-5180 *website:* www.kensington-palace.org.uk
Former residence of Diana, Princess of Wales, part of the spacious palace is used as a private home for members of the Royal family. The other part is open to the public. It is situated near the middle of the Broad Walk, some distance from the nearest roads. By phoning in advance, disabled visitors may get permission to park outside the palace.

Main entrance is step free. An audioguide with a hearing aid (induction loop) facility is included in admission price. The tour takes about two hours, but there is seating at regular intervals. The signposted route involves $-14-6$ steps to the exhibition of Princess Diana's dresses in the basement. Alternative step-free access is possible via sloped ground around the outside of the building, through a side entrance; ask staff. The state apartments are on the first floor $+22$. **Wheelchair cubicle (D75 ST115)** in the Gents and an **adapted cubicle (D75 ST62)** in the Ladies, both on the GF. Both are located in the shop accessed by alternative entrance $+1+1+1$. Café at the Orangery about 50m away, $+6$ with a portable ramp available.

Regent's Park area

Described in one section of the *Eyewitness* guide. The area includes the north end of Baker Street, Marylebone Road, the Regent's Canal, Little Venice and Camden. Pay-and-display parking is possible round the Inner Circle, and on Chester Road. There are a substantial number of BB spaces on the Inner Circle (not marked in the *Blue Badge User Guide with Map of Central London*). There is also pay-and-display parking around long stretches of the Outer Circle.

Note the **wheelchair toilets** in Regent's Park and the one opposite Madame Tussaud's.

Camden is just northwest of Regent's Park, and the canal passes through. There are many shops and stalls stretching about 1.5 km along Camden High Street and Chalk Farm Road. Camden Market, opposite Inverness Street, is open Thursday to Sunday and is flat. Much of it is covered. It can be congested, with narrow gaps between stalls. Camden Lock Market, across the canal, has three courts: east, middle and west. There are two levels, but both have (steep) ramped access from Chalk Farm Road. A lift from Camden Lock Place goes to the upper level. The surfaces are rough in places, and it's often crowded. There is an **adapted toilet (D85 ST60)** on the first floor of West Court, accessed via the road or the lift. The key is available from the nearest shop. *Lloyd's No 1 Gastro Pub* is located across the canal from Camden Lock Market on the towpath (there is a step-free bridge over the canal, although it is cobbled and very steep), which has a **wheelchair toilet (D80 ST85 NKS)**.

On Camden High Street between Greenland Street and Delancey Street, there's a *McDonald's* with a **wheelchair toilet (D80 ST80)** and step-free access, and also a *Burger King* with a **wheelchair toilet (D80 ST70)** labelled 'Ladies'.

Little Venice. The Regent's Canal was opened in 1820, joining the Grand Union Canal and the busy port at Paddington Basin to the River Thames at Limehouse. A hundred years ago it was busy with horse-drawn barges. Now it is a quiet waterway taking people on a scenic route through parts of London not otherwise seen.

Little Venice itself provides a quiet retreat from the general 'rush' in London. Near the junction of Blomfield Road and Warwick Avenue are the Rembrandt Gardens. Opposite 60 Blomfield Road, near the junction with Clifton Villas, is *Jason's Canal Trip* ticket office and restaurant (*Tel*: 020 7286-6752). There is a high kerb outside the entrance, but step-free access inside. There are two **wheelchair toilets (D75 ST70)** in the restaurant. Getting on and off the boat involves going through a gap 60cm wide and ±3 steps. Staff there are used to carrying chairs and their users. They use a narrower plastic chair to carry you in if your chair is too wide to get through the gap, and you can transfer back into your own once you are on board. On the boat the chairs and tables are movable.

There are two nearby pubs, the *Warwick Castle*, on Warwick Place, with +1+1 steps at the entrance, and the *Bridge House*, on Westbourne Terrace Road with +1. Neither had adapted toilets. From Westbourne Terrace Road Bridge there is steep ramped access down to the towpath where the *Waterside Café* has −1−3 and movable tables and chairs. The Canal Bus (*Tel*: 020 7482-2550) departs from here and the one we saw, *Water Buffalo*, had +1−3 to get on board and fixed seating so that a chair user would have to transfer.

London Central Mosque see chapter on *Places of worship*.

Madame Tussaud's and the Planetarium see chapter on *Museums and galleries*.

Primrose Hill rises gently up from Prince Albert Road, and you can get fine views over London on a good day. **Two adapted toilets (D85 ST60 NKS)** in the Children's Playground at the bottom of the hill, about 100m from the park entrance.

Regent's Park
Manager's Office, The Storeyard, Inner Circle, Regent's Park NW1 4NR
Tel: 020 7486-7905 *website:* www.royalparks.gov.uk

A large and attractive area just north of Marylebone. The park was enclosed in 1812, and Nash developed a grand design consisting of a garden suburb including a pleasure palace for the Prince Regent. Only eight villas were ever built. It is fairly flat, and most of the paths are tarmac. There's a largish lake with facilities for boating, and in the northeast corner is London Zoo. The ring road round the outside is nearly 8km long. The **Information office** is on the Inner Circle close to the junction with Chester Road. They publish a programme of summer entertainments, including recitals in Queen Mary's Rose Garden, performances on the bandstand and children's events in the playgrounds. There are BB spaces along Chester Road, and a few around the Inner Circle by Chester Road and Holme Green only.

To the north is **Primrose Hill** and, off the Inner Circle, there's a small **open-air theatre** with step-free access – an attractive spot during warm summer evenings. Queen Mary's Garden has an attractive rose garden. We found four places selling refreshments: a cafeteria on the Broad Walk (near Chester Road); a restaurant on the Inner Circle in Queen Mary's Garden, near the theatre; another cafeteria by the tennis courts towards York Gate; and another restaurant by Hanover Gate. All have step-free access, and both outdoor and indoor seating. There are also several refreshment stands scattered around the park.

There are several wheelchair toilets in Regent's Park:

- just off Chester Road where it is crossed by Broad Walk, **cubicles (D90 ST90)** in both Ladies and Gents;
- by the boating lake, **unisex (D90 ST120)**, near Hanover Gate;
- by York Bridge (near the cafeteria), **cubicle (D75 ST100)** in Ladies. Gents not seen, but probably similar.
- in the restaurant by Queen Mary's Garden **(D80 ST110)**.

There are **adapted cubicles (D90 ST45 NKS)** in both Ladies and Gents, in Queen Mary's Garden near the end of Chester Road, and an **adapted toilet (D75 ST60)** in the Children's Playground just inside Gloucester Gate. *All of them seem to be kept locked with a nearby attendant who has the key.*

London Zoo
Regent's Park NW1 4RY
Tel: 020 7722-3333 *Fax:* 020 7586-5743
website: www.londonzoo.co.uk

The zoo is in the northern part of Regent's Park, and the Regent's Canal passes alongside. The Zoological Gardens, opened in 1828, was the first institution in the world dedicated to the study and display of animals. It has recently been in danger of closure, and has had to rethink its functions and the way it works, particularly in the field of conservation. A considerable amount has been done to improve the facilities for disabled visitors, although some problems remain. Both power and manual chairs are available for hire near the main entrance, which is useful as the zoo is big. You are advised to book in advance, on extension 576. Volunteers may be available on request to help people in chairs get around. Guide dogs are not allowed on site. On busy days, disabled visitors who might find the crowds at the entrance a problem can arrange to enter via the east service gate (*Tel:* 020 7449-6573).

The main entrance is on the Outer Circle. Parking facilities for disabled visitors are poor, considering the size and importance of the zoo. For BB holders there is a single space on the road outside, plus five BB spaces in the CP opposite the main entrance. The main zoo CP is nearly 500m away. There are usually taxis available outside when you leave, so if this is a viable option for you, you could save yourself a long walk/wheel.

The zoo is triangular in shape with sides approximately 500m × 500m × 800m. The main entrance is, oddly enough, somewhere near the middle of the triangle, because the road (the Outer Circle) passes through the triangle, and the various houses and terraces on the far side are reached via one or other of two ramped tunnels. A green line marked on the ground shows a recommended route around. A full visit could well take you between 2 and 3km, and there are some steepish slopes, particularly through the tunnels (each of which has a 30m slope at both ends), and also on the far side of the Outer Circle. A chair user would need to be very fit to get round on a solo basis.

This write-up splits the zoo into three areas, and it would be perfectly feasible to reduce the distances involved and still see a lot which is of interest, by concentrating on the displays within about 400m of the main entrance to the south.

Just to the right of the entrance is the **Information kiosk** with a list of daily events. Large print information is available, as is a map which details the location of wheelchair toilets but includes no other access features. There are plenty of maps around, and some sign-posting, but the maps are somewhat stylised and diagrammatic rather than precise and 'access-friendly'. In addition there is information about events that day and about animal feeding times, which may help you plan an itinerary.

There are quite a number of animal enclosures where hedges or walls may obstruct your view if you use a chair. One important thing to note is that, with modernisation, physical entry to buildings, although desirable, is no longer essential in order to see the animals. Many of the displays can be seen by walking round outside. If the animals or birds happen to be on the ground when you are going past, you'll find some of them difficult to see from a chair user's eyeline. Fortunately, of course, you'll find many of the animals are up in branches or high up in their cages.

Our description starts with the buildings and houses near the entrance; then those further away to the southeast, and finally those accessed by the tunnels under the Outer Circle.

Near the main zoo entrance

The **Reptile House** has ramped access, bypassing + 2 steps.

The **Aquarium** has + 5 at the entrance and − 8 at the exit (neither with handrail). It also has a low level of lighting, but you rapidly get accustomed to this, and after a couple of minutes can see very adequately. For an alternative step-free route, which is 150m from the entrance and uneven in places, ask at the information kiosk (about 30m away).

The **apes and monkeys**, **cranes and birds** are all seen from outside. Further over, past the restaurant, the same is true of the **flamingos, parrots and macaws**, although the flamingos are particularly difficult to see from a chair because of the hedges.

The **café/restaurant** by the fountain has ramped bypasses to the + 2 at its entrance. It does, however, have fixed seating inside, as do many of the on-site catering facilities.

The **shop** by the fountain is step free throughout.

The **amphitheatre** has step-free access to the front rows with wheelchair spaces.

There are **wheelchair cubicles** in the Gents **(D90 ST90)** at the side of the Aquarium, and in the Ladies **(D90 + ST70 +)** to the east of the main entrance by the birds of prey. There is a **wheelchair toilet (D90 ST130)** by the *Fountain Café*. This is in the coffee shop, on the left of the counters.

Further away, on the main site

The view of the big cats (**leopards**, **lions and tigers**) is good, as there are big glass panels coming down to about 40cm off the ground. A ramped route leads through from the **macaws** down to the **penguins**, and there's plenty of cover in this area. There are, however, some steps, and it isn't always easy to identify the step-free access routes. In particular, as you approach the penguin enclosure this way there are -5, and you have to go some way round to the right to bypass them.

The **penguin** enclosure presents problems for a chair user, simply because it has a 130cm high wall around it. The **Children's Zoo** is step free throughout, and well laid out. There are lots of farm animals, with opportunities to touch and even hold them. There is -1 to the Discovery Education Centre. The **Tropical Bird House** has a flat entrance at one end and $+2$ at the other.

The **Web of Life** is an ecological exhibition centre focusing on conservation, with interactive educational facilities. It is step free throughout and there is a **wheelchair toilet (D85 ST75)** next to it.

Wheelchair toilet (D90 ST95) in the Children's Zoo near the Discovery Centre.

Across (or under) the Outer Circle

As already mentioned, the ramps for the tunnel are quite long and steep. This side of the zoo is slightly more hilly than the main part.

Giraffes and zebras may be seen outside but, if they're not, you can enter the house via a ramp and $+1$. On a dry day, you can see the **pigs and oryx** from the canal bridge. On the other side of the canal is the **Snowdon Aviary** with outdoor cages. There is also a route which takes you inside via $+1$. All the other birds can be seen from outside. The **small mammals** can be seen under cover and with step-free access. There are -21 to the **Moonlight World**. To get into the **Invertebrate House**, the normal route is via $+14$, but there is an alternative, up a steep and somewhat bumpy ramp. This is signed and some 60m to the right. The house is step free inside.

Areas with a reasonable amount of cover and interest in the event of rain include the 'big cats' enclosures and the Tropical Bird House, the Aquarium and Reptile House, the Small Mammals House and the Cotton Terraces. Note that the only exit from the zoo which does not involve negotiating narrow revolving gates is back via the main entrance.

Outer London

Barnes, Brentford and Chiswick

Chiswick House
Burlington Lane, Chiswick W4 2RP
Tel: 020 8995-0508
Situated just off the A4 some 500m past the Hogarth roundabout on the left as you are going towards Heathrow. Well signed. However, **disabled visitors should use the main gate**, which is about 30m BEFORE the well-signed entrance for the CP. It's very easy to overshoot the main entrance gates, and a long way round to get back to them, so approach with some care.

From the official CP there's a 600m walk over a roughish path, and including a step. However, if you go through the main gates, you can follow the drive all the way round to the forecourt of the house and BB holders can park there

The house is a Palladian villa built around a central octagonal room with several interesting 18thC portraits. Entrance from forecourt is + 1 step then + 1 bypassed by ramp. The rest of GF is step free but first floor holds the main interest. There are + 16 spiral stairs or grand staircase outside (+ 7 + 6 + 6) if you ask staff to remove 'No Entry' sign. If you ring in advance they can charge up a stairclimber to bypass these. **Wheelchair toilet (D85 ST70)** to right if you are facing entrance in modern annexe opened on request. Alternatively there is a **wheelchair toilet (D80 ST130 NKS)** on left side of step-free café 50m from house. Some paths around house and through gardens are gravelled.

Hogarth's House
Hogarth Lane, Great West Road W4 2QN
Tel: 020 8994-6757
A Georgian house now a gallery housing many of Hogarth's engravings. Parking is possible by the Reckitt & Coleman office building, as well as in the grounds of Chiswick House (see above). The − 3 steps through the gate can be bypassed. The path to the house is over roughish ground. Entrance + 1, and the GF is flat. There are + 13 narrow steps to the first floor. The main attraction is the collection of prints.

Kew Bridge Steam Museum
Green Dragon Lane, Brentford, Middx TW8 0EN
Tel: 020 8568-4757 *website:* www.kbsm.org

Housed in a 19thC water pumping station, it has five Cornish beam engines, some of which are 'in steam' at weekends. It's a fascinating place including an exhibition of the importance of water in our lives. CP outside. Flat entrance, and then there is ramped/lift access to a large part of the museum. They have gone to considerable lengths to make it accessible. From the entrance area there are ramps down into the basement exhibition area. An open lift (D80 W90 L130) bypasses + 16 steps to the main floor around some of the engines. The *Babcock Café* is up a steepish ramp, D72 and then −2 with a portable ramp readily available. While there are + 5 to see the Bull engine, it is possible to go around the outside of the building and then there are only + 2 with a portable ramp. From the main floor there are + 17 spiralled steps to an upper gallery. **Wheelchair toilet (D70 + ST70 +)** in the workshops across the CP some 40m from the entrance. It is to the left of the Diesel House Studios, and down a little corridor, just outside the Ladies toilets on the left.

Public Record Office (PRO)
Ruskin Avenue, Kew, Surrey TW9 4DU
Tel: 020 8876-3444 *DisEnq:* 020 8392-5363
e-mail: enquiry@pro.gov.uk *website:* www.pro.gov.uk
The PRO is the UK's national archive, and preserves the records of central government and of the courts of law. Documents such as the Domesday Book, Guy Fawkes' confession and the last telegram from the *Titanic* are on display in the Visitor Centre. Many special exhibitions and events are held. If you want to inspect any documents, you must bring proof of identity with you to get a reader's ticket, at reception.

Entrance off the South Circular Road at a junction with traffic lights; the road leads towards the Kew Retail Park. There are four BB spaces at the rear of the building from which there is step-free access to the main foyer. A café, shop and reception are on the GF. Lift (D85 W105 L150) on the GF to the first and second floors, where records are kept. **Wheelchair cubicles (D75 ST90)** on the GF and **wheelchair toilets (**not seen **NKS)** on the first and second floors. Wheelchairs are available to get around this large building. Staff are very helpful and a range of reading aids are available.

The Wetland Centre
Queen Elizabeth Walk, Barnes SW13 9WT
Tel: 020 8409-4400 *e-mail:* info@wetlandcentre.org.uk
website: www.wetlandcentre.org.uk

A unique reserve for wild birds created on decommissioned reservoirs. As well as facilities that allow keen birdwatchers to look out for periodic visitors, there are a number of rare and endangered species kept there for breeding. The entrance is about 200m down Queen Elizabeth Walk from the junction with Castelnau by the *Red Lion* pub. The 283 bus, which is accessible, runs to the Centre from Hammersmith Bus Station, where there is step-free access to the Underground stations: other bus routes stop near the *Red Lion*.

The CP is about 100m from the entrance, just beyond the bus stop, with twelve BB spaces. From the CP the route leads over a small wooden hump-backed bridge. We are told it becomes rather slippery in winter, but that remedies for this are being considered.

Step-free entrance to the ticket office. This leads into a courtyard. To the left of the door you have come through is the entrance to the shop, which is step free. To the right of the door from the ticket office is the entrance to the **Discovery Centre**. This includes the 'Secrets of the Wetlands' exhibit and entrance to the GF section of this is step free. The 'Wetlab' section of the exhibition with interactive displays, is $+10+9$ steps, but there's a lift to bypass these. A further door from the courtyard leads to the **Observatory**, a large glass-fronted room with views over the Wetlands. Step-free entrance, with a ramp bypassing -4 to the front of the room. Gallery level $+9+10$. Between the Observatory and the Discovery Centre is the Tower, where a lift (D80 W110 L150) provides step-free access to the 'Wetlab', and via high-level open-air walkways, to the gallery in the Observatory and the binocular shop (which is above the souvenir shop). The second floor of the tower, also accessible by lift, contains a children's area. **Wheelchair toilets (D80 ST80)** are on the GF and first floor, ahead and to the right out of the lifts.

The **theatre** is opposite the main building and has step-free access. It shows a short film about wetlands. Chair users can either sit in front of the front row of seats (which possibly restricts their view of the edge of the screen), or transfer to the front row, which is step free from the entrance.

The **café** can be entered from the GF of the Tower or from outside, towards the Waterlife walk, and has step-free access with movable tables and chairs.

The **Waterlife** walk is reached from beyond the café, and consists of a number of areas with examples of wetland life and flora, as well as a number of hides with views over the main lagoons. It is approximately 500m to the far end of the walk, by the most direct route, but rather longer if you wish to divert off the main path to the hides or exhibits. The main paths are tarmac, but a few outlying paths have loose compacted surfaces. These, however, are generally flat and should not pose problems to most chair users. All the hides and the Wetland Living hut have step-free access and low-level viewing holes at 100 to 115cm from the ground. The Wader Scrape hide has +3, bypassed by a ramp, to the viewing area. The Peacock Tower, at the far end of the route contains a lift (D80 W110 L150) to the viewing levels. **Wheelchair toilet (D90 ST80)** in a block about two-thirds of the way around the route, before the sheltered lagoon and not far from the WWF hide.

The **World Wetlands and Wildside** walk is reached from behind the theatre, and consists of a series of gated areas which try to create different international habitats, in which several endangered species of birds are being bred in captivity. Distances and the state of the paths are similar to the Waterlife walk, and a large (though not particularly heavy) gate separates the Wetlands and the Wildside areas. The Wildside Hide at the far end of the walk has +8+8 steps to the upper viewing level and no lift. There are no low-level viewing windows on that level (although there are on the GF level, which has step-free access). The Headley hide has step-free access and low-level viewing holes.

Signage is reasonably good throughout the centre. The map provided has been criticised for being unclear, but it is apparently to be replaced in the near future. Our (non-twitcher) surveyors enjoyed their visit there, and would recommend the centre to bird-watchers and interested non-birdwatchers alike.

Greenwich

Greenwich is situated a few km to the east of London, and has some spectacular classical buildings, as well as a large park and the (Old) Royal Observatory with its famous meridian. Its history is tied up with the Tudors, with things naval and the study of navigation.

You can get there by river, which can be a pleasant way to come; by using the DLR or by National Rail.

Small covered CP near the *Cutty Sark*, on your left as you approach the riverside by road. The *Gipsy Moth* pub has a **wheelchair toilet**; there's one off the foyer in the Ibis Hotel, and in the public toilets by the junction of Carlton Road and The Avenue. There are also **wheelchair toilets** in the National Maritime Museum. The riverside and the area around the Maritime Museum and Royal

Naval College is all fairly flat. In the park, and towards the Old Observatory and Blackheath, there's a very steep hill.

Tourist Information Centre
2 Cutty Sark Gardens SE10 9LW
Tel: 0870 608-2000
Near the *Cutty Sark* by the pier with step-free entrance. There's an **adapted toilet** in the nearby Visitor Centre for the Naval College.

Cutty Sark
King William Walk SE10 (by Greenwich Pier)
Tel: 020 8853-3589 *website:* www.cuttysark.org.uk
A famous tea clipper that sailed both the Atlantic and the Pacific in the 19thC. The middle deck has flat access via a cobbled area. The shop is on this level. There are −16 steps to the lower deck. The cabins have D55 and a threshold 23cm high. There are +5 to the bows. The upper deck is +12 (steep) with a 46cm threshold at the top.

Gipsy Moth IV
King William Walk SE10
This is the boat in which Sir Francis Chichester sailed around the world in 226 days in the 1960s. It is a tiny vessel, and a visit involves steep steps (+9−4) to the cockpit which has W66. Inside there are more steep steps and some narrow gaps.

A **riverside walk** goes from the two ships past the pier and the Royal Naval College to the *Trafalgar Tavern*. This is about 400m long. The walk is flat or ramped throughout, but there are some cobbles. The *Cutty Sark* (pub), *Yacht Tavern* (in Crane Street) and the *Trafalgar Tavern* all have seating areas on the GF. The *Cutty Sark* and the *Yacht* have **adapted toilets**.

Greenwich Park
Park Office, Blackheath Gate SE10 8QY
Tel: 020 8858-2608 *website:* www.royalparks.gov.uk
A large expanse of over 200 acres stretching up the hill from Greenwich and linking with Blackheath. The park was originally the grounds of the royal palace, while Blackheath was common land and was often a meeting point for groups entering London from the east. These included Wat Tyler's group of rebels at the time of the Peasants' Revolt. The park includes the Royal Observatory at the top of the hill, and Ranger's House in the southeast corner. The

shortest route to the top from the river involves a very steep path with 10 single steps. There is a gentler, step-free route from the gate at the end of King William Walk, following the road up to the car park at the top. In total this is 750m long, but from March to October an adapted shuttle bus runs this route half-hourly.

In parts of the park the squirrels are so tame that they will eat out of your hand, but be careful, some may bite! There is a bandstand, with occasional performances, and a superb view of London from the end of Blackheath Avenue near the Observatory. There's alternative car access from Blackheath to the viewpoint, where you can park. There is a small café by the car park, which includes an **adapted toilet (D80 ST120** with inward opening door).

National Maritime Museum and Queen's House
Romney Road, Greenwich SE10 9NF
Tel: 020 8858-4422 (access information line: 020 8312-6608) *website:* www.nmm.ac.uk *e-mail:* bookings@nmm.ac.uk

An extensive museum whose exhibits illustrate the key role that seafaring has played in British history. Built in the 19thC as a school for sailors' children, it was completely renovated in 1998 when some of the outside walkways were enclosed under a large glass canopy. There is limited parking for BB holders on the east side of the site, approached from the end of Park Row (off the A206 Romney Road). Spaces are bookable 24 hours in advance. It's some 200m from the CP to the main entrance, where you can drop off a passenger if that's necessary. The immediate area around the museum is flat, but there's a steep hill in Greenwich Park up to the Observatory.

The main entrance is flat, and a diagrammatic *Floor Plan* is available at the information desk just inside. There is an alternative ramped entrance on the other side of the building which takes you into level two of the exhibition, via a café area. The whole building is about 100m deep and a little over 150m wide in places, and the exhibitions are on several floors. The newest part is a large covered atrium, designed in a similar way to the one in the British Museum. A two-level central area is linked by walkways to older wings which contain most of the exhibits and form a horseshoe around the atrium.

Three levels are set out in this way though levels two and three are themselves split into lower and upper levels. Nearly all the exhibits can be reached step free, but this includes the use of a number of lifts which connect various split levels in the older buildings. The horseshoe is split into streets, beginning in East Street. There are three lifts, one at the southeast junction (D80 L125 W180), one to all levels at the southwest junction (D115 L245 W145), one just west of this (D125 L270 W135). **Be warned! The lifts get 'confused' according to staff, if you press too many buttons**. One of our survey team was trapped for a while in one of them! You can reach the café and some exhibits on level two by taking a lift (D80 L170 W125) to the left past the ticket desk. Signposting is not particularly good: it looks as though it was designed to look pretty, rather than to give clear directions. The staff are friendly and well-informed.

There are two **wheelchair toilets** on the GF. One **(D85 ST80)** by the ticket desk and one **(D85 ST70)** in the opposite corner of the atrium. Another **wheelchair toilet (D85 ST100)** is on level two in the southeastern library area.

Adjacent to the Maritime Museum back towards the CP is the **Queen's House**. This was designed by Inigo Jones for Anne of Denmark who was James I's queen. The other buildings towards the river were carefully sited so that the queen had an unobstructed view of the river. It has been restored and furnished as it would have been in the 17thC and the upstairs rooms are exquisite. Entrance is step free leading to the ticket office in the basement. To the right is a lift (D100 W205 L100) that goes up to the GF and the first floor. On the GF −3−1 steps from the Great Hall will take you into a roadway and then +1+3 take you to the Orangery, with a lovely view of Greenwich Park. On the first floor there is a 2cm threshold leading to the balcony. **Wheelchair toilet (D100 ST70)** in the basement to the left of the entrance. There may only be timed (hourly) entry to the Queen's House in the winter.

Old Royal Naval College Visitor Centre
King William Walk, Greenwich, SE10 9LW
Tel: 020 8269-4747 *Fax:* 020 8269-4757
Off King William Walk opposite the junction with College Approach, the visitor centre is to the left through the main entrance to the Royal Naval College. Both entrances are step free and everything is on one step-free level with a shop and a café to the side of the main room. **Adapted toilet (D95 ST125** inward door) in the far right corner from the main entrance.

Royal Naval College
King William Walk SE10
Tel: 020 8269-4747
These impressive buildings were designed by Sir Christopher Wren, and replaced the old Tudor palace. They are now used by Greenwich

University. The only parts open to the public are the hall and the chapel. It is about 100m from the road, and parking is difficult both because the roads are busy and for security reasons. The normal route to the hall involves +15 steps, then +3+15 and there's a further +6 to a raised section. If you ask at the entrance lodge, someone will escort you across the face of the building, round the side and down the back. By this route you can have flat (if somewhat bumpy) access and avoid the first +15, but it's about 100m further. The entrance to the chapel is opposite that of the hall, and involves −1+1+3+14. They have a caterpillar-type stairclimber for chair users available if you ring and ask in advance.

The Old Royal Observatory and Flamsteed House
Greenwich Park SE10 9NF
Tel: 020 8858-4422 *website*: www.nmm.ac.uk
Famous for the meridian (0° longitude line) which passes through it. Just over a hundred years ago, Greenwich Mean Time became the basis of time measurement for most of the world. The CP in the park is described above and is level with the Observatory entrance. The path leading up from the Maritime Museum is very steep with about 10 +1 steps towards the top. The site has been refurbished, but is step free only in parts.

Flat entrance, followed by −1 step into the courtyard (where the meridian is). Part of the courtyard is cobbled. From the entrance, the Meridian Building is some 80% step free. This includes the telescope used to take readings at zero longitude. There's then +1 and −3 to other rooms on the GF. A first-floor gallery is +19. There's flat access to the shop from the entrance hall, but you have to get a door opened. There's a **wheelchair toilet (D70 ST80)** which is between two buildings and is signposted from the courtyard. It is down a small dead-end passage off a triangular garden. A visit to **Flamsteed House** involves +4, D74 and then +17 to the first floor where there's a D60. Stairs −3−7−7. The route continues via the basement −20+16, to the gardens.

Ranger's House
Chesterfield Walk SE10
Tel: 020 8853-0035 *Fax:* 020 8853-0090
Situated in the southwest corner of Greenwich Park, some 300m from the main south entrance to the park, off Charlton Way. Closed on Mondays and Tuesdays. The CP in front of the house operates on a first come, first served basis, though staff will open their yard to BB

holders if all the spaces are taken. The main entrance has $-2+7+2$ steps. There is an alternative step-free route if you press the bell on the railings. Staff will escort you to an exterior platform stairlift (W100 L140) which bypasses $+9$. From here, the GF is step free, including a shop and **wheelchair toilet**. The upper floor is $+22$, though this can be bypassed by a staff-operated Stannah stairlift with a seat into which to transfer. Staff will carry your wheelchair upstairs. From here the upper floor is step free. Audio tours available.

Thames Barrier Visitor Centre
Unity Way, Woolwich SE18 5BR
Tel: 020 8305-4188
The Thames Barrier is a key part of the system that protects London from flooding. It is 500m wide, and consists of ten huge moveable steel gates. The viewing point and visitor centre is situated off Woolwich Road (A206), just past Charlton Station if you are coming from the west, down Eastmoor Street. From CP, which has five **BB** spaces, there is $+1$ step to the visitor centre. From the CP there's a well-signed lift (D90 W100 L120) to the top of the embankment. This bypasses $+9+9$. When we visited the lift wasn't working, but we have been told that it has been fixed. Small café with flat access on the top where you buy a ticket for getting into the visitor centre. There is a good view of the Barrier 40m along the embankment from the café. You can get down nearer the river edge, via $-11-11$ or, further back, -27. Notices helpfully warn chair users of the dangers of flooding, but this doesn't happen too often, or too suddenly, so you'd probably get a bit of warning! The exhibition consists of a video and a few small displays, and is not of as much interest as the Barrier itself. **Wheelchair toilet (D70 ST75 NKS)** with a broken handrail, on the ground level by the exhibition.

Hackney

Sutton House
2 Homerton High Street, Hackney E9 6JQ
Tel: 020 8986-2264
A Tudor house, surviving in something like its original form, in spite of having been, among other things, a girls' school in the 17thC, and a squat in the 1980s. Limited opening times. Parking in Sutton Place or Isabella Road, off the High Street. It is built around a courtyard. Small lip at the main door. On the GF there is a small concert hall, several rooms, a shop, café and a **wheelchair toilet (D90 ST80)**. There

are four floors, but no lift. The chapel is in the basement, down about 20 steps. First floor + 6 + 13, second floor + 16. The main part of the house is the GF.

Nearby is **Victoria Park**, which was the first public park in London created for ordinary people and not for royalty. Because of this, it has become known as the People's Park.

Hampstead and Highgate

Hampstead Heath

The Heath is a huge area covering nearly 800 acres, just 7km from the centre of London. It includes the Kenwood estate. It is quite hilly in parts, and the approach through Hampstead village is up a steep hill. The Corporation of London, Guildhall EC2, who are responsible for the Heath, publish an excellent diary/guide (available at several places on the Heath) which lists various events. These include performances in the bandstands and at Kenwood, children's activities and fairs. In the middle of the guide is a map showing the principal facilities.

Information Centre (*Tel:* 020 7482-7073) off Gordon House Road near Gospel Oak Rail Station.

The entrance is 10m away to the right of the Lido. A ramp bypasses + 2 steps. CP with three BB spaces shared with the Lido. There is also an electric buggy available which can be booked a week in advance and they hope to have more soon. They can also provide a good map showing the paths over most of the Heath with an indication of the steepness of the slopes and the roughness of the terrain.

The Heath is best approached from its lower reaches near Parliament Hill. There is a CP in East Heath Road at the South End Green end, from where it is possible to enjoy a pleasant wander across the Heath without encountering severe slopes. Another recommended access point is at the end of Parliament Hill which is a Mecca for kite-flying enthusiasts. If you can climb up, you can get an excellent view over London; or, if you feel less athletic, you can take the path to the left and enjoy a less exacting amble towards Highgate Ponds.

Six wheelchair toilets are shown on the Corporation of London listing/map mentioned above, and these are:

- in the heath 'extension' to the north. It is in the red tile complex next to the sports pitches, some 400m from Wildwood Road and 600m from Hampstead Way **(D80 ST130 NKS)**. The paths are rough and muddy when wet;

- 100m from the entrance on North End Road (on the West Heath) **(D85 ST90 NKS)**; there is nearby parking for BB holders;
- on what is called East Heath, almost due south from *Spaniards Inn*. Gravelly paths, and in a hilly area. The toilet (not seen) is in a brick hut complex hidden amongst some trees;
- about 200m from the Nassington Road entrance, to the south of the heath. It is between the athletics track and the playground. About 800m from Gospel Oak station **(D100 ST150+ NKS)**;
- those shown next to Highgate Road on the east side by the tennis courts **(D80 ST120 NKS)**;
- by Highgate Ponds by Millfield Lane. Down a steepish ramp **(D75 ST115 NKS)**.

Highgate Cemetery
Swain's Lane N6 6PJ
Tel: 020 8340-1834 *website:* www.highgate-cemetery.org
Full of graves and tombs that reflect high Victorian taste, and best known for being the burial place of Karl Marx. Admission charge. It is divided into two sections, west and east. There is a flat entrance to the east side and the main path is smooth. Long distances of over 500m may be involved, depending on what you want to see. The west section is on a steepish hill, and there are few paths. Most chair users would need assistance in the western part, but there's plenty of interest. The cemetery is always closed during funerals, so call beforehand. The western part is only open to prearranged groups.

Kenwood House (The Iveagh Bequest)
Hampstead Lane NW3 7JR
Tel: 020 8348- 1286
Kenwood House is on the northernmost edge of the Heath. It is a handsome period house with a fine picture collection. Open-air concerts are held in the grounds, and concerts and poetry readings are held in the Orangery on the GF. Access for disabled visitors is from the East Lodge on Hampstead Lane via an intercom as the gate is normally closed. It is then about 200m to a small CP with two BB spaces by the house. The normal route via the West Lodge involves a 400m walk from the road. There is ramped access to the GF if you go about 60m round to the front from the BB spaces. This bypasses +15 steps. The GF is flat, and includes various displays of paintings and antiques, as well as a shop. The first floor is +3+18+6. The cafeteria and **adapted toilet (D85 ST74** but inward opening door) are both near the BB spaces.

The audience area for concerts is about 450m from the house reached by gently sloping gravel paths. The orchestra perform under a shelter on the other side of the small lake.

Spaniards Inn
Spaniards Road NW3
Tel: 020 8455-3276
Where the road joins Hampstead Lane. Famous pub that Dick Turpin is said to have frequented, and also numbers famous poets amongst its previous patrons. On-site CP, and then flat to left-hand entrance. 75% is step free from this entrance. +13 steps to the Turpin Bar. Garden is −3 from the pub although there's a ramp from the CP.

Places of Worship

London has an enormous number of historic and important places of worship, of which we have only surveyed a selection. Most were built with inherent architectural barriers of one kind or another and our experience has been that ecclesiastical authorities have been generally slow in providing ramps or stairlifts to bypass these. However, many famous churches now have step-free entry routes, and these bypass obstacles that have been there for many years and are an integral part of the Gothic architecture.

Westminster Abbey, Westminster Cathedral, St Paul's Cathedral, St James's Piccadilly and St Bartholomew-the-Great provide sharp contrasts in style and beauty. If churches are your special interest, get a copy of *A Guide to London's Churches* by Mervyn Blatch, published by Constable (a reprint is currently under consideration). Note that some of the smaller churches are locked during the day, especially those in the City. If you want to see a particular church, it might be worth phoning in advance. There's a useful website www.london-city-churches.org.uk which includes details about many of the City churches, and a location map. Apparently there were 111 in the 16thC, of which 80 were destroyed in the Great Fire of 1666. 51 were subsequently rebuilt under the direction of Sir Christopher Wren. There are also a number of churches, some outside the City that were built to designs by John Nash in the Regency period.

Reflecting the fact that both Londoners and visitors to the city have a wide variety of beliefs and practices, we have included descriptions of some of the more prominent mosques, synagogues and temples. Of particular interest, and with good access, are the Brahma Kumaris World Spiritual University, the London Central Mosque, the Peace Pagoda in Battersea Park and the Swaminarayan Hindu Mission. Most synagogues are kept locked except at the times of meetings or services. It is therefore essential to ring first.

Abbeys and cathedrals

St George's RC Cathedral
Lambeth Road SE1 7HY
Tel : 020 7928-5256

The cathedral, opposite the Imperial War Museum, was rebuilt after its destruction in World War II. Step-free entrance, then flat inside with plenty of space for chair users at the sides and front. Induction loop.

St Paul's Cathedral
Ludgate Hill EC4
Tel: 020 7236-4128 *website:* www.stpauls.co.uk
Admission charge, except for services. Christopher Wren's masterpiece still dominates London's skyline. The dome is thought to be the second largest in the world and contains the famous Whispering Gallery. BB holders can use the coach space on Ludgate Hill. The floor area is approximately 80m by 200m.

The main entrance has +10+14 steps, with either revolving or swing doors to go through at the top. A **step-free way in** is 60m away, to the right of the main stairs. Go down the side of the cathedral, and find the door tucked away in the corner where the South Transept joins the Nave. The entrance is locked, but ringing the bell will usually bring assistance. The bell rings in the verger's office, and if there is nobody there you might have to send a messenger up the main stairs. Inside, a platform stairlift (W65 L85) or service lift (D80 W105 L135) bypasses +22 (spiral). These give access to the main floor which has flat access throughout, except for the American Memorial Chapel which is +4, and to the Choir which is also +4. A new wooden structure with an altar has recently been placed under the dome, to bring the centre of worship nearer the congregation, but no attempt has been made to ramp the steps up to the choir.

The crypt is also reached by the service lift (bypassing −38 from the main floor or −20 from outside). It contains Nelson's tomb, a large chapel, the cathedral Treasure, a shop and a café. There are **wheelchair toilets (D80 ST75)** just inside the doors of both Ladies and Gents. The −3 steps down to Nelson's tomb have been ramped. To get through to the chapel beyond, ask one of the staff to open the barrier just past the Treasure exhibition.

There are hundreds of narrow steps from the first floor to the other galleries: +259 to the Whispering Gallery, +116 to the Stone Gallery, and +155 to the Golden Gallery. The service lift goes to within about 30 steps of the Whispering Gallery, but we were told that it is strictly for 'private' use.

Just outside the cathedral past the coach park on the south side, and near the junction with New Change there is a 'Tardis' **wheelchair toilet (NKS)**, available 24 hours a day. The churchyard area at the east end can be reached step free, and is a good shady spot with a large number of seats. Note that City Thameslink Station (which is accessible) is nearby, and also the *Hogshead* pub, see page 331.

Southwark Cathedral
Borough High Street SE1
Tel: 020 7367-6700 *Fax:* 020 7367-6725
website: www.dswark.org/cathedral
e-mail: cathedral@dswark.org.uk
The cathedral is situated beneath and to the southwest of London Bridge. Though much restored, the building retains its traditional Gothic style. William Shakespeare's brother Edmund is buried here. The entrance can be reached step free from Cathedral Street (if approached from the southwest corner). There's a ramp to the right to bypass −6 steps. The entrance itself is step free. Inside some 70% is step free. The Ambulatory is reached via +1+3 on the right side. The first step is permanently ramped, and there are portable ramps available to get up the others. The shop, refectory and exhibition 'The Long View of London' are accessed via +7 but with an open lift (D120 L200) to bypass them. All are step free, and the ±4 in the shop can be avoided by using a ramped passage outside. **Wheelchair toilet (D70+ ST70+)** near the top of the open lift. There's a second **wheelchair toilet (D70+ ST70+)** in the basement, reached by the lift (D70 W110 L140) next to the refectory. Induction loop in the church. A great deal of thought has gone into making the facilities accessible. The refectory can also be approached step free by going round to the north side of the Cathedral, though the route is well cobbled. There's a large attractive courtyard outside the refectory, with tables there during the summer.

Westminster Abbey
Broad Sanctuary SW1
Tel: 020 7222-5152 *website:* www.westminster-abbey.org
Admission charge to parts of the Abbey. The church is used for many national occasions and royal events. It contains the tomb of the Unknown Warrior and those of many famous people. Some parking is available for BB holders by prior arrangement, in the Dean's Yard, 150m away. The main way in is through the north entrance which is step free. An audio tour guide available. Once inside, much of the ground level is flat.

Exceptions are: the Chapel of Our Lady of the Pew, leading to St John the Baptist Chapel (+1+2 steps); the Chapel of St Nicholas

(+ 1 + 2); and the Chapel of St Edmund (+ 2). The upper chapels have + 12 + 1 + 2. These include the Henry Vll Chapel.

From the abbey interior, the cloisters are − 5. There used to be a ramp here, making a valuable link. There is step-free access to the cloisters from Dean's Yard, by the West Gate, but the removal of the ramp makes the Abbey considerably less accessible. The cloisters give access to the Chapter House (+ 10), the Abbey Treasures Exhibition (− 3 are bypassed by portable ramp), and to the Abbey Gardens, which have flat access.

The main visitors' exit is via − 2 − 1 steps at the West Door, which may also be the entrance for those wanting to come to a service. A portable ramp is available, but visitors wanting to avoid the steps may find it easier to exit through the North Door.

The Abbey Bookshop has flat access on the right of the West Gate. **Wheelchair toilet (D80 ST80 NKS)** across the road, in front of the Queen Elizabeth Conference Centre, by Storey's Gate, has a slightly cobbled pathway. Induction loop in the church for services. There is a Scalomobile with an attached chair to help anyone who can use the facility to get to the upper chapels, but we were told that it hasn't been used for the past two years, and that you still can't see much when you get up the first set of stairs.

Westminster RC Cathedral
Ashley Place SW1P 1QW
Tel: 020 7798-9055 *website:* www.westminstercathedral.org.uk
One of London's rare Byzantine-style buildings, its red-brick tower stands in sharp contrast to the nearby Abbey. Entrance + 2 + 2 steps, bypassed by a long ramp 30m to the right of the building. Flat inside to all main areas. Numerous side chapels are + 1 or + 2. The book and souvenir shop are − 3. Induction loop.

The tower lift (D80 W120 L140) goes to the top, but there is + 1 − 1 to the balconies. The views are interesting, but partially obstructed by metal bars.

Churches

All-Hallows-by-the-Tower see chapter on *Places of interest*.

All Souls
Langham Place W1
Tel: 020 7580-3522
Opposite Broadcasting House at the top end of Regent Street, the

church is often used as a recording studio. The + 7 steps at the entrance can be bypassed by a ramp on the left. Inside, a lift (D74 W135 L105) bypasses + 3 into the church, and also − 18 to the lower floor which contains a meeting hall, the reference library and an **adapted toilet (D70 ST68)**. Induction loop in the church.

Brompton Oratory
Brompton Road SW7
Tel: 020 7808-0900 *website:* www.brompton-oratory.org.uk
A quiet and attractive church with a stunning interior, located almost next to the Victoria and Albert Museum. It is also known as the London Oratory. Entrance + 6 + 1 steps. If you go about 30m down the side of the church on the left, there's a ramp on the left to an alternative entrance. To get the door unlocked, ask at the house, or ring the bell which is set in the wall by the drainpipe, and near the bottom of the ramp.

Central Hall
Storey's Gate SW1H 9NH
Tel: 020 7222-8010
e-mail: visitorservices@c-h-w.co.uk *website:* www.c-h-w.com
Built in 1912, Central Hall is the 'Cathedral' of Methodism, used on Sundays for worship and at other times for meetings and exhibitions. It is located opposite Westminster Abbey. Entrance + 3 + 13 steps, bypassed through a side door about 75m away by the corner between Tothill Street and Matthew Parker Street. This has + 1, but there is a portable ramp just inside. Ring the bell for assistance. Flat from here to two lifts (D80 W95 L100 and D200 W300 L350) which give access to all five floors. Although most floors have split levels, roughly 95% of the building is step free, although quite long distances may be involved. The Lecture Hall and Library have + 5, bypassed by a platform stairlift. The Great Hall on the third floor has four chair spaces, and an induction loop. Café in the basement has movable tables and chairs. **Wheelchair toilet (D85 ST105)** on the third floor by the foyer and **adapted toilet (D100 ST55)** on GF by side entrance. The website has an excellent page describing disabled facilities and mentions an accessible toilet in the basement, which may be the one we have described as being on the GF.

Church of the Holy Sepulchre (St Sepulchre without Newgate)
Holborn Viaduct EC1 ·
Tel: 020 7248-3826
At the junction of Holborn Viaduct and Snow Hill. Sir Henry Wood,

the founder of the 'Proms', is buried here. Entrance $+1+2$ steps, then swing doors. Flat inside.

City Temple
Holborn Viaduct EC1
Tel: 020 7583-5532
The City's main Nonconformist church. Entrance $+3$ steps, bypassed through a side door, normally locked. The GF contains the chapel, church and the hall. Lift (D85 W180 L185) goes to all six other floors, which contain conference halls and meeting rooms. **Adapted toilet (D63 no ST** with fixed handrail) down a twisty corridor on first floor, reached by a lift. Infrared hearing system in the church.

Farm Street Church
Farm Street W1
Tel: 020 7493-7811
Also called the **Church of the Immaculate Conception**. By the junction with Carlos Place. Entrance $+5$ steps, but there is a step-free alternative from Mount Street via the church gardens. Bookshop -7.

St Bartholomew-the-Great
West Smithfield EC1A
Tel: 020 7606-5171 *website:* www.greatstbarts.com
Apart from the Tower Chapel, this is London's oldest church. There are twelve BB spaces outside. The main entrance is 50m along a passage just off the West Smithfield Roundabout. Flat, then $-1(3cm)-1(4cm)$ steps into the church. Level throughout with uneven surface, except for the Lady Chapel $(+1)$, then $+5$ to the choir. **Wheelchair toilet (NKS)** on the West Smithfield Roundabout.

St Bride's
Fleet Street EC4
Tel: 020 7427-0133
A Wren church with strong journalistic links, about 500m from St Paul's Cathedral. Fleet Street entrance $+2+1$ steps, but there is level access from Salisbury Court. Flat inside. The crypt (-21) contains remnants of earlier churches on the site, and a section of Roman pavement.

St Clement Danes
Strand WC2
Tel: 020 7242-8282

Another Wren church, best known for its oranges and lemons. Blitzed in the Second World War, it has now become the RAF church. It stands on an island in the middle of the Strand. Entrance + 1 step, then level. The balcony is + 25, and crypt − 22.

St Giles
Cripplegate, St Giles Terrace, Fore Street EC2 8DA
Tel: 020 7638-1997 *website:* www.stgilescripplegate.com
Milton's burial place. St Giles is situated in the middle of the Barbican development. A ramp bypasses + 2 steps at the entrance. Step free inside.

St James's
197 Piccadilly W1J 9LL
Tel: 020 7734-4511 *website:* www.st-james-piccadilly.org
On the south side of Piccadilly, opposite Swallow Street. The poet and visionary William Blake was baptised here. It was supposedly Wren's favourite church. There are − 3 steps from Piccadilly to the church-yard, where small fairs are frequently held, and a further + 2 into the church itself. Both these flights of steps are normally ramped. The ramp is W68 at its narrowest. There are + 2 + 2 (not ramped) from Jermyn Street . Step free inside to about 80%. The Wren Café, on the right of the church, has + 1 small step from Piccadilly.

St John's
Waterloo Road SE1
Tel: 020 7633-9819
Located on the big roundabout at the end of Waterloo Bridge. A ramp to the right of the entrance bypasses + 3 steps. Small threshold (± 3cm) at the main entrance door. Inside the church is largely step free, and there's a **wheelchair toilet (D70 + ST70 +)** towards the front on the left side.

St Lawrence Jewry
Gresham Street EC2
Tel: 020 7600-9478
The church of the Corporation of London with a fantastic ceiling. Step-free entrance then flat throughout except for − 2 to small private chapel. Induction loop.

St Magnus the Martyr
Lower Thames Street EC3
Tel: 020 7626-4481

There has been a church on this site just next to London Bridge for more than 1,000 years. Wren completed this building in 1676. Flat entrance and level access throughout.

St Margaret's
Parliament Square SW1
Tel: 020 7222-5152
The parish church of the House of Commons, where Sir Winston Churchill was married. The main entrance on the west side has +3 +1 steps. There's a permanent ramp at the north entrance. You may have to ask the security staff at the main entrance to open the north door. Flat inside except for +1 to the information desk.

St Mary Abbots
Kensington High Street W8 4HN
Tel: 020 7937-2419 *Fax:* 020 7937-4317
website: www.stmaryabbots.freeserve.co.uk
Situated on the corner of Kensington High Street and Kensington Church Street, this pretty church has a peaceful garden at its rear. The entrance from the south porch leads through a short sloped cloister corridor, from where +3 steps to the main church can be bypassed using a portable ramp. The main church area is step free except for +2 to the altar. A slope down from the north porch bypasses −3 from west door to garden. Then, +6 to upper tier of the garden can be bypassed by a sloped path (which is 100cm wide) near the west door of the church.

St Mary-le-Bow
Cheapside EC2
Tel: 020 7248-5139
Houses the Bow Bells, 'within whose sound a true cockney is born'. Entrance +5 steps. Flat inside. The Court of Arches, which decides ecclesiastical law cases and confirms the election of bishops, is held in the Crypt, which is −17.

St Mary-le-Strand
Strand WC2
Tel: 020 7836-3126
An 18thC building in Baroque style. Entrance +1 +9 steps, then flat inside.

St Martin-in-the-Fields
St Martin's Place WC2N 4JJ
Tel: 020 7930-1862 *website:* www.stmartin-in-the-fields.org
On the northeast corner of Trafalgar Square, off St Martin's Lane. Often called the 'Parish Church of London'. The main (west) entrance has a minimum of +5 steps, bypassed by the ramped north entrance. This gives flat access to the nave. The crypt with café is −3−10 from Duncannon Street or −2−27 from the antechapel. There are regular concerts.

St Mary Woolnoth
Lombard Street EC3
Tel: 020 7626-9701
Between Lombard Street and King William Street. Sumptuous interior by Hawksmoor. Entrance +8 steps.

St Marylebone Parish Church
17 Marylebone Road NW1
Tel: 020 7935-7315
Where poets Elizabeth Barrett and Robert Browning were married after they eloped. Entrance +5 steps, bypassed by a ramp on the right, which leads to +1, for which there is a temporary ramp. The inside is level. Lift (D75 W95 L120) to the crypt, where there is a pastoral centre, a small chapel, a café, and a **wheelchair toilet (D70 ST80)**. The balcony has +20.

St Olave's
Hart Street EC3
Tel: 020 7488-4318
The church where Samuel Pepys is buried. Entrance −2 steps. Flat inside, but rather cramped.

St Paul's Church see write-up on Covent Garden in the chapter on *Places of interest*.

St Peter-Upon-Cornhill
Cornhill EC3
Tel: 020 7283-2231
Used as a Christian study centre, and only open to the public by prior arrangement with the caretaker. Only the back entrance, in St Peter's Alley, is used, which has +1 step into the courtyard, then +1 into the church.

St Saviours
Walton Place SW3 1SA
Tel: 020 7823-8979 *website:* www.stsaviours-intermission.org.uk
Just a short distance from Knightsbridge tube station, down Basil
Street. Step-free entrance to the lower room, chapel and galleries. A
series of exhibitions is held in the White Space Gallery on the GF.
Lift (D90 W110 L300) to the first-floor worship space which is step
free. **Wheelchair toilet (D70+ ST70+)** on the GF to the left of the
main foyer. The lift to the church is large enough to take a coffin!

St Stephen Walbrook
39 Walbrook EC4
Tel: 020 7283-4444
Most famous as the place where the Samaritans were founded in
1953. Entrance +1+13 steps then step free apart from +2 to the
altar.

Temple Church
Inner Temple Lane EC4
Tel: 020 7353-8559/3470
One of the few circular churches still in existence. South side entrance
with +1 step.

Wesley's Chapel see chapter on *Places of interest.*

Mosques, synagogues and temples

Al Khoei Mosque
Chevening Road NW6 6TN
Tel: 020 8960-6378
Near the junction with Salusbury Road. CP can be used if you
telephone in advance. Entrance +5 steps, then flat. **Wheelchair users
may use the prayer room without removing shoes or transferring from
chair**. We were told that stick users must use a wheelchair, although
presumably disabled walkers can only use the prayer room if they
remove their shoes.

Brahma Kumaris World Spiritual University
Global Co-operation House, 65 Pound Lane, Willesden NW10 2HH
Tel: 020 8459-1400 *e-mail:* london@bkwsu.com
website: www.bkwsu.org.uk
The international centre for Brahma Kumaris was opened in 1991. A

worldwide organisation with an emphasis on meditation and spiritual development. Courses run daily, weekly, or more long term. UGCP on Pound Lane with twenty-two spaces of which only four are not on a steepish incline. The main entrance and GF are flat. A lift (D80 W110 L138) gives step-free access to all other floors. The seven floors contain numerous rooms, including a seminar room and an auditorium. Roof garden $-3+25-1$ steps. **Wheelchair toilets (D85 ST90)** on the GF and on the third floor **(D85 ST85)**.

Central Synagogue
36-40 Hallam Street W1W 6NW
Tel: 020 7580-1355
Entrance $+7$ steps. The GF is level. Chair spaces are available at the rear of the main worship area. Women normally use the upper gallery (about $+30$ steps), but if this causes a problem, they can remain at ground level. Hall for meetings -24. Induction loop.

London Buddhist Vihara
The Avenue, Chiswick W4 1UD
Tel: 020 8995-9493
50m from the junction with Bedford Road. Entrance $+3$ steps, then flat to the main hall, shrine, sermon hall and shop. Library $+1$. Staff said that all visitors, including chair users, must remove their shoes before entering the shrine room.

London Central Mosque (Islamic Cultural Centre)
146 Park Road NW8 7RG
Tel: 020 7724-3363 *website:* www.islamicculturalcentre.co.uk
e-mail: islamic200@aol.com
A fine building with a bronze dome, southeast of Regent's Park, by the junction with Hanover Gate. CP available for visitors, controlled by security gate, beside which is the pedestrian entrance. There are $+3$ steps to the main square, bypassed by a ramp 15m away, along the left side. To the right of the main square is the reception to the mosque.

Once inside, there is a bookshop to the right, and an enquiry desk to the left, as well as a prominent display, with clocks showing the five times of prayer: dawn, noon, mid-afternoon, sunset and night. Flat access to the bookshop, enquiry desk and main area of worship for men. 10m in front of the main entrance are the mosque doors. Inside these there is an uncarpeted (non-sacred) area where shoes must be removed before going on the carpet to pray. However, everything is visible from this area, including the fine carpet, chandelier and dome. Although women pray in a separate gallery (+ 20), women visitors are allowed to look inside from this non-sacred area, provided they are suitably dressed. Women are asked to cover their heads.

For praying, the main GF part of the mosque is for men only. Gents toilet and *wudhu* in the basement are − 20 or so. *Wudhu* is ritual washing before praying, principally of the feet. For disabled men there is a toilet available on the GF for washing, or there is a lift (D75 W75 L100). Women pray in an upper gallery (+ 20). Unadapted Ladies toilet and *wudhu* on the GF. The lift bypasses the + 10 + 11 to the first-floor library and upper gallery (for women).

The new administrative block, to the left of the security gate at the main entrance, contains a **wheelchair toilet (D85 ST110)** on the second floor to the left of the lift (D80 W100 L130). Staff are friendly and welcoming.

London Peace Pagoda see write-up on Battersea Park in the chapter on *Open air activities*.

London Jamme Masjid
Brick Lane E1 6QL
Tel: 020 7247-6052
Between the junctions with Princelet Street and Fournier Street. Entrance + 5 steps, then flat to the main prayer hall. Worshippers must first visit washing rooms for *wudhu* (see write-up on the London Central Mosque). These are − 3 or − 5.

New London Synagogue
33 Abbey Road NW8 0AT
Tel: 020 7328-1026 *Fax:* 020 7372-3142
e-mail: administrator.nls@masorti.org.uk
Four parking spaces in the driveway (phone in advance). Entrance + 2 steps, then + 5 − 5 to the prayer hall. Alternative entrance + 1 at the side of the synagogue. **Wheelchair toilet (D85 ST75)**.

Swaminarayan Hindu Mission
105-119 Brentford Road NW10 8GB
Tel: 020 8965-2651 *Fax:* 020 8965-6313
e-mail: shm@swaminarayan-baps.org.uk
website: www.swaminarayan.org
A new and beautiful temple complex. Visitors from all religions are

welcomed. We were told that BB spaces are provided near the main entrance. There are two main buildings, linked by a 20m ramp. **Note that all visitors should remove their shoes before entering either building**.

The prayer hall contains a reception point, shop, function rooms and areas for worship, all on one level. There are seats and wheelchair spaces on both sides of the worship area. **Wheelchair cubicle (D80 ST85)** in both the Ladies and Gents loos. The temple is on two floors, with a lift (D85 W105 L160). On the first floor there is an exhibition called 'Understanding Hinduism' and an area for worship. Assistance for disabled visitors should always be available.

West London Synagogue for British Jews
33 Seymour Place W1H 5AU
Tel: 020 7723-4404 *website:* www.wls.org.uk
Flat access through main gate for services. At other times the only entrance is via 33 Seymour Place with + 1 step. Step free inside using a lift (D75 W120 L120). All worship is on the GF. The sanctuary has a split level of − 4 bypassed by a portable ramp if advance warning is given. **Wheelchair toilet (D75 ST85)** on the GF. Induction loop.

Museums and galleries

London has one of the greatest collections of museums and galleries in the world. The variety of subject, size and interest is vast. As a result of recent changes, most of the big museums are free, and you only have to pay when there are special exhibitions on. Most large museums and galleries have wheelchairs available that can be borrowed.

Much effort and thought has been put into providing improved access for disabled visitors. Staff are usually helpful, although not always aware of all the facilities provided. **Many museums now provide facilities for visitors who are partially sighted to touch and feel some exhibits. These facilities are generally available by special arrangement, so it's worth phoning in advance**.

Patience is occasionally required to get special step-free access routes opened up. Art collections and historical artefacts are valuable, and security is important, so it is not always possible to leave particular doors open. It may also take a little time to find the right person to operate stairlifts to bypass steps.

Some major museums and galleries are large, making it difficult to walk or wheel all the way round in a single visit. You would do well to look at the plan, either by writing in first, or using the plans in a standard guidebook. Then you can choose some of the things of greatest interest and go and see those.

The presentation of many exhibits has been improved, and facilities, such as catering and the provision of toilets, have been upgraded.

If you require more detailed information, there are many guidebooks around. *London Museums and Galleries* published by Insight Guides, and the *Museums and Galleries of London* by Abigail Willis from Metro Publications are two which stand out. They are both well presented and informative.

Inner London

Apsley House see Wellington Museum.

Bank of England Museum
Threadneedle Street EC2R 8AH
Tel: 020 7601-5491 *website:* www.bankofengland.co.uk

Historical and financial displays, including some real gold bars! The
nearby Bank Station has step-free access from the DLR. Entrance in
Bartholomew Lane +4+3 steps, then ±3 to exhibits. All can be
bypassed by portable ramps, available on request. If you ring first,
you won't have to wait until someone can come and put the ramps
down. **Wheelchair toilet (D90 ST85)** at the rear of the museum. The
cinema, used by groups, has chair spaces and an induction loop.

Bankside Gallery
48 Hopton Street, Blackfriars SE1 9JH
Tel: 020 7928-7521
It is situated on the South Bank to the east of Blackfriars Bridge just
before Tate Modern. From the Riverside Walk, a ramp near the pub
bypasses the −7 steps outside. The small gallery is all on one floor.
Ramps bypass +2 steps at the entrance, and there is flat or ramped
access throughout. There is a **wheelchair toilet** in the *Founders Arms*
pub less than 100m away.

Barbican Art Gallery see section on *Arts centres*.

Bramah Tea and Coffee Museum
40 Southwark Street, Bankside SE1 1UN
Tel: 020 7403-5650 *website:* www.bramahmuseum.co.uk
Just west from London Bridge on the north side of Southwark Street,
this small museum highlights the social and commercial history of
two of the world's most important commodities. It smells gorgeous.
Parking may be difficult but there is a drop-off point outside the
entrance to the café with twenty minutes' waiting allowed. The café is
+1 step from the street (a ramp should be forthcoming). The small
GF museum is on the right and is flat throughout. **Wheelchair toilet
(D75 ST80)** at the back opposite the entrance.

Britain At War Experience see chapter on *Places of interest*.

British Library
96 Euston Road NW1 2DB
Tel: 020 7412-7332 *Textphone:* 020 7387-0626 *website:* www.bl.uk
On the north side of Euston Road, between Midland Road and
Ossulston Street. Both of these roads have BB spaces. The library
houses the national collection of books, manuscripts and maps, as
well as the National Sound Archive. Its books are available to
registered readers who are doing bona fide research, and who cannot

get their material through other public libraries. It also contains some public exhibition galleries (John Ritblat) where the Magna Carta, the Lindisfarne Gospels and Shakespeare's First Folio can be seen. There is an interactive workshop. Public tours take place four days a week.

From Euston Road, there is a large courtyard (stepped) with a step-free route about 100m around the edge. The main entrance is step free, with an information desk (straight ahead) in the foyer. To the left is a shop, and to the right is the office for reader registration. The isometric diagram/map available is useful but it takes a bit of getting used to. Working upwards, the floors are described as LG (lower ground), GF, UG (upper ground), first, second and third.

The public galleries are accessed by going to the left of the information desk. Some exhibits are on the GF, and others on the UG and first floors, reached by one of the two lifts (D105 W180 L130). The John Ritblat galleries measure roughly 50m by 30m. The UG has a large café at the back, and there's a restaurant on the first floor.

The whole building is step free (as one would expect), and there are as many as ten lifts. Six of them are on the right side of the building, described below, two link the public galleries, and two are on the far left towards Ossulston Street (and not shown clearly on the isometric plan available).

The easiest route for readers who want to use the library is to go straight down to the LG using either the ramp or the lift (D75 W85 L180). Both are to the right of the information desk. There is a cloakroom there, where bags are left. From the LG level, there are three lifts opposite and two adjacent (all D110 W150 L130). These access every floor except the GF, thus reaching the reading rooms. **Wheelchair cubicles (D80 ST70)** are located in the Ladies and Gents next to the lifts from the cloakroom on the UG, first and second floors. **Wheelchair toilets (D85 ST110)** are also available on the left of the building (towards Ossulston Street) on the LG, UG, first, second and third floors.

British Museum
Great Russell Street WC1B 3DG
Tel: 020 7323-8000 *info:* 020 7323-8299 *Textphone:* 020 7323-8920
website: www.thebritishmuseum.ac.uk
e-mail: information@thebritishmuseum.ac.uk
One of the largest museums in the world, approximately 200m

square on three main floors. It houses the national collection of archaeological remains which covers two million years of world history. A central feature is the Great Court, which is now covered over with a glass roof and incorporates the old Reading Room of the British Library. There are nearly 100 galleries, and some 4km of walking to see all the exhibits. Almost all the museum now has step-free access via the various lifts, and **where there seems to be a problem, ask one of the staff**, who are generally helpful.

Parking for up to four BB holders can be arranged in advance (*Tel:* 020 7323-8288). The spaces are in the museum forecourt off Great Russell Street near the open lift mentioned below. There are plans of the different floors in the museum available from the information desk. You can also print the plans from the website. There is a leaflet for disabled visitors. To make the best use of a visit, you'd do well to get hold of these before coming, and choose which parts of the museum to have a look at. Alternatively, join one of the excellent guided tours that take place regularly, three times a day; take an audio tour or join one of the eyeOpener Tours which go to a particular part of the museum.

The main museum entrance from Great Russell Street has + 12 steps, bypassed by a well-hidden open lift (W115 L200) to the left. If that lift is not operational, staff can take you to another entrance about 40m away to the left, giving access to an inside lift from the basement level. The alternative entrance in Montague Place has flat access, but you are dependent on another single lift for getting through to the main part of the museum.

Coming in from Great Russell Street, the first hall is quite gloomy, and then you reach the dazzlingly white Great Court with its four classical porticos. In the centre is the Reading Room, which is very atmospheric, and has step-free access. Try out the Compass Computer System where you can look up details of 4000 items in the museum on computers.

There are also shops and cafés. To the left, as you come in, is the information desk, and to the right is the box office for special exhibitions and for the audio guides. Also to the left is access to the largest galleries.

There are five main lifts and four others of importance. All have D75+ W95+ and L120+, but note that you sometimes come in through one door and go out from another. The main lifts are the two south lifts, off the Great Court, as you come in from the main entrance. The east and west lifts around on either side of the oval-shaped central construction, and the North lift which links to

Montague Place. They are quite well 'hidden'. In addition the numbering of floor levels is inconsistent. On the four new lifts, the Great Court Main Floor is Level 2, and the Upper Floors are Level 6. However, on the old north lift, Great Court Level is 0 (with the street entrance at -1) and the Upper Floors are Level 3.

The whole of the GF has step-free access, except for Gallery 16 (where there are ± 17), and there are $+3$ at either end of Gallery 18, although you can see pretty well from the lower level. The upper and lower floors are nearly all step free as well.

There are **cafés** on the GF of the Great Court, and the Gallery Café by Room 12 (in the southwest corner). This as reached via $+12$. There is a staff-operated lift D90 W130 L130) to bypass these, but no sign at all saying that it is possible. Only about 25% of the Gallery Café is step free, and much of it is on a raised gallery $+4$. The **Court Restaurant** is on Level 6 at roof level of the Reading Room, and reached by the east or west lifts (or from Level 3 of the north lift). At certain times, the cafés and restaurant get very crowded.

The various **wheelchair toilets (all D70+ ST70+)** are not particularly well signed or marked. There are:

- two on the GF of Great Court on either side of the oval structure, just before you get to the shops (coming from the main entrance);
- two at Levels 3 and 5, one on either side of the oval structure by the east and west lifts;
- one by Room 5 in the 'special exhibitions' area, but this is not always available;
- one by Room 12;
- two in the Clore Education Centre on the lower floor.

The museum is huge and has limited seating, but is a fascinating place to visit. Wheelchairs are available for use. With the redevelopment, access has improved enormously, but a second platform lift is needed in the forecourt (on the right-hand side), and we found that not all the lifts inside the building were working when we visited.

Cabinet War Rooms

Clive Steps, King Charles Street SW1A 2AQ

Tel: 020 7930-6961 *website*: www.iwm.org.uk

Admission charge. This is where Winston Churchill held many vital Cabinet meetings during World War II. The rooms are laid out as they were when the war ended. Step-free access from Horse Guards

Road, or via −15 steps from King Charles Street. Step free to the ticket office, then a lift (D80 W110 L150) bypasses −16 to the rooms. Step free throughout at lower level. The 150m route ends in a small shop. **Wheelchair toilet (D90 ST70 NKS)** opposite the lift on the lower floor. Key available from lower floor reception. Free audio/printed guides. Two wheelchairs for hire. Some narrow passages, high displays, and dim lighting.

In 2003, an extension will allow access to more rooms, and the museum will expand to three times its present size. The physical layout will be much the same. A new education facility and café will open with **two wheelchair toilets** and **one wheelchair cubicle**. The architect is currently undertaking an access audit.

Crafts Council Gallery
44A Pentonville Road N1 9BY
Tel: 020 7278-7700 *website:* www.craftscouncil.org.uk
On-site parking if you phone first. Ramped entrance bypasses +6 steps, then lift (D90 W105 L145) access between the two floors. **Wheelchair toilet (D70+ ST70+)** on GF. Induction loop in the conference room.

Design Museum
Shad Thames SE1 2YD *website:* www.designmuseum.org
Tel: 020 7403-6933 *info:* 020 7940-8790
The museum highlights classic design from the past 100 years, and state-of-the-art innovations from around the globe, with changing exhibitions. CP in Gainsford Street or two BB spaces in Shad Thames. Entrance +5 steps with a ramped bypass. Displays on the first and second floors, reached via a lift (D80 W125 L165). Ask staff. Coffee shop on the GF, and a **wheelchair cubicle (D85 ST75)** in both the Ladies and Gents toilets. Wheelchairs available.

Florence Nightingale Museum
2 Lambeth Palace Road SE1 7EW
Tel: 020 7620-0374
Admission charge. Small museum on the site of St Thomas's Hospital, celebrating the life and achievements of the Lady of the Lamp. Six BB spaces opposite. Flat entrance and step free throughout. It is roughly 100m around the museum. Small cinema with one chair space. **Wheelchair toilet (D80 ST120)** by the Gents to the right of reception.

Freud Museum
20 Maresfield Gardens, Hampstead NW3 5SX
Tel: 020 7435-2002
Admission charge. Sigmund Freud moved to this house in 1938, and
the museum contains the famous couch on which his patients lay for
analysis. Parking space can be reserved. Entrance +1 (8cm) step,
then level through the GF. First floor +21.

Guards' Museum
Wellington Barracks, Birdcage Walk SW1E 6HQ
Tel: 020 7414-3271/3428
Admission charge. Displays of various army costumes and weapons.
Entrance +6 steps, then −41. Both can be bypassed by a lift (D75
W120 L165). Phone in advance for use. Inside, the museum is level,
and is about 100m around. **Wheelchair toilet (D90 ST120)** in the staff
area. The GF shop is +1.

Hayward Gallery see section on *Arts centres* under the South Bank.

ICA (Institute of Contemporary Arts) see section on *Arts centres*.

Imperial War Museum
Lambeth Road SE1 6HZ
Tel: 020 7416-5320 *RecM:* 0900-1600140 *website:* www.iwm.org.uk
A fascinating collection of historical military equipment, with numerous changing exhibitions. It is housed in a building that, more
than 150 years ago, was a lunatic asylum. Parking for visitors with
disabilities can be arranged. The main entrance is 50m from the road
on a tarmac path through Geraldine Mary Harmsworth Park, and
has +9+1+3 steps leading to the GF. These are bypassed by using
the west entrance reached by going to the right of the big guns, and
then continuing nearly 150m down the right side of the building. This
leads to the lower GF/basement. The diagram of the building on
your ticket, which you get on entering, has an isometric diagram
showing the main central lifts and the location of the disabled
persons toilets. There is also a lift (D80 W90 L250) by the west
entrance which gives access to the picnic room, where there are two
wheelchair toilets (D70+ ST70+).
    **There is flat, ramped or lift access to virtually all exhibits on all six
    floors**. The pair of lifts (D90 W160 L150) by the main staircase serve
    the lower ground, ground and first floors, and a separate lift (D80
    W110 L150) must be used to reach the second floor. This goes from

the first floor – turn right from either of the main lifts until you reach the far wall, and go through the door marked 'disabled lift'.

The self-service café and the shop are both step free from the GF. There are **wheelchair toilets (all D70+ ST70+)**, reasonably well marked on the plan, and signed. The museum has gone to considerable lengths to make the building step free via the new lifts, and there are plans to provide an open lift to bypass the steps at the main entrance.

Jewish Museum
Raymond Burton House, 129-131 Albert Street NW1 7NB
Tel: 020 7284-1997 *Fax:* 020 7267-9008
website: www.jewishmuseum.org.uk
Admission charge. Pay-and-display parking outside. Displays of ceremonial art and the history of the British Jewish community. Step-free entrance then lift (D80 W100 L140) access between all three floors of exhibits, and a lecture room on the first floor. **Wheelchair toilet (D80 ST80)** in the basement.

London Dungeon see chapter on *Places of interest*.

London Planetarium
Allsop Place, off Marylebone Road NW1 5LR
Tel: 020 7487-0200
To the left of Madame Tussaud's with its own entrance 30m down Allsop Place, which is flat. Lift (D80 W110 L155) at entrance takes you to first floor, which contains the dome where you can see a show illustrating how the stars and planets were formed and how they move in the sky. Step-free access to auditorium which has two chair spaces and an induction loop. An exhibition called 'Mars Departures' is on a mezzanine, which is −21 steps from first-floor planetarium, bypassed by a platform stairlift (not tried). **Wheelchair toilet (D90 ST75)** on the first floor, 10m to left of lift.

London Transport Museum
Covent Garden WC2
Tel: 020 7565-7299 *website:* www.ltmuseum.co.uk
Located between Russell Street and Tavistock Street. Admission charge. Museum detailing the history of the capital's transport system. Full of old trains and buses. Ramped entrance to GF and step free throughout, although it is quite cluttered, and there are some tram lines to get over. A lift (D135 W105 L145) links to the two other floors. In the shop, staff can open the ramped exit to avoid −3

steps. **Wheelchair toilet (D90 ST75)** at the back of the GF, and another **(D85 ST105)** off the café which is by the exit.

Madame Tussaud's

Marylebone Road, London NW1 5CR
Tel: 0870 400-3000 *Fax:* 020 7487-0200
website: www.madame-tussauds.com
e-mail: cfc@madame-tussauds.com
Situated 50m left from main exit of Baker Street tube, this is one of London's most popular tourist attractions. Admission charge. **The museum is strict about only allowing three chair users to visit at any one time** and it does get extremely busy. *It is therefore sensible to telephone and book in advance to ensure entry.*

There is a drop-off zone outside the main entrance.

From the entrance there are + 16 steps to the three lifts (D110 W125 L180) which take walkers to the third floor from where they can continue downwards on the designated route using the stairs. There are about 30 steps between each floor.

There is step-free access for wheelchair users using a staff lift (D80 W110 L185) behind reception, which goes to all floors. The tour begins on the third floor and continues down the floors to the GF. Chair users can use the lift, although this means that you take a slightly different route from everyone else. There is step-free access throughout except for + 3 steps to a mezzanine including an information desk on the second floor (Grand Hall). On the GF, the excellent Spirit of London ride is + 9, although there's a slightly easier route going up only + 4 through an unmarked door on the right, just before the + 9. The ride has to be boarded while it is moving, and that might be a problem for some.

The Chamber of Horrors interactive exhibits involve an additional admission charge. They are situated in the basement and can also be accessed step free via a lift.

The building tends to be very crowded and the layout somewhat confusing; staff have a few problems coordinating their guidance. **Wheelchair toilets (D85 ST85)** on the second floor (Grand Hall) and on the GF just past the end of the Spirit of London ride, and before the shop.

Museum of Garden History (Tradescant Trust)

Lambeth Palace Road SE1 7LB
Tel: 020 7401-8865 *website:* www.museumgardenhistory.org
Located just south of Lambeth Bridge, and situated in an old church,

this small museum is famous for having Bligh of the Bounty buried in its garden. Entrance + 1 step to the shop, then + 2/ramped to the museum. Restaurant is ramped and on one level. Flat access to the small garden with a bumpy paved surface. Limited opening times.

Museum of London
London Wall EC2Y 5HN
Tel: 020 7600-3699 *DisEnq:* 020 7814-5777 *Fax:* 020 7600-1058 *e-mail:* info@museumoflondon.org.uk
website: www.museumoflondon.org.uk
The museum includes some fascinating displays covering the history of London, dating from the very earliest times, including wartime London, and coming right up to date with more recent developments and discoveries. A considerable effort has been made to ensure that the museum is readily accessible, and it was extensively redeveloped during 2002. When we visited, part of it was a building site.

It is located at an upper level (the Podium level of the Barbican development) at the junction between London Wall and Aldersgate Street. Chair users are asked to phone in advance on 0870 400-3000. There are three BB spaces which are reached by taking the first left turn off London Wall (going east from the roundabout), just past the MSCP. You need to reserve a space in advance, and a staff member will come down and operate the lift which will provide access to the building.

Pedestrians can either approach the museum across the Podium from the Barbican, or via the mini-foyer just opposite where Little Britain meets Aldersgate Street. At this entrance there is a lift going up to the Podium/upper level.

From here, the main museum foyer/entrance is step free, and there is an information desk, a shop and café. The museum is on four main levels, with the upper/entrance level being Level 5. The Museum measures very approximately 70m by 80m and is built around the Ironmongers' Hall. The Lord Mayor's ceremonial coach is one of the prime exhibits, but there are many other interesting things to see. Most of the exhibits, which are arranged in chronological order, starting with the oldest, are on Levels 5, 4 and 3. All are connected either by ramps or lifts. There are two main lifts, but as the site was under construction when we visited we were unable to measure them. Both should be very adequate for chair users. There is a hall for special exhibitions on Level 3. Level 6 includes the education department and meeting rooms for the Museum Friends. There are **wheelchair toilets (D70+ ST70+)** on Levels 3, 4 and 5.

National Army Museum
Royal Hospital Road, Chelsea SW3 4HT
Tel: 020 7730-0717 *website:* www.national-army-museum.ac.uk
Quiet museum with an excellent *Story of the Army* gallery. Access
has improved immensely. Entrance +3 steps with a ramped bypass.
The turnstile can be bypassed. Step-free access is possible to most of
the museum by using two lifts. The first (D120 W200 L135), on the
right after the entrance, serves the upper levels of each floor. The
other lift (D80 W100 L140), reached by a steep ramp from the GF,
serves the rest of the museum. There are +7 at the exit of the
Victorian Soldier gallery, which can be avoided by doubling back.
The lifts do not serve the small gallery and lecture theatre on the
lower level, but a platform stairlift (W70 L85) can be used to bypass
the −8, and there is another open lift to the lecture theatre. The
museum has a shop and café. The **wheelchair toilet (D80 ST110)** on
the GF is signposted.

National Gallery
Trafalgar Square WC2N 5DN
Tel: 020 7747-2885 *Fax:* 020 7747-2423
website: www.nationalgallery.org.uk
e-mail: information@ng-london.org.uk
Charge for special exhibitions. Fine collections of various painting
schools from the 13th to the early 20thC. Limited parking only
available for pre-arranged groups (*Tel:* 020 7747-2854). The current
main entrance from Trafalgar Square has +35 steps. There are flat
entrances in Orange Street or through the new Sainsbury Wing, 50m
left of the main entrance. With the pedestrianisation of the area on
the north side of the Square, it is planned to have another step-free
route through an entrance in the right-hand corner of the building
towards the National Portrait Gallery, leading into a large foyer with
café and shop, and a lift leading up to the main gallery level.
   The forty-six galleries on the GF of the main building all have flat
access. There are three lifts, each serving different sections of the
lower floor. The lifts at Orange Street (D80 W130 L115) and near the
Central Hall (D80 W105 L140) serve more galleries, and the lift (D80
W105 L140) near the main entrance gives access to the café and an
adapted toilet (D100 ST60 NKS). To gain flat access to this lift it is
necessary to avoid the Central Hall, and go via room 45. There is a
wheelchair cubicle (D80+ ST85+NKS) in both the Ladies and Gents
toilets by the Orange Street entrance.
   The Sainsbury Wing has five floors, with the middle one at

entrance level. The top floor contains the galleries which link to the main building. All floors are accessible via the lift (D115 W170 L180). The restaurant is on the first floor, near a **wheelchair toilet (D85 ST85 NKS)**. A second **wheelchair toilet (D85 ST85 NKS)** is on the lower ground floor. Signposting is good, as is the detailed floorplan available. Both shops are step free, although the smaller one has a platform stairlift (W80 L125) to bypass +5 to part of it. The Gallery has a theatre with three chair spaces at the back, and a new entrance at basement level via a lift gives access to four spaces near the front. The cinema has eight chair spaces. Induction loop in both. It also has a touch sensitive Micro Gallery. CD Rom guides are for hire, giving details of every single artefact. The building is large, with a frontage on Trafalgar Square about 200m long.

Natural History Museum
Cromwell Road, Kensington SW7 5BD
Tel: 020 7942-5000 (Mon-Fri) or 020 7942-5011 (Sat-Sun)
website: www.nhm.ac.uk
Massive museum full of models and remains, of all types of animals, plants, gems and minerals. The exhibits explain both the evolution of the planet, and how humans and other species evolved. Well presented. Most famous for the dinosaur skeletons and the model of a blue whale. The Romanesque frontage is hugely impressive, and the interior is cathedral-like, designed to show off the wonders of creation. The museum is split into the **Life Galleries** covering both existing and extinct animals, and the **Earth Galleries** (the former Geological Museum) which tell the story of the development of the earth. A whole new section is being built at the Queen's Gate end called the **Darwin Centre** with 22 million zoological specimens and opportunities for meeting museum scientists.

There are four BB spaces with time limits outside in Exhibition Road and four more across the road outside the V and A. **Prebooked parking can be arranged** in the CP at the end of Museum Lane alongside the museum off Exhibition Road (*Tel:* 020 7942-5888). A map of the museum is available at the information desk near both entrances. It is based on an isometric diagram, and it's quite difficult to follow where the lifts go (a rather important feature for the disabled visitor). There is a useful printed *Access Guide*, but little detailed information (about access) on the website. The *Access Guide* does mention all kinds of useful things, but fails to say how big the museum is!

There are three ways in. At the main entrance on Cromwell Road, there is a 40m long sloped approach, and then + 10 steps. **The entrance on Exhibition Road to the Earth Galleries provides step-free access**. If you use the Museum Lane CP, you will enter in the basement, and a lift (D110 W180 L140) brings you up to room 35.

Nearly all of the galleries are flat or ramped, but the distances involved are considerable. Using the Exhibition Road entrance, it is around 400m to the Mammals Gallery – which is one of the places that most people want to go, and it's slightly further to the Darwin Centre. The signposting is quite good, and with the map it is reasonably easy to find your way around. The Darwin Centre which has temporary (step-free) access isn't quite so easy to find. The Exhibition Road entrance has been redesigned, so that you go straight in, and the lift (D90 W100 L110) to take you up to the main GF level is away to your left bypassing the + 15 + 3 steps in front of you. In the lift you are confronted with eight bright red buttons, only three of which are relevant (the bottom three on the left). The main floor is one level up. Once on the main level (GF), you can either proceed through Gallery 60 past the long escalator to the Life Galleries, or if you want to see the Earth Galleries, take the lift which you will find by going along Gallery 60 and turning right near the end. This route is poorly signed. The Earth Galleries are on the first and second floors and are step free.

If you go through to the Life Galleries, go down through Gallery 40 to Waterhouse Way, and then along to the main entrance hall with the dinosaurs, in Gallery 10. The room numbers are clearly marked. There are some steps in the Mammals Gallery to get to the upper level, but there are instructions for finding the lift prominently placed at the bottom. It is not shown on the isometric map.

The main central lift just off Gallery 30 (near the entrance hall) leads to the first floor, with step-free access, and to the second, which only gives access to part of the gallery – the great sequoia, and the Botany Library.

There are restaurants/cafés with movable chairs and tables off Galleries 60, 35 and 11. The provision of toilets is limited, considering the size of the museum. There are **wheelchair toilets all (D70+ ST70+)** on the GF at the end of the dinosaur hall, just before Gallery 11, and en route to the mammals, off Gallery 14, and in the Darwin Centre just past the information desk. Another is in the basement and accessed by a lift (D75 W85 L120) which you reach off the Mammals Gallery through a door marked 'Woolfson Laboratories'. There is also one in the basement by the service/CP entrance. As mentioned above, the one in the Earth

Galleries was closed when we visited. The GF shops all have step-free access.

We hope that when the next phase of the Darwin Centre is completed, there will be step-free access from Queen's Gate thus reducing the distances disabled people have to go to reach some of the interesting galleries.

National Portrait Gallery

2 St Martins Place WC2H 0HE

Tel: 020 7306-0055 *Fax:* 020 7306-0056 *website:* www.npg.org.uk

Situated to the north of Trafalgar Square towards Charing Cross Road and behind the National Gallery, it houses a remarkable collection of portraits of those who have shaped British history. It has recently been extensively modernised and extended, with much improved access. One BB space can be booked through the National Gallery. The main entrance has + 2 steps, but there are alternative step-free ways in, either via the Gift Shop (25m to the left of the main doors) or using a ramped route in from Orange Street. **Inside, nearly all the galleries are accessible without steps**. There are six lifts. One (D80 W100 L150) simply links the Gift Shop with the main entrance (bypassing + 4) and the basement, which contains a café and some exhibits. The second (D80 W160 L170) goes from the main entrance to the lower GF, GF, first floor and second floor. Three lifts (D80 W100 L140) near the Orange Street entrance go to the upper floors, including the top floor where there is a restaurant with superb views. A single lift (D75 W90 L140) near the Orange Street entrance links the GF with the IT gallery.

Everywhere is step free, except the Royal Landing (+ 20 from the GF or − 17 from the first). A manually-operated stairclimber (of the Scalomobile type for manual chairs only) is available. There are **four wheelchair toilets**: in the basement **(D80 ST100 +)**; the lower GF **(D80 ST70)**; on the GF near the Orange Street entrance **(D90 ST75)**, and on the top floor by the restaurant **(D90 ST70)**. Facilities include a touch tour of various sculptures, large print guides and sound guides, induction loop in Ondaatje theatre and wheelchairs on request, as well as a good access leaflet and good signposting.

Percival David Foundation of Chinese Art

53 Gordon Square WC1H 0PD

Tel: 020 7387-3909 *website:* www.pdf.org.uk

Houses a fine collection of Chinese ceramics. Entrance + 4 steps, although if you ring in advance, they can put a ramp down. There is then flat or lift (D69 W120 L85) access to three floors of galleries. **Wheelchair toilet (D70 ST200 +)** on the third floor.

Photographers' Gallery
5 and 8 Great Newport Street WC2H 7HY
Tel: 020 7831-1772 *Textphone:* 020 7379-6057
website: www.photonet.org.uk
Small and interesting gallery with changing displays, housed in two separate buildings. No 5 has a steepish ramp, but is step free to reception, two galleries, the café and **two wheelchair cubicles**, Ladies **(D80 ST100)**, Gents **(D80 ST80)**. The print sales room and the library are +19 steps. No 8 is step free throughout, and contains another gallery and the bookshop.

Pollock Toy Museum
1 Scala Street W1P 1HL
Tel: 020 7636-3452
Admission charge. A small and fascinating museum, with entrance in Whitfield Street. It occupies two small houses joined together, with small rooms connected by narrow winding staircases. Entrance +1 step to two sections of the museum shop, linked by a narrow corridor (D65). The museum is on the first and second floors, with a minimum of +15.

Public Record Office Museum see chapter on *Places of interest.*

Queen's Gallery
Buckingham Palace, London SW1A 1AA
Tel: 020 7321-2233
website: www.royal.gov.uk
e-mail: buckinghampalace@royalcollection.org.uk
Located just south of Buckingham Palace. Admission charge and pre-booking is probably necessary. Gallery shop, ticket counter and e-gallery are all step-free on the GF. Lift (D70 W125 L150) gives step-free access to the first floor which contains all the exhibits, which are from the Queen's extensive collection. **Wheelchair toilet (D90 ST80)** under the stairs on the GF. Some rooms in the gallery are very small, but as the gallery's policy is to limit visitor numbers to avoid crowding, it is possible to see the various exhibits.

Royal Academy Of Arts
Burlington House, Piccadilly W1J 0BD
Tel: 020 7300-8000 *website:* www.royalacademy.org.uk
Admission charge. The oldest and most prestigious fine arts institution in Britain, known particularly for its summer exhibition,

although it has its own permanent collection. Two **BB** spaces in the forecourt if reserved in advance. Ramp bypasses +4 steps at the entrance. The main exhibition on the first floor can be reached by a glass lift (D80 W135 L280), which is itself worth having a look at. Lift access also to smaller second-floor galleries. Flat access to other first-floor galleries is available by passing through private rooms. Most exhibitions have taped commentaries, and there are seats available throughout the 200m route around the main gallery. Shop on first floor. Ramped access to the restaurant, and there is a **wheelchair toilet (D95 ST80)** by the Gents on the GF.

Science Museum
Exhibition Road, South Kensington SW7 2DD
Tel: 0870-870-4868 *Textphone*: 020 7942-4445 DisEnq 020 7942-4446
website: www.sciencemuseum.org.uk
One of the country's most popular museums, with some excellent 'hands on' galleries for children, including:

- 'Launch Pad' on the lower GF;
- 'Pattern Pod' on the GF;
- 'On Air' on the 3rd floor.

The museum shows centuries of continuing scientific and technological development, and includes steam engines, spacecraft and the first mechanical computers. Access has been carefully thought about, and the management have an ongoing programme to make all areas fully accessible. The museum is on seven floors, and over fifty galleries cover a total area of some eight acres. **A Guide for Disabled Visitors is available at the entrance**. The isometric map of the entrance foyer and the access to the main hall is both inaccurate and misleading. The isometric in the Eyewitness guide is much clearer. What the official map needs is an old-fashioned ground plan drawing to supplement the isometric.

There are four BB spaces directly outside the museum in Exhibition Road, and others down the road outside the other museums. Prior arrangement can be made to use the museum's own CP. Flat entrance. Just inside, on the right is an information desk. The long foyer (to the left of the entrance) can be quite confusing when it's crowded. You go along some 60m past the −8 steps down to the shop, past a ticket counter, and on towards the glass lift at the end. On your right is the main museum hall containing several old steam engines and the space exploration exhibits. The foyer is on a raised level (a sort of mezzanine) above the main floor level which is -8, bypassed by a ramp which is on the right hand side when you come to the main exhibition, well before you get to a second information desk.

There are not many seats around (although there are a few). The main hall is over 250m long, as are the floors above.

The museum is effectively in two parts. The main floors, linked by the first three pairs of lifts you come to, and the separate Wellcome Wing linked by the fourth pair of lifts. All the lifts are D100+ W150+ L150+. On the GF, the glass lifts at the end of the entrance foyer link part of the lower GF, GF, first, second and third floors. The second pair of lifts are well hidden on the right side of the main museum hall, behind a wall with a big notice saying 'Exit and Stores', just before you get to the Museum Café. These lifts link all the floors, including the fifth and sixth. After the space exhibition, the third set of lifts in the centre of the hall gives access to the basement, and floors 1 to 3. If you look very closely, there are some discreet signs pointing to various facilities, but they are so self-effacing that you can easily miss them (we did!).

Finally, at the beginning of the **Wellcome Wing**, which has step-free access from the GF, two lifts on the left give access to all the Wellcome floors (basement to Floor 3). At the upper levels, there can be problems. To make the link shown on the map as being on Level 3 you have to use the left-hand lift which goes to the mezzanine on Level 2, and then use the ramp which takes you on to the main Level 3 'Flight' area. This wasn't signed or indicated anywhere as far as we could see. The IMAX cinema has four chair spaces, and an induction loop.

There are a good number of **disabled persons' toilets** in the museum, and they are reasonably well marked on the map. They are, however, slightly variable in terms of their accessibility. The main GF one just past the second set of lifts (behind the Exit and Stores sign) was absolutely stuffed with bins when we surveyed it. There were four of them! In some of those in the (new) Wellcome Wing, the door opens inwards, although they're all D70+ ST70+. Some also have large bins which affect the ease of access if you are a chair user.

The step-free access to the **shop** is from near the second pair of lifts on the lower part of the GF. There are two cafés with movable chairs and tables on the GF, while the catering areas in the basement and on Level 3 are more suited to school parties having picnics.

Serpentine Gallery
Kensington Gardens W2 3XA
Tel: 020 7402-6075 *Fax:* 020 7402-4103
website: www.serpentinegallery.org
Located some 400m north of the Alexandra Gate and the Albert
Memorial, a small gallery all on one level with changing exhibitions
of contemporary art: four spacious rooms with a shop. The entrance
is flat. There's a **wheelchair toilet (D85 ST80)** through the main
entrance and left past the counter.

Shakespeare's Globe Exhibition and Theatre
21 New Globe Walk SE1 9DR
Tel: 020 7902-1400 BO 020 7401-9919
website: www.shakespeares-globe.org.
The theatre is a reconstruction of the open-air playhouse where
Shakespeare worked. The exhibition entrance is on the riverside past
the theatre and towards Tate Modern. It is in a huge 'Undercroft'
beneath the theatre. Ramps bypass −7−3 steps in the ticket office
area. A lift (D75 W110 L150) takes you down to the bottom level
with an extensive and well-presented exhibition covering both the
theatre of Shakespeare's time and the London in which he worked.
Theatre tours start from here, and use a second lift (D100 W200
L200) to reach the theatre above. There are **wheelchair toilets (D70 +
ST70 +)** near the first lift at the upper level, another on the bottom
level, and on the GF level near the shop and theatre foyer where the
tour finishes. All the toilet doors are quite heavy to open. Access to
theatre performances is described in the *Theatres* section.

Sherlock Holmes Museum
221b Baker Street NW1 6XE
Tel: 020 7935-8866 *website:* www.sherlock-holmes.co.uk
Admission charge. Celebratory museum of Sir Arthur Conan Doy-
le's fictional detective. Situated opposite the corner of Regent's Park,
access is difficult as this is a listed building. Entrance + 1 step, then
no exhibits but an impressive shop on GF. First floor + 17, then + 18
to the second and + 16 to the third.

Sir John Soane's Museum
13 Lincoln's Inn Fields WC2
Tel: 020 7405-2107
The house was left to the nation in 1837, with a stipulation that
nothing should be changed. Full of artefacts of this great collector,

but access is (inevitably) poor. The entrance has $+2+5+1$ steps, and 80% of the GF is flat. The other 20% is $-3+3$. There are some narrow doorways, including one W52. The basement is -17 (winding), the first floor $+27$. Even though only about 40% of the collection is visible from the GF, it is well worth a visit to step back into the dreamy and eclectic world of this great collector and architect. When one of our surveyors visited, he was not allowed to use his own wheelchair, but was requested to one of the museums small-wheeled chairs. That meant bringing a pusher. The reason given was that the corridors were too narrow, but clearly the policy has changed, because the same surveyor had visited some years before without problems.

Tate Britain
Millbank, SW1P 4RG
Tel: 020 7887-8000 *Textphone:* 020 7887-8687
website: www.tate.org.uk *e-mail:* information@tate.org.uk
Charge for special exhibitions. One of the major art collections, with roughly fifty galleries including a fine exhibition of Turners in the Clore Gallery. Parking for visitors with disabilities can be booked (020 7887-8888). CP entrance in John Islip Street opposite Bolinga Street. Using the entrance by the CP, disabled visitors are escorted to the Clore Gallery, where a public lift (D135 W175 L430) gives flat access to the main galleries through the Turner collection.

There are three pedestrian entrances. The main entrance has $+21$ steps, while the Manton entrance on Atterbury Street is accessed by a ramp. There are three BB spaces by this entrance. The flat entrance to the Clore Gallery is 50m to the right of the main entrance. From here the route to the main galleries is the same as that described above.

There is an information desk at the Manton entrance where good access guides, large print maps and a selected number of large print captions accompanying works in the collection are available. From this desk there is step-free access to the whole gallery. The café and restaurant are accessed by a ramp while the main galleries can be reached by a lift (D165 W175 L290) to the left of the desk. **Adapted toilets (D75+ ST80** inward doors) at the Clore entrance, two on the café level and one in the Linbury Galleries. There is seating available throughout. The pictures and captions are generally at a good height for wheelchair users. Wheelchair spaces are available in the auditorium and Studio One which both have an induction loop.

Tate Modern

Bankside, SE1 9TG

Tel: 020 7887-8888 *Textphone:* 020 7887-8687 *Fax:* 020 7887-8898
website: www.tate.org.uk *e-mail:* information @tate.org.uk

The gallery is housed in a huge building that used to be a power station, and exhibits art which is post-1900. Parking is restricted, but there are eight BB spaces off Hopton Street, which can be reserved in advance. The BB spaces are by the building wall, just to the right of the long ramp, and you get to them through a barrier. There's an intercom to alert the staff that you're there.

The museum can be reached either from the south bank Thames Walk, or across the Millennium Bridge from St Paul's. Southwark tube station, which is on the accessible Jubilee Line Extension, is about 600m away. If you come from the riverside, there is a flat entrance by the corner café on the GF (Level 2). This is also the easiest one to use from the BB spaces, via the walkway over the long ramp. At the West Entrance, there is a long wide slope down to the bottom level with steps and a handrail down the right hand side. At this lower level, there are the ticket offices for special exhibitions, and just inside the doors to the left there is an information point. You can get a gallery plan there, and an access leaflet. The plan takes a little getting used to. Four lifts (D120 W150 L250) go to all floors, but these can get quite busy. There are escalators as an alternative.

Although step free, the galleries are around 180m long and some 40m wide, so if you go to more than one level, **there can be long distances involved** as there is only one block of lifts. A wheelchair can be borrowed if you need one, and there are benches scattered throughout the galleries. There are many interesting and provocative exhibits. The descriptions of various exhibits are sometimes not designed for someone who is even slightly visually impaired, and some are not at a very friendly height for a chair user. There are **wheelchair toilets (D80 ST80)** on most levels, adjacent to the main toilet blocks. There are also **wheelchair toilets** in the special exhibition areas, but these are very discreetly signed, and it's easiest to ask a staff member. The ST space is blocked by a large bin in most of the toilets. There are three cafés, on Level 2, Level 4 and Level 7. In the one on Level 4 the counters are quite high. From the top floor, there's an outside balcony/gallery giving some fine views, but recently the one at the City end has been closed, severely limiting access. Special tours and facilities for visually impaired visitors, those with learning disabilities and those wanting to access reference materials available on request. Note the accessible *Founders Arms* pub on the riverside.

Theatre Museum
1e Tavistock Street WC2E 7PR
Tel: 020 7943-4700 *website:* www.theatremuseum.org
No admission charge. The main entrance is on Russell Street. The museum celebrates 400 years of British theatre with changing exhibitions. Regular guided tours and make-up demonstrations. Flat or ramped access through most of the two floors which are connected by a long ramp. GF has interactive exhibits with pulleys, but the main exhibits are in the basement. + 3 steps to play area with bean bags on the GF. **Wheelchair toilet (D80 ST70 NKS)** to the right of the entrance. Ask for the key.

Victoria and Albert Museum
Cromwell Road, South Kensington SW7
Tel: 020 7942-2000 or *RecM:* 0870-4420808 *DisEnq:* 020 7942-2197
Textphone: 0207942-2002 *website:* www.vam.ac.uk
Vast museum with 11km of galleries and literally thousands of exhibits, some of them very famous. The building measures about 250m along the Cromwell Road by 200m along Exhibition Road. Collections cover furniture, jewellery, china, prints, drawings, sculpture and dress from Britain and all over the world. There is a broad division between the galleries devoted to art and design, and those concentrating on materials and techniques. You might take advantage of the regular (free) guided tours and specialist talks.

Most London guidebooks will have a summary of what is where, and if you write in the museum will send you a detailed floor plan and an access leaflet. These can also be obtained from an information desk near either entrance. If you're making a first visit, it's really difficult to work out how to use them and, for example, which lifts go where. Not all the lifts go to all floors, and some of the upper galleries are only on one side of the building. In the description here, we will try to 'talk you through' the basic access details. Ideally, you need to choose two or three areas which might be of particular interest. You can then work out how to get there, and check your route with a member of staff when you arrive. The routes we describe should enable you to get to any part of the GF (Level 1). **On the diagram, we have marked which lifts link to which floors**.

There are four BB spaces outside the Exhibition Road entrance and four more on the other side outside the Natural History Museum Earth Galleries entrance. The main entrance in Cromwell Road is now ramped and the revolving doors can be folded back quite quickly to facilitate entry by a chair user, though you'll have

V & A Museum

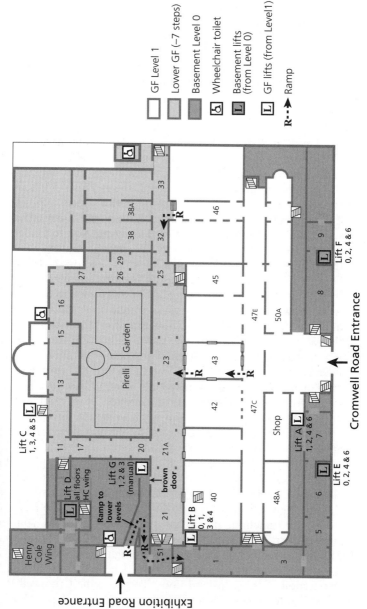

Exhibition Road Entrance

Cromwell Road Entrance

Henry Cole Wing

Lift C
1, 3, 4 & 5

Lift D
all floors
HC wing

Lift G
1, 2 & 3
(manual)

Ramp to
lower levels

brown door

Lift B
0, 1,
3 & 4

Lift A
1, 2, 4 & 6

Shop

Lift E
0, 2, 4 & 6

Lift F
0, 2, 4 & 6

Garden

Pirelli

GF Level 1

Lower GF (–7 steps)

Basement Level 0

Wheelchair toilet

Basement lifts
(from Level 0)

GF lifts (from Level1)

R···➤ Ramp

to attract the attention of a staff member. The entrance in Exhibition Road also offers step-free access. Access around the museum is quite complicated and poorly signed but, with a little planning, you can reach roughly 95% of the exhibits step free.

Starting from the Cromwell Road entrance, you are on Level 1. The foyer is spacious, but the GF involves a split level, and the whole of the area around the Pirelli Garden is lower than the front of the building (by −7 steps). There are two ramped routes to bypass the steps. As an alternative route from the foyer, the lift over to the left serves Levels 1, 2, 4 and 6 on the left side of the upper galleries.

If you want to get orientated, to understand the museum layout and the link between the two entrances, then follow this route. If you go straight ahead from the foyer, the −4 and −3 steps into and out of the Medieval Treasury are both ramped, although the first ramp is roped off because it's a bit steep, and you need to get a staff member to move the barrier. This brings you to Gallery 23, where you turn left. Alternatively, go through Gallery 48 where there is both a ramp and an open lift at the end on the left. From Gallery 23, go to 21A which has an open rectangular balcony in the ceiling. A little further along, in the wall on the right, there is a small brown door with a tiny white plaque on it. Go through this door, and it gives you access to a split ramp (to the left). If you take the ramp upwards, it leads you to the Exhibition Road entrance (go right at the top of the ramp). If you take the ramp downwards, it leads either to Galleries 1 to 7 on Level 0 (if you turn left at the end) or to the lift in the Henry Cole Wing (if you turn right).

Starting from the Exhibition Road entrance, turn right past the information desk. Then the ramp is on your left through a glass door. Go down the sloped corridor to the junction which is Y-shaped. If you turn very sharp right and go on downwards, it'll lead you either (if you then turn right at the door at the end) to the lift for the Henry Cole Wing, or (if you turn left at the end of the ramp) to Galleries 1-7 on Level 0 via a further ramp bypassing −5.

Alternatively, when you go down the first part of the ramp and come to the junction, if you go straight on, it leads you to a manually-operated service lift (accessing Levels 2 and 3, (although the lift buttons say 1 and 2). If you go through the brown door on the right of the lift, you come out on Level 1 near Gallery 21A in the lower section of the split-level floor. To get to the Cromwell Road entrance, go to Gallery 23, and use the ramps through the Medieval Treasury, or go on to the end of Gallery 32 where there's a ramp or an open lift leading up to Gallery 46.

From the GF (Upper Level 1, near the Cromwell Road entrance):

- Level 0 is reached using the ramps, through 43, or via 46/32, to get to the lower part of Level 1. Then go through the small brown door just past 21A. Alternatively use lift B, or by changing lifts using lift A, then lift E. To get to Room 8 (Level 0), you take lift A to Level 6 and then go across to lift F;
- Level 2, left, is reached from lift A, and Level 2 right by taking lift A to Level 6 and going down in lift F;
- the largest part of Level 3 is reached from lift C, and while most of it is accessible step free, the ironwork and musical instruments collections both involve a minimum of some 10-15 steps. The step-free rooms stretch from 73, via 70A, 69, and round to 84 (where there are +4 to 85). From 84 the staff can open a door for you to go through to see the jewellery in 91/93 which is protected by separate security and has revolving security doors at each end. It is also step free round through 81, 95, 99, 107 etc. There are +9 up to 111 and through to the ironwork gallery, and from 114A, −14 to 40A with the musical instruments.

Room 74 can be reached by using lift G which has a heavy manual door. Flat access can be arranged in advance to the National Art Library (Rooms 77/78) from room 74;

- Level 4, left, is reached using lift A, Level 4 right is reached using lift A to Level 6, then lift F
- Level 5 has the lecture theatre which is normally reached via +21, although there is now lift access from lift C.
- Level 6 is reached using lifts A, E or F, and is a floor where there is a link between the left and right sides of the main building;
- the **Henry Cole Wing** is reached using lift D, accessed from Level 0. In the building, on Level 2 there are +5 to rooms 207-9, −4 to 202 and +6 to 220. Level 3 has −3 to all rooms except 305, and Levels 4, 5 and 6 have flat access except for +8 to the Panorama of Rome on Level 4.

There are **wheelchair toilets (D70+ ST70+)** in the following places:

- on the GF (Level 1), off Room 33 and off Room 16 – reached in both cases via the ramp or lift at the end of 46;
- on Level 0 (the basement), between the bottom of the big ramp, to the right towards the shop, where there are two cubicles just before the entrance to both the Ladies and Gents;

- on Level 2, left side, off Room 56;
- on Level 3, off the lift lobby leading to the Whiteley Silver Galleries;
- on Level 4, left side, off Room 123.

The **restaurants** in the Gamble Room (Level 1), and the one beneath the Henry Cole Wing (Level 0) both have flat access. The **Pirelli Garden** is a pleasant area for sitting outside in the summer, accessed step free from room 23 on the lower part of Level 1.

Wallace Collection
Hertford House, Manchester Square W1U 3BN
Tel: 020 7563-9500 *Textphone:* 020 7935-9570
website: www.wallace-collection.org.uk
Situated on the north side of Manchester Square, this is an extensive private art collection bequeathed to the nation by Lady Wallace in 1897. Two BB spaces for which it is advised to phone in advance. There is an excellent access guide called *Welcome to the Wallace Collection*. It includes a local map showing BB spaces. Entrance has + 3 steps bypassed by ramp to reception area where a remote control device which opens awkward doors can be obtained. Shop and restaurant, accessible by ramp, on GF, as well as lift (D80 W120 L155) to LGF and first floors. **Wheelchair toilet (D95 ST75)** on the LGF through two doors. Frequent tours. There is a braille map, and the audio guides have a T setting for those with a hearing aid. Lecture theatre on the LGF with two chair spaces. An induction loop can be provided if you ask in advance.

War Museum see write-up on Imperial War Museum.

Wellington Museum (Apsley House)
149 Piccadilly W1J 7NT
Tel: 020 7499-5676
Admission charge. The Duke of Wellington's former residence, known as 'Number 1 London'. It is situated on the north side of Hyde Park Corner, and somewhat isolated because of the swirl of traffic on almost all sides. You can now reach the house step free across the roads from Grosvenor Place. The easiest alternative approach is from Hyde Park. Parking can be booked in the forecourt. The entrance has + 7 steps then − 9 to the lift (D85 W100 L105) which serves the other two floors. The main rooms are on the first floor and are step free. In the basement there are − 3 to a small gallery. Audio guides are available.

Outer London

Bethnal Green Museum of Childhood
Cambridge Heath Road, Bethnal Green E2 9PA
Tel: 020 8980-2415
A museum with all kinds of things of interest to children, and various holiday activities. A parking space at the back can be booked in advance. Entrance +4 steps but there is a flat way in at the back. There is a goods lift (D110+ W100+ L100+) which serves all four floors. There is a mezzanine level with ramped access from the ground floor.

The coffee shop is on the GF, as is the **wheelchair toilet (D80 ST80)**.

Dulwich Picture Gallery
Gallery Road, Dulwich Village London SE21 7AD
Tel: 020 8693-5254 *Fax:* 020 8299-8700
website: www.dulwichpicturegallery.org.uk
Admission charge. This building, designed by Sir John Soane, provides a wonderful setting for an art gallery, with large and peaceful grounds. CP for disabled visitors reached from Gallery Road. It does not have marked spaces but can take approximately six cars. Ring in advance to book a space. Main entrance from College Road +3 steps, bypassed by a ramp to the right of the entrance. There is an alternative ramped access from Gallery Road. Step free everywhere, except −2+2 to the mausoleum of the gallery's founders.

Café by the main entrance. **Wheelchair toilet (D85 ST80)** near the café.

Geffrye Museum
Kingsland Road, Shoreditch, London E2 8EA
Tel: 020 7739-9893 *Fax:* 020 7729-5647 *e-mail:* info@geffrye-museum.org.uk *website:* www.geffrye-museum.org.uk
Situated between Pearson Street and Cremer Street, the museum, built as almshouses in 1715, now details the history of the evolution of interior design.

Parking is very difficult although we were told that cars with **BB** badges may park in the 'Coaches' area on Kingsland Road right outside the main gates. The −3 steps at the main entrance can be bypassed by ramps 20m away on either side. Ramped entrance to the museum itself, then apart from a threshold to a small seating area, the museum has 100% flat access. The lift (D80 W100 L145) is at the top of the stairs in a modern extension at the far right of the building, past the café. This takes you to a downstairs exhibit which is step free. **Wheelchair toilet (D90 ST90)** on lower floor to the left of the lift.

The garden at the rear of museum has step-free access.

Horniman Museum and Gardens

100 London Road, Forest Hill SE23 3PQ
Tel: 020 8699-1892 *website:* www.horniman.ac.uk
A museum about world arts, craft, religion and history. The entrance is 50m to the left of the main building and reached by a steep hill through the gardens. Limited parking on site is available if requested in advance. The entrance and access throughout the museum is step free. A lift (D120 W130 L200 +) serves all three floors. The aquarium can be reached from the LG floor via a platform stairlift (W69 L80) or from the GF by a door at the back of the Natural History Gallery. **Wheelchair toilets** by the entrance on the GF **(D75 ST145)**, on the lower GF **(D75 ST130)** reached from the main atrium, and in the Library (not seen). There is another **wheelchair toilet (D70 ST120)** in the gardens near the museum. A café on the GF serves light snacks.

Kenwood House see chapter on *Places of interest.*

Kew Bridge Steam Museum see chapter on *Places of interest.*

National Maritime Museum see chapter on *Places of interest.*

Orleans House Gallery see chapter on *Places of interest.*

Royal Air Force Museum see chapter on *Days out.*

Whitechapel Art Gallery

80-82 Whitechapel High Street, London E1 7QX.
Tel: 020 7522-7888 *Fax:* 020 7377-1685 *Textphone:* 020 7522-7854
e-mail: info@whitechapel.org *website:* www.whitechapel.org
Just next to the north entrance to Aldgate East tube station, this is a fine exhibition space for modern art. Parking may be difficult, but there is apparently one BB space outside the gallery (to book it call 020 7481-5955). There is an NCP in Spreadeagle Yard about 75m from the gallery. Step-free access from the high street, with Zwemmers art

bookshop inside on your right, information desk on the left and gallery ahead. An *Access Guide* is available. There are three floors all of which can be reached through a service lift (D200+ W200+ L300+) operated by staff. Flat access to the whole of the first floor including the restaurant. **Adapted toilet (D85 ST65)** on the second floor. Staff are helpful, and large-print guides and audiotapes are available.

William Morris Gallery
Lloyd Park, Forest Road, London E17 4PP
Tel: 020 8527-3782
Situated 100m west off 'The Bell' junction with the A112, just after the turn-off to Bedford Road. A listed building celebrating the Victorian designer and craftsman who was also a great socialist. He is of particular interest to us as some of the planning for this book took place in a pub named the *William Morris*. The gallery is attached to an attractive public park. There are some parking spaces within the grounds as well as a CP on Bedford Road, but there are no BB spaces. The main entrance has +4 steps which can be bypassed by a portable ramp. From the foyer there is step-free access to all of the GF, where 75% of the collection is housed. +25 to first floor, which has a few paintings. No lift. Toilets on GF, no wheelchair toilet. There is a public **wheelchair toilet (D75 ST75)** outside the main entrance on Forest Road.

Wimbledon Lawn Tennis Museum
Church Road, Wimbledon SW19 5AE
Tel: 020 8947-2825.
Admission charge. Part of the All England Lawn Tennis and Croquet Club. Parking available inside the gates with advance warning. Step free via a lift (D76 W103 L130) to museum and shop which are on the second floor. **Adapted toilet (D75 ST105** but with an inward opening door) opposite the cash desk. Tea room on the GF, with −4 steps or a ramp from outside the building, or −5 with a platform stairlift from inside. On request chair users can be shown the Centre Court but there are −5+9 steps from the 1st floor. There is an induction loop in the audio-visual area. For details of the Championships, see the chapter on *Sport*.

Days out

Around London there are numerous castles, country houses, gardens, theme parks, and the extensive developments in the Lee Valley. The variety is immense and we have included just a small selection of places. We describe first those places outside the North and South Circular ring roads, then those beyond the M25, and finally facilities in the Lee Valley.

There is an excellent guide, updated annually, on *Facilities for Disabled and Visually Handicapped Visitors at National Trust Properties* available from the NT, 36 Queen Anne's Gate SW1H 9AS (*Tel:* 020 7222-9251). The NT have gone to some lengths to improve the access at their properties.

Many places charge for entry, although there are commonly reductions for chair users. The two theme parks listed (Chessington and Thorpe Park) have a substantial entrance charge, after which the rides are all free. As a result it's probably worth making it a whole day's visit.

Beyond the North and South Circular roads

Chessington

Chessington World of Adventures
Leatherhead Road, Chessington, Surrey KT9 2NE
Tel: 0870 444-7777 *website:* www.chessington.com
A substantial theme park which has developed from what used to be a small zoo. Besides the zoo, there are many rides, a pub, a playground, cafés and numerous other attractions. Queues for the rides will be much shorter if you get there early. Closed during the winter months.

The main CP is well signed off the A243, and has twenty-two BB spaces near the entrance. As the CP is huge, these are of considerable value. Flat/ramped access throughout the 35 acre site, with undulating paths that are mainly tarmac. A limited number of wheelchairs are available for hire, requiring a substantial deposit. Phone first to book.

They provide a very useful *Guide for Guests with Disabilities* which describes access to the rides, and to restaurants and toilets. In order to get easy access to some of the rides, often via the exit, you can get a special wristband from the Medical Centre (located behind Tomb Blaster in the Forbidden Kingdom). The majority of the rides have ramped access, but virtually all have + 1 or + 2 to get into the cars or carriages, and this is not mentioned in the leaflet. All the rides require transfer out of a wheelchair, and you need a friend or carer to effect this. To get to five out of the twenty-two rides you must be able to walk unaided, but these are generally the most demanding/vomit inducing ones(!). Certain height restrictions apply on some of the rides, the largest minimum being 1m 40cm. People with spinal problems would need to be cautious. There are numerous cafés and restaurants with step-free access and movable tables and chairs. Six disabled persons' toilets are listed in the information leaflet. Most have a small lip or threshold at the door. Only two are **wheelchair toilets (D70 + ST70 +)** located by the South admissions turnstiles, and next to *McDonald's* in Transylvania.

There are **adapted toilets:**

- by the turnstiles at North admissions **(D75 ST52** and inward opening door**)**;
- by the Chessington Shop in Market Square **(D95 ST68)**;
- by the Medical Centre in Forbidden Kingdom **(D75 ST42)**;
- in *KFC/Pizza Hut* in Market Square **(D85 ST75** but blocked by two large bins**)**.

Chislehurst

Chislehurst Caves
Caveside Close, off Old Hill, Chislehurst, Kent BR7 5NB
Tel: 020 8467-3264
An extraordinary complex of caves, cut through chalk and flint. Exhibits include part of an Ichthyosaurus fossil, and an area associated with the Druids and Romans. During World War II the caves were used as a massive air-raid shelter with thousands of people living there. You can see the church and hospital, and where people kept their belongings by their bunk beds.

CP 50m away; rail station about 300m. At the entrance to the caves there's a gate (D68). Note that even the short tour will take you about 1km, with no seats. Inside, the caves are cool (always 8°C) and access is step free, although the surface is really rough and bumpy in places. Even the hardiest chair user would need a good pusher.

Ramp at the main door to the ticket office and café. **Adapted toilet (D70 + ST57)** off the café area with flat access.

Enfield

Forty Hall Museum
Forty Hill, Enfield, Middx EN2 9HA
Tel: 020 8363-8196
A small museum of fine art and local history set in pleasant grounds. Two BB spaces immediately outside the house. Main entrance +2 steps, side entrance +1, and there is a ramp available. The GF, including the tea-room, is flat; the first floor has +22. **Wheelchair toilet (D75 ST110)** in a toilet block 20m from the main entrance.

Hendon

Royal Air Force Museum
Grahame Park Way, Kingsbury NW9 5LL
Tel: 020 8205-2266
Britain's national museum of aviation housing one of the world's finest collections of historic aircraft. Large CP. The bulk of the museum is in the Main Aircraft Hall and the Bomber Command Hall. Flat entrance and step-free access almost everywhere, except to the chapel (+1 step) and to one small exhibition (+2). There is ramped access to a flight simulator, and a theatre with two chair spaces. There are galleries on the first floor, reached by lift (D78 W140 L120), as well as a cinema with room for chair users at the back. The **wheelchair toilet (D90 ST70)** is between the two halls, next to the Gents.

The separate Battle of Britain Hall has two flat entrances, one to the display galleries and one to the restaurant, again, step free throughout. Lift (D85 W110 L145) to the first floor of display galleries. There is a mezzanine level containing a 'Sunderland Flying Boat', which is +13 from the GF. The restaurant contains a second **wheelchair toilet (D90 ST85)**.

Richmond and Kingston

Ham House
Ham Street, Ham, Surrey TW10 7RS
Tel: 020 8940-1950 *e-mail:* hamhouse@ntrust.org.uk.
Magnificent house by the river, built in 1610. CP (only for BB holders) in the forecourt. The main entrance has +4+5 steps which can be bypassed by a stairclimber (you should apparently phone in advance to use this) then +1+1. The house is on three floors, with a

small lift (D67 W85 L84) to the basement and first floor, bypassing −13 and +27 respectively. Most areas on the GF have +1.

The shop on the right-hand side of the house has step-free access. The route to the restaurant bypassing −5 is signposted, with a ramp to get inside. Paths around the gardens are gravelled, and you may prefer to use the grass. There are plenty of seats and wheelchairs available for use. **Wheelchair toilet (D85 ST80)** opposite the shop and well signed.

Hampton Court Palace and Gardens

East Molesey, Surrey KT8 9AU
Tel: 0870 752-7777 *website:* www.hrp.org.uk
A magnificent riverside Tudor palace with 50 acres of formal gardens surrounded by extensive wooded parklands. The main palace covers an area of about 200m by 100m. CP, with eight BB spaces, approached from the main entrance near the end of the bridge. Hampton Court rail station is about 400m away across the bridge, and has +2 steps with a ramped alternative.

You can walk through some of the courtyards in the palace, and there are routes through the gardens at the side. The main formal gardens are behind the palace, and are free to enter, and although the area is generally flat many of the paths consist of thick crunchy gravel. There is a useful leaflet entitled *Palace Tour for Visitors Avoiding Stairs*.

To see the palace, the ticket office (with +2 steps) is near the CP and main entrance. The garden shop near the back entrance is step free, and also sells entrance tickets, but it is some 500m from the main entrance, and about half the distance is across crunchy gravel. Note that only six chair users are allowed on the first floor of the palace at any one time in case of the need for an emergency evacuation.

From the main entrance, visitors proceed through the Base Court and Clock Court, both of which are cobbled. The information centre is at the far side of Clock Court. There is step-free access to the Chapel Royal off Clock Court. There are a substantial number of stairs involved on the way to the main sections of the palace. Disabled visitors can use the lift (D90 W140 L190) by the far left corner of Fountain Court, although this means taking a slightly different route from other visitors. All four main sections of the palace can then be seen with step-free access, with warders opening any necessary doors. The only step is −1 to the video room. The Wolsey Rooms and Renaissance Picture Gallery are +24 −1 from the courtyard, but warders will unlock a door in the King's Apartments on request from where they are only −3.

The Tudor Kitchens are at ground level, with +1 at the entrance in Clock Court, then −4 to see a model of the palace and a commentary. These steps can be bypassed by using an entrance in Base Court with −1−1 and then step-free access to most of the kitchens. The wine cellar is −8 from the kitchens, but most of it can be seen from the top of the stairs. The Coffee Shop/Café in the kitchens has a ramped entrance, bypassing +1. The seating is −2 but is step free by coming in through the exit.

The Gift Shop is off Clock Court, and the easiest access is via +1+1+1 from a door by **wheelchair toilet (D70 + ST70 +)** between Base and Clock Courts. There's another **wheelchair toilet (D85 ST80)** through a door leading to the Ladies off Fountain Court.

Other noteworthy details are:

- the **Tiltyard Tea Rooms** have step-free access;
- the **Tudor Tennis (Real Tennis) Court** has −1 at the entrance and +1 at the exit. It can only be reached across 100m+ of gravel;
- the **Privy Gardens** have step-free routes, and within them both the **Vine** and the **Mantegna Exhibition** have step-free access;
- the **Maze** is in an area called The Wilderness, and is step free, although some of its tarmac paths are quite narrow with tightish turns. Our survey team managed to get lost in it for half an hour;
- **adapted toilet (D80 ST40)** 150m to the east of the Maze, and a **wheelchair toilet (D85 ST90)** about 300m to the south of the Maze.

We were told that the funding is in place for a five-year development plan to improve access, including laying flagstones to provide cobble-free routes and a scheme to improve access from the railway station.

Kew Gardens

Royal Botanic Gardens, Kew, Richmond TW9 3AB
Tel: 020 8332-5655
website: www.kew.org.uk *e-mail:* info@kew.org.uk

Admission charge. The Royal Botanic Gardens is a world leader in plant research and conservation. The gardens are large, covering over 300 acres, and with distances of over 1.5km. Wheelchairs are available for use, but if you want one it is best to ring in advance (*Tel:* 020 8332-5121). There are quite a few benches and seats, and also some shelters in the event of rain. There are BB spaces near the Main Gate off Kew Green, and in the CP by the Brentford Ferry gate.

Three of the entrances are along the Kew Road, one off Kew Green and one by the river and CP. The area is fairly flat, and there are tarmac paths through much of the gardens. **The Visitor Centre is by the Victoria Gate** on Kew Road, opposite Lichfield Road. It comprises the main information point, a shop and **a wheelchair toilet (D85 ST70)**. There is a ramp to bypass + 3 steps. They have a large print map. The leaflet *Welcome to Kew* gives information on which plants are in bloom at different times of the year and gives advice on which places are 'inaccessible' as well as showing the location of ramps.

The *Kew Explorer* mini-train runs a regular hop-on/hop-off service around the outside of the gardens. It has one wheelchair space, but can also take folded chairs and buggies. For more information, *Tel:* 020 8332-5615. In addition, a free *Discovery Tour* in a special bus which can accommodate up to twelve chair users is available. This must be booked in advance on *Tel:* 020 8332-5643.

Going round clockwise on the map from the riverside (Brentford) gate:

- **White Peaks** contains a shop, café and art space. **Wheelchair toilet (D80 ST70)** on the other side of the art space, through double doors;
- **Kew Palace** was closed for restoration when we visited. It has + 2 + 1 at the entrance and + 11 + 3 + 11 to the first floor. The route to the 17thC garden is via some bumpy cobbled ramps (bypassing steps). It is hoped that access will have been improved when it reopens. **Wheelchair toilet (D75 ST90)** nearby;
- **Orangery shop and restaurant**, both + 2 but with ramped bypass. **Adapted toilet (D75 ST68)** around the back;
- **Gallery**, + 2 at the entrance;
- **Alpine House**, ramped access;
- **Princess of Wales Conservatory** gives a unique glimpse of tropical flora in a house divided into ten habitats. Although the main route is flat, some parts can only be reached via stepped ramps (one step at a time);
- **Museum No 1** plants and people exhibition;
- By the Cumberland Gate there's an **adapted toilet (D80 ST42)**;
- **Waterlily House**, with a ramp bypassing + 4. Hot!
- **Palm House**, built in 1850. A ramp bypasses + 5, then mainly flat. Spiral staircase to marine display (− 26) and to gallery (+ 52). Hot, and possibly difficult for someone with asthma;
- **Temperate House**, a ramp bypasses + 9 + 3. Spiral stairs to the gallery (+ 45);

- **Marianne North Gallery**, a ramp now bypasses the $+5+5+1$ steps up to Victorian paintings of plants and landscapes. Flat inside;
- **Wheelchair toilet (D75 ST85)** between the gallery and the Lion Gate. Unisex, though signed as for Gents;
- **The Pavilion restaurant/café**, flat access. **Adapted toilet (D70 ST55)**;
- **Evolution House**, which opened in 1995, takes you on a journey from Precambrian times, over 500 million years ago right through to the present. Step free throughout, including the shop. The surface is mainly smooth, except for some large 'footprints' set in the path
- **Wheelchair toilets (D80 ST70)** over towards the lake.

Kingston has a town centre which has been extensively redeveloped, see chapter on *Shops*.

Osterley Park House
Jersey Road, Isleworth, Middx TW7 4RB
Tel: 020 8232-5050
Fine neo-classical house set in a large park. The entrance to the park is off the A4 via Thornbury Road. CP some 300m from the house, and there is a shuttle bus. It is possible to reserve a parking space by the house itself.

The entrance is $+10+10+1+3$ steps, leading directly to the first floor. A Stairclimber is available, which should preferably be pre-booked. Most of the rooms are on the first floor, but there's also the GF (-23) and second floor ($+36$).

On the right of the house the shop has $+1$/ramped, and the tea room and information desk have flat access. **Wheelchair toilet (D95 ST150)** behind the shop. Wheelchairs available, and on some days there are powered buggies for use in the grounds. Ring first to confirm.

Richmond Park
Park Office, Holly Lodge, Richmond Park, Richmond, Surrey TW10 5HS
Tel: 020 8948-3209 *website:* www.royalparks.gov.uk
The park, to the west of London, provides a huge area (over 2000 acres) of rough but attractive open ground and is well-known for its herds of deer. Parts are wooded but the park is mainly grassy and hilly. It was created by Charles I, and given over for public use by

Edward VII in 1910. It's definitely a place to go to by car as there's no public transport in or through the park. There is a road running all the way round and several entrances and CPs, whose surfaces are uneven and gravelly. **Refreshments** are available near the Roehampton Gate and at Pembroke Lodge (between the Richmond and Ham Gates) with step-free access. The **Isabella Plantation** contains a magnificent collection of azaleas. Even out of season it's a lovely place, with a network of paths passing small streams and waterfalls. Most chair users would need a little assistance to get round. The main CPs for the plantation are about 300m away over rough ground. There are BB spaces in a special CP reached from the Ham Gate and near Peg's Pond.

In the park, there are **wheelchair toilets (all D70+ ST70+ NKS)** by the Kingston Gate, Robin Hood Gate, Roehampton Gate and Sheen Gate, and there's another in the CP at Pembroke Lodge.

Pembroke Lodge is surrounded by level tarmac paths, and offers fine views over the river from an outside part of the restaurant. CP off the road with six BB spaces. You can drive up to the Lodge if you need to. A poorly-signed **wheelchair toilet (D70+ ST70+)** outside the Lodge is at the back of the main toilet block. The area is particularly attractive during May with the rhododendrons. Near the **Roehampton Gate** there is ramped access to the Pavilion restaurant. There are some awkward gates in the area designed to keep the deer out.

Thorpe Park
Staines Road, Chertsey, Surrey KY16 8PN
Tel: 01932-562633 *website:* www.thorpepark.com
A leisure park for the family which is increasingly catering for older children and teenagers, featuring logflumes and rollercoasters. The signposts along the A320 always seemed to appear at the last minute. Admission charge. Our survey team was unimpressed by the fact that we had to pay the full price of admission just to make our brief assessment. **A comprehensive guide for visitors with disabilities is available**, although this is simply a listing with advice about accessibility. Signage on-site was relatively poor.

Large CP with BB spaces to the right of the entrance. Once inside it is generally flat or ramped, but is quite big, covering about 1km. Wheelchairs are available by the main entrance.

The first thing you come to is the upper level of the 'Dome', with a restaurant, bar, and shops, all with flat access. There are numerous eating places throughout the complex.

Access to many of the rides is very difficult. It is the policy of the management, however, that, although some rides are not recommended, if you are with friends who can assist you, it is your choice as to which rides you go on – and that is something that we thoroughly approve of. Although the access guide produced by the management is useful, it does not detail the steps involved.

There are **wheelchair toilets (D70 + ST70 +)**:

- opposite *Burger King* in the Canada Creek;
- behind the Thorpe Park Shop in the Octopus Garden;
- on the lower floor of the Dome, accessed from the beach area;
- outside the complex just before the entrance point (to the left).

There are **adapted toilets**:

- on the upper floor of the Dome (where the door width was potentially restricted by a grab bar);
- opposite Detonator in Calypso Quay;
- near the Farm Gift Shop.

Outside the M25

Bedfordshire

Whipsnade Wild Animal Park
near Dunstable, Bedfordshire
Tel: 01582-872171 *website:* www.whipsnade.co.uk
On the B4540 and well signed from J9 on the M1. A large zoo on the edge of the Chiltern Hills, with some species roaming freely. There's a big CP about 100m from the main entrance on the right, but you can take your car and drive round the main circuit (a distance of about 2km), which is undoubtedly the best way to see the park. It's a good idea to buy the *Park Guide and Map*, as the free map gives limited information.

Many of the animals can be seen from the road or from tarmac paths, and there is parking near some of the pens. There are a few rough and hilly paths, difficult if it's just been raining; to get to some places a chair user would need a strong pusher. The **train** which goes round most of the site has two coaches each providing three wheelchair spaces. There's just a 7cm gap between platform and train. This is a good way to get an overview, and you'll see some things you cannot see from a car.

Attractions include the Discovery Centre which has step-free access (although there is −1 step at the exit). Some 80% is visible to a chair user. There is step-free access to arenas 1 and 2 at the Sea Lion House, and space at the front for chair users. The two gift shops and two cafés are also step free.

There are **three wheelchair toilets (D80+ ST80+)** shown on the guide book map. One is by the Discovery Centre, one by the Café on the Lake, and the third by the Reindeer Enclosure. There are **wheelchair cubicles (D80 ST100)** in the M/F toilets near the main Gift Shop.

Berkshire

Windsor and Windsor Castle are a great draw for visitors with the riverside, the castle, the Great Park and Eton just across the river. By car it is some 50km from central London. Alternatively you can take a Network SouthEast train to Windsor and Eton Riverside, a station with flat access but situated at the bottom of Castle Hill (and it is a long steep hill); or take a Western Region train to Windsor Central (changing at Slough), which is higher up and nearer the castle. Only the westbound platform at Slough is step free.

Tourist Office
24 High Street, Windsor SL4 1LH
Tel: 01753-743900 *website:* www.windsor.gov.uk
Step-free access. We were told that there is a disabled person's toilet on the first floor (presumably with lift access!). The *Access Guide to Windsor and Maidenhead* is available as a handout, but this is mainly for residents. It will tell you where there are some wheelchair toilets in the area and give some details about parking. There's a *Shopmobility* (*Tel:* 01753 622-330) in Bachelors Acre off Peascod Street with an Information Point beside the Library. Windsor Central Station has flat access. In the forecourt there's a lively shopping and café/restaurant area.

Windsor Castle
Tel: 020 7321-2233, the central number for the Royal Collection
website: royal.gov.uk.
Parking in the vicinity of the castle is difficult and the main CPs are at the bottom of the hill. Unfortunately no provisions can be made for disabled people to park inside the castle grounds, even though there is space in the Middle Ward. There's a CP in the Central

Station, and three BB spaces on the High Street about 150m from the castle. Quite a good ploy is to use the CP close to the coach park (which is well signed), and use the lift (D70+ W70+ L70+) up to the Central Station. Access to the castle grounds is generally fairly good, although it's hilly and big. Most chair users would need a pusher. To see most of it you have to go 400/500m from the top of Thames Street. There are cobbles by the main gate, but most of the paths are then tarmac. The courtyard areas are largely accessible to chair users.

St George's Chapel has superb perpendicular architecture and houses the tombs of George VI and of the Queen Mother. Entrance +2+1 steps. Alternative flat access from the north entrance. Inside, there are 3 single steps which were not ramped when we visited. One side chapel has −3 and D55.

Albert Memorial Chapel, with beautiful marbled walls, has +2−2 inside, avoided by ignoring the one-way system.

Tickets for entrance to the castle including the **State Apartments**, are obtained from the Admission Centre which is just past the main castle gate on the right. You then go up the hill and into the castle grounds near the Round Tower.

The main route is then via the North Terrace and +20 to the China Museum followed by a further +28 to the State Apartments. **It is possible to bypass these steps using an entrance from Engine Court**. A ramp bypasses +2 and leads to the China Museum level, then a lift (D80 W100 L105) with a 90° turn on exit takes you to the State Apartments. There is then step-free access, and you can get a good view of the area damaged by the fire and since restored. Chair users are not allowed into the newly-opened apartments in the East Wing, even though there are only about 5 steps en route.

There are **two wheelchair toilets (D80 ST90 NKS)**, on the right hand side of the route up from the Admissions Centre to the entrance. Other **wheelchair toilets (D85 ST70 NKS)** are located in Engine Court, next to the shop, and another **(D85 ST80)** is on the north terrace to the left of the Doll's House entrance.

The **Gallery** is +7+2+1 from the north terrace, but there is an alternative step route. Ask a warden for assistance.

In Windsor itself, there is a **wheelchair toilet (D85 ST80 NKS)** in Windsor Station between *La Tasca* and *Costa Coffee*.

Eton College Chapel is nearby (over half a mile on foot, but considerably further by car). Gravelled or cobbled access to the front entrance, then +5+7+5+5+2 steps, and +1 in the main body of the chapel. The general area of Eton College school is flat and well worth a visit. Visiting is curtailed during the school term, and if you want to find out when it is open *Tel:* 01753671-224. If you make contact in advance, there's a platform stairlift around the back which it should be possible to use.

About 75m further on there's the cloister, via cobbles and −1. There are then +2 to the GF of the Brewhouse. Stairs to the upper levels. In the cloister the museum has −1, with a video presentation. **Wheelchair toilet (D80 ST75).**

Savill Gardens

Windsor Great Park. *Enquiries to:* Keeper of the Gardens, Crown Estate Office, The Great Park, Windsor, Berks
Tel: 01753-860222 *website:* www.savillgarden.co.uk
These are some delightful and varied gardens, covering some thirty-five acres of woodland stretching over a km from the entrance. The terrain is variable and is hilly in places. Well signposted. Large CP with four BB spaces and a slightly gravelly surface.

Ramped access to the main entrance, labelled 'Savill Garden Entrance'. The paths through the gardens are mainly tarmac, although some of the routes are grassed. The Temperate House is step free. **Wheelchair toilet (D80 ST85)** with a high pedestal, on the right just after the entrance. The shop alongside has flat access, and sells a wide range of plants as well as gifts and books. There's an excellent restaurant/tea room, with a splendid view, about 60m from the garden entrance/shop. It has a small threshold at the entrance, and some outdoor seating. **Adapted cubicles (D70 ST70** but inward opening doors) in the toilets round to the right from the restaurant.

Legoland

Windsor, Berkshire SL4 4AY
Tel: 01753-626111 *Fax:* 01753-626160 *website:* www.legoland.co.uk
Some 3km from Windsor off the B3022, and well signed. A large and impressive theme park covering about 800m by 600m. Admission charge. CP with more than fifty BB spaces about 100m from the entrance. The park is built on a hillside, with the entrance near the top. Disabled visitors can make their way gently downwards via various rides and attractions, and then take the **Hill Train** back to the top. The train is step free to get on board, but there is a 10cm gap. It includes a compartment that can take up to four chair users. There is a comprehensive *Special Needs Guide* to be used in conjunction with the standard *Park Guide* which has a map. The *Special Needs Guide* is

generally helpful and positive. It does, however, include a couple of references to the need for 'official documentation' to prove (for example) your inability to join a queue. We hope that this is included just to cover the operators in the event of people making unreasonable claims relating to special needs, and that such documentation would not normally be asked for. For quite a number of the rides, chair users would need a friend with them who can assist with transfer. For some rides, you would need full upper-body control. These things are well explained in the leaflet, and our impression is that the staff are generally both helpful and positive. There are chair spaces if you want to see any of the shows. The Ferris Wheel and Adventurers' Express are both fully wheelchair accessible.

All the main cafés/restaurants and shops have step-free access.

Each of the six toilet blocks marked on the map has at least one **adapted toilet**. The guide claims that there are two disabled persons' toilets in each block, but variations in design (for example some only have ST60 and some have inward opening doors) mean that **adapted toilets** is a better description.

Buckinghamshire

Bekonscot Model Village
Warwick Road, Beaconsfield, Bucks HP9 2PL
Tel: 01494-672919 *website:* www.bekonscot.com
A remarkable miniature 'world', dating from the 1930s, with an enormous amount of detail, including a working model railway. Closed in winter. Well signed from the M40, Junction 2, except the last turning into Warwick Road. There are BB spaces in the CP by the church, 120m from the entrance. The village includes rather narrow and slightly hilly tarmac paths and bridges, in keeping with the 'model' concept. We were told that the paths had been slightly widened, and can now accommodate a chair 75cm wide. There are wheelchairs available for use, but they are not currently suitable for self-propelling. The route around the village is about 300m long, and there's a tea shop about halfway round. Two new **wheelchair toilets** are due to be built in 2003. A really interesting visit for children.

Hertfordshire

St Albans
St Albans is about 40km north of London. It has a combination of both old and modern shopping facilities (in and around the Malt-

ings), a cathedral and unique Roman remains in Verulamium. Some parts of the city, such as St Peter's Street and High Street are hilly, and some streets are cobbled. The various sites are some way apart, and the best way to come is by car. If you come by train, the station is more than 1km from the city. There are several wheelchair toilets, including in the Maltings, and at the station on Platform 1. The main sites are shown on the diagram.

Tourist Information Office
Town Hall, Market Place, St Albans AL3 5DJ
Tel: 01727-864511
The Town Hall is at the end of St Peter's Street and the office is step free. They have some literature about local attractions, and their mini-guide indicates which of them have a nearby disabled persons' toilet.

St Albans Cathedral
Sumpter Yard, St Albans AL1 1BY
Tel: 01727-860780
The abbey church can be approached from three directions. The first, for pedestrians only, is via the Waxhouse Gate which is off the High Street opposite the clock tower. By going to the left (east) around the end of the abbey to the large cedar tree, there is flat access. The second way in is from Holywell Hill into Sumpter Yard, where there is limited parking. The third route, through the west entrance by way of George Street and Romeland has $+2+1+5$ steps.

Once inside, there are several small groups of steps (up to 5 max) but these are nearly all ramped, giving step-free access to about 90% of the interior. The shop, bookstall, refectory and tea shop all have flat/ramped access. **Adapted toilet (D80 ST57)** to the right of the entrance, in the South Presbytery aisle with ramped access from the South Transept. There is a touch-and-hearing centre in the South Quire aisle. Ask a verger for a key. There are normally wheelchairs available for use in the cathedral. There are grassy slopes around the abbey but the paths include the odd step or so.

Museum of St Albans
Hatfield Road, St Albans AL1 3RR
Tel: 01727-819340
Adjacent CP. A side entrance opened on request bypasses $+2$ steps. The staff will open locked doors, giving step-free access to the GF. First floor $+9+9$, second floor $+5+7$. **Wheelchair toilet (D70 ST95)** on the ground floor.

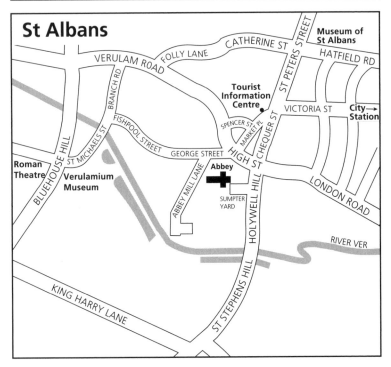

St Albans

Museum of St Albans

CATHERINE ST

ST PETERS STREET

HATFIELD RD

VERULAM ROAD

FOLLY LANE

BRANCH RD

Tourist Information Centre

ST PETERS ST

VICTORIA ST

City → Station

FISHPOOL STREET

SPENCER ST

MARKET PL

CHEQUER ST

ST MICHAELS ST

GEORGE STREET

HIGH ST

Roman Theatre

Verulamium Museum

BLUEHOUSE HILL

Abbey

ABBEY MILL LANE

SUMPTER YARD

HOLYWELL HILL

LONDON ROAD

RIVER VER

KING HARRY LANE

ST STEPHENS HILL

Verulamium is what remains of Roman St Albans. Verulamium Park is a large area, and is generally flat/ramped. Verulamium includes the remains of houses, a theatre, and a hypocaust as well as parts of the town walls. What you see is mainly the building foundations, and some impressive mosaics. The **hypocaust** has a bumpy approach, +1 step and a narrow entrance (W66).

Verulamium Museum St Michael's Street, St Albans AL3 4SW *Tel:* 01727-751810. Two BB spaces in the CP about 50m from the museum. Step-free access throughout. The museum is on the GF, and there's a **wheelchair toilet (D85 ST85)** in the basement, accessed by a lift (D75 W95 L130).

The Roman Theatre is under separate ownership. It is about 200m from the museum and has a step-free entrance. There are bumpy grass slopes inside with some quite steep ramps.

Other interesting places in the area which are said to be fully wheelchair accessible, with adapted toilets, are the **Garden of the**

Rose, Chiswell Green *Tel:* 01727-850461, and the **Mosquito Aircraft Museum**, Salisbury Hall, London Colney *Tel:* 01727-822051. These are not always open, and if you want to visit, you should either ring the number given, or the tourist office.

Hatfield House
Hatfield, Herts AL9 5NQ
Tel: 01707-287010 *website:* www.hatfield-house.co.uk
A Jacobean mansion built in 1611 for the Cecil family, who still live there. Regular Elizabethan banquets are held there (*Tel:* 01705-262055). The house lies just off the A1000 and is less than 1 km from Hatfield town centre. Parking directly in front of the house. Hatfield NR Station is nearly 400m away. The entrance has + 15 steps bypassed by a detour of about 150m right round the back of the house using an uneven stone path. However, you have the opportunity of entering the house through the original front door. Small lift (D70 W95 L115) to all relevant floors for the tour (otherwise it involves + 31 and − 31). Sometimes visiting is restricted to 'regular' guided tours, while on other days people can wander around as they wish. In view of the special arrangements needed to bypass the steps, it's probably sensible to ring first.

About 150m away is the 'Old Palace' with an adjacent courtyard (Palace Yard) containing a café and a small shop, both with ramped access. The beautiful grounds and garden are nearly all on the same level. **Adapted toilet (D75 ST100**, but the door opens in**)** in the courtyard. The normal guided tour lasts about an hour.

Kent

Chartwell
near Westerham, Kent TN16 1PS
Tel: 01732-868381 *RecM:* 01732-866368
website: www.nationaltrust.org.uk/places/chartwell
Winston Churchill's country home from 1924. Well signed from Westerham, off either J5 or J6 on the M25. At busy times, entry is by 'timed ticket', and you may have to wait (an incentive to book in advance). Large CP with eleven BB spaces, eight by the visitor centre and three by the restaurant. As the house and gardens are set on a hill with steep slopes and many steps en route, you can arrange either to drop off or park directly in front of the house if necessary. You need either to ring in advance or to ask at the visitor centre, as it involves going back on to the main road and a staff member has to open the main gates. This is an occasion where a mobile phone might be really valuable.

From the visitor centre which is step free from the CP, the route to the house is uphill, and includes $+15$ steps. The $+2$ at the entrance can be bypassed using a portable ramp. The GF is step free apart from ±1 to the terrace and $+2$ to the small lift (D70 W85 L80) which goes to the first floor, bypassing $+21$. Chair users would need to transfer to a stool, and there's a 'loan' chair on the first floor for use. Only one chair user at a time is allowed on the first floor. There is an unavoidable $+1$ on this level. There are -16 from the GF to the basement dining room and finally -2 at the official exit. Chair users can use the portable ramp at the GF entrance.

Churchill had a studio in the gardens, and some of his work is on display. This is best approached from the front of the house. Take the slightly uneven path next to the exit gate and follow it around the croquet lawn to the side of the house. Then take a short cut across the grass. It's quite a difficult route, and most chair users would need a pusher. At the studio door there is $+1-1$ to the GF, which is mainly flat apart from -6 to a small display of gifts that Churchill received.

The restaurant/café and shop are $+6$ from the CP, but there is a ramped route to the left of the shop, or there's a step-free side entrance from beside the three BB spaces. A **wheelchair toilet (D90 ST75)** is located beside the doorway to the visitor centre.

Ightham Mote
Ivy Hatch, Sevenoaks, Kent TN15 0NT
Tel: 01732-810378
Near the M20 junction 2A, and signed from the A25. Medieval stately home with a moat. On-site CP with six BB spaces, and a bumpy, stony surface. It is possible to negotiate a slightly closer dropping-off point near the shop if necessary. The easiest route to the cobbled central courtyard is to go down a stony path behind the house, about 100m long, and with -1 step at the start. The GF rooms have step-free access, but with $+1-1$ between some of them. First floor is $+17$. A restaurant with an accessible toilet is due to be opened at the end of 2002 in a separate building.

Around the house are some attractive lawns, grounds and ponds, reached by gravel paths, or a steep grass verge. The tea lounge near the CP has step-free access but fixed seating. The shop has a flat entrance through D67 then a $+3$ split level and an upstairs section ($+14$), so that only about 40% has step-free access. **Wheelchair toilet (D85 ST110)** near the shop, just before the entrance gate to the stony path described.

Leeds Castle
Maidstone, Kent ME17 1PL
Tel: 01622-765400 *website:* www.leeds-castle.com
The castle dates back nearly 900 years, and the setting, in the middle of a lake, is breathtaking. It has been owned by monarchs, including Henry VIII, and by famous families including those of Sir Anthony St Leger, Lord Culpeper and Lord Fairfax. The last owner, Lady Ballie, left the castle to the nation. Since then, considerable efforts have been made to make the site accessible. A detailed leaflet and a braille guide are available. Special events, such as wine festivals, concerts and a flower festival, are held from time to time.

The castle is well signposted from Junction 8 on the M20. Large CP about 400m from the castle with BB spaces, and a minibus with lift access goes near to the entrance if necessary. Wheelchairs are available. The drawbridge has 45m of cobbles, and leads past the Dog Collar Museum with a ramped entrance, to a circular 'courtyard' called the Inner Bailey. A ramp bypasses −15 into the castle, and the GF has been made accessible by the use of a platform stair lift by the Heraldry Room bypassing −6. Part of the route takes you against the flow of people doing a standard tour, so you may have to wait a little. The upper floors are +2+14+14, then −15−15 (spiralled).

The grounds have occasional steps and slopes, and a good number of seats. The Duckery has an artificial lake with a wooden walkway. Past the castle entrance the Culpeper Garden is ramped throughout; the Aviary is up a gentle slope, and in the centre of the Maze there's a grotto with −15−7+13. There is also a nine-hole golf course which can provide facilities for blind or partially sighted players (*Tel:* 01622-880467.)

About 150m from the drawbridge around the Fairfax Courtyard are the restaurant (with ramp bypassing +2), and the shop. Both have split levels inside. **Adapted toilets (D75 ST67)** by the BB spaces in the CP. There are **three wheelchair toilets (D85 ST85)** just before the Fairfax courtyard.

Surrey

Claremont Landscape Garden
Portsmouth Road, Esher KT10 9JG
Tel: 01372-467806
One of the earliest surviving English landscape gardens, dating from before 1720. On the opposite side of the road from West End

Lane. CP by the entrance. The gravel path and grassland immediately around the lake are flat and firm. Tea room and shop by the CP, and **adapted toilet** (not seen).

Guildford is a picturesque town with a steep cobbled High Street. Not an obvious place to recommend for accessibility. It does, however have step-free access at the main station, and a *Shopmobility* (*Tel:* 01483-453993) scheme based in the Friary/Bedford Road CP about 400m away. **Wheelchair toilet (D70+ ST70+ NKS)** on the GF of the Friary Shopping Centre. A pedestrian bridge goes to the Friary Shopping Centre with lift access to all levels. You can then get to North Street and the High Street (which is pedestrianised for most of the day), as well as the castle and the river.

The town has a 'wheelchair tourist trail', with details available from the Tourist Information Centre in Tunsgate (*Tel:* 01483-444333). This is some 700m up a cobbled route from the Friary Centre, and has +1 step at the entrance. Shopmobility may have copies of the route.

Guildford Cathedral
Stag Hill, Guildford GU2 7UP
Tel: 01483-565287
Situated well outside the town on the top of Stag Hill, the cathedral dominates the skyline. It is one of only four cathedrals built in Britain in the 20thC. CP outside, and a permanent ramp bypasses the steps at the entrance. Flat inside, except for +4 steps to the Lady Chapel, and −4 to the Brass Rubbing Centre. The shop and refectory, by the parking area, are step free. **Wheelchair toilets (D90 ST70+)** by the shop.

Polesden Lacey House
Polesden Lacey, Great Bookham, Dorking, Surrey RH5 6BD
Tel: 01372-452048 *RecM:* 01372-458203
Approached from Junction 9 on the M25, and well signed from the A24 to Dorking. An elegant 19thC house with formal Edwardian gardens. Open-air theatre performances in the summer. BB parking spaces next to the shop and café, about 100m from the house. The main entrance is ramped bypassing +2 steps, and all the rooms with displays are on the GF with step-free access. The shop, plant sales and restaurant have a ramp bypassing +2. **Wheelchair toilet (D80 ST120)** nearby.

The **garden** has gravelled or grass paths, and is generally flat. The only steps are those to the former kitchen garden (+ 4). There is a wheelchair route with a hard surface which covers a distance of well over 1km. Most chair users would need a strong pusher.

The **open-air theatre** (*Tel:* 01372-457223) is about 200m from the house, and chair users are asked to book spaces in advance. Wheelchairs, including one powered chair for use in the garden, are available.

Wisley Gardens
A3, Woking, Surrey GU23 6QB
Tel: 01483-224234 *Fax:* 01483-211750
website: www.rhs.org.uk/gardens/wisley/index.asp
The Royal Horticultural Society Gardens are about 10km north of Guildford off the A3. Members only on Sundays. CP with more than thirty BB spaces near the entrance. The main CP is very large with an uneven surface in places, and if it's crowded, you could be more than 300m from the entrance. Wheelchairs and five Batricars are available. In the summer you may have to book a powered buggy one or two weeks in advance. The gardens have been well adapted for disabled visitors, although the toilets were designed and installed some years ago to standards that have been superceded.

Step-free entrance to the site which is spread out over 240 acres. Over half the gardens are readily wheelchair accessible and a map is available showing hard surface paths, link routes over grass areas, and where the paths are steep. The map issued at the ticket office included access information, but with one glitch showing a step-free route at the end of the canal where there were, in fact, − 8 − 8 steps. A second, more accurate map was then made available for disabled visitors. Broadly speaking, the northern part of the gardens is fairly flat while the southern part is hilly. Most chair users will need a pusher. It's not a bad idea to do the hilly bit first and then trundle gently down towards the restaurant. The Glasshouses have a longish push up, but flat access throughout.

The restaurant and gift shop are both step free throughout. **Adapted toilet (D75 ST50)** just outside the entrance by the picnic area. There are **two adapted toilets (D80 ST65)** near the glasshouses, and another **(D70 ST45)** just past the canal. There's a **wheelchair toilet (D80 ST70)** near the restaurant. In parts of the gardens, there are not many seats.

Lee Valley

A remarkable series of developments, established in 1967 to regen-
erate the then derelict valley into a 'green chain' stretching from
London's East End (around Stratford), through Walthamstow and
Tottenham right up past the M25 to Broxborne and Ware. Its extent,
and some of the key facilities, are shown on the map. The river along
which the Park has been developed is variously called the Lea or Lee.
For the sake of consistency, we refer to everything here as Lee.
**Because many facilities have the prefix 'Lee Valley' it is not always
clear, initially, which part of the valley they are in**. Some of them sound
very similar, and yet are 15km apart, and we have tried to use
descriptive names to clarify their location. There is an excellent *Access
Guide to the Lee Valley Regional Park* which can be obtained from the
Lee Valley Park Information Centre, Abbey Gardens, Waltham
Abbey, Essex EN9 1XQ *website:* www.leevalleypark.org.uk *e-mail:*
info@leevalleypark.org.uk *Tel:* 01992-702200 *Fax:* 01992-702230.

The Park area provides a wide range of activities. There are nature
reserves, sports and entertainment facilities, an excellent choice of
places for fishing, a boating centre and camp sites. The *Access Guide*
referred to above includes detailed maps and descriptions, and
covers:

- countryside sites;
- countryside activities;
- fishing sites;
- sports and recreational facilities.

Because of the range of facilities, and the care taken to make as many
of them as possible accessible to all, we have made a detailed survey
of the area, and included descriptions of the various places, starting
from the inner London part, and working outwards.

The south end of Lee Valley, around Stratford, Leyton and Hackney

Sports Centre
Quarter Mile Lane, Leyton E10
Tel: 020 8519-0017
Off the A106 Eastway, and well signed as Lee Valley Sports Centre.
On-site CP. Ramped main entrance, and most facilities are step free,
except the viewing gallery for the squash courts which has + 14 steps.

Lee Valley

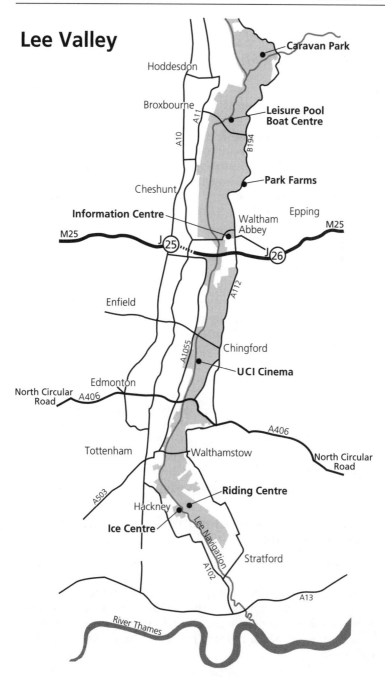

Caravan Park

Hoddesdon

Broxbourne

Leisure Pool
Boat Centre

A11

A10

B194

Park Farms

Cheshunt

Information Centre

Epping

Waltham
Abbey

M25

M25

J 25

J 26

Enfield

A112

A1055

Chingford

UCI Cinema

Edmonton

North Circular
Road

A406

A406

North Circular
Road

Tottenham

Walthamstow

Riding Centre

A503

Hackney

Lee Navigation

Ice Centre

Stratford

A102

A13

River Thames

Health Suite + 1. No adapted changing/shower facilities. Café/bar to the left from reception. **Wheelchair cubicle (D90 ST80)** in the Gents; **adapted toilet (D85 ST52)** in the Ladies.

Ice Centre
Lea Bridge Road, Leyton E10 7QL
Tel: 020 8533-3154
Situated on the east side of the River Lee Navigation, on the A104. On-site CP. Ramped main entrance to an ice rink, changing area and bar. Only 20% of the bar is step free. Limited space for chair users at the corners of the rink, with relatively poor view. The easiest seats have + 3 to the back row, then − 2 towards the front. Induction loop. **Adapted toilet (D70 ST120** inward opening door**)** behind reception. Key from reception.

Riding Centre
Lea Bridge Road, Leyton E10 7QL
Tel: 020 8556-2629
Some 100m east of the Ice Centre. On-site CP. Step-free access throughout. There is a specially-designed mounting block for riders with disabilities. **Wheelchair cubicles (D75 ST75)** in both the Gents and the Ladies opposite reception.

Middlesex Filter Beds Nature Reserve
Tel: Information Centre 01992-702200, or the South Area Ranger Base 020 8533-6937. South of Lea Bridge Road (A104) not far from Chatsworth Road. There is a CP behind the *Princess of Wales* pub giving step-free access to the towpath. All paths are surfaced, and ramps are provided along the 500m route. Panels describe the natural, industrial and archaeological history of the Beds. Described by our surveyors as 'lovely'! Nearest adapted toilet in the Ice Centre.

Mid-valley, between Chingford and Edmonton. Picketts Lock area.

The **Picketts Lock (Lee Valley) Sports and Leisure Centre** was closed early in 2002.

The UCI cinema is about 30m from the main entrance (see section on *Cinemas*). **Wheelchair toilet (D90 ST80)** at the bar and restaurant by the petrol station next to the cinema. Also on site is a **Deep Pan Pizza** Restaurant which has step free access and a **wheelchair toilet (D85 ST75)**.

North of the M25

Lee Valley Park Information Centre
Abbey Gardens, Waltham Abbey, Essex EN9 1XQ
Tel: 01992-702200
Situated inside the grounds of Waltham Abbey, the entrance is off
the roundabout where Sewardstone Road (A112) meets the Crooked
Mile (B194), and also Parklands. The Abbey Gardens consist of a
small orchard, a moat and grass areas with picnic tables.

On-site CP about 80m from the Centre with five BB spaces. Flat
main entrance and step-free access via ramps to meeting rooms.
Information centre and shop on the GF. **Wheelchair toilet (D80
ST70)** behind the information point. **Note that arrangements may be
made at the Centre for making wheelchair access possible in various
parts of the Lee Valley Park**.

Waltham Abbey Church
Church Street, Waltham Abbey, Essex EN9 1XQ
Tel: 01992-767897
About 300m from the Countryside Centre described above. Flat
access to a gate where there is + 1 − 1 step, but this can be bypassed if
another door is opened for you. Step-free access inside, but − 8 to the
crypt, and Visitors' Centre. **Wheelchair cubicles (Gents D95 ST120,
and Ladies D95 ST120)** in the toilets just opposite the church.

Lee Valley Park Farms
Hays Hill Farm, Stubbins Hall Lane, Holyfield, Waltham Abbey,
Essex EN9 2EG
Tel: 01992-892781
CP about 100m away, and then there's a steepish slope up to the
farm. There is a wide variety of cattle, sheep, pigs, goats, poultry and
rabbits, including a few rare breeds. The shop and information point
both have + 1 step. **Adapted toilet (D85 ST75** but obstructed by fixed
rail). There's also a picnic area.

Leisure Pool
New Nazeing Road, Broxbourne, Herts EN10 7AX
Tel: 01992-467899
Just off the B194 Nazeing New Road. On-site CP. The main entrance
is some 100m via a ramp (bypassing steps), and the foyer has step-
free access to a café, a poolside balcony, and beauty treatment
rooms. The pool is reached by lift (D100 W150 L150). There is

an alternative flat (and shorter) route if you go to the double doors at the foot of the steps between the CP and the main entrance. This entrance is normally locked, so you either have to ring first, or get someone to 'alert' the staff of your need.

The pool level is flat. There are changing rooms for disabled swimmers on your right as you come out of the lift. There are two **adapted loos (D70 ST40)** at this level. During the summer there is access to an outdoor area, and it is possible to get there step free through a door by the entrance to the disabled changing room. The GF also contains a wet sauna (+ 1 step D62) and a dry sauna (+ 1 + 1 D53). The jacuzzi is + 6.

Boat Centre
Old Nazeing Road, Broxbourne, Herts EN10 6LX
Tel: 01992-462085
Boats are available for hire. There are small four-seater motor boats available, with obvious access challenges, but if people can help you on and off, it could be a fun activity. There's nothing quite so relaxing as a trip on the river. Our group has enjoyed several week-long holidays in the past, and with judicious choice of boat, it is possible to minimise any access problems. There's a fully adapted passenger vessel called the *Lady of Lee Valley* with an **adapted toilet** which does regular short trips, and may be available for hire as well (*Tel:* 01992 466-111). In addition, the '72 Club have a fully-accessible boat for holiday hire, with accommodation for eight people, including three chair users in electric chairs. It has a lift on board to facilitate access. For booking information, ring the main contact number above. **Wheelchair toilet (D75 ST75)** in the *Crown* pub about 100m away, reached by going round the outside of the pub to the back. Inside, there's a split level of ± 3 to part of the GF bar. The ramped entrance on the side leads to the upper level, and the bar while the toilet is on the lower level. There's another **wheelchair toilet (D75 ST70 NKS)** at the Old Mill and Meadows site. There are four riverside chalets for hire by the mill. One is adapted for chair users with a shallow ramp at the front. See chapter on *Accommodation*.

Rye House Gatehouse and Marsh Nature Reserve
Rye Road, Hoddesdon, Herts
Tel: 01992-460031 (at the Information Centre)
The gatehouse is a 15thC moated building. CP with two BB spaces. Access inside involves + 23 spiralled steps to a first floor exhibition and then a further + 31 to the roof. The Nature Reserve is run by the

Royal Society for the Protection of Birds (RSPB), and has an information centre open every weekend. Most of the paths are well surfaced. There's a wheelchair-accessible bird hide on the site overlooking the lake and marsh. It is possible to arrange similar facilities on the nearby Thames Water Sewage Works. **Wheelchair cubicles** in both Ladies and Gents **(D80 + ST110 +)** toilets across the road from the main CP.

Dobbs Weir Caravan Park, see *Accommodation* chapter.

Opportunities for fishing: angling sites with step-free access.
There are areas allocated for fishing throughout the Lee Valley Park. All the normal regulations apply, which you will know about if you fish regularly. You need an NRA Rod Licence, for example. There are eleven species to be caught. **A special permit for anglers with disabilities is available from the Information Centre**. They publish an excellent leaflet summarising where the sites are, and what you can catch, and there are fuller details in the information pack mentioned at the start of the Lee Valley write-up.

If you need to get any gates unlocked so that you can get your car nearer to a particular site, contact the Information Centre in Waltham Abbey. There will be local rangers who can organise this.

We looked at several sites, but bear in mind that some are quite large. There are some allocated angling 'stances' near to parking, but it will depend on what you want to do, and how much effort is involved, as you may wish to go further up the bank, or to another part of the gravel pit. By far the best thing is to talk to the experts in the Countryside Centre.

Entertainment

The chapter is split into sections on:

- Arts centres where there are several adjacent facilities
- Cinemas
- Music venues
- Theatres

These are subdivided into:

- Central venues
- Outer areas inside the North/South Circular Roads
- Between the North/South Circular Roads and the M25

- BBC and ITV audience shows

Much of the information was originally gathered by visit, by Artsline with whom we have worked closely, and by our own survey teams. The data has been updated by phone calls to venues which have already been visited, and by visits to new places, and to others where there has been major change.

For the central London theatres, there are location maps readily available, and most London guides have one. The **Society of London Theatre (SOLT)**, 32 Rose Street WC2 9ET *Tel:* 020 7557-6700 *Fax:* 020 7557-6799 *e-mail:* enquiries@solttma.co.uk publishes a fortnightly *Official London Theatre Guide* which includes a detailed location map. SOLT were partners, with Artsline, in producing the *Access Guide to London's West End Theatres*. This access information is now also held on the SOLT *website*, www.officiallondontheatre.co.uk/solt although it is not entirely clear how often it is checked and updated. Each write-up includes a venue description, telling people how many steps there are to different parts of the theatre. It then tells you about wheelchair access, signed performances, facilities for those with hearing impairment and suggests the best place for disabled walkers. Almost the only thing missing is details of the adapted toilet/s provided.

All this is a far cry from the struggles we had fifteen and twenty years ago in getting this information properly presented (see our 1983 edition). The high quality of the current data is due to the longstanding partnership between Artsline and SOLT, on the collection of data by visit, and on much greater awareness. The SOLT presentation on its website provides a good model which shows other service providers how to approach 'access' information, and we particularly like the initial venue description used. The only real snag is that downloading and printing the information is quite a slow business.

Gaining access to entertainment has got considerably easier over the years, although there's still room for improvement and in a few places the provision has got worse rather than better. This is largely to do with perceived safety issues, and the more rigorous application of fire regulations. Local authorities are almost paranoid about the criticism that would be made in the media if something went wrong, and by the increasing tendency for people to copy America with an immediate rush to litigation if there's a hassle. In this context, the DDA is something of a mixed blessing – mainly good, as it encourages people to do all kinds of things they would otherwise not have done, but bad if it stops people from doing something because it cannot (for example) be made entirely wheelchair compatible. The biggest ongoing problems in relation to access to entertainment in London are to do with parking and the transport system together with some at the oldest venues, which were built long before access was an issue. There are also problems in finding a suitable restaurant or pub near the venue that has step-free access and a disabled persons' toilet. There is information about this in the chapter entitled *Pubs and bars*, but most places in central London don't fulfil that basic requirement.

Artsline (*Tel:* 020 7388-2227) can provide additional and updated information about most venues. They will have, or can get, information about signed performances, concessionary prices, and whether or not guide dogs can be admitted to the auditorium. The staff there have lots of experience and are interesting people to talk to. Concessions for disabled walkers are not as common as for chair users. Pensioners can often go to matinee performances at reduced rates, and some venues have concessions for the unwaged. Many venues admit chair users and/or registered disabled patrons at a reduced price. Artsline can advise about the details.

We have not attempted to cover these issues in the guide, as concessions are based on a variety of criteria, and signed performances only happen occasionally.

One tip when making arrangements by phone to book seats is *always* to find out *who* you are talking to, and make a note of it. Also note the time and date of the conversation. It's so much more convincing to say, 'Elaine told me that...', than it is to say, 'Someone said...'.

Note that special arrangements cannot normally be made through ticket agencies. The Really Useful Theatre (RUT) group, however, have a central booking system which is not an 'agency' like Ticketmaster, and booking through RUT should be secure, as they have a dedicated line for bookings for disabled theatregoers. **For anyone with special needs, it is necessary to negotiate access with the venue management when booking**. This is particularly true in places where seats have to be removed, which takes a little time. Fortunately for theatregoing, the culture is such that booking in advance is quite normal. That is not quite so true for going to the cinema, where people are more used to taking decisions on the spur of the moment. However, the new multiplexes do offer disabled cinema goers much more choice about where they can go, and an environment where there are virtually no access difficulties.

Many venues provide for people who have impaired hearing. A good number of theatres now have infrared systems and will lend you a headset, while cinemas tend to use induction loops. The newest cinemas (like the Odeon, Kingston) are now using infrared systems. A few places can provide you with a 'necklace-type' induction loop. Commonly there is good reception for both induction loops and infra-red systems in only part of the auditorium. There is occasionally a problem with the output from loops overlapping between screens in a cinema, so that you see one film and hear the soundtrack of another! It is usually possible to get round this by moving to a different seat, but it may be that the loop needs adjustment, and you will have to ask the staff. Try to get it tuned during the adverts before the main film if necessary. If the system doesn't work, *tell the management*. It may well be that they don't know. There are occasional signed performances for deaf people; both Artsline and the venue concerned will have details.

For people who are partially sighted it is normally best to sit at the front of the stalls. Chair users have to use the chair spaces provided unless they can transfer to a seat. Many venues offer concessionary prices because of this.

Because of difficulties of classification in the cinemas and theatres listing, **we have taken the following postal districts as being central**: **EC1**, **EC4**, **SE1**, **W1**, **W2**, **WC1** and **WC2**. As elsewhere in the guide we have not generally tried to describe parking for central venues, but have a look at the *Blue Badge User Guide*, and the section in the guide on central London CPs. If you have problems getting through, check the number in the phone book or in *Time Out*.

In our descriptions we have described the relation between the auditorium and the street level by which you would normally arrive. Quite a few theatres have the circle at street level, so you go down to the stalls and up to the upper circle. Fringe theatres and music venues are highly variable. Some are in a room over a pub, with only stepped access. Some cinema screens are on upper floors. Where possible, we've described the physical layout.

We would urge ALL venue managers to produce a short access leaflet, which can be based on the kind of information included here. It should highlight accessible public transport routes, and give practical information about parking. The venue description should be much the same as the write-up in the guide, possibly with a little amplification. Ideally it should be brief and to the point, but also practical and informative. The access leaflet should be available either on the web (and any extra information can be incorporated into the SOLT website) or by post.

Organisations that produce an access guide themselves are urged to make them practical and user-friendly. They should never consist of more than two sides of A4 paper, even for complex venues like the Barbican. The Barbican Access Guide is a very worthy document, but it's nearly forty pages long, and the one to the National Theatre is similarly wordy. Such guides are more of a bureaucratic list which says that every aspect of access has been considered, and less of a user-friendly guide to the intending visitor. Part of the reason for this is that the management of the organisation is trying to meet its perceived legal obligations to disabled people. We'll be very happy if the management of such venues borrow the abbreviated material here and use it.

Price concessions

A few venues are no longer making it a condition of entry that a chair user should be accompanied, although many still do. It may be a condition attached to their licence. Ask the venue and/or Artsline. Quite often disabled people need to sit in the most expensive part of the auditorium, and that is part of the basis of 'two for the price of one' which is relatively common. The requirement is usually associated with the rules about the ease of evacuation of the building in the event of an emergency, thus limiting chair users to the ground level.

In parallel with the variable cost is the fact that your special requirements often preclude a wider choice of seat. In a few venues the chair spaces provide only a restricted view, or are at the very front.

Arts centres

Many sites and venues have multiple functions and include a cinema, theatre and a display space for exhibitions. The South Bank has more than ten important venues all in the same area, and it seems sensible to list and describe these together. The Barbican Centre similarly has several venues and exhibition spaces, this time in one building. Some arts centres are smaller, but have theatre, cinema and exhibition spaces all under one roof.

All the centres provide a place to eat, and most have parking space. Many of the buildings are relatively modern, or have been well adapted.

We describe the South Bank group of venues first, with the National Theatre and Festival Hall among other places, then we describe the Barbican, followed by those in Croydon. Finally we list the smaller centres in alphabetical order.

South Bank Complex

website: www.southbanklondon.com
This includes the National Theatre, Royal Festival Hall (RFH), National Film Theatre (NFT), Hayward Gallery and the nearby IMAX cinema. The National Theatre has the Olivier, Lyttleton and Cottesloe auditoria, and there are the Queen Elizabeth and Purcell Room concert halls as well. It's a huge concentration of arts-related venues on a site overlooking the Thames on either side of the south end of Waterloo Bridge. Recent developments include a number of accessible eating and drinking places in the area, and just along the river are the London Eye and Aquarium in one direction, and Gabriel's Wharf and the OXO Tower in the other.

The Festival Hall was built for the Festival of Britain in 1951, so it is remarkable that it incorporated a substantial number of chair spaces, since access and disability issues were not much thought about at that time. The pedestrian bridges on either side of Hungerford Bridge are new. There have been several attempts to devise schemes to update and upgrade the site around and within the Festival Hall, and this is discussed later in this section.

The riverside frontage is attractive, and there is now a step-free riverside walk which stretches from County Hall and the London Eye to as far away as Tower Bridge. It is described in more detail in the chapter on *Recommended itineraries.*

There is an UGCP under the National Theatre with lift access, which is probably the best place to park. There are BB spaces in

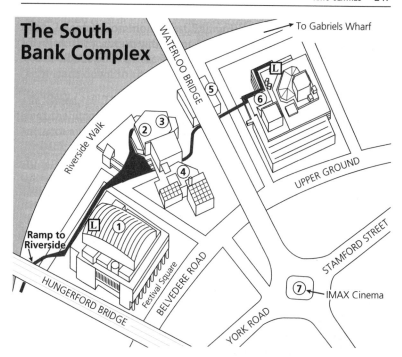

The South Bank Complex

To Gabriels Wharf

WATERLOO BRIDGE

Riverside Walk

UPPER GROUND

STAMFORD STREET

Ramp to Riverside

HUNGERFORD BRIDGE

Festival Square

BELVEDERE ROAD

YORK ROAD

IMAX Cinema

① Royal Festival Hall **RFH1**
② Queen Elizabeth Hall **RFH2**
(Main entrance, upper level
Wheelchair access, ground level)
③ Purcell **RFH3** (upper level)
④ Hayward Gallery (upper level)
⑤ National Film Theatre
⑥ Royal National Theatre
⑦ IMAX Cinema
⑧ London Eye

━━━ Step-free access at upper level

---- Step-free routes to and from Waterloo

L Lift

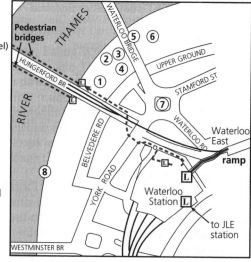

THAMES

WATERLOO BRIDGE

Pedestrian bridges

HUNGERFORD BR

UPPER GROUND

STAMFORD ST

RIVER

BELVEDERE RD

WATERLOO RD

Waterloo East

ramp

YORK ROAD

Waterloo Station

to JLE station

WESTMINSTER BR

the road in front of the Festival Hall, but the development plans envisage moving them to the area underneath the Hayward Gallery. There are also a limited number of BB spaces on Belvedere Road.

To get there from Waterloo station use the central exit opposite Platform 12 by the big clock. It is a vital route, as both Waterloo and Waterloo East stations have step-free access and both lead on to the main station concourse. From the exit, turn left down the pavement past the main station steps. There are about 40 steps down to a subway, with a lift bypass leading to the IMAX cinema and a step-free (and traffic-free) route to Belvedere Road, and the riverfront. Alternatively you can now cross the roads just past the station steps using step-free road crossings. This means that you can get to the riverfront via the pavement leading under the railway arches called Sutton Walk. This takes you into Concert Hall Approach and on to the GF foyer of the Festival Hall. The National Theatre is further along Belvedere Road/the river, to your right. The distance from the station to the RFH is about 500m. If distance is a hassle, take a black cab. All other exits from Waterloo involve steps, except the very long road/ramp to the right towards Westminster; the road/ramp leading down to the end of Lower Marsh and the road/ramp leading away from Waterloo International.

Note that to get back to Waterloo from the RFH, there's quite a long steady slope up from York Road – much of which can be bypassed. Just go straight ahead from the second zebra crossing on your way up the hill. After a narrow and rather foul-smelling alley, you reach Waterloo International Station, and you can use the lifts on the concourse to get up to the main station. Alternatively, if you go around into Waterloo Road (about 100m on from the big roundabout) just past the Underground station entrance there are lifts going up to the station concourse.

Watch out for some local maps, including the one in the Festival Hall access guide, which incorrectly show a junction between Waterloo Bridge and Belvedere Road. The 'junction' involves a 25m drop, and the pedestrian link is essentially around the roundabout, both at road level, and from around the IMAX cinema.

To get there from the Jubilee Line station, which exits into Waterloo Road under the railway bridge, simply turn left, and go around the roundabout (dominated by the IMAX cinema), finding Concert Hall Approach on the other side leading to Belvedere Road and the riverside. Note that the only accessible entrance/exit for the Jubilee

Line is the one in Waterloo Road. The distance to the RFH is about 600m, and it's fairly flat.

From Westminster which now has a fully-accessible tube station, it's considerably further, but there's step-free access via Westminster Bridge, and, turning left, along the back of County Hall to Belvedere Road. Similarly, there is step-free access using the new Hungerford Bridge footways **from Charing Cross**.

How to get around

At ground level, the Riverside Walk links step free to Level 1 of the Festival Hall with flat access to the NFT restaurant and the NFT1 cinema. It also links to the GF of the National Theatre, including the Cottesloe, around the corner.

The upper level links across to the first floor of the National Theatre, and gives access to the main concourse of the Festival Hall (Level 2), the Hayward Gallery, the Purcell Room and the main entrance to the Queen Elizabeth Hall (although **not** the chair-users' entrance, which is at ground level off Belvedere Road). Until autumn 2003 this upper-level link will be blocked off because of building work at the Hayward Gallery. We hope that the proposal for a ramp to be provided at the back of the Hayward Gallery will go ahead. Then it will be possible to reach the upper level from Waterloo Bridge without steps.

It is one of those typical nonsenses that in the lifts, labelling is US-based in one case and UK-based in the other. In the RFH, the GF is Level 1, so the terrace is at Level 2, whereas in the National Theatre the GF is the GF (using UK conventions), so the terrace is at Level 1, the first floor.

Future developments

Two pedestrian bridges have been built on either side of Hungerford Bridge. On the west (Parliament) side there is a lift at each end of the bridge. On the east (City) side there is step-free access from Charing Cross Station, and a lift down to the Festival Hall. We very much hope that a ramp will also be provided here, as dependence on the operation of a single lift is most unsatisfactory. It is hard to exaggerate the importance of this bridge link. On one end is London's busiest rail station and its biggest arts complex. On the other is Charing Cross, Trafalgar Square, the National Gallery and theatreland. It is extra-ordinary that proper access facilities have not been built in, and the perception that providing a lift solves all problems is incorrect. Currently (in March 2003), the lifts only work about half the time.

They are hydraulic lifts which are less expensive but also tend to be less robust and reliable than their conventional counterparts. The mid-level lift exit to the terrace has not been built yet. Ramps are so much better, because they cannot break down, and about the only thing that might be a problem is ice formation in the winter.

Other developments are planned, but while several schemes have been proposed, none has planning permission. One important feature of these developments is that an *Access Users Group* is involved with a wide variety of people commenting on the plans and pushing for improvements. Members of the group have different disabilities.

This is a welcome concept, and contrasts with the usual situation where an able-bodied access liaison officer is expected to know about all the disabilities. The key thing is that one size cannot fit all, AND there is no substitute for experience, however well someone is trained.

It is currently planned to close the RFH from mid 2005 through most of 2006 for major refurbishment. Among the features planned are:

- closing the BB parking area by the RFH riverside entrance, and transferring this to under the Hayward Gallery. There would either be a ramped pedestrian exit from this, or one involving a platform stair lift. It would be about 30m from the CP to a new entry to the Hall;
- providing a long ramp from the Hungerford Bridge walkway down to the terrace level of the RFH, thus bypassing the single (somewhat unreliable) lift;
- providing a new main entrance to the Hall to face the Hayward Gallery, with a new large lift to link all floors. Platform lifts will provide links to the front of the building;
- more wheelchair toilets will be provided with two on each level where there are chair spaces;
- the building will be reconfigured in the public areas and the ballroom floor (on the terrace level) will be accessed by platform lift rather than a ramp.

Venue details
Hayward Gallery
South Bank Centre, Belvedere Road SE1 8XX
Tel: 020 7960-4242 *Textphone:* 020 7960-5266
website: www.hayward.org.uk

On the south bank of the Thames between the National Theatre and the Royal Festival Hall.

The gallery holds regular special exhibitions for which there is normally an admission charge. The main pedestrian entrance is from the upper walkway/terrace around the Festival Hall. This can be reached from the NT, RFH or from the Hungerford Bridge walkway originating in Charing Cross Station. There's a CP immediately under the gallery off Belvedere Road with a lift (D105 W150 L300) to the main entrance. This is a service lift operated by staff, and there's an intercom in the CP for attracting someone's attention. The gallery is step free throughout, with a ramped bypass to some steps on the lower level. At the upper level there is a café and small shop. Between the CP and the lower gallery level is a mezzanine level with an **adapted toilet (D80 ST80** inward opening door). A staff escort is required to access the toilet. Wheelchairs are available and the audio guide has a T-setting for hearing aids. There are plans for refurbishment during 2003, and it is expected that this will include a new disabled persons' toilet, and a café.

IMAX Cinema
1 Charlie Chaplin Walk, South Bank SE1 8XR
Tel: BO 020 7902-1234 M 020 7960-3100
website: www.bfi.org.uk/imax
This is a huge circular protrusion sticking up from the sunken centre of the roundabout at the south end of Waterloo Bridge. It is the UK's largest cinema screen with superb sound and picture quality. The seats are quite steeply raked in front of a huge, slightly concave screen. The cinema is reached either from the riverside by the National Film Theatre or Festival Hall, or from Waterloo Station by using the lift just past the big staircase (see earlier description). Main entrance flat, leading to the box office and café. Two lifts (D85 W105 L140) on either side of the box office going to the screen on the fourth floor. Eight wheelchair spaces around the top row of seats. **Wheelchair toilets (D90 ST80)** to the left of the box office on the GF, and next to the lifts on both the first and fourth floors.

National Film Theatre (NFT)
South Bank SE1
Tel: 020 7928-3232 M 020 7815-1374
website: www.bfi.org.uk/nft
There are two entrances, and three cinemas. The main entrance is accessed from Belvedere Road and leads to the box office, NFT2 and

NFT3. NFT3 is situated above the box office, and reached either via
+ 35 steps or up an external ramp (negotiated with staff assistance).
The other entrance is on the riverside, under Waterloo bridge and
provides step-free access to NFT1. Inside the building there is a split
level with ± 8 steps. To get to NFT1 from the box office you either
have to use the steps, or go right round the outside of the building
(about 100m) and use the step-free route through the restaurant.
Each cinema has two chair spaces. There are adapted toilets on both
the box office and riverside levels. At the lower level there's a large
adapted toilet (D70 ST0) to the right of reception, 10m down the
corridor. The ST0 (no space for side transfer) is because of a vertical
pole placed immediately adjacent to the WC which is an old design
presumably intended to help those with arthritis. From the riverside,
there is a **wheelchair toilet (D75 ST80)** just to the left after you have
gone down the passage towards NFT1. The door is very difficult to
open. All the cinemas have an induction loop.

National Theatre
South Bank SE1 9PX
Tel: 020 7452-3400 BO 020 7452-3000 *Textphone:* 020 7452-3009
DisEnq: 020 7452-3540 *website:* www.nationaltheatre.org.uk
The complex contains an UGCP, three theatres, bars, buffets, a
restaurant, a bookshop, and a GF foyer with temporary exhibitions
and free evening performances. An access guide is available with a
good cutaway diagram. BB holders have free parking if using the
UGCP on presentation of a performance ticket. The **Lyttelton/
Olivier** main entrance is at ground (riverside) level facing the river.
The **Cottesloe** theatre entrance is some 80m round the corner of the
building.
    In the main building the levels are connected by lifts (D100 W210
L160), including the UGCP and the upper walkway. Several
mezzanine levels are reached by steps, but there are now slow
platform stairlifts to bypass these. Ask one of the staff if you need
help.
    All three theatres have infrared hearing systems using headsets.
Alternatively, for people with a hearing-aid T switch, necklace-type
sensors can be provided, giving you your own induction loop. Both
systems work anywhere in the theatre.
    Olivier The box office is on a mezzanine, reached via + 11 steps
from level 1 or − 23 from Level 2. While there are stairlifts, using
them is a hassle, and you can arrange to pick up Olivier tickets at the
Lyttelton box office on the GF. The theatre is an amphitheatre on

two levels, linked by the main lifts. Three chair spaces in the rear stalls accessed by lift on Level 2. The bar is also on this level. **Wheelchair toilet (D80 ST75)** outside the rear stalls.

Lyttelton Box office and foyer on the GF. A traditional proscenium arch theatre, also on two levels. Flat access on the GF to rear stalls where there are four chair spaces. **Wheelchair toilet (D90 ST85)** off the foyer, next to the Ladies. To the right of this, there is a lift (D75 W115 L90) to the circle (Level 2), bypassing $+22$.

Cottesloe Ramped entrance, bypassing $+5$, 100m to the left of the Olivier/Lyttleton main entrance. It is alongside the IBM building. Step free to foyer and box office. A small studio-style theatre where a variety of layouts are used. The auditorium has three seating levels. It is flat from the foyer to two chair spaces, and six possible transfer seats. There are steps to both higher and lower seating levels. **Adapted toilet (D65 ST80)** on the right inside front entrance.

In the National Theatre, the **Mezzanine Restaurant** has lift access via the glass lift opposite the Long Bar or is -13 steps from Level 1 with a platform stairlift. **Wheelchair toilet (D85 ST95)** adjacent to the restaurant.

The **Terrace Café** (bistro style) has lift access via the glass lift.

The **Circle Café** is between levels 2 and 3 and you would need to use a platform stairlift to bypass the ± 22 steps to get there.

The **Lyttelton Long Bar** is on the GF with flat access and sometimes has free entertainment of one kind or another, often prior to evening performances.

Backstage tours of the theatre are organised three times a day, and we are told that they are step free and accessible.

South Bank Centre SE1
Tel: 020 7960-4242 *Textphone:* 020 7921-0921 *DisEnq:* 020 7921-0926
website: www.rfh.org.uk e-mail: boxoffice@rfh.org.uk
A detailed access guide is available in the form of quite a large 'directory' and with an inaccurate map showing the local area (with a non-existent junction between Waterloo Bridge and Upper Ground). There are BB parking spaces on the road by the riverside entrance to the Festival Hall. Step-free access both from riverside level, and from the upper walkway/terrace.

Royal Festival Hall
Belvedere Road SE1 8XX
Tel: 020 7921 0600 **BO** 020 7960-4242 *Fax:* 020 7928-0063
website: www.rfh.org.uk

The box office is to the left of the riverside entrance. There is a single lift linking the riverside level with the main concourse and auditorium. It was out of action when we surveyed, but this rarely happens. Bypassing it involved going round the building to the stage door and using a service lift (D300 W300 L300). From the main concourse (Level 2, upper walkway level) there are three large lifts (D170 W170 L220) up to most of the auditorium. To get to Levels 3 and 4 there are two smaller lifts (D80 W160 L90). One is just past the cloakroom on Level 2, and the other is behind a small bar on the other side of the concourse. There are chair spaces with flat access in the balcony (Level 5) and terrace (Level 4). Level 5 is reached using the large lifts. To get to Level 4 use the smaller (separate) ones. Note that there is no wheelchair toilet on this level. Row AA has the most leg room. On most floors the lifts lead to split levels and steps to the auditorium. Twin track Sennheiser system.

On the **Main Concourse** (Level 2) there are free music and dance performances at various times, a bookshop, bar (− 4 steps) and several food counters. The **People's Palace Restaurant** on Level 3 can only be accessed without steps using the smaller lift by the cloakroom. The lift is on the right of the building (looking from the riverside).

The **Poetry Library** and **Voice Box** which host readings and literary events, are on Level 5 accessed using the smaller lift on the left of the building.

Wheelchair toilets (D85 + ST80 +) on Levels 1, 3 and 5. On Level 1, by the riverside, turn to the right as you come in through the main doors, and the toilet is on the left opposite the lift.

Festival Square

A new café is being built on the Belvedere Road side of the building with a piazza outside. It will be open in mid-2003. There will be a new **wheelchair toilet** at GF (road) level.

Queen Elizabeth Hall

Main entrance on the upper walkway level, and from the foyer, there are − 11 steps to the hall. Access for people with disabilities is via the Artists' Entrance at Riverside/Belvedere Road. This gives step-free access via a large lift to five chair spaces in the front row. It is by no means an ideal spot for the wide variety of entertainment provided. Sometimes the sound balance is very poor. **Wheelchair toilet (D80 ST75)** by the Artists' Entrance. Row AA has good legroom. Infrared system.

Purcell Room
Entrance on the upper walkway level. The QEH and Purcell Room share the same entrance. Then +4 steps bypassed by a platform stairlift. There are two chair spaces, and good legroom in rows A and D. There is a well hidden **wheelchair toilet (D70 + ST70 +)** near the entrance to the auditorium. The signage is poor, but you'll find it just outside the Ladies. Infrared system.

The Barbican

Barbican Centre
Silk Street EC2Y 8DS
Tel: 020 7638-8891 *Textphone:* 020 7382-7297 Restaurant (*Searcy's*) 020 7588-3008 Library 020 7638-0569 *website:* www.barbican.org.uk
The Centre is in the northeast corner of the City in a complex which includes hundreds of flats, the Guildhall School of Music and Drama, and two Exhibition Halls. It is surrounded by a large pedestrian area on two levels which now has much-improved maps at all the entry points. Car and taxi access to the Centre is from Silk Street.

While this centre for theatre, concerts, cinema and art exhibitions was opened in 1982, access was considered only after all the main design parameters were fixed. There have been recent improvements, but it's an extremely confusing building. Signposting inside is not at all clear, and we found that the plans and listings, which have been put in strategic places to clarify things, were cluttered, and contained far too much information. An *Access Guide for the Barbican* is available, but see earlier comments. There is a cutaway diagram of each floor in the *Barbican Centre Pocket Guide*.

The centre provides unique facilities. It is compact, and there are lots of things to see and do. Virtually everywhere can be reached reasonably easily via the four main lifts, and the management have gone to some lengths to overcome the design shortcomings.
Parking: CP3, entered off Silk Street has eleven BB spaces and CP5 approached off Beech Street has three spaces. The CPs form a multi-storey stack, and are linked by lift E. From the bottom level CP3, you come out, on Level −1, and can go directly to the theatre and concert hall foyer. Signing is poor. From the upper level, CP5, you can come out on the lakeside on Level 0, and enter the building near the *Waterside Café*. Again, signing is poor. From the BB spaces, go directly *away* from lift E, and find an exit to your left. For badge holders, take your parking ticket and get it stamped at the venue you are visiting to waive the parking charge.

Getting there by foot is now somewhat easier. There are good maps at each of the fourteen gates to the upper podium, five of which have ramps. See the write-up in *Recommended itineraries*. There is a step-free route from the Museum of London over the upper podium.

The **main entrance** to the centre is at the junction of Silk Street and Whitecross Street. Unfortunately, it is a bit of a mess. Even if you arrive in Silk Street right opposite it you can be confused. To the left is a road leading down into the building which is the route down to CP3. To the right is a two-lane covered road. Signs to the Main Entrance are not prominent. Follow the two-lane 'road' about 30m, apparently into the building, and then the main door is on your left. There's a plan and listing just outside. Go through the doors, and you are on Level 0, the main GF level. In front of you is the bridge link (an enormous improvement) which gives flat access to the GF foyer and to the lifts. To your right is the ticket office and information desk, and there is a platform stairlift to bypass the -8 steps.

Since the building is big, it is important that you know where you want to go and how to get there. **People with disabilities are basically dependent on the four main lifts (D105 W160 L150)**, which are grouped together. By sticking to these lifts you can probably avoid getting lost! It is assumed that you start either on Level -1 (CP3 level); on Level 0 from the main entrance, linked to the lifts by the bridge; on Level 0, reached from CP5; or on Level 2 from the high-level walkway. For both the Barbican Hall and the Theatre, you need to make your way to Level -1 with the main foyer for major performances.

There are **wheelchair toilets** on every level except the GF, Level 0:

- Level -2 **(D90 ST70)** close to the lifts;
- Level -1, sited off the foyer near the exit to CP3;
- inside the theatre area there are two toilets **(D75 ST70)** at the circle level. Note that the wheelchair spaces are in the upper circle, one floor higher, so you have to use the lift (D79);
- Level 2 **(D90 ST70 +)** from the lifts go out to Frobisher Crescent, and it's on your right; this one is slightly smaller than some of the others, and some chair users may have difficulty in turning;
- Level 3, outside the Art Gallery;
- Level 4 **(D75 ST70)**; again a slightly smaller cubicle.

Details of facilities in the centre
Barbican Hall Used mainly for concerts. Level -1 is the main foyer.

If you arrive by the main lifts on Level −1, you must then cross the service road. Sixteen chair spaces and seats for disabled walkers are in Row U in the stalls which are reached step free from level −1. There are also four chair spaces at the back of the circle reached via the main lifts. Induction loop.

Barbican Theatre Foyer on level −1. It has a unique design with most seats reached via stepped access. There are eight chair spaces, four at the back of the stalls and four in the upper circle on Level 0, reached via the internal theatre lift (D75 L95 W110). In the upper circle, each chair position has a device which can lower the floor to improve sight lines. However you are left with a stage view that is slightly obstructed. There is only one row of seats (Row T) with step-free access in the main part of the theatre. It is at the back of the stalls (on Level −1) and has a good amount of leg room. The wheelchair toilets are on the circle level inside the auditorium; to use them during the interval you've got to be pretty quick, as they're on a different level from both sets of chair spaces. Infra-red sound system.

The **Pit Theatre** and **Cinema 1** are on Level −2, reached via the main lifts. The **Pit** has one chair space, and step-free access to front row seats. Infrared headsets available. In **Cinema 1** there are boxes for two wheelchairs. Induction loop, which does not work in the boxes.

Cinema 2 is on Level 4. The foyer can be reached by using the main lifts to Level 2 and then lift D from Frobisher Crescent. One chair space on Level 5 at the back of the raked auditorium. This is accessed via lift A (D80 W105 L150) either from outside the Silk Street entrance, or from the cinema foyer on Level 4. To find the lift at street level you have to go back from the main entrance to Silk Street, and then into the administrative area through the glass panels. The security guard will show you. Induction loop.

Concourse Gallery, **The Curve** on Level 0, alongside the ticket/information desk just inside the Silk Street entrance. Numerous free exhibitions. Use the platform stairlift to bypass the −8. Alternatively it is step free at the other end from the main GF foyer.

Barbican Art Gallery on Level 3, right by the main lifts. The gallery is on two levels with −56 between them. We were told that an open lift has been installed to link the floors.

Searcy's Brasserie, near the main lifts on Level 2, the library floor. View out over St Giles' church and the lake. Flat access.

Conference suites are on Level 4 which is a section primarily for private functions and conferences. You can get there from Level 2. There are two lifts going to Level 4: lift E which you can take from

CP3, and lift D which you can take from Frobisher Crescent on Level 2.

Library (a public library with a reference section) is on Level 2. Flat access. Membership is open to those who live, work or study in the City, and to regular Barbican Centre visitors. The library has a CCTV magnifying machine to help those with visual impairment and Zoomtext software on the public internet PCs for magnifying text on screen. The Music Library is accessed via a platform stairlift (W85 L70), bypassing −22.

Waterside Café is on Level 0, with tables and chairs alongside the artificial lake. This is particularly attractive in the summer. The café is buffet-style and serves a variety of food. Flat access, but it can get congested.

Conservatory normally open at weekends and bank holidays. There is a 'garden in the sky' on Level 3, reached via the main lifts. Flat/ramped access through most of the area, although a few narrowish gaps and D66.

In the centre **foyer** there is a varied programme of free early evening and Sunday lunchtime concerts, and also occasional exhibitions.

Croydon

Clocktower
Katharine Street, Croydon, Surrey CR9 1ET
Tel: 020 8253-1030 *Textphone:* 020 8253-1027
website: www.croydon.gov.uk/clocktower
The building is joined to the Town Hall and contains a library, cinema, museum, art gallery and music venue as well as two cafés and the Tourist Information Centre (*Tel:* 020 8253-1009). Parking in the Surrey Street CP (entrance on Scarbrook Road), with eight BB spaces, and street parking on Fell Road by St George's Walk. East Croydon Station is about 800m away, and there's a Tramlink stop in George Street about 400m away. The centre has an excellent access guide which has a local map, and floor plans, as well as a clear description of the main facilities. It tells you where there are seats. It also includes details of the Mobile Library which visits various parts of the borough and has a wheelchair lift.

A ramp to the right of the main entrance bypasses −11 shallow steps to the foyer. On the GF there is Tourist Information, a shop, and a **wheelchair toilet (D90 ST85)**. The +3 to the café has a ramped alternative on the right. All the floors can be reached by lift (D105

W100 L200 +). Second **wheelchair toilet (D90 ST80)** on the first floor to the right of the lift.

Library Entrance from the foyer, then a separate lift (D110 W170 L160) or escalator access between all four floors. **Wheelchair toilet (D90 ST75)** on the first floor, and another **(D85 ST80)** on the third floor. Ask at the enquiry desk for key.

Riesco Gallery Step-free access from the foyer. Small gallery with a permanent exhibition of Chinese pottery. Seats available.

Exhibition Gallery Flat access from the foyer and throughout. Small gallery with changing exhibitions.

Lifetimes Museum Small museum situated mainly on the first floor but with a small mezzanine level (+ 18) which can be reached with staff assistance by lift.

Braithwaite Hall Step-free access from first floor. Small jazz, chamber music and comedy venue.

David Lean Cinema Flat access from the first floor. Art House film theatre. Removable front row seats which can accommodate three wheelchairs if advance warning given. Infrared hearing units available for hire.

The **Shop** is quite small and congested, but staff members are always happy to help.

Fairfield Halls
Park Lane, Croydon, Surrey CR9 9EE
Tel: 020 8688-9291 *website:* www.fairfield.co.uk
Comprises three major venues. It is about 500m from East Croydon station and a similar distance from the tram stop in George Street. Some BB parking by the entrance, on the corner of Park Lane and Barclay Road. UGCP is just behind Halls on Barclay Road. From UGCP a steep ramp bypasses + 28 steps to the ground level, then left and 70m to the entrance. Flat main entrance to the box office and gift shop. Open lift (W85 L130) to the right of box office bypasses + 6 to a mezzanine, where there is the Arnheim Gallery, a bar and a restaurant. All other floors are reached by two lifts (D100 W185 L115), one to the left and one to the right of the box office. The Ashcroft Theatre is to the left of the box office on all floors. The Fairfield Concert Hall is to the right on the first and fourth floors. **Wheelchair toilet (D90 ST70)** opposite the entrance to the restaurant on the mezzanine. There is a **wheelchair cubicle (D75 ST80)** on the second floor in the Ladies, by the lift on the left. Another **wheelchair cubicle (D75 ST70)** is in the Gents on the third floor, by the lift on the right.

Arnheim Gallery For public functions. Flat from the GF.

Ashcroft Theatre Three wheelchair spaces in a separate box on the second floor. Circle seats are −2 then −2 for each row. Induction loop.

Fairfield Hall (concert hall) Eight wheelchair spaces on Level 3 with seats in between. Front row of the lower stalls (Level 2) has step-free access, as do the front six rows on Level 1. Sennheiser system.

Other arts centres

Battersea Arts Centre (BAC)
Old Town Hall, Lavender Hill, Battersea SW11 5TF
Tel: BO 020 7223-2223 *Textphone:* 020 7223-5311
website: www.bac.org.uk
Located by the junction with Theatre Street. Parking congested. Ramped entrance, bypassing +4 steps. It's an old Town Hall with a grand entrance and staircase. There are several performance areas, some accessed by lift (D75 W100 L140). Café and bar on the GF. There are +3+12+11 to the first floor, then more to the **theatre** but it is step free via the lift and stage. Two chair spaces. Both **Studios One** and **Two** have step-free access, and two chair spaces. The **gallery** for exhibitions of pictures, photography and sculpture is on the first floor, with step-free access. **Adapted toilets** on either side of the main stairs, **Gents (D67 ST70), Ladies (D70 ST60)**, both on the GF. Induction loop system in all three performance areas.

ICA (Institute of Contemporary Arts)
The Mall SW1Y 5AH
Tel: 020 7930-3647 *Textphone:* 020 7839-0737
website: www.ica.org.uk
Modern gallery with changing exhibitions, films, and productions reflecting current ideas and themes. Located close to Admiralty Arch. Parking on the Mall is restricted but there are three spaces available at the rear of the building, on Carlton House Terrace, that must be booked in advance. The main entrance on the Mall is step free and gives flat access to the GF. The Carlton House entrance is +5 steps and gives access to the first floor. The routes around the outside of the building from rear to front are either −40 or 300m step free via Admiralty Arch.

GF entrance gives flat access to the box office, shop (cramped) and café (cramped with fixed chairs and tables). The bar, with movable tables and chairs, is on two levels. There is flat access to the lower level and +10 to the actual bar. There is an intercom system to order drinks, which can be brought down.

The theatre has flat access with six wheelchair spaces inside and an induction loop fitted. Cinema One is ramped with two wheelchair spaces. Cinema Two (D74) is ramped, but notice needs to be given for seats to be removed to create wheelchair spaces. Both cinemas have an infrared hearing system with free headsets available from the box office. The Lower Gallery is −7, bypassed by an open lift (D80 L140 W85) and the new Media Centre is −5, bypassed by going through the Lower Gallery.

The first floor houses the Upper Gallery. This is +30 from the GF or +5 from the rear entrance or accessed by a tiny lift (D56 W85 L80) reached by going through the kitchen (ask the chef first!). We managed this (just) by transferring to a chair placed in the lift and carrying the wheelchair up the stairs.

Wheelchair toilet (D80 ST100) on the left by the entrance on the GF.

Riverside Studios

Crisp Road, off Queen Caroline Street, Hammersmith W6 9RL
Tel: 020 8237-1111 *website:* www.riversidestudios.co.uk
An active fringe theatre in an old warehouse. Close to Hammersmith Broadway where there are CPs. Parking near the theatre can be congested. Hammersmith tube station has lift access from platform to pavement, and is about 400m away. Flat to the foyer and café. Studios one, two and three have flat/ramped access to the front row. The ramp bypasses +2 steps from the foyer. The cinema is up about +45, but there are plans to install a lift. There are normally chair spaces in Studios one, two and three, at the front, and there's a **wheelchair toilet (D70+ ST70+)** just by the ramp from the foyer.

Stratford Circus

Theatre Square, Stratford E15 1BX
Tel: 020 8279-1000 *Fax:* 020 8279-1099
website: www.stratford-circus.org.uk
Set back 40m from Great Eastern Road. Step free from the north exit of the Stratford shopping centre, this new arts centre was designed with accessibility in mind. No parking attached but there are fourteen BB spaces in the MSCP above the shopping centre, and a CP up a steep ramp behind the centre. Otherwise, there are two BB spaces in a CP on Salway Street, 50m to the right from the main entrance. There's step-free access to the GF, with a café/bar, a studio theatre (Circus 2) with movable seating, and the main auditorium (Circus 1) with eighteen possible chair spaces and an induction loop. A lift (D75

W105 L140) goes to the two other main floors and to mezzanines. The first floor contains the balcony to Circus 1, which has chair spaces, as well as Circus 4 and 5, respectively a meeting room and an editing suite. The second floor contains Circus 3, a dance studio. **Two wheelchair toilets (D80 + ST80 +)** on the GF, and **one (D80 + ST80 +)** on the first floor. Stage and backstage areas also claimed to be accessible via a lift (not seen).

Note the Stratford Picture House and Theatre Royal which are very nearby. See page 335 for accessible Stratford pubs.

Watermans Arts Centre
40 High Street, Brentford TW8 0DS
Tel: 020 8232-1010 *Fax:* 020 8232-1030
e-mail: info@watermans.org.uk *website:* www.watermans.org.uk
The Watermans is a small centre with a theatre, cinema, gallery and open performing space, bar and café. It is by the junction with the South Ealing Road, and overlooks the Thames. On-site UGCP with six BB spaces. The centre is on several levels. There is a flat entrance from the CP mid-level, near three of the BB spaces. The main entrance at an upper level can be reached up a ramp to the left, and is some 80m from street level. From here there is a lift (D80 W90 L125) down to the main level. There is step-free access throughout, with ramps to bypass the split levels.

The theatre has six chair spaces. The cinema has three. The bar and café are fully accessible, and there is an outside eating area and riverside balcony. Infrared sound system in both the cinema and theatre. **Wheelchair toilet (D75 ST75)** up the ramp and past the bar and theatre entrance.

Cinemas

Since the guide was first published, provisions at cinemas have improved enormously. Initially it was the UCI group who introduced multi-screen cinemas with chair spaces in every screen and step-free access. Then Warner Brothers came on the scene, and largely set the pace and the standard. Their Leicester Square cinema is fully accessible although without easy parking. The ones in the suburbs at places like Croydon, Finchley, Harrow and Park Royal are good in every way. They are unequalled from an access viewpoint in that there is nearby parking with BB spaces, step-free access to all screens, which also have chair spaces, and there are disabled persons' toilets off the foyers. At many sites there are other nearby facilities, including bowling alleys, restaurants and popular fast food outlets. Add to those the UCI multiscreen cinemas at Whiteleys (Queensway), Lee Valley and Sutton; and the UGC at Staples Corner, and it is clear that things are improving. Now the Odeon group has opened its first multiplex in Kingston.

Other cinemas which have really good access include the Curzon Soho, Premier in Peckham, the Ritzy in Brixton, the Rio in Kingsland and the Showcase and Cineworld in Wood Green.

There are still problems because older 1930s cinemas have been converted into cinemas with several screens. The main screen is often in the circle of the old cinema and accessed only by steps, often 30 +. However, a good number of the GF screens (usually 2 and 3) have chair spaces with step-free access, possibly through a side exit.

We have listed cinemas by location and name, putting the chain name after, where applicable. Cinemas do change their numbers and booking arrangements from time to time. If you have trouble, check in *Time Out, Metro* or with another cinema in the chain. Note that the *Reel Guide* was published by Artsline early in 1996, and this includes more details about the cinemas than we have room to include. Artsline will also have updated information.

The main chains are now identified by their websites and their call centre numbers. This is another change since 1996, and not an entirely positive one, as it has become more difficult to speak to someone who actually knows the particular cinema and who may understand access issues.

Odeon *RecM:* 0870 5050-007 *website:* www.odeon.co.uk
UCI *RecM:* 0870 010-2030 *website:* www.uci-cinemas.co.uk
UGC contact local cinema or Head Office *Tel:* 020 8987-5000
website: www.fox.co.uk/cinema/ugc.html

Warner Village *RecM:* 0870 240-6020
website: www.warnervillage.co.uk

On the **Odeon** number (above), you are asked to name the cinema you want to ask about. Then you get the choice of hearing the programme details, booking tickets, or you are given the cinema's number for making other enquiries. You need a pen and a piece of paper to hand to jot down the number. This seems to be a really good system, though it's not clear how well the voice recognition software will work for someone who has a strong accent, nor for someone with a speech impediment.

On the **UCI** number, you select the cinema you want using the star button on the phone, and after a couple of minutes of (possibly unwanted) instructions, you are offered the possibility of making direct contact with the cinema by pressing 0.

On the **Warner Village** line, you are offered the option of speaking to an operator quite quickly.

Multiplexes with wheelchair spaces in all screens

These cinemas are described in more detail on pages 265–282.

Central London

Shaftesbury Avenue, Trocadero (UGC), Shaftesbury Avenue W1B 7FE *Tel:* 020 7434-0032 BO 0870 907-0716
Warner West End, 3 Cranbourn Street, Leicester Square WC2H 7AL *RecM*: 020 7437-4347 BO 020 7437-4343 **M** 020 7437-3484
Whiteleys (UCI), Second floor Whiteleys Shopping Centre, Queensway W2 4YL *Tel:* 020 7792-3147

Outer areas inside the North/South Circular Roads

Acton Park Royal (Warner), Royale Leisure Park, Kendal Avenue W3 0PA *Tel:* 0870 240-6020
Finchley Road (Warner), O2 Centre, 255 Finchley Road NW3 6LU *Tel:* 020 7604-3059 *RecM*: 0870 240-6020
Fulham Broadway (Warner), Unit 18, Fulham Broadway Retail Centre SW6 1DN *Tel:* 020 7385-2025
Greenwich Filmworks (UCI), Bugsbys Way, Greenwich SE10 0QJ *RecM*: 0870 010-2030 **M** 020 8853-3282
Islington (Warner), Parkfield Street N1 0PS *Tel:* 020 7226-2848
Shepherd's Bush (Warner), West 12 Shopping and Leisure Centre, Shepherd's Bush Green W12 8PP *Tel:* 020 8749-5014
Staples Corner (UGC), Geron Way, Staples Corner NW2 6LU *Tel:* 020 8208-1367 *RecM*: 0870 907-0717
Wood Green Cineworld, Shopping City, High Street N22 6YQ *Tel:* 020 8829-1400 *website:* www.cineworld.co.uk

Between the North/South Circular Roads and the M25

Bluewater Showcase, Water Circus, Greenhithe DA9 9SG *RecM*: 01322 422-700 BO 0870 242-7070

Croydon Purley Way (Warner), Valley Park Leisure Complex, Hesterman Way, Croydon CR0 4YA *Tel:* 0870 240-6020

Croydon Grants (Warner), 14-20 High Street, Croydon CR0 1GT *Tel:* 0870 240-6020

Dagenham (Warner), Dagenham Leisure Park, Cook Road, Dagenham, Essex RM9 6UQ *Tel:* 0870 240-6020

Enfield (UGC), Southbury Leisure Park, 208 Southbury Road, Enfield EN1 1YQ *Tel:* 020 8366-1550 *RecM:* 0870 907-0745

Harrow (Warner), St George's Shopping Centre, St Ann's Road, Harrow HA1 1AS *Tel:* 0870 240-6020

Hemel Hempstead (Odeon), Jarman Park, Herts HP2 4IW *Tel:* 01442-292220

Kingston (Odeon), Clarence Street, Kingston KT1 1QP *Tel:* 020 8974-5197

Lea Valley UCI (Picketts Lock Centre), Picketts Lock Lane, Edmonton N9 0AS *Tel:* 0870 010-2030

North Finchley Lido (Warner Bros), Great North Leisure Park, Chaplin Square N12 0GL *Tel:* 0870 240-6020

Romford Ster Century, The Brewery Shopping Centre, Waterloo Road, Romford RM1 1AU *Tel:* 01708 759-100

Sutton (UCI), St Nicholas Centre, St Nicholas Way, Sutton, Surrey SM1 1AZ *Tel:* 020 8395-4488 *Fax:* 020 8395-442

Uxbridge (Odeon), The Chimes Shopping Centre, 302 High Street UB8 1GD *Tel:* 01895-237490

Wimbledon (Odeon), The Broadway, Wimbledon SW19 1QB *Tel:* 020 8944-6890

Main Cinema Listing

An increasing number of cinemas are using automatic computerised booking systems via the phone, where you can pay for your ticket by credit card and simply collect it on arrival. Some have an enquiry method for disabled patrons which puts you through to the management to make necessary arrangements.

Central London

We have taken the following postal districts as being central: EC1, EC4, SE1, W1, W2, WC1 and WC2. As elsewhere in the guide we have not tried to describe parking for particular central venues.

Barbican Cinema see section on *Arts centres*.

Covent Garden (Odeon)

135 Shaftesbury Avenue WC2 8AH

Tel: 020 7836-6514

By the junction with St Giles Passage. Four screens. Front entrance has +3 steps, bypassed via a side door to the left (ring the bell if necessary). Screen One has step-free access via a lift, and two chair spaces, while Screen Two is +20. Screens Three and Four are down around 30 steps. **Wheelchair toilet** on the GF. Induction loop for all screens.

Curzon Soho

99 Shaftesbury Avenue W1D 5DY

Tel: **BO** 0871 871-0022 *RecM:* 020 7439-4805

website: www.curzoncinemas.com

By the junction with Frith Street. Three screens. Flat entrance to the BO and café on the GF, then a lift goes down two floors to all three screens. The big screen has two chair spaces. The two smaller screens have one and two wheelchair spaces respectively. All are held until fifteen minutes before the film. All the chair spaces are created by removing seats, so advance warning is appreciated. There is a bar on the floor above the screens, which is step free from the lift. **Wheelchair toilet (D95 ST80)** to the right of the lift on screen level. Induction loops in all screens.

Empire (UCI)

Leicester Square WC2H 7NA

Tel: 020 7734-8222 *RecM:* 0870 010-2030

One of London's premier cinemas. Three screens. On the north side of the square. Main entrance +14 steps, but there's an alternative for Screen One (which has several chair spaces) via a steep ramp accessed from Leicester Street. Screen Two is +35 and Screen Three −48. **Wheelchair toilet (D80 ST90)** off the main foyer, level with Screen One, step free if you have come up the ramp. Induction loop in all screens.

ICA see section on *Arts centres.*

Leicester Square (Odeon)

22-24 Leicester Square WC2H 7LQ

Tel: 020 7930-6111

Situated on the east side of the square. Six screens. The main cinema has one large screen, and the Mezzanine next door has five screens.

The entrances are separate. In the main cinema it is step free to the stalls, with six chair spaces. Screen One of five Mezzanine screens is step free, though 24 hours' notice should be given for three possible seats to be removed. The other four screens are up two flights of stairs. **Wheelchair toilet** in foyer of Mezzanine building. Infrared system available in all screens.

Marble Arch (Odeon)
10 Edgware Road W2 2EN
Tel: 020 7723-8072
Situated very near the Marble Arch roundabout. Five screens. One small step at the entrance reaches the box office. From here, you are escorted to a service lift up to Screens Two and Three. Screen One is +12 steps from GF, Screens Four and Five approximately +35. **Wheelchair toilet (D85 ST80)** level with Screens Two and Three. Induction loop in all screens.

National Film Theatre see section on *Arts centres.*

Other Cinema
11 Rupert Street W1V 7FS
Tel: 020 7734-1506 *RecM:* 020 7437-0757
website: www.picturehouse-cinemas.co.uk
Between Shaftesbury Avenue and Coventry Street. Two screens. Entrance −19 steps, but an exit to the left gives flat access to both screens via a small lift. Screen Two has one chair space, and there are plans to provide spaces in the other screen. **Wheelchair toilet (D85 ST100)** next to the lift, at screen level. No induction loop yet, but it is planned to provide one. There is an access leaflet.

Shaftesbury Avenue, Trocadero (UGC)
Shaftesbury Avenue W1B 7FE
Tel: 020 7434-0032 BO 0870 907-0716
Built on the upper floors of a large complex described in the chapter on *Places of interest.* Access for a chair user is via a lift (D80 W100 L120) which is accessed from Great Windmill Street outside the building. There is an intercom near the junction with Shaftesbury Avenue. Go past the window displaying the cinema programmes, and you will find three doors – a double and a single. By the single door is a 'press button and hold' intercom. This lift goes to all four floors of the cinema. Seven screens.

Using the lift, screens one to five have step-free access and designated chair spaces (though we're a little doubtful about the size of these, and you may have to sit sideways). Screen Six has step-free access to part of the auditorium, but Screen Seven has −2 then −1 inside. **Wheelchair toilet (D85 ST85)** near the lift on the fourth floor. The route for walkers from the Trocadero entrance to the screens is via steps and escalators. These can be avoided by using the lift.

In the smaller screens the chair spaces are created by removing seats, and it is not clear that the seats are always 'out'. If you ring first, they can remove seats to increase the number of chairs accommodated. All screens have an induction loop.

The main entrance to the cinema is via an escalator from Shaftesbury Avenue, but the ticket office can be reached step free from Coventry Street using the staff lift from the shopping centre. Then it is +3 to the screens.

Wardour Street (Odeon)

10 Wardour Street W1V 3HG
Tel: 020 7437-2096
Located inside the Swiss Centre. Four screens. There are +1+2 steps to reach three lifts to entrance which gives step-free access to Screen Two, while there are a maximum of five steps to Screens One, Three and Four. Induction loops in all screens. No wheelchair toilet.

Warner West End

3 Cranbourn Street, Leicester Square WC2H 7AL
RecM: 020 7437-4347 BO 020 7437- 4343 **M** 020 7437-3484
50m from Cambridge Circus NCP. Nine screens. Flat entrance into foyer, where there is a lift (D80 W100 L140) to all levels. All screens have four or more chair spaces. **Wheelchair toilets (D70+ ST70+)** off the foyers on all levels except the GF. All screens have an induction loop. *It's a very good facility access-wise.*

West End (Odeon)

40 Leicester Square WC2H 7LP
Tel: 020 7930-4994
On the south side of the square. Two screens. Flat main entrance gives step-free access to Screen Two via platform stairlift, with wheelchair spaces. Induction loop in both screens. Screen One is up a large number of steps, and is described as 'highly not recommended'.

Whiteleys (UCI)
Second floor Whiteleys Shopping Centre, Queensway W2 4YL
Tel: 020 7792-3147
On-site parking at the centre with the entrance in Redan Place, and
three BB spaces on the second floor, level with the cinema. There is
+1 step en route. Eight screens. The centre is described in the
chapter on *Shops*. To get to the second floor, use the main lifts in
the centre of the building. The cinema is level with a number of eating
places. Screens Five, Six, Seven and Eight are on the second floor.
The larger screens One, Two, Three and Four are on the third floor
reached by lift (D75 W105 L135). All screens have at least two chair
spaces. **Wheelchair toilet (D85 ST80)** in the foyer. All screens have
induction loops except Screen Four.

Outer areas inside the North/South Circular Roads

Acton Park Royal (Warner)
Royale Leisure Park, Kendal Avenue W3 0PA
Tel: 0870 240-6020
Situated within a large leisure complex. On the left of the A40
Western Avenue after Gipsy Corner. It is just east of Park Royal
tube station and the Hangar Lane underpass. You can approach it
from one side of the A40 going out of London towards Oxford or
from behind, from the residential area via Westfields Road and
across the bridge. There is also a new way of getting there if you're
coming from the west, from the gyratory system or the underpass.
There is a slip road on the left signed to the A40 Oxford, just past
the BP garage, which takes you past the complex, but then enables
you to turn right and right again to get across the A40. Nine
screens. On-site CP with more than twenty BB spaces, but the
place gets very congested at weekends. It is a compact development including the cinema, a large bowling alley, a nightclub and
several restaurants. The Megabowl bowling alley and entertainments centre has step-free access to almost everywhere, and now
incorporates a pub. **Wheelchair toilet (D70+ ST70+)** by the other
toilets. Virtually all the other eateries have flat access and **wheelchair toilets**.

   The cinema has a flat entrance and a spacious foyer, with step-free
access to all screens. All have several chair and transfer spaces.
They can take out additional seats if you ring and ask. **Two
wheelchair toilets (D80 ST75)** off the foyer. All screens have an
induction loop.

Camden (Odeon)

14 Parkway NW1 7AA

Tel: 020 7482-4051

Situated 50m west of Camden Town tube station. Five screens. Step free at the main entrance, and to Screens One, Two, Three and Four via a lift. Screen Five has approximately +10 steps. **Two wheelchair toilets**. Induction loop in all screens.

Clapham Picture House

76 Venn Street, Clapham Common SW4 0AT

RecM: 020 7498-2242 BO 020 7498-3323

website: www.picturehouse-cinemas.co.uk.

100m from Clapham Common tube. Four screens. Flat entrance, and step free to Screens Three and Four, each with two chair spaces. Screen One has +26 steps, Screen Two has 40+ and chair users are not permitted. **Wheelchair toilet (D85 ST70+)** in the foyer. Induction loop in all screens.

Electric Cinema

191 Portobello Road W11 2ED

Tel: 020 7908-9696/020 7229-8688 *website:* www.the-electric.co.uk

Near the junction with Cobble Terrace. One screen. Entrance +2 steps, but there is step-free access via the club next door, which also has a **wheelchair toilet** upstairs. Access to the toilet is via a lift, and staff assistance is necessary. Two chair spaces.

Everyman

5 Holly Bush Vale, Hampstead NW3 6TX

RecM: and BO 0870 066-4777

website: www.everymancinema.com

One screen. Entrance +3+5 steps then +8 to the auditorium. Side exit allows step-free access into the auditorium. Two chair spaces. **Wheelchair toilet** to the left of the screen. Induction loop.

Finchley (Phoenix)

High Road, East Finchley N2 9JP

Tel: 020 8444-6789 *RecM:* 020 8883-2233

By the junction with Fairlawn Avenue. One screen. From street level, +3 steps to the box office bypassed by a ramp. Then there is a lift to the auditorium bypassing +21. Three chair spaces. **Wheelchair toilet** opposite the lift. Induction loop.

Finchley Road (Warner)
O2 Centre, 255 Finchley Road NW3 6LU
Tel: 020 7604-3059 *RecM*: 0870 240-6020
Situated on the first floor of the O2 Centre, which is 50m left from
Finchley Road tube station. There is a large CP off Rosemont Road for
the centre. Access from Finchley Road is through two large revolving
doors (200cm opening) and then up to the first floor in a circular lift (D70
Radius200) to the right of the escalators. From the CP on the lower level,
there is a lift (D100 W110 L120) to the left of the escalators up to ground
level, and then a 30m corridor to the main gallery and circular lift.
   Eight screens. The cinema itself is all on one level, with step-free
access to all screens, and at least two chair spaces in every screen.
Two wheelchair toilets (D80 ST110) opposite Screen Five, and **one
(D80 ST75 NKS)** in the *Wetherspoons* pub next to the cinema.
Induction loop in all screens.
   The O2 Centre has bars and restaurants on the GF and first floor;
the lower level has a large *Sainsburys*.

Fulham Broadway (Warner)
Unit 18, Fulham Broadway Retail Centre SW6 1DN
Tel: 020 7385-2025
Situated within the shopping centre, the entrance to which is 100m to
the left from Fulham Broadway tube station. It has three floors with
shops on the GF, restaurants, bars and the cinema on the first floor
and a fitness club on the second floor. A lift halfway down the central
corridor goes to all floors, including a **wheelchair toilet** in the basement. There is another **wheelchair toilet (D90 ST100 NKS)** at the
back of *Lloyd's No 1* pub, on the first floor. The cinema itself is at the
back of shopping centre on the first floor, with step-free access via lift
and ramp which bypasses + 5 steps. Nine screens. All screens are step
free on one floor. All have two, four or six chair spaces. **Two
wheelchair toilets**, one **(D95 ST110)** by Screen Five, the other
(D95 ST100) by Screen Seven. All screens have induction loops.

Fulham Road (UGC)
142 Fulham Road SW10 9QR
Tel: 020 7370-2110 BO 0870 907-0711
Near the junction with Drayton Gardens. Limited on-site parking on
request. Six screens. Entrance + 1 step, then flat to Screens Four and
Five, each, we were told, with five chair spaces. Other screens are
reached by over 35 steps. Infrared system in Screens Three and Four.
Wheelchair toilet situated between Screens Four and Five.

Genesis Cinema

93 Mile End Road E1 4UJ

Tel: 020 7780-2000 *website:* www.genesiscinema.co.uk

Located on Mile End Road, between Cephas Avenue and Cleveland Way, about 500m left from Stepney Green tube station. Five screens. Step free entrance, leading straight to the box office. Screen One is +11+11 steps. An open lift (D80 L110), situated behind the box office, bypasses −4 to give access to Screens Two to Five. All have five/six spaces. **Wheelchair toilet (D80 ST100)** next to the lift. Induction loop in all screens.

Greenwich Filmworks (UCI)

Bugsby's Way, Greenwich SE10 0QJ

RecM: 0870 010-2030 M 020 8853-3282

A part of the Leisure Park by the corner of Bugsby's Way and Blackwall Lane. Large outdoor CP. Fourteen screens. The step-free entrance to the cinema is down a short alley between *Pizza Hut* and *McDonald's*. The box office and a bar are on the GF, while the screens are spread over four floors, reached via a lift behind the ticket barrier. All have step-free access and between four and eight chair spaces. **Four wheelchair toilets (D80+ ST80+)**, one on each floor. Infrared system for all screens.

Hammersmith (UGC)

207 King Street, Hammersmith W6 9JT

Tel: 020 8748-2388 *RecM*: 0870 907-0718

200m from Ravenscourt Park tube, opposite Studland Street. Four screens. Step free to the foyer and Screens Three and Four. Both have chair spaces. Films are rotated to the accessible screens. About +**40** steps to Screens One and Two. **Wheelchair toilet (D85 ST75)** in the foyer. Induction loops in all screens.

Holloway (Odeon)

419-427 Holloway Road, Islington N7 6LJ

Tel: 020 7281-1228

At the junction with Tufnell Park Road. Eight screens. Step-free through the foyer to Screens Four, Five Six, Seven and Eight. Each has at least three chair spaces. Screens Two and Three are via +45 steps; with +27 to Screen One. **Two wheelchair toilets (D90 ST85)** in the foyer. Induction loop in all screens.

Islington (Warner)
Parkfield Street N1 0PS
Tel: 020 7226-2848
Located on the first and second floor of the N1 Shopping Centre, opposite Angel Tube Station, on the corner of Upper Street and Liverpool Street, with pedestrian entrances on both. UGCP accessed from Parkfield Street, with eleven BB spaces. The GF has shops, the first floor has restaurants, the cinema and the new Marquee Club. Two lifts (D110 W140 L135) halfway along the arcade serve both floors and the UGCP. There is a **wheelchair toilet (D85 ST150 NKS)** next to the lifts on the first floor, and **adapted cubicles** in both Ladies and Gents, as well as others in *Borders* and *Lloyd's No1* pub.

Nine screens. The first floor entrance to the cinema leads to the box office. There is a lift (D110 W140 L155) to the right of the box office, which gives access to all the screens which are on the second floor. All are step free and have between two and twenty chair spaces. **Three wheelchair toilets**, one **(D95 ST95)** in the foyer, one by Screen Four **(D80 ST90)**, the other by Screen Nine **(D95 ST95)**. All screens have an induction loop.

Kensington (Odeon)
Kensington High Street W8 6NA
Tel: 020 7602-6460
Opposite the Commonwealth Institute, near the junction with Earls Court Road. Six screens. A fire exit bypasses +6 steps at the entrance giving step-free access to Screens Four and Five, which have three chair spaces each. From the foyer: Screen One has +46 steps; Screen Two +39; Screen Three +72 and Screen Six +12. **Wheelchair toilet (D85 ST75)** in the main foyer. Induction loop in all screens.

Muswell Hill (Odeon)
Fortis Green Road, Muswell Hill N10 3HP
Tel: 020 8883-3547
Near the junction with Muswell Hill. CP at the rear. Three screens. Ramp at main entrance, then flat to Screens Two and Three. Each have two transfer and three chair spaces. Screen One +26 steps. **Wheelchair toilet** on the GF. Induction loop in all screens.

Premier
95A Rye Lane, Peckham SE15 4ST
Tel: 020 7732-1313 020 *RecM:* 020 7732-1010

About 150m from Peckham Rye NR Station. CP behind the cinema. Six screens. Step free to all screens. Screen One has two chair spaces, and Screens Two to Six have one chair space each. **Wheelchair toilet (D85 ST90)** by the entrance to Screen Six. All screens have an induction loop.

Putney (Odeon)

26 Putney High Street SW15 1SN
Tel: 020 8780-1200
Situated about 100m from Putney Bridge. Three screens. Only Screen Two has step-free access, with approximately +15 steps to Screens One and Three . There is a **wheelchair toilet** in the foyer and induction loops in all screens.

Rio

107 Kingsland High Street, Kingsland E8 2PB
Tel: 020 7241-9410 *website:* www.riocinema.org.uk
At the junction with John Campbell Road. Step free to the stalls with four permanent chair spaces, as well as removable seats. **Wheelchair toilet (D85 ST85)** by the stalls entrance. Infrared system.

Ritzy

Brixton Oval, Coldharbour Lane, Brixton SW2 1JG
Tel: 020 7733-2229 *website:* www.ritzycinema.co.uk
The phone number connects you to a series of computerised options. Choose Option 1 to book tickets and speak to a human! 50m from Brixton tube station. Five screens. Step free to all the screens via the main entrance. One to Four are on the GF. Screen Five on the first floor is reached by a lift (D80 W105 L140). All screens have removable seats, so phone in advance to ensure that a chair space is available. Induction loop in all screens. Step free to the Ritzy Bar on the GF; Ritzy Canteen on the first floor has some tables with flat access. **Wheelchair toilet (D85 ST80)** on the GF.

Shepherd's Bush (Warner)

West 12 Shopping and Leisure Centre, Shepherd's Bush Green W12 8PP
Tel: 020 8749-5014 *RecM:* 0870 240-6020
Situated opposite Shepherd's Bush Central Line tube station, the cinema is part of a leisure complex including fitness centre, pool hall, bar and restaurants. The nearby NCP has limited parking. Twelve screens. The entrance to the cinema is on the GF, while the box office

is on the first floor and the screens are on the second floor, accessed by lift (D79). All have wheelchair spaces. **One wheelchair toilet (D85 ST100)** on the second floor, to the right from the lift. Infrared system in all screens.

Staples Corner (UGC)
Geron Way, Staples Corner NW2 6LU
Tel: 020 8208-1367 *RecM*: 0870 907-0717
Just 400m south along the Edgware Road, on the left. The other developments in the area are mainly shops and stores. On-site parking. Ramped entrance, and then step free to all screens. Every screen has three or more chair spaces. **Two wheelchair toilets (D70 + ST70 +)** in the foyer. All screens have an induction loop.

Stratford Picture House
Gerry Raffles Square, Salway Road E15 1BN
Tel: 020 8555-3366 *Textphone:* 020 8522-0043
BB spaces in CP on Salway Road, and the shopping centre CP is about 400m away. Four screens. Flat entrance to box office and kiosk. Lift to the left of the box office takes you to the first floor which has a bar and the screens. All screens have at least four chair spaces. **Two wheelchair toilets**, one past the kiosk on the GF, the other on the first floor between the Ladies and Gents. Induction loop in all screens.

Surrey Quays (UCI)
Redriff Road SE16 1LL
Tel: 020 7232-4400 *RecM:* 0870 010-2030
Huge CP for the retail centre (see *Shops* section) has BB spaces outside step-free cinema entrance. Nine screens, all step free, with wheelchair spaces. Screens One, Three, Four, Five and Nine are accessed via a lift (D75 W100 L140) at the back of the foyer. **Three wheelchair toilets (D80 ST80)**, two off the foyer on the GF, the other on the first floor to the right of the lift. All screens have induction loops.

Swiss Cottage (Odeon)
96 Finchley Road NW3 5EL
Tel: 020 7586-1269
50m from Swiss Cottage tube. Ramp at entrance. Six screens. Flat route to Screens Three, Five and Six. Each has at least one chair space. The other screens are all up at least two flights of stairs. **Wheelchair toilet (D90 ST90)** in the foyer. Induction loop in all screens.

Tricycle Cinema
269 Kilburn High Road NW6 7JR
Tel: 020 7328-6611 M 020 7372-6611
Part of the same building as the *Tricycle Theatre* (see *Theatres*). One screen. Step-free entrance; lift bypasses flight of steps down to cinema, which has two chair spaces. **Wheelchair toilet (D70 + ST70 +)** to the left of the entrance. Infrared system.

West India Quay (UGC)
11 Hertsmere Road E14 4AL
Tel: 020 7517-7860 BO 0870 907-0722
Located halfway along Hertsmere Road, next to a MSCP. Nine Screens. Step-free entrance from the street, with box office on the GF. A lift (D75 W105 L135) to the right of the box office goes to all four floors. Screens One to Five are on the first floor, while Screens Six to Nine are on the third floor. All screens have four wheelchair spaces. **Four wheelchair cubicles (D75 ST85),** two each on floors one and three. Infrared system in all screens.

Willesden Green Belle-Vue Cinema
Willesden Green Library Centre, 95 The High Road NW10 2ST
RecM: 020 830-0822 BO 020 8830-0823
CP behind the Centre has BB spaces. One screen. Ramped entrance. Flat route via fire doors bypasses + 7 steps into the cinema. Please ring first. Two chair spaces and room for up to fifteen at the front. **Wheelchair toilet (D85 ST80)** in main concourse.

Wood Green Cineworld
Shopping City, High Road N22 6YQ
Tel: 020 8829-1400 *DisEnq:* 020 8829-9762
website: www.cineworld.co.uk
Shopping City is located along both sides of Wood Green High Road, between Lordship Lane and Westbury Avenue. The pedestrian entrance is 250m along from Lordship Lane. The MSCP is accessed from Noel Park Road, and covers floors two to nine with four BB spaces on each odd-numbered floor. Three lifts (D115 W170 L120) serve all floors, immediately to the right from the pedestrian entrance. There are shops and eateries on the GF and first floor.

Twelve screens. The cinema shows quite a number of Asian films. The box office is on the first floor, to the left of the lifts. Screens One to Three are at box office level, with an open lift (D80 W110) bypassing − 6 steps. Screens Four to Twelve are on the GF, accessed by a lift (D80 W100 L140) next to the open lift, at the bottom of the −6. All have chair spaces. **Two wheelchair toilets (D90 ST110)**, one to the right of the box office, the other on the GF by Screen Eight. Induction loops in all screens. The Cineworld website does not appear to include any access information.

Wood Green Showcase
Hollywood Green, High Road N22 6EJ
Tel: 020 8829-9546 *RecM:* 0870 162-8960
On the corner of Wood Green High Road and Lordship Lane, immediately opposite the tube station. Six screens. The box office and screens are on the first floor, accessed by escalators or by a lift (D75 W90 L110), but a key is needed from the box office to operate the lift. There are a minimum of five chair spaces in each screen. **Two wheelchair toilets (D95 ST75)**, one to the right of the popcorn counter, and another by the screens. Induction loops in every screen.

Between the North/South Circular Roads and the M25

Barnet (Odeon)
Great North Road, Barnet, Herts EN5 1AB
Tel: 020 8440-9970
Near the junction with Station Road. Five screens. A ramp at the entrance gives step-free access to Screens Two, Three and Four. Transfer spaces in these screens and a seat can be removed (with notice) in Screens Three and Four for a chair space. Screens One and Five have more than +30. **Wheelchair toilet** on GF off foyer. Induction loop in all screens.

Beckenham (Odeon)
High Street, Beckenham, Kent BR3 1DY
Tel: 020 8658-7114
Some on-site parking. Six screens. A ramp to the left of entrance gives step-free access to Screens Three, Four and Five, with chair spaces. Screens One and Two are up two flights of stairs, while Screen Six is +15 steps. **Wheelchair toilet** by Screen Four. Infrared system in all screens.

Bluewater Showcase
Water Circus, Greenhithe DA9 9SG
Tel: BO 0870 242-7070 *RecM:* 01322 422-700

Parking available nearby in Bluewater Centre. Twelve screens. Step free to box office on GF, which also contains six screens. Lift to first floor, where five screens can be reached step free; the other one is up a staircase. Eleven screens have wheelchair spaces. **Two wheelchair toilets**, one on the GF, one on the first floor. Induction loop in all screens.

Bromley (Odeon)
242 High Street, Bromley, Kent BR1 1PG
Tel: 020 8313-9599
Near Beckenham Lane. On-site parking possible if you phone first. Four screens. Step-free access through main entrance, then flat to Screens Two and Three with chair spaces in each. Screen One +42, Screen Four +18. **Wheelchair toilet** in foyer. Induction loop in all screens.

Croydon Clocktower see section on *Arts Centres*.

Croydon Purley Way (Warner)
Valley Park Leisure Complex, Hesterman Way, Croydon CR0 4YA
Tel: 0870 240-6020
In the Valley Park Leisure Complex, near Waddon Marsh Station (and IKEA). On-site CP. Step-free access to all eight screens with at least four chair spaces in each. **Two wheelchair toilets (D95 ST85)** in the foyer. Induction loop in every screen. Nearby, in the Leisure Complex is a *Burger King*, *Frankie and Benny's* New York Italian Diner and the *Chiquito* (Mexican) restaurant and bar. All have step-free access and a **wheelchair toilet (D70+ ST70+)**.

Croydon Grants (Warner)
14-20 High Street, Croydon CR0 1GT
Tel: 0870 240-6020
Located opposite the junction with Park Street. Parking in the UGCP behind Fairfield Halls, 500m from the cinema via a subway under the main road. *Edwards* to the left of the entrance has a **wheelchair toilet (D85 ST75)**. Lift behind escalators (D105 W140) gives access to all floors of the cinema. Ten screens. Box office only on the first floor, with Screens One to Three on the second floor and Screens Four to Ten on the fourth floor. All screens have four wheelchair spaces. **Two wheelchair toilets (D95 ST75)**, one to the left of lift on the second floor, the other on the fourth floor. All screens have an induction loop.

Dagenham (Warner)
Dagenham Leisure Park, Cook Road, Dagenham, Essex RM9 6UQ
Tel: 0870 240-6020
Located within a leisure complex which includes restaurants, bars, a bowling alley and a bingo hall, the cinema is at the junction of Cook Road and Ripple Road (A13). Nine screens. All can be reached step free, and have chair spaces. Induction loop in all screens.

Ealing (UGC)
61 Uxbridge Road, Ealing W5 5AH
Tel: 020 8579-4851 *RecM:* 0870 907-0719
Opposite the Town Hall, about 500m from Ealing Broadway tube station. Three screens. Small step at the entrance, then flat to Screens Two and Three (three chair spaces in each). Screen One is reached via + 30 steps. **Wheelchair toilet (D90 ST200 +)** by Screen Three. Induction loop in all screens.

Enfield (UGC)
Southbury Leisure Park, 208 Southbury Road, Enfield EN1 1YQ
Tel: 020 8366-1550 *RecM:* 0870 907-0745
Fifteen screens. The cinema is on three floors, and all screens are step free via a lift and have varying numbers of chair spaces. **Three wheelchair toilets**, one on each floor. Infrared system in all screens.

Harrow (Warner)
St George's Shopping Centre, St Ann's Road, Harrow HA1 1AS
Tel: 0870 240-6020
On the first floor of the shopping centre, which has a MSCP attached. The centre has several lifts (D120+ W160+ L160+). Nine screens. Screens One to Five have four chair spaces, Screens Six to Nine have two; staff said they could easily fit more in at the front of all screens. **Wheelchair toilet (D90 ST100)** towards Screens Five to Nine on the left. Induction loops in all screens.

Hemel Hempstead (Odeon)
Jarman Park, Herts HP2 4IW
Tel: 01442-292220
Eight screens. Ramp at main entrance gives step-free access to all screens, with two spaces in each (advanced booking is advised). **Wheelchair toilet** in the foyer. Induction loop for all screens.

Kingston (Odeon) see section on *Shops*.

Lea Valley UCI (Picketts Lock Centre)

Picketts Lock Lane, Edmonton N9 0AS

Tel: 0870 010-2030

Large on-site CP with ramps and BB spaces. Flat entrance and step free to all twelve screens. All have at least two chair spaces. **Wheelchair toilets (D90 ST80)** either side of the foyer. There are several other wheelchair toilets in the complex; see the *Days Out* chapter. Induction loop in each screen and at the box office.

North Finchley Lido (Warner)

Great North Leisure Park, Chaplin Square N12 0GL

Tel: 0870 240-6020

Just north of the junction of High Road and the North Circular Road. Part of a large development with restaurants and a bowling alley. Large CP with ten BB spaces just outside the cinema, and six more elsewhere in the CP. Eight screens. Step-free access to the box office, with a lift (D80 W105 L135) to all eight screens. All screens have four chair spaces. **Wheelchair toilet (D90 ST75)** on the first floor. All screens have induction loops.

Richmond Filmhouse

3 Water Lane, Richmond, Surrey TW9 1TJ

Tel: 020 8332-0030

Opposite the *Watermans Arms* pub. The street is slightly cobbled. Entrance + 1 step with difficult camber. Then flat to the one screen. One chair space. **Wheelchair toilet (D85 ST95)**. Infrared system.

Richmond Hill Street (Odeon)

72 Hill Street, Richmond, Surrey TW9 1TW

Tel: 020 8940-3040

The entrance is opposite the bridge. Parking is difficult. The two Richmond Odeons are run together, and this one contains Screens One to Three. Flat entrance, then step-free access to Screens Two and Three, both with three chair spaces. Screen one is + 44 steps. Induction loops only in Screens One and Three. The Studio is about 300m away down the hill.

Richmond Studio (Odeon)

6 Red Lion Street, Richmond, Surrey TW9 6RE

Tel: 020 8332-6435

The entrance is next to the police station. The other half of the Richmond Odeon. Entrance + 6 steps, bypassed via a door on Red

Lion. Four screens (four to seven). From the street there is step-free access to Screens Four and Five. Each has two chair spaces. Screens Six and Seven are +22 from the box office. **Wheelchair toilet (D85 ST75)** near the Red Lion Street entrance. Induction loop in Screens Four and Five.

Romford Ster Century

The Brewery Shopping Centre, Waterloo Road, Romford RM1 1AU
Tel: 01708 759-100
Located on the first and second floors of the shopping centre above *Sainsbury's*, beyond the eateries. Sixteen screens. Box office only on the first floor, then lift (D85 W95 L130) to the left takes you up to the foyer and step free to sixteen screens. This cinema has adopted the policy of providing one chair space for every 100 seats in the screen. **Two wheelchair toilets**, one **(D85 ST100)** to the left of the foyer, the other **(D85 ST100)** to the right.

South Woodford (Odeon)

60 High Road, South Woodford E18 2QL
Tel: 020 8989-4066
On the corner of George Lane. Seven screens. Entrance +1 step. Ramped access to Screens One, Two and Three. The other screens are up two flights of stairs. **Wheelchair toilet** on GF near box office.

Streatham (Odeon)

47-49 Streatham High Street, Streatham SW16 1PW
Tel: 020 8769-2221
By the junction with Pendennis Road. Eight screens. Ramped entrance, then step-free access to Screens Four to Seven. Screens One, Two and Three are up two flights of stairs, while Screen Eight is up one flight of steps. **Wheelchair toilet** in GF foyer. Infrared system in all screens.

Sutton (UCI)

St Nicholas Centre, St Nicholas Way, Sutton, Surrey SM1 1AZ
Tel: 020 8395-4488
Part of the shopping centre, see write-up on Sutton in the chapter on *Shops*. Adjacent MSCP. Lift (D105 W110 L135) to the GF. Six screens. Flat entrance, and open lift (W80 L170) bypasses +12 steps to all screens. All screens have six chair spaces. **Two wheelchair toilets (D95 ST80)** in the foyer. Induction loops available.

Uxbridge (Odeon)
The Chimes Shopping Centre, 302 High Street UB8 1GD
Tel: 01895-237490
Nine screens, all with chair spaces. Step-free access to all via a lift in
the shopping centre. **Two wheelchair toilets** off the foyer. Induction
loop in all screens.

Watermans Art Centre see write-up in section on *Arts centres.*

Wimbledon (Odeon)
The Broadway, Wimbledon SW19 1QB
Tel: 020 8944-6890
This cinema has been relocated from the site of the previous
Wimbledon Odeon. It is now situated 150m from the Centre Court
exit of Wimbledon Station, in the middle of the Broadway. The
entrance is hidden behind the front of *Safeway.* From here, a lift
(D110 W155 L180) takes you to the first floor, where the box office
and the twelve screens are situated. All have between two and four
chair spaces. **Two wheelchair toilets (D95 ST95)** to the left and right
past the box office. Induction loop in all screens.

Music venues

A multi-purpose venue has been built in Docklands, which we list
first, along with Wembley.

London Arena
Limeharbour E14 9TH
Tel: 020 7538-8880 BO 020 7538-1212 *DisEnq:* 020 7538-2288
website: www.londonarena.co.uk
e-mail: angela.ivey@londonarena.co.uk
By the junction with East Ferry Road, and 50m from Crossharbour
DLR Station. The Arena is a huge modern multi-purpose venue. It
has a capacity of 13,000, and puts on a variety of events. As a result,
various layouts are used. The ASDA CP about 200m away has ten
BB spaces. Depending on the event, there are up to thirty-six BB
spaces less than 100m away, under the DLR bridge.
   The management have gone to some lengths to ensure adequate
access for both chair users and disabled walkers. Disabled patrons
will normally use the flat VIP entrance some 25m from the main
entrance. Flat access everywhere on the GF to all bars, kiosks and
toilets. Lift (D80 W100 L150) to the first floor. There are usually up

to thirty chair spaces, and seats with step-free access. **Five wheelchair toilets** (all **D70 + ST70 +**) on the GF, one in the south stand, and two each in the west and east stands.

Wembley Arena
Engineers Way, Wembley HA9 0DN
Tel: 020 8902-8833 BO 0870 739-0739
Used mainly for concerts and shows (sporting and children's events). There are 30 + BB spaces next to the Arena. The entrance for wheelchair users is to the left of the booking office. This bypasses the normal turnstiles for getting in. The main area around the arena has step-free access, and there are fast food kiosks and refreshment stalls.

For pop concerts there are four areas by Gates 6, 12, 26 and 36, for chair users and friends. Each can accommodate up to seven chairs and has step-free access. Other events may involve different layouts. There are relatively few seats with step-free access, but if you want one, ask when booking.

Two wheelchair toilets (D85 ST70) with a tight 90° turn en route by Gates 17 and 38 (there are plans to move these). The restaurant/bar on the second floor is reached by + 12 + 12 steps (plans to provide step-free access).

Rock, jazz, rave and folk

Note that most of the venues listed have significant access barriers. All we can do is to tell you what they are. In many cases the venue management and staff will be helpful in assisting people to get in to enjoy the music and the atmosphere. As with some other things, it may be that it's more difficult for disabled walkers than it is for a chair user.

Inside the North/South Circular Roads

Amersham Arms
288 New Cross Road, New Cross SE14 6TY
Tel: 020 8692-2047
Opposite New Cross Tube Station. Step-free access via side doors to bar and music. **Wheelchair toilet (D85 ST100)**.

Archway Tavern
1 Archway Close, Archway Roundabout N19 3TD
Tel: 020 7272-2840

The pub is opposite Archway Tube. Side door on the right with a small step.

Astoria
157 Charing Cross Road WC2H 0EL
Tel: 020 7434-9592
Entrance $+3+4$ steps. The auditorium is well above street level. The lowest part is the dance floor which is $+27$ from the foyer. Best viewing is from the balcony which has two flat areas with tables and seats, with space for a couple of chair users to get a good view of the stage. This involves $+50-8$ from the foyer, and the staff are willing to help if needed. No hearing system, as the music is likely to be very loud!

BAC see section on *Arts centres.*

Borderline
Orange Yard (off Manette Street) W1U 5LB
Tel: BO 020 7734-2095
NCP at Centre Point. Step free from Manette Street. Then -23 steps to the venue, bypassed via a service lift (D150 W150 L150) reached from Goslett Yard. The dance floor is -1.

Brixton Academy
211 Stockwell Road, Brixton SW9 9SL
Tel: 020 7771-3000 BO 0870 771-2000 *website:* www.brixton-academy.co.uk
One of London's premier venues. Opposite the junction with Bellefields Road. Entrance $+5$ steps, and staff will offer to carry chair users up these. Alternative step-free entrance about 150m round to the left. Once inside, step free throughout GF to bars and the main auditorium, which has a raised viewing area on the left with priority use for chair users. Excellent viewing point. First floor circle $+20$.
Wheelchair toilet (D85 ST90) in the foyer.

Bull and Gate
389 Kentish Town Road NW5 2TG
Tel: 020 7485-5358
Intimate venue for up-and-coming bands at the back of a pub with $+1$ step at entrance. To the left of the main pub entrance, there is ramped access. Alternatively, there is step-free access through the toilets (!) to the music area. There are plans to install a wheelchair toilet next year.

Bull's Head
Lonsdale Road, Barnes SW13 9PY
Tel: 020 8876-5241
Jazz. Near the junction with Barnes High Street. Entrance has +1 step then +4 to the music venue. A side entrance in Barnes High Street has an easier +4. Maximum of three chair users.

Dingwalls see **Jongleurs** in *Theatres.*

Dublin Castle
94 Parkway, Camden NW1 7AN
Tel: 020 7485-1773
About half way along Parkway. The pub has +1 step, then +2 to the venue.

Earls Court see chapter on *Exhibition halls.*

Forum
9 Highgate Road, Kentish Town NW5 1JY
Tel: 020 7284-1001
Rock. 80m from Kentish Town tube and NR station. No restriction on chair users. It can get very crowded, so arrive early. Entrance +1 step. The hall floor has three levels. From the entrance there are −2 to the first level, then −4−4 to other levels. Very little seating. There are +30 to the circle, which has transfer seats.

Garage
20 Highbury Corner N5 1RD
Tel: 020 7607-1818
Rock. 50m from Highbury and Islington tube and BR. No restriction on number of chair users. Flat entrance then +3 steps to the hall, which has few seats. Portable ramp available. There are +2 steps to the bar, bypassed by a steep ramp at the far side of the hall. **Adapted toilet (D80 ST75 inward opening door)** to the left as you go in. It also contains **Upstairs at the Garage**, which is +25 from the GF. Rock, folk. No restriction on chair users. Very few seats.

Half Moon Putney
93 Lower Richmond Road SW15 1EU
Tel: 020 8780-9383
Rock, Blues and Folk. Pub and music hall +1 step, or flat around

the back. Flat inside apart from $+1$ to the raised sections at either side of the hall. Some gigs are seated, some not.

Hammersmith (Carling) Apollo
Queen Caroline Street, Hammersmith W6 9QH
Tel: BO 020 7416-6022 M 020 8748-8660
On the corner with the Fulham Palace Road. Parking in nearby NCP on Glenthorpe Road. Entrance $+3$ steps to foyer and bars. Step free from foyer to auditorium. Ramped access via a side exit can be arranged. There are two chair spaces on a raised platform with a ramp at the rear of the auditorium, and three seats for transfer. Row L has good legroom. **Wheelchair toilet (D85 ST90)** to the back left of the auditorium.

Hope and Anchor
207 Upper Street N1 1RL
Tel: 020 7354-1317
Historic venue where U2 once played. Located on the junction of Upper Street and Islington Park Street. Entrance from Islington Park Street to bar level via lip. 40% is -1 step. Entrance from Upper Street is $+1$, then -16 to the venue, which is step free with little seating.

Jazz Café
5 Parkway, Camden NW1 7PG
Tel: 020 7916-6000 *website:* www.jazzcafe.co.uk
Jazz. Ticket office outside, then $+1$ step to enter the building which is flat apart from two small raised seating areas which are both $+3$. The split level balcony bar and restaurant have $+15$. **Adapted toilet (D80,** opening in **ST75)** next to the stage through the double doors.

Marquee Club
16 Parkfield Street, N1 Centre, Islington N1 0PS
Tel: 020 7288-4400 BO 0870 120-2221
website: www.themarquee.com
At the back of the N1 Shopping Centre, on two floors. The GF entrance is opposite the lifts for the N1 Centre CP, and gives step-free access to the box office and cloakroom only. To bypass the steps up to the venue, you must exit the building, take the lift opposite to the first floor, then re-enter the Marquee at this level. From here, an internal lift takes you down to the venue level, above

the box office stairs. This level also contains a bar and grill. There are **two wheelchair toilets** (not seen) by the internal lifts on both levels.

Ocean

270 Mare Street, Hackney E8 1HE

Tel: 020 8533-0111 BO 020 7314-2800 *website:* www.ocean.org.uk

Vast four storey venue located on Mare Street between Morning Lane and Paragon Road. There are nearby BB spaces outside the Town Hall. Step-free main entrance leads to the box office, as well as a bar/restaurant. Behind the box office is the main lift which goes to all floors. Ocean 1 is on the first floor, and includes **two wheelchair toilets**. Ocean 2 and 3, on the second and third floors, are much smaller, and each have one **wheelchair toilet**. All venues have an induction loop, and have a maximum of over twenty chair spaces.

Paradise Bar

460 New Cross Road, New Cross SE14 6TJ

Tel: 020 8692-1530

On the corner of Florence Road. Step free via a narrow door (W65). **Wheelchair cubicle** in Ladies.

Rock Garden

The Piazza, Covent Garden WC2E 8HE

Tel: 020 7240-3961

Rock. 50m from Covent Garden Tube Station. There are −20 steps to the venue, and bar (+1). Little seating. Maximum of four chair users. Restaurant at street level.

Ronnie Scott's

47 Frith Street W1D 4HT

Tel: 020 7439-0747 *website:* www.ronniescotts.co.uk

World famous Jazz venue. Entrance +3 steps, then +2, and −3 to a lower level. Quite cramped. There are −15 to the TV room/social bar and +24 to the dance club. Two chair users allowed.

Royal Standard

Blackhorse Lane, Higham Hill E17 6DS

Tel: 020 8503-2523

Rock. 15m from Blackhorse tube station with on-site parking (phone early to reserve a place in the CP). Entrance +1 step, then step free to the bar and music hall apart from +2 to raised section. Phone in advance to reserve a place.

Shepherd's Bush Empire
Shepherd's Bush Green, Shepherd's Bush W12 8TT
Tel: BO 0870 771-2000 M 020 8354-3300 *website:* www.shepherds-bush-empire.co.uk
Converted theatre near the corner of Goldhawk Road. Step free to the ticket office, then +2 steps to the foyer and −6 to a raised section at the back of the stalls where there is space for four wheelchair users and a bar. Alternative route via fire door, which is +2 from street (portable ramp available) and then −2 inside (due to be ramped). From the raised section to the dance floor is −6. From the foyer: circle +21; upper circle +40−5; balcony +40−5+30. **Wheelchair toilet** was due to be installed at the left of the raised section at the back of the stalls in January 2003, though at the time of going to print nothing had materialised. **Wheelchair toilet (D90 ST75 NKS)** 50m away on the pavement.

606 Club
90 Lots Road, Chelsea SW10 0QD
Tel: 020 7352-5953 *website:* www.606club.co.uk
Jazz and blues. Non-members must book a table for dinner. Entrance via −17+1−2 steps, then +1 to the bar. Two chair users allowed. Staff trained to help wheelchair users up stairs.

Swan Pub
215 Clapham Road, Stockwell SW9
Tel: 020 7978-9778
Opposite Stockwell Tube Station. Flat throughout.

Union Chapel
Compton Terrace N1 2XD
Tel: 020 7226-1686 *website:* www.unionchapel.org.uk
A converted church near Highbury Corner featuring various genres, including jazz, indie, folk and world music. Two venues; the main venue is accessed via Compton Terrace, with a portable ramp to bypass +3 steps. The sloped auditorium has 100% fixed seating (pews) with wheelchairs accommodated at the back. **Wheelchair toilet (D75 ST85)** through a door to the right of the stage and then signposted on the right. The bar is via a door to the left of the stage

with −1 bypassed with a portable ramp, then a stairlift (W77 L85) and a sloped corridor.

The studio venue can be reached step free from Compton Terrace. It is step free inside and has 100% movable seating.

Vortex Club
139 Stoke Newington Church Street N16 0UH
Tel: 020 7254-6516
Opposite Grove Lordship Road. Entrance to the club is +15, then +1 to a seating area.

Between the North/South Circular Roads and the M25

Cartoon
179 London Road, Croydon CR0 2RJ
Tel: 020 8239-1616
Rock. Near the junction with St James's Road. Step free throughout.

Classical music

Barbican Centre see section on *Arts centres.*

Blackheath Concert Halls
23 Lee Road SE3 9RQ *Tel:* BO 020 8463-0100 M 0120 8318-9758.
By the corner of Blackheath Park. Parking by prior arrangement only. The +4 steps at the front entrance can be bypassed via a ramp on the left leading to the foyer, and **wheelchair toilet (D80 ST100)**. The music hall is on the GF, with varying numbers of wheelchair spaces. Three flights of stairs lead to the recital rooms. Induction loop.

Conway Hall
25 Red Lion Square, Holborn WC1R 4RL
Tel: 020 7242-8032 *website:* www.conwayhall.org.uk. Used for classical music recordings and public meetings. Step free to the main hall. **Wheelchair toilet (D75 ST75)** and plenty of chair spaces. Ring first. Balcony +27 steps. Plans to install induction loop.

Purcell Room see section on *Arts centres.*

Queen Elizabeth Hall see section on *Arts centres.*

Royal Albert Hall

Kensington Gore, London SW7 2AP

Tel: BO 020 7589-8212 *DisEnq:* 020 7589-3853 *Textphone:* 020 7589-4447 *website:* www.royalalberthall.com *e-mail:* access@royalalberthall.com

The Hall was completed in 1871, and provides a grand and well-loved venue for a wide variety of events. Notably, during the summer, it is the host to the Henry Wood Promenade Concerts (see www.bbc.co.uk/proms). There is currently an extensive development and building programme which includes improvements for disabled visitors. The major work involves re-landscaping the South Steps and providing a new underground service yard. When the work is complete, the Hall will be open to visitors throughout the day, with restaurants, shops and a Hall tour available.

Eight on-site BB spaces can be booked. There are also BB spaces in Exhibition Road near the big museums. There's a CP in Prince Concert Road for people coming to concerts, but spaces there must be booked. Parking in the area is tightly controlled.

Ramped entrances are currently sited at Doors 2, 8 and 12, bypassing +4 steps at other entrances. By 2004 more entrances will have ramps.

Most of the interior of the building is now step free and accessible by lift, except for parts of the basement, and the central area called the Arena. There's a large forty-person lift by Door 11, two eight-person lifts (D75 W105 L140) by Door 2, a goods lift at Door 5, and an eight person lift (D90 W125 L145) by Door 8. All the lifts go from the GF to upper floors. There's a platform stair lift (W95 L140) to the Arena foyers by Door 2.

Most seats have stepped access; however, there are fourteen wheelchair spaces at the back of the Stalls at ground level. These are on both sides of the Hall, close to the stage. In addition there are now eight chair spaces in the Circle. These are in sections R,P,W and Y and those in R and W have better sightlines as they are more central. Four wheelchairs can be accommodated at Gallery level for certain events. All the wheelchair spaces have room for a companion to sit nearby. There is also step-free access to a number of the boxes, but box doors at Grand Tier and Second Tier are generally 66cm wide although some have door widths up to 140cm. There is normally a step or two inside the box itself.

There are **wheelchair toilets** (all **D70+ ST70+**) at ground level by Door 8, at Grand Tier level by Door 5, and at Circle level by Door 5.

The hall has a Sennheiser infrared sound system (headsets can be obtained at the Door 6 information desk). There is an audio description for certain events and an induction loop system. Seating can be provided near the stage for visually impaired patrons, and the best thing is to ring the Access Line 020 7589 3853.

There are several restaurants and bars, all with step-free access. These currently only open two hours before a performance, but when the Hall is open through the day, opening times may be extended.

Royal Festival Hall see section on *Arts centres*.

Covent Garden Royal Opera House (ROH)
Bow Street WC2E 9DD
Tel: **BO** 020 7304-4000 *Fax:* 020 7212-9460 *DisEnq:* 020 7212-9123 *Textphone:* 020 7212-9228 *website:* www.royaloperahouse.org.uk *e-mail:* boaccess@roh.org.uk

The ROH is the main centre for both opera and ballet in London, with an international reputation. It is situated in the northeast corner of the (old) Covent Garden Market, now extensively redeveloped, and opposite the famous Bow Street Police Station. Over the millennium period the Opera House was extensively redeveloped, and facilities for disabled patrons were greatly improved.

A free mailing list is available to disabled people, but advanced booking is essential for most performances. A detailed layout plan is available showing the seating arrangements. Parking is a potential problem. There are BB spaces in Bow Street and in Great Queen Street. There's also an NCP in Drury Lane. After 18.30 there are currently some single yellow line areas where BB holders can park.

There are step-free entrances from the Covent Garden Piazza, and from Bow Street. The Opera House has nearly twenty wheelchair spaces, which are in the Stalls Circle, Grand Tier, Balcony and Upper Amphitheatre. In addition, a good number of seats can be reached step free, adjacent to these spaces. Given the architectural limitations, they have made a very good job of providing spaces. All can be reached by lift. Most of the chair spaces are reached by using the large lifts on the left side of the building which you come to on your left if you enter through the box office area. These lifts also go to the Floral Hall bar and restaurant. For the Upper Amphitheatre, use the lifts on the right side of the building, to the right of the main foyer. If you come in from the box office, go straight on across the foyer, and the lifts are in front of you.

There are **wheelchair toilets (D70 + ST70 +)** on most floors where there are chair spaces, near the lifts. There's also one off the Ampitheatre Bar.

Note that if you want an interval drink in the Floral Hall, you will have to use the lift, so allow a little extra time.

The **Linbury Studio Theatre** has step-free access via a lift, and four wheelchair spaces. There are two chair spaces in the **Clore Studio Upstairs**.

Sadler's Wells Theatre
Rosebery Avenue EC1R 4TN
Tel: BO 020 7863-8000 *DisEnq:* 020 7863-8128 *Textphone:* 020 7863-8015 *website:* www.saddlerswells.com
The theatre is some way away from London's main theatreland, and is situated at the north end of Rosebery Avenue, near St John's Street. During the millennium, the theatre was closed for a massive redevelopment, during which the needs of disabled patrons were thoroughly addressed. Apart from the provision of chair spaces, the management have developed what they call an 'Access Address (AA) Book'. This is a way in which patrons can register their needs, and be provided with appropriate seat locations and prices. The AA Book is open not only to people with physical, sensory and cognitive disabilities, but also to over-60s, full time students, unwaged people, and to family groups. It is an approach which provides an interesting model for others to learn from.

There is a small CP in Arlington Way alongside the theatre, where disabled people can park without charge, but as there are only fifteen spaces, booking is essential. There are currently some nearby streets with single yellow lines which means that parking is possible after 18.30.

There is step-free access to the main theatre foyer, and 50m further up Rosebery Avenue to the Lilian Baylis (LB) theatre and to the café. The stalls of the main theatre are at ground level, while in the LB it is step free to the back row of the small auditorium.

In the main theatre there are four wheelchair spaces in the middle of the Stalls, and three more at the back of the First Circle, reached by a lift. The main route to the stalls involves $+2+1 -4-9$ steps to get to the row where the chair spaces are. There's an alternative route just to the right of the main Stalls entrance. In the foyer, it's quite confusing and crowded just before a performance, and we saw several elderly and disabled walkers who went up and down the steps unnecessarily, because they didn't know about the easier route. The passage also goes past the lift for getting to both the First and

Second Circles. There are some seats with step-free access near the chair spaces.

There are **wheelchair toilets (D70+ ST70+)** on the GF near the chair spaces in the Stalls (although this one tends to get used by others, because it is the only one around); on the First Circle level and through the café by the LB theatre.

St John's Smith Square Concert Hall
St John's Smith Square SW1P 3HA
Tel: BO 020 7222-1061 *Fax:* 020 7233-1618 *website:* www.sjss.org.uk
An atmospheric Georgian church in the middle of an attractive square. It is a regular concert venue, hosting a wide range of classical concerts. Unfortunately, there is a minimum of +16 steps to get in, and there are more steps to the crypt restaurant. Induction loop.

St Martin-in-the-Fields see chapter on *Places of worship.*

St Paul's Cathedral see chapter on *Places of worship.*

Wigmore Hall
36 Wigmore Street W1U 2BP
Tel: BO 020 7935-2141 *website:* www.wigmore-hall.org.uk *e-mail:* boxoffice@wigmore-hall.org.uk
Step free to foyer. A lift (D110 W160 L140) serves the main floor of the auditorium, where the three chair spaces are situated at the back. Chair users can also transfer on to aisle seats. The lift also goes to the basement restaurant, the Bechstein Room. There is a **wheelchair toilet (D85 ST75)** in the basement. Induction loop.

Theatres

London offers a huge range of theatre, and there is a somewhat blurred distinction between mainstream performances in the mainly Victorian and Edwardian theatres, and those in generally smaller venues, many of which are away from the West End, and are called the 'fringe'. We have adopted a strictly geographical approach, and the theatres listed as central are those in the West End and City areas. The theatres listed here can nearly all accommodate chair users, mostly with step-free access, but where there are barriers, these are described. Many of the venues have an adapted toilet and a good number have an infrared sound system. Just a few in very old Victorian and Edwardian buildings cannot yet accommodate chair users who need to stay in their chairs.

Trying out some of the fringe shows has always been a slightly haphazard pleasure. The really brilliant shows tend to get noticed and are booked out very quickly. If you want to get to these, keep your eyes open on the weekly *Time Out* reviews, among others. There are many other good shows, and others that don't quite come off, but may be interesting nonetheless.

Theatre staff tend to be able to recognise the needs of a chair user fairly readily, as they're relatively clear. The needs of disabled walkers are rather more varied, and you're more likely to have to spell out what you need, and to ask more questions. **Usually the easiest (step-free) access will be the same as for a chair user, and the easiest seats to get to will be on the same level as any chair spaces**. However, you may also need a reasonable amount of legroom, and some seats have more than others. You may alternatively want to be near a toilet, and may prefer to book an outer aisle seat which is well placed in that respect.

The SOLT/Artsline *Access Guide to London's West End Theatres* contains a great deal of additional information. The SOLT website www.officiallondontheatre.co.uk will be regularly updated.

Central

Adelphi
The Strand WC2E 7NA
Tel: BO 020 7379-8443 or via Ticketmaster 7344-0055
A 1930s theatre which has been refurbished, with the stalls at street level. Entrance + 1 step. A ramp is available. Then step free to the Stalls, with two chair spaces with a slightly restricted view. The Stalls are sloped, and transfer is possible to an aisle seat. **Wheelchair toilet (D70 ST70 +)** off the foyer.
 From the foyer: Dress Circle + 40; Upper Circle + 80. Infra-red hearing system.

Albery
St Martin's Lane WC2N 5AV
Tel: BO 020 7369-1730
A Victorian/Edwardian theatre with the Royal Circle at street level. Main entrance + 3 steps, then + 3 to the Royal Circle where aisle seats are available for transfer (in row G). Box M at Royal Circle level is available for chair users. It is accessed from a side exit, then + 3 (which can be temporarily ramped, though it's quite steep). No adapted toilet.

From the foyer: Stalls -30; Grand Circle $+30$; Balcony $+50$. Infrared hearing system.

Aldwych
Aldwych WC2B 4DF
Tel: BO 020 7379-3367
Entrance $+1+5$ steps, then flat to the Dress Circle and boxes. Easier entry via Drury Lane exit door with ramped access. One chair space beside seat C1. There is a **wheelchair toilet** near seat C1.
From the foyer: Stalls -25; $+15$ to rear Dress Circle; Upper Circle about 50.

Apollo, Shaftesbury Avenue W1V 7DH
Tel: BO 020 7494-5070
Entrance $+1$ (8cm) step. Alternatively, enter through an exit door on Shaftesbury Avenue. From here it is -12 to Stalls with 2 transfer seats. No chair spaces.
    From the foyer: Stalls -22; Dress Circle $+12$; Upper Circle $+40$; Balcony $+60$. Infrared headsets.

Apollo Victoria
17 Wilton Road SW1V 1LL
Tel: BO 020 7828-7074
Two entrances, each with $+4$ steps. Alternatively, use an exit on Wilton Road, which gives access via a ramp to the Dress Circle with four small chair spaces; you may have to sit slightly sideways-on as the space is only 85cm deep. Eight transfer seats. No adapted toilets.
    From the foyer: Stalls -30; Dress Circle $+15$. Wheelchair toilets in Victoria Station and on the corner of Victoria Street and Bressenden Place.

Arts
6 Great Newport Street WC1E 7HF
Tel: BO 020 7836-3334
Small theatre, partly sunk below street level. Flat entrance, but $+5$ steps to the Circle and -19 to the Stalls. The $+5$ can be bypassed by a ramped entrance. A seat can be removed to accommodate one chair user at the back of the Circle. **Adapted toilet (D75 ST60)** by the back of the Circle.

Bloomsbury

Gordon Square WC1H 0AH

Tel: BO 020 7388-8822.

Small theatre with its auditorium well above street level. The seats are steeply raked. Ramped entrance, bypassing +4 steps, and a platform stairlift bypasses +7 to the box office and café. There is a further stairlift to the auditorium passing a further +7. Three chair spaces at the front of the Stalls. Lift (D80 W135 L105) to the basement, where there are **adapted cubicles** in Gents **(D80 ST40** with fixed rails) and Ladies **(D80 ST120)**.

From the foyer +7+28 to the Circle and another +28 to the Rear Circle.

Cambridge

Earlham Street WC2 9HV

Tel: BO 0870 890-1102.

1930s theatre with the Stalls at street level. Flat entrance, then −5 steps to the Stalls. Alternatively step free to the Stalls using a side door in Earlham Street. Two seats in row N can be removed to make chair spaces, and aisle seats are available for transfer. **Wheelchair toilet (D80 ST80)** by rear Stalls. From the foyer: Royal Circle +30; Upper Circle +65. Infrared headsets.

Cochrane

Southampton Row WC1B 4AP

Tel: 020 7269-1606.

A small theatre on the corner with Theobalds Road. Ask about parking. Flat main entrance. Lift inside (D75 W130 L140) to bar on the first floor. Up to four chair spaces in the Stalls, although seats need to be removed. Infrared hearing system. **Wheelchair toilet (D80 ST75)** on the GF near the CP entrance.

Coliseum

St Martin's Lane WC2N 4ES

Tel: BO 020 7632-8300 *Textphone:* 020 7836-7666

Large Edwardian-style theatre used mainly for opera and dance. Stalls at street level. Ramped front entrance. Step-free access to boxes at the back of Stalls (D75), with up to two chair users per box. Aisle seats in the Stalls seats available for transfer but there are −2 steps into the area, and then each row is stepped. Seven chair users allowed. **Wheelchair toilet (D80 ST100 +)** off the corridor leading to the Ladies, by the Stalls bar.

From the Foyer: Dress Circle +35; Upper Circle 60+, and Balcony 90+ from an outside entrance. There is a service lift from the foyer which you may use with permission. It goes to within 4 steps of the back of the Dress Circle and within 14 steps of the rear Upper Circle. Both circles are themselves steeply stepped. The management are somewhat reluctant to allow those who really cannot manage stairs to use this facility, because of possible difficulty in the event of an evacuation. They are, however, both helpful and flexible. Infrared hearing system.

Comedy
Panton Street SW1Y 4DN
Tel: BO 020 7369-1731.
A medium-size Victorian theatre with the Dress Circle at street level. Entrance +2 large steps. Alternative via an exit on Oxenden Street with a temporary ramp to the Dress Circle. One chair space (E17) plus transfer spaces.
From the foyer: Stalls −25; Upper Circle +35; Balcony +55.

Criterion
Piccadilly Circus W1V 9LB
Tel: BO 020 7413-1437 *DisEnq:* 020 7839-8811
The theatre is built below ground level. There is +1 (15cm) step to foyer. An alternative entrance next to the stage door in Jermyn Street can be opened. It gives sloped access to the rear Upper Circle with one chair space next to C20, and is also the easiest access for a disabled walker. **Wheelchair toilet (D80+ ST80+)** off the passage behind the Upper Circle. Induction loop.
From the foyer: −20 to the Upper Circle and −32 to the Dress Circle. It is further down to the Stalls.

Dominion
269 Tottenham Court Road W1P 0AL
Tel: BO 020 7636-2295
50m from St Giles Circus. Flat entrance, then −10 steps to the Stalls bypassed by a platform stairlift. Three chair spaces in the rear right-hand side with a slightly restricted view. Aisle seats available for transfer. Adapted toilet towards the front left of the Stalls.
From the foyer: Royal Circle +32; Centre Circle +60.

Donmar Warehouse
Thomas Neal's, Earlham Street WC2H 9LX
Tel: BO 020 7369-1732

A small new theatre in the heart of theatreland. It is in a block that has been rebuilt and is all above road level. The box office has +1 step, although you can gain flat access via the adjacent shopping precinct. Lift, (D75 W80 L100) staff operated in the evenings, to the Stalls (first floor) and Circle (second floor). This bypasses +25 to the Stalls or +40 to the Circle. One chair space (D31) in the Stalls plus transfer seats. **Wheelchair toilet (D75 ST80)** off the Circle bar. Induction loop.

Drill Hall
16 Chenies Street WC1E 7ET
Tel: BO 020 7307-5060
In a turning off Tottenham Court Road. Step free to auditorium, using a ramped bypass to +2 steps at the entrance. Up to twelve chair spaces by taking out seats. **Adapted toilet (D75 ST56)** off the foyer. There are +23 to the first floor, with a rehearsal room, and a further +22 to the second floor. A lift goes down to the darkroom in the basement. Bar on the GF. Induction loop.

Drury Lane Theatre Royal
Catherine Street WC2B 5JF
Tel: BO 020 7494-5470
This has been a theatre site since Restoration times, and the current one is the fourth. It is very 'grand' with Edwardian and Victorian imperialism. It has been home to a series of hit musicals. Entrance +6 steps to the box office, then +3 to foyer. Flat access through side exit door on Russell Street, leading to the Stalls which have four chair spaces. **Wheelchair toilet (D75 ST90)** near the Russell Street entrance.

From the foyer: Stalls −17 +17; Grand Circle +40; Upper Circle +60, Balcony even higher and very steep. Infrared hearing system.

Duchess
Catherine Street WC2B 5LA
Tel: BO 020 7494-5070
Small theatre built at the end of the 1920s. Entrance +1 step, then −21 to Stalls, with two chair spaces. Alternatively, +12 to Dress Circle where aisle seats are available for transfer (but note the steep steps). Row A is nearest (up 3 steps). **Adapted toilet (D73** opens in, **ST55**, but the cubicle is quite long) on Stalls level. Infrared hearing system.

Duke of York's
St Martin's Lane WC2N 4BQ
Tel: BO 020 7361-1791
Victorian-style theatre with the Royal Circle at street level. Flat
entrance, then step-free access into the back of the Royal Circle
which has seats that can be removed to make two chair spaces. They
put in a small platform to create an adequate area. A wooden rail
prevents your chair from sliding down the slight slope. Restricted
view sometimes, depending on the production. For walkers, there is
step-free access to row D seats. **Wheelchair toilet (D80 ST70)**.
 From the foyer: Stalls −20; Upper Circle +23. Infrared headsets.

Fortune
Russell Street WC2B 5HH
Tel: BO 020 7836-2238
A small art deco style theatre built in the 1920s. It is one of the smallest
West End theatres. Flat entrance. Easiest chair access through Crown
Court Alleyway side exit door, then +5 steps to the Dress Circle with
a transfer seat at the right hand end of row F. No chair spaces.
 From the foyer: Stalls −21; Dress Circle +7; Upper Circle +40.

Garrick
2 Charing Cross Road WC2H 0HH
Tel: BO 020 7494-5470
An old Victorian-style theatre, partly sunk below road level. Entrance +2 small steps. One chair space at the back of the Dress
Circle, when seat E25 has been removed. It is necessary to negotiate
an awkwardly angled step to get into the space, and as there is no
'depth' it is necessary to sit side-on to the stage. Seat number E1 is
available for transfer.
 From the foyer: −30 to Stalls and +35 to the Upper Circle.
Infrared headsets.

Gielgud (Globe)
35 Shaftesbury Avenue W1D 6AR
Tel: BO 020 7494-5470
An Edwardian theatre with the Dress Circle at street level. Recently
renamed. Entrance +1 step. Two chair spaces, B1 and B21 in the
Dress Circle or transfer seats. Access to these is via +1 and through
an exit door in Rupert Street.
 From the foyer: Stalls −22, Dress Circle +3, Upper Circle +35.
Infrared headsets.

Globe Theatre

New Globe Walk, Southwark SE1 9DT

Tel: 020 7401-9919 *website:* www.shakespeares-globe.org.uk

The reconstruction of the Shakespearean theatre at Bankside has now opened for performances in the summer. There are two BB spaces 40m away on New Globe Walk, and the accessible Southwark tube station is about 600m away. Step-free access to box office. A lift (D75 W100 L150) serves several levels, including the shop and café (with movable tables and chairs) on the Piazza level. The theatre is accessed from the Piazza level, with flat access to the Yard (open standing area). Note that no electric chairs are allowed here. A huge lift at the back of the theatre gives access to the Lord's Rooms above the stage and the Gentlemen's Rooms either side, both of which can accommodate more chair users under cover. You need staff assistance to get there as the route is through a restricted area.

Views can be slightly restricted by the rails (and an extra cushion is a good idea for a chair user to get you a bit higher), and if the rain is blowing your way, you might get wet. In addition, the chair spaces are in effect to the side of and slightly behind the stage. Some of the action may be difficult to see because of the pillars. The wheelchair spaces are partially covered. What is needed is a platform in the pit to enable some chair users to get a better view, and to enjoy a play like others. There is a restaurant on the first floor via D75. There is a **wheelchair toilet (D85 ST75)** on the Piazza level down the corridor, past the other toilets near the shop.

Haymarket, Theatre Royal

Haymarket SW1Y 4HT

Tel: BO 020 7930-8800

A beautiful Victorian theatre which was completely refurbished and redecorated, restoring its original grandeur. Unfortunately the refurbishment did not go so far as to include the planned adapted toilet or an improved hearing system. Stalls on street level. Main entrance + 3 steps. Step free through exit doors leading to the Stalls. There is one chair space at X18. Aisle seats in Stalls are available for transfer.

From the foyer: Stalls −20 + 10; Royal Circle + 25; Upper Circle + 55; Balcony + 60.

Her Majesty's

Haymarket SW1Y 4QR

Tel: BO 020 7494-5470

Victorian/Edwardian theatre with the Stalls at street level. Flat entrance. A side exit door off Charles II Street gives step-free access to the Stalls with two chair spaces beside S12. The view is slightly restricted, with a pole in the way. Stalls aisle seats available for transfer. **Wheelchair toilet (D80 ST70)** by Rear Stalls.

From the foyer: Stalls −22 + 18; Dress Circle + 32. Infrared headsets.

Lilian Baylis see Sadler's Wells in *Music venues*.

Logan Hall
University of London, 20 Bedford Way WC1H 0AL
Tel: 020 7612-6401
Main entrance ramped, then an open lift (W110 L175) bypasses + 13 steps leading to reception on Level 4. Lift (D110 W110 L175) to Level 1, with seven chair spaces when seats are removed. Induction loop. **Adapted cubicles** in the Gents toilets **(D75 ST45)**, and Ladies **(D75 ST69)** on Level 1.

London Palladium
Argyll Street W1V 1AD
Tel: BO 020 7494-5470
Huge theatre, associated with 'variety', and recently with musicals. The Stalls are at ground level. Front entrance + 4 + 8 steps. Box Office + 5. Ramillies Place exit almost gives step-free access (there's a tiny step) from street level to the Stalls. This is right round the other side of the theatre, and about 300m from the entrance via Oxford Street. Seats can be removed to create a chair space at V35 in Stalls (restricted view sometimes). Other spaces at L46, S49 and W49, with side views. Stalls aisle seats are available for transfer. **Wheelchair toilets (D80 ST80)** by rear Stalls.

From the foyer: Stalls −23; Circle + 15; Upper Circle + 50. Infrared headsets.

Lyceum
Wellington Street WC2E 7DA
Tel: 020 7420-8112
A Victorian music and dance hall which became a theatre. The Stalls are at ground level. Entrance + 3 steps to lower foyer. Eight chair spaces in the Stalls reached step free via an exit to the left. **Two adapted toilets (D70 + ST70 +)** by the step-free entrance/exit. These have rather heavy split hinged doors and a staff operated key pad to open them.

From the foyer: Stalls −7: Royal Circle +32; Grand Circle +85. There's a lift to all levels, but there are still steps to all seats.

Lyric
Shaftesbury Avenue W1V 7HA
Tel: BO 020 7494-5470
A traditional Victorian theatre with the Dress Circle on street level. Entrance +1 step, then +3 to the foyer. Shaftesbury Avenue royal entrance/exit leads step free to three boxes which can each accommodate a chair user and companion. All have D74 and a side view. Transfer seating in the dress circle +6 from the royal entrance. **Wheelchair toilet (D70+ ST70+)** inside the royal entrance.

From the foyer: Stalls −18; flat to the back of the Dress Circle, and a minimum of +2 into seats; Upper Circle +25; Balcony +45. Infrared headsets.

National Theatre see section on *Arts centres.*

New Ambassadors
West Street, Cambridge Circus WC2H 9ND
Tel: BO 020 7369-1761
Small Victorian theatre with the Dress Circle at street level. Entrance +1 step, then +5 into the Dress Circle where seats F4 and F5 are available for transfer.

From the foyer, Stalls −21.

New London
Parker Street, Drury Lane WC2B 5PW
Tel: BO 020 7404-4079
A modern and versatile theatre in the upper part of a modern block. UGCP next door with two BB spaces. Flat entrance. For people with disabilities, there is step-free access (two steps are ramped) through the stage door in Parker Mews, leading to a small lift (D60 W80 L105) which goes to Level 3 for the Stalls. A larger service lift goes to the second floor, where the original lift can be entered via a larger door (D70) to get to Level 3. The alternative is that there are +18 steps to the Stalls from Level 2. Stalls seat number D38 can be removed to make a chair space. Stalls seats J15 and J18 are available for transfer.

From the foyer, there is an escalator or +32 to the Stalls, then a further +50 to the Circle. Infrared headsets.

Old Vic

Waterloo Road SE1 8NB

Tel: 020 7928-2651 (stage door)

The BO number varies with the production. Forever associated with the name of Lilian Baylis, who took over the theatre in 1912 and established its classical tradition. Refurbished in 1983. Entrance +1+4 steps. Alternative entrance through Webber Street side exit with +2. Portable ramp available, giving step-free access to the Stalls and four chair spaces. Aisle seats in Stalls available for transfer. **Wheelchair toilet (D85 ST100)** inside the Webber Street entrance.

From the foyer: Stalls +3; Dress Circle +32; Upper Circle +60.

Open Air

Inner Circle, Regent's Park NW1 4NP

Tel: BO 020 7486-2431

Outdoor auditorium which can be delightful on a fine summer's evening. Open May to September. BB spaces on the Inner Circle opposite Chester Road, and also opposite Regent's College. Flat entrance via the box office, or via a steepish ramp opposite 'The Holme'. Step-free access to four chair spaces on either side of Stalls. **Adapted cubicles (D85 ST65)** in both Ladies and Gents on the same level as the chair spaces. **Adapted toilet** (unisex) near the chair spaces.

Palace

Shaftesbury Avenue W1V 8AY

Tel: BO 020 7434-0909

In Victorian times, the Royal English Opera House, now a home to many successful musicals. Entrance +2 steps. Alternatively go through a side exit (+1) to the rear Stalls. One chair space. **Adapted toilet** by the side exit.

From the foyer: the Stalls are normally −23+23, but these can be bypassed via −3, on request; Dress Circle +30; Upper Circle +55; Balcony approx +75. Infrared headsets.

Peacock

Kingsway WC2A 2HT

Tel: 020 7863-8222

Main entrance on Portugal Street +4 steps. The Dress Circle is at street level. Use a side entrance on Kingsway where a ramp bypasses 3 steps inside leading to two chair spaces at the back of the Dress Circle. Transfer seats available. No adapted toilet.

From the foyer: −22+7 to Dress Circle; −44 Stalls.

Phoenix
Charing Cross Road WC2H 0JP
Tel: BO 020 7369-1722
A theatre strongly associated with Noel Coward, with the Dress
Circle at ground level. Entrance +4 steps. Flat access through an
exit, giving step-free access to a box (D79), which can hold a chair
user and companion. Slightly sideways view. Dress Circle seats
available for transfer. **Wheelchair toilet (D75 ST85)** next to the box.
   From the foyer: Stalls −13; Dress Circle +21; Upper Circle +40.

Piccadilly
Denman Street W1V 8DT
Tel: BO 020 7369-1734
Entrance +1 step. The Royal Circle is at street level. Two side exits in
Sherwood Street without steps. One (on the right) leads to the Royal
Circle with +1 (8cm) en route, and one transfer seat at A28. The other
on the left, leads via a ramp to Box C (D65), on left of Circle. This
holds up to two chair users and three companions. For some produc-
tions it may house technical equipment and be unavailable.
   From the foyer: Stalls −15; Royal Circle +11−10, Grand Circle
+70.

Place
17 Dukes Road WC1H 9AB
Tel: BO 020 7387-0031 *Textphone:* 020 7387-7246 *Fax:* 020 7387-3504
About 200m from Euston Station, left down Euston Road and then
south down Duke's Road. Small theatre and predominately dance
venue. Step-free entrance to the foyer and box office, then two lifts
(D80 W120 L100) either side of the auditorium service all seats and
the café/bar. Wheelchair spaces available. **Three wheelchair toilets
(D80 ST75)** are well signposted on each level.

Playhouse
Northumberland Avenue WC2N 5DE
Tel: BO 020 7369-1721
Recently refurbished medium-size Victorian theatre. Stalls at street
level. The +3 steps to the foyer can be bypassed by a portable ramp.
Then step free to the Stalls, where two chair spaces can be provided.
Wheelchair toilet (D75 ST75) at Stalls level.
   From the foyer: Dress Circle +29; Balcony +80. Induction loop
for the Stalls with best reception in the centre.

Prince Charles see section on *Cinemas*.

Prince Edward
Old Compton Street W1V 6HS
Tel: BO 020 7447-5400
Large 1930s theatre with the front of the Circle at street level. Flat entrance. Easiest entrance for people with disabilities via a side exit door in Greek Street, giving step-free access to Row A in the Dress Circle, where seats A2-A5 are available for transfer. The Royal Box has space for two chair users and companions. Slightly side-on view, but otherwise good. **Wheelchair toilet (D70+ ST80+)** through the main foyer on the right.
From the foyer: Stalls −22 steps; Dress Circle +13; Upper Circle +80. Infrared hearing system.

Prince of Wales
Coventry Street W1D 6AS
Tel: BO 020 7839-5972/5987
Built in the 1930s on a grand scale. Stalls at street level. Flat entrance, then −4 steps to the Stalls with one chair space and transfer seats. No adapted toilet.
From the foyer: Stalls −4, Dress Circle +23/40. Infrared sets available.

Queen's
Shaftesbury Avenue W1V 8BA
Tel: BO 020 7494-5470
Large Edwardian theatre partly reconstructed after the war. Dress Circle at street level. Flat entrance. Side exit gives access via one small step to the Dress Circle with two chair spaces. There's an adapted toilet signed, but it is in fact a standard size cubicle.
From the foyer, Stalls −18 steps; Dress Circle −3 and Upper Circle +19. Infrared hearing system.

Royal Court, Jerwood Theatre Downstairs (JTD) and Upstairs (JTU)
Sloane Square SW1W 8AS
Tel: 020 7565-5000 *Textphone:* 020 7565-5085 *Fax:* 020 7565-5001
website: www.royalcourttheatre.com *e-mail:* boxoffice@royalcourt-theatre.com
The whole building with its two auditoria has been extensively refurbished, and access issues have been thoroughly addressed. An excellent access guide is available. Although there are +4 steps

at the main entrance, just to the side (on the right) there's a step-free entrance leading to the main lift (D78 W90 L130) which links to virtually every level. Street level is described as LG. The foyer is G (ground).

The JTD has its Circle at ground level. From the foyer, there are −4−16 to the stalls (in the basement), and a further −11 to a bar and restaurant area. Alternatively there are +11 to the Balcony bar. The JTU has +64. The lift bypasses all the steps, and goes to every level, although in the basement there's a staff-operated open lift (D90 W140 L180) to bypass the final −11 and get to the bookshop and restaurant. The JTD has three chair spaces in the Stalls and one in the circle, and the JTU has at least one chair space. There are **three wheelchair toilets (D70+ ST70+)** near the chair spaces, although they have heavy doors, and in the one by JTU the door opens inwards (though to a big cubicle). Infrared system in both theatres, and the JTD has a loop as well.

Sadler's Wells see section on *Music venues*.

St Martin's
West Street, Cambridge Circus WC2H 9NZ
Tel: BO 020 7836-1443
Small Edwardian-style theatre with the Dress Circle close to street level. Entrance +3 steps, then +3 to Dress Circle. Alternatively use an exit from Tower Court with +5 steeply ramped. At this level, Box C (D76) holds one chair user and companion. Two seats in Row F at the back of the Dress Circle are available for transfer. **Adapted toilet** by the Tower Court exit.

From the foyer: Stalls −29; Upper Circle +45. Infrared headsets.

Savoy
Savoy Court, Strand WC2R 0ET
Tel: 020 7836-8888
Built for the Gilbert and Sullivan's light operas, the theatre has been refurbished, providing improved access. The theatre lies under the Savoy building, and the street is level with the Upper Circle. Step-free access from the Strand to the box office. Ramped access is possible from Carting Lane (which is quite steep) to the Dress Circle. It's best to go there *first* if you need to use this entrance as it's a long way round the block from the box office. Contact the stage door in Carting Lane to gain access. Step-free access to two chair spaces in the Dress Circle, and to Row F seats. The **adapted toilet (D70 opening**

inwards, ST50) near the chair spaces has restricted space, particularly because of the door.

From the foyer: Upper Circle $+2-2$ steps; Dress Circle -30 and Stalls -63. Infrared headsets.

Shaftesbury
Shaftesbury Avenue WC2H 8DP
Tel: BO 020 7379-5399
An Edwardian theatre with a somewhat troubled history. In 1973, part of the ceiling collapsed. The front of the Royal Circle is at street level. Entrance $+1$ small step, then it is step free to the Royal Circle row A (right side) in which seats are available for transfer; -3 to Boxes A and B (D70) which can hold either one or two chair users and a companion. **Wheelchair toilet (D70+ ST70)** near the boxes and transfer seats.

From the foyer, Stalls -25; Royal Circle (front) step free, (rear) $+30-5$; Grand Circle $+60$. Infrared headsets.

Strand
Aldwych WC2B 4LD
Tel: BO 020 7930-8800
An Edwardian theatre, built as a 'pair' with the Aldwych on either side of the Waldorf Hotel. Circle at street level. Entrance $+8$ steps. Easier access through Catherine Street side exit, with -4. From here it is step free to two chair spaces in Box A and transfer seats at the front of the Dress Circle.

From the foyer: Stalls -32; Dress Circle -7; Upper Circle $+40$.

Theatre Museum see chapter on *Museums and galleries*.

Theatre Upstairs see write-up on the Royal Court.

Vaudeville
Strand WC2R 0NH
Tel: BO 020 7836-9987
Originally built in 1870, it was completely refurbished in 1969. The Stalls are close to street level. Main entrance $+1$ step. No chair spaces, but transfer is possible for two chair users to an aisle seat in the Stalls. This is reached via -6.

From the foyer to the Dress Circle is $+27$; Upper Circle $+57$.

Victoria Palace
Victoria Street SW1E 5EA
Tel: BO 020 7834-1317
Built as an Edwardian music hall, it has the Stalls on street level. Flat entrance over a tiny lip. Step-free access through Allington Street exit, to the Stalls. Staff can remove Stalls seats M36 and O36 to make two chair spaces. Alternatively you can transfer to these seats. **Adapted toilet NKS** by the exit.

From the foyer: Stalls −4; Dress Circle +28; Upper Circle +75. The theatre is licensed to accommodate up to six wheelchair users. Infrared hearing system.

Whitehall
Whitehall SW1A 2DY
Tel: BO 020 7369-1735
Entrance +1 step. No chair spaces. The Royal Circle has +14 and some transfer seats.

From the foyer: Stalls −25.

Wyndham's
Charing Cross Road WC2H 0DA
Tel: BO 020 7369-1736
An intimate theatre built for Charles Wyndham, a famous Victorian actor-manager. The Stalls are just below ground level. Entrance +1 step to the foyer. An exit on the Charing Cross Road gives access to technicians' box via −3. This has chair space, limited by the fact that it's quite cramped with a restricted view. Transfer seats in the Stalls using an alternative exit involving only −9.

From the foyer: Stalls −18; Royal Circle +12; Upper Circle +21; Balcony +40. Infrared hearing system.

Young Vic
66 The Cut SE1 8LZ
Tel: BO 020 7928-6363
Located just opposite Short Street. Flat access to the main entrance, and 'downstairs' has two chair spaces, and possibilities for transfer. The balcony has 20+ steps. The café is −3 from the foyer, with a platform stairlift. This has had some reliability problems, but is said to be working well now. It provides a good example of where a ramp would have been a much better solution to bypass the steps. **Wheelchair toilet (D85 ST70)** just past the stairs in the foyer. Sennheiser sound system downstairs.

Outer areas inside the North/South Circular Roads

Some small-scale theatre takes place in a room over a pub or in a basement, and these involve the barrier of more than 15 steps, as well as restricted space in the venue itself. These are listed below:

Baron's Court Theatre at the **Curtain's Up**, Barons Ale House, 28 Comeragh Road W14 9RH *Tel:* 020 7602-0235
Canal Café, Bridge House, Delamere Terrace, Little Venice W2 6ND *Tel:* 020 7289-6054
Etcetera, Oxford Arms, 265 Camden High Street NW1 7BU *Tel:* 020 7482-4857
Finborough, 118 Finborough Road, West Brompton SW10 9ED *Tel:* 020 7244-7439
Gate, 11 Pembridge Road, Notting Hill W11 3HQ *Tel:* 020 7229-5387
Greenwich Playhouse, Prince of Orange, 189 Greenwich High Road SE10 HAA *Tel:* 020 8858-9256
Hen and Chicken, 109 St Paul's Road N1 2NA *Tel:* 020 7704-2001
Pentameters, 28 Heath Street, Hampstead NW3 6TE *Tel:* 020 7435-3648. Above the *Three Horseshoes* pub. Has three chair spaces

Albany, Douglas Way, Deptford SE8 4AG *Tel:* BO 020 8692-0231 *Fax:* 020 8469-2253
Step-free access at the entrance and to the GF of the venue. Inside there is a lift (D75 W110 L125) to get to most other parts of the theatre. No restriction on the number of chairs. **Wheelchair toilet (D85 ST100)** on the GF opposite the front door. Induction loop.

Almeida, Almeida Street, Islington N1 1TA *Tel:* BO 020 7359-4404 M 020 7226-7432 *website:* www.almeida.co.uk
Near the corner of Upper Street, on the left hand side. NCP about 50m away. Entrance is step free, then there is ramped access to the Stalls. Six chair spaces, and five possible transfer seats. The Circle has +27 steps. **Wheelchair toilet (D80 ST90)** off the foyer. Infrared system. We are told there will soon be a dedicated access helpline.

BAC see section on *Arts centres*.

Broadway Theatre, Rushey Green, Catford SE6 4RU *Tel:* BO 020 8690-0002
On the corner of Catford Road. MSCP with BB spaces at the back of the theatre about 200m away. Entrance +11 steps. This goes to the

Stalls with four chair spaces. Steps up to the Circle, and − 10 to the **Studio Theatre** which also has four chair spaces.

There are **wheelchair cubicles (D85 ST80)** in both Ladies and Gents toilets off the foyer. We were told that there's an adapted toilet in the Studio Theatre, accessible by ramp. Induction loop.

Chats Palace, 42-44 Brooksby Walk, Hackney E9 6DF *Tel:* BO 020 8533-0227

Opposite Homerton Hospital. A venue putting on cabaret, comedy, poetry, jazz, soul and theatre performances. They involve people with disabilities in workshops and performances as well as spectating. Level access to foyer and bar. Step free to performance area with chair spaces. There are + 27 steps to the first floor where there are meeting rooms and where some of the workshops take place. **Wheelchair toilet (D75 ST85)** off the bar. Infrared sound system available on request.

Cockpit, Gateforth Street NW8 *Tel:* BO 020 7258-2925 M 020 7258-2920 *Fax:* 020 7258-2921 *e-mail:* cockpit@cwc.ac.uk

Situated just off Church Street. Some on-site parking possible. Step free to the foyer and bar. The − 6 steps to the auditorium can be bypassed via exit door in Samford Street. Four chair spaces. **Adapted cubicle in the Ladies (D65 ST70 obstructed by a fixed handrail inside the door)**. Apparently induction loop to be installed.

Courtyard, 10 York Way, King's Cross N1 9AA *Tel:* BO 020 7833-0870 *website:* www.thecourtyard.org.uk

About 30m north of King's Cross station. Step free throughout. Two chair spaces.

Greenwich, Croom's Hill, Greenwich SE10 8ES *Tel:* BO 020 8858-7755 M 020 8858-2265

On the corner with Nevada Street. Entrance + 1 step. Lift (D80 W100 L140) to the auditorium. Two chair spaces if seats are removed. Access to the front of the theatre is via + 33. Induction loop. **Adapted toilet (D75 ST60)** on the GF. Seats reserved at the front for visually-impaired customers. Book in advance.

Hackney Empire, 291 Mare Street, Hackney E8 1EJ *Tel:* BO 020 8985-2424 M 020 8510-4500 *e-mail:* info@hackneyempire.co.uk *website:* www.hackneyempire.co.uk

Opposite Morning Lane, by the Town Hall. Step-free entrance on

Mare Street. There is step-free access to around twenty possible chair spaces in the Stalls, and four more spaces on other levels, accessed by a lift (D120 W140 L240). **Eleven wheelchair toilets (D70+ ST70+)**, three of which are on the GF. Infrared system in main theatre, induction loop in studio.

Hampstead Theatre, Eton Avenue, Swiss Cottage NW3 3EU *Tel:* BO 020 7722-9301
150m from Swiss Cottage Station. Step free to up to twelve chair spaces in the main theatre. Some chair spaces in a smaller auditorium. There is a **wheelchair toilet**. Provision of an induction loop or infrared system is under discussion and at least one of these will be provided.

Hoxton Hall, 130 Hoxton Street N1 6SH *Tel:* BO 0171 739-5431 Admin: 020 7684-0060
Nearly opposite Homefield Street. Parking at the Britannia Leisure Centre 100m away. Ramped entrance, and step free to the café, theatre auditorium and most workshop spaces. Balcony +20 spiralled. Induction loop in theatre, and in GF workshop space. **Wheelchair toilet (D80 ST85)** at the rear of theatre.

Jackson's Lane, 269a Archway Road, Highgate N6 5AA *Tel:* BO 020 8341-4421
Opposite Highgate tube station. Two BB spaces. Steep ramp to the entrance. Level inside to the café, bar and theatre. Plenty of chair spaces and transfer opportunities. **Adapted cubicles** in both Gents and Ladies, and there's a **wheelchair toilet (D85 ST80)** by the Gents. Induction loop. There's also a backstage changing room for disabled performers with a **wheelchair toilet** and shower **(D85 ST100)**.

Jongleurs Comedy Club, Middle Yard, Camden Lock, Chalk Farm Road NW1 8AB *Tel:* 020 7924-2766
Underneath Bar Risa, with a cobbled ramp down from Camden Lock Place. Chair spaces at street level, where the bar and food counter are situated. Other levels drop down (with −2 steps) towards the stage. **Wheelchair toilet (D85 ST80)** at street level. As a music venue, it goes by the name of *Dingwalls*.

Little Angel Theatre 14 Dagmar Passage, Cross Street, Islington N1 2DN *Tel:* 020 7226-1787
Neatly tucked away between Cross Street and Dagmar Terrace. Two

BB spaces on-site if booked in advance. Entrance + 1 step, but a step-free alternative is available. The venue is all on one level, including the café. Up to four chair spaces if benches are removed. **Wheelchair toilet (D75 ST70)** just off the foyer. Induction loop.

Lyric, King Street, Hammersmith W6 0QL *Tel:* BO 020 8741-2311 M 020 8741-0824
Next to Hammersmith Grove with an NCP about 200m from the theatre. Step free to the box office. Two lifts (D80 W100 L110) go to all floors. On the first floor, there's a bar, café and outside garden. The **Studio** is on this level with level access, but no chair spaces. The second floor is the Stalls level of the main theatre, with three chair spaces. The lift goes to both the Circle and Upper Circle, but there are steps involved. **Adapted toilet (D69 ST90)** on the first floor next to the lifts; if locked, the key is in the café on the same floor. **Wheelchair cubicles** in Ladies **(D70 ST90)** and Gents **(D75 ST70)** on the second floor next to the lifts. Both theatres have induction loops.

Oval House, 52-54 Kennington Oval SE11 5SW *Tel:* **BO** 020 7582-7680 M 020 7735-2786
Right by the cricket ground. CP space if booked in advance. Level access to the foyer, café and Theatre Downstairs. Plenty of room for chair users. Induction loop. Theatre Upstairs is + 17 (steep and narrow). **Two unisex toilets,** labelled Gents **(D75 ST42)** and Ladies **(D75 ST110)** on the GF.

Riverside Studios see section on *Arts centres.*

Southwark Playhouse, 62 Southwark Bridge Road SE1 0AS *Tel:* 020 7620-3494
Near to the corner of Unison Street. Entrance + 1, then flat to the auditorium. Up to four chair spaces. There is a **wheelchair toilet** though it is apparently difficult to reach because the passageway is used for storage.

Theatre Royal, **Stratford**, Gerry Raffles Square, Stratford E15 1BN
Tel: BO 020 8534-0310 *Fax:* 020 8534-8381
e-mail: marketing@stratfordeast.com
About 150m from Stratford Station on the DLR. Opposite Angel Lane. On-street BB spaces outside and CP about 100m away. Level to the box office. The Stalls have − 2 steps, but a step-free route can be opened if needed. Six chair spaces in the Stalls. Induction loop.

Wheelchair toilet (D100 ST70) next to the bar at the end of the corridor. From the foyer: +18 to the Circle; +35 to the Upper Circle.

Theatro Technis, 26 Crowndale Road NW1 1TT *Tel:* 020 7387-6617 Situated off Camden High Street, halfway down the road. Ramped access available, and the venue is all on one level. Six chair spaces. **Wheelchair toilet (D70+ ST70+)** near the bar. Induction loop.

Tower, Canonbury Place, Islington N1 2NQ *Tel:* 020 7226-5111 *website:* www.towertheatre.org.uk
Level entry to one chair space; one row has step-free access so it is possible to transfer. Other parts of the theatre at different levels. The bar has +2 steps. Induction loop.

Turtle Key, *Tel/Textphone:* 020 8964-5060 *fax:* 020 8964-4080 *website:* www.turtlekeyarts.com
Formerly a theatre, now a travelling company with disability arts productions. Details of productions and venues are available by phone.

Walthamstow Assembly Hall, Town Hall, Forest Road, Walthamstow E17 4SY *Tel/Textphone:* BO 020 8521-7111
BB spaces outside. Ramped entrance and step free to the auditorium. Up to twenty chair spaces. **Wheelchair toilet (D75 ST90)** off the foyer. Induction loop.

Between the North/South Circular Roads and the M25

Beck, Grange Road, Hayes, Middx UB3 2UE *Tel:* BO 020 8561-8371 M 020 8561-7506.
Turn right at the *Crown* if travelling east on the Uxbridge Road. Large CP with two BB spaces. Step-free access throughout, and up to eight chair spaces. Bar/bistro. **Adapted cubicles** in both Ladies and Gents toilets. Induction loop.

Charles Cryer, 39 High Street, Carshalton, Surrey SM5 3BB *Tel:* BO 020 8770-4950 M 020 8770-4960
Parking available in High Street. Ramp to main entrance bypasses +4 steps. Lift (D75 W110 L150) to the auditorium on the first floor. Four chair spaces. Induction loop. **Wheelchair toilet (D85 ST110)** on the first floor.

For those interested in the production side of theatre, the lift goes up to the lighting box, and there is a **wheelchair toilet** and shower **(D75 ST70)** in both dressing rooms. The production studio behind the theatre is step free to the main GF area.

Chingford Assembly Hall, Station Road, Chingford E4 5EN *Tel:* BO (*Textphone*) 020 8521-7111 M 020 8529-0555
On-site CP with three BB spaces. Step-free access to hall, toilet, and ten chair spaces. Induction loop. **Adapted toilet (D75 ST150 + NKS door opens inwards but spacious)** off the foyer. **Wheelchair toilet (D85 ST100 + NKS)** outside.

Churchill, High Street, Bromley, Kent BR1 1HA *Tel:* BO 020 8460-5838 M 020 8464-7131.
    In the pedestrian precinct, by the corner with Churchill Way. Five BB spaces in Churchill Place. Level access and step free to nine chair spaces in the Circle, which is at street level. A staff lift (D80 W100 L140) serves both floors. Sennheiser sound system. **Adapted toilet (D75 ST75, but fixed handrails)** off the Circle foyer.

Kenneth More, Oakfield Road, Ilford, Essex IG1 1BT *Tel:* 020 8553-4466
About 400m from Ilford Station. Step free to the auditorium. Three chair spaces. Induction loop. **Adapted toilet** near the chair spaces.

Millfield, Silver Street, Edmonton N18 1PJ *Tel:* BO 020 8807-6680
At the junction of the North Circular and the A10. On-site CP with two BB spaces, but ring if you want to reserve a slot. Level access on the Silver Street side to four chair spaces and transfer possibilities. Bar inside. Induction loop. **Adapted cubicle (D75 ST40)** in Gents and **wheelchair cubicle (D75 ST155)** in Ladies off the foyer.

Orange Tree, 1 Clarence Street, Richmond, Surrey TW9 2SA *Tel:* 020 8940-3633 *Textphone:* 020 8940-7323
100m from Richmond Station (which has step-free access to and from all lines). Possible on-site parking if booked. Entrance + 5 + 6 steps. The normal route from the foyer to the theatre is via + 7 steps, or about + 25 if you are going to the gallery. Alternative ramped entrance from the courtyard CP, giving step-free access to the chair spaces (up to four chairs, where seats are removed) in the main auditorium. Only one row is accessed this way without steps. The courtyard entrance also leads to the lift (D80 W110 L160) which goes

to the foyer/bar and up to the third floor. **Wheelchair toilet (D80 ST80)** on the third floor, through two doors into the dressing room area. Induction loop.

Paul Robeson, Centre Space, Treaty Centre, High Street, Hounslow, Middx TW3 1ES *Tel:* BO 0845 456-2840
Treaty Centre MSCP, about 200m away. Theatre box office on the GF. Lift (D110 W155 L140) gives level access to the front row of first floor auditorium with up to six chair spaces. Step free to the café. Induction loop. **Wheelchair toilet (D85 ST75)** on the first floor.

Polka, 240 The Broadway, Wimbledon SW19 1SB *Tel:* 020 8543-4888
    A unique children's theatre some 600m from Wimbledon Station (which is fully accessible). Step-free access to the GF where there is a café, play area and a workshop for children with special needs. The *Adventure theatre* of the GF is a studio theatre. There are exhibitions from time to time in a separate step-free area, as well as signed performances in the main theatre. Lift (D75 W100 L130) to the auditorium with six chair spaces. Induction loop. **Wheelchair toilet (D80 ST110)** on the GF.

Questors, Mattock Lane, Ealing W5 5BQ *Tel:* BO 020 8567-5184 M 020 8567-0011
A long-established theatre club about 500m from Ealing Broadway Station. Small on-site CP with four BB spaces. Level entrance and lift (D90 W110 L150) to the back of the auditorium with four chair spaces. The lift bypasses about +30 steps. Step free to bar and gallery via the lift. The lift also gives access to the Grapevine Bar (for members) and a **wheelchair toilet (D85 ST85)**. Sennheiser infrared sound system. The small **Studio** Theatre has flat access, and uses movable seating.

Richmond, The Green, Richmond, Surrey TW9 1QJ *Tel:* BO 020 8940-0088 M 020 8940-0220
Richmond Station (which is fully accessible) is about 400m away. Parking difficult, although there's a CP off the A316 Twickenham Road, also some 400m. A traditional-style theatre, recently reno-vated. There are +5 steps at the main entrance, then step free to the rear Stalls; +23 to the Dress Circle and +40 to the Upper Circle. Alternative entrance to the left gives level access to the rear stalls with four chair spaces. Step free to the bar. **Wheelchair toilet (D70 ST80)** next to the rear Stalls entry. Infrared system.

Studio, 28 Beckenham Road, Beckenham, Kent BR3 4LS *Tel:* BO 020 8663-0103
About 150m from Clockhouse Station. There are +9 steps at the entrance, but once inside, the venue is on one level. Some chair spaces. **Adapted toilet (D75 ST30)** between the front entrance and box office.

Tara, 356 Garrett Lane, Earlsfield SW18 4ES *Tel:* 020 8333-4457
A small arts centre opposite Earlsfield station. There is +1 step at the entrance. Six chair spaces can be provided by removing a row of seats.

Tricycle, 269 Kilburn High Road NW6 7JR *Tel:* BO 020 7328-1000 020 7372-6611
    A fringe theatre with good access. Entrance ramped. There are +6 steps into the theatre, but given notice, some seats can be removed and there is a lift for chair users giving access to four spaces. The catering facilities, bar and exhibition space all have flat/ramped access. Induction loop available. **Wheelchair toilet (D70+ ST70+)** to the left of the entrance.

Waltham Forest Theatre, Lloyd Park, Forest Road, Walthamstow E17 5EH *Tel/Textphone:* BO 020 8521-7111
Off Forest Road, by the park, with on-site CP and BB spaces. Step free throughout including the bar. Four chair spaces in the theatre. Induction loop. **Wheelchair toilet (D85 ST80)** to the right of the auditorium as you face the stage.

Watermans Arts Centre see section on *Arts centres.*

Wimbledon, The Broadway, Wimbledon SW19 1QG *Tel:* BO 020 8540-0362 M 020 8543-4549
About 250m from Wimbledon Station (which is fully accessible) by the junction with Russell Road. Small on-site CP. There are +7 steps to the box office and +6 to foyer bar. Alternative route for chair users via a fire exit on Russell Road involving −5 steep steps, with a platform stairlift to bypass them. Eight chair spaces. **Two wheelchair toilets (D95 ST90)** at the back of the Stalls step free from the chair spaces.

Going to BBC and ITV shows

BBC Television Centre
Wood Lane W12 7RJ
Tel: 020 8743-8000 *website:* www.bbc.co.uk

The main entrance is about 100m south of the White City tube station. There are four BB spaces which should be pre-booked. Tours of the Centre are run regularly throughout the week. Pre-booking is essential. Tours cover some distance and involve lifts (D90 W115 L180) but a wheelchair is available on request. Information sheets for hearing-impaired visitors are also provided. There are eight studios that have audience shows in the Centre. For tickets contact BBC Audience Services *Tel:* 020 8576-1227 *Textphone:* 020 8225-8090 *website:* www.bbc.co.uk/tickets. The audience entrance is step free and + 14 steps to the audience foyer can be bypassed by an alternative (longer) sloped route via the CP. Those who have arranged parking are met at their cars and escorted to the foyer. Access to all eight studios is step free. Wheelchair spaces are located at the front and to the side of each studio (with a maximum of four, but more usually two per studio). It is necessary to phone in advance to ensure a chair space. It is also advisable to ask in advance if you require an induction loop. There are **four wheelchair toilets (D70 + ST70 +)** on the GF, though at least one has an inward opening door.

London Television Studios
Upper Ground SE1 9LT
Tel: 020 7737-8888 *Fax:* 020 7261-8027 *e-mail:* LWT.Tickets@granadamedia.com
Located on the South Bank east of the National Theatre. There are three studios for shows with an audience. The normal entrance is to the left of the building, from Upper Ground. There are + 5 steps to the ground level of Studio One, and to Studios Two and Three. Access to upper level of Studio One is via a lift (D140 W170 L195) bypassing + 11 + 11 + 3. **Step free access for chair users is via the main entrance** on Upper Ground. From here you will be escorted via lifts (D95 W170 L175). Wheelchair spaces are located on either the ground or upper level of Studio One. In Studios Two and Three the number of spaces varies according to the show, and advance notice is requested so they can cater appropriately. There isn't a permanent induction loop but one can be provided on request. **Wheelchair toilets** on the GF next to Studio One **(D90 ST100)**, and at main reception **(D90 ST70)**. **Adapted toilet (D90 ST125** inward door**)** on the first floor next to the studio.

Pubs and bars

The English pub is a unique institution, but pubs and bars vary a great deal. Some have a mainly local clientele while others are full of passing trade. Many have a core of regulars. Some depend on business trade. A great many pubs now serve food, and also coffee, as well as alcohol and soft drinks. **Many in and around the City and Docklands are closed at weekends**, while others only serve food during the week. *We have included phone numbers, so if you want to find out about eating or are in doubt as to opening hours, you can ring to check.*

This listing has seen enormous change during the past ten years or so. We are now able to list well over 250 pubs inside the M25 which have either flat or single-step access, and which have a well-adapted toilet. In 1989, that number was just four. Several of the brewers have made it a policy to include a disabled persons' toilet in the specification for all new premises. Sometimes they will include one when a pub is refurbished. Companies that have pursued a consistent policy of providing access and a disabled persons' toilet in their pubs include Wetherspoons and All Bar One. With refurbishment, O'Neill's and Fullers have provided these facilities wherever possible. Some useful websites if you are looking for more pubs are:

www.pubs.com
www.pubs247.co.uk
www.fullers.co.uk
www.youngs.co.uk
www.jdwetherspoon.co.uk
www.hogshead.com

However, the accessibility data on these websites is somewhat variable and does not always meet our basic criteria.

All the toilets listed are unisex unless specifically described as being inside the Ladies or Gents area. Regrettably, some managers regard the disabled persons' toilet as a convenient store cupboard. This seems to happen slightly less often than it did in 1995, but it can be very irritating when you need to use a facility which has been provided, but is not readily available.

Note that some pubs are adopting a strict 21+ policy, particularly at busy times. Also, some pubs tend to attract a particular clientele, for example, from the gay community. Rarely are these in any sense exclusive. As these things tend to change we have not mentioned age restrictions nor described anything other than physical access. If you need to find out about age restrictions, or about anything else, ring first.

The *Time Out Pubs and Bars Guide* has good pub descriptions, and includes some information about access. Unfortunately, as with other pub guides, they have not adopted any specific criteria, and so some of the information is misleading. This is because they are dependent on information supplied by pub managers and owners, who will have different ideas about what 'disabled access' involves. The CAMRA *London Pubs Guide* indicates 'disabled access' but gives no toilet information. Many of the premises listed as being wheelchair accessible have a step or two at the entrance, and more importantly have NO easy access toilets. Of the pubs in the *Time Out* guide, only about half of the ones described as having a disabled persons' toilet were deemed by our survey teams to be worth mentioning in this chapter.

We have included several bars attached to restaurants, where they have gone to the trouble of providing a disabled persons' toilet, but some of these may be quite upmarket and pricey. No doubt very good places, but a tad more expensive than your average pub.
We have not attempted to survey and list the accessible restaurants in central London. Unfortunately, there are relatively few of them, since most restaurants are small, and the toilets are either in the basement or upstairs.

Other places that offer accessible eating facilities with a nearby wheelchair toilet include the big museums, the big department stores, the Festival Hall and the National Theatre, and during the day, Covent Garden Opera House. There's also the Oxo Tower, Shakespeare's Globe and Somerset House. Southwark Cathedral has an attractive refectory with tables and chairs outside during the summer. We hope that from the suggestions we can offer, including the pubs and bars list, you can find somewhere pleasant and interesting to eat.

In order to make the list easy to use we have grouped the pubs in geographical areas:

London's West End and centre comprising:
the postal districts W1, WC1 and WC2, SW1, SE1, W2, NW1 and N1;
the **City area** comprising:
postal districts EC1, EC2, EC3, EC4 and E1;
inner areas including:
the northern Docklands, and the Isle of Dogs (E14), and inner postal districts E, N, NW, W, SW, SE;

outer areas north of the river comprising:
Brentford, Greenford, Hayes, Hounslow, Teddington and Whitton,
Denham, Ickenham, Rickmansworth, Ruislip and Uxbridge,
Borehamwood, Edgware, Harrow, Kenton, Stanmore and Wembley,
Barnet, Chingford and Enfield,
Chigwell and Loughton,
Barking, Brentwood, Dagenham, Hornchurch, Ilford and Romford;
outer areas south of the river comprising:
Chessington, Kingston, Richmond, Surbiton, Walton and Worcester
Park;
Barnes, Mitcham, Morden, Putney, Roehampton, Wandsworth and
Wimbledon;
Croydon,
Banstead, Cheam, Purley, Sutton and Wallington;
Beckenham, Bickley, Bromley, Orpington and West Wickham;
Bexley and Dartford.

London's West End and centre (W1 and WC2, WC1, SW1, SE1, NW1 and N1)

W1 and WC2

These areas cover London's main theatreland and shopping areas. In order to make the listing as helpful as possible, we have grouped the pubs as being around:

- Oxford Street and Shaftesbury Avenue including Leicester Square and St Martin's Lane. This includes a few places that are in the WC2 postal district;
- Covent Garden and Aldwych, to the east of St Martin's Lane.

Around Shaftesbury Avenue and Oxford Street
All Bar One, 36 Dean Street W1 *Tel:* 020 7479-7921
Opposite the junction with Meard Street. Step-free entrance and then to 95% of interior: a small area has +2 steps. A large, spacious pub, but only around 30% of the chairs and tables are at an appropriate height for chair users. Well signed **wheelchair toilet (D90 ST85)** at the back of the pub through the double doors. When we surveyed, however, there were two large tables stacked in it.

All Bar One, 3 Hanover Street W1 *Tel:* 020 7518-9931
Near the junction with Regent Street. Ramped entrance and step-free access in spacious interior. **Wheelchair toilet (D90 ST85 NKS)** on the left-hand side towards the back of the pub. Key at the bar.

Bar Monaco, 39 Shaftesbury Avenue WC2 *Tel:* 020 7437-0847
Next door to the Queen's Theatre. The main bar is on the GF, which is
step free. The first floor has a brasserie. No lift. **Wheelchair toilet (D85
ST70)** to the right of the bar – the key can be obtained from the bar.

Bar Red and Restaurant, 5 Kingly Street, London W1B 5PF Tel: 020
7434-3417
30m from the junction with Beak Street, with flat access to the main bar.
Wheelchair toilet (D80 ST75) on the left (contained movable cleaning
equipment at time of survey). Downstairs bar via − 7 − 10 steps.

Blues Bistro and Bar, 42-43 Dean Street, Soho W1V 5AP *Tel:* 020
7494-1966 *website:* www.bluesbistro.com
Situated 20m from the junction with Old Compton Street. Step-free
entrance to GF bar area with tables and bar food. There is − 1 step to
the restaurant. Ladies toilet also used as **wheelchair toilet (D70 ST80)**.

Cheers, 72 Regent Street W1B 5RE *Tel:* 020 7494-3322
American bar and restaurant about 50m from Piccadilly Circus.
About 20% of the seating is step free. **Adapted toilet (D80 ST60)** to
the right of the central steps.

Corney and Barrow, 116 St Martin's Lane WC2N 4BF *Tel:* 020 7655-
9800 *website:* www.corney-barrow.co.uk
Situated on the corner of St Martin's Lane and William IV Street.
There are + 3 steps to the GF bar, which has high tables throughout.
Restaurant on the first floor + 16. **Wheelchair toilet (D70 ST75)** on
the GF to the right of the bar.

Jack Horner, 236 Tottenham Court Road W1 *Tel:* 020 7580-1882
On the junction with Bayley Street. Ramped entrance and **wheelchair
toilet (D80 ST90)** on the GF. Key at bar.

Manto, 30 Old Compton Street, W1 6AR *Tel:* 020 7494-2756
Situated 30m from the junction with Greek Street. The entrance and
GF bar are step free. There are + 24 steps to the first floor bar.
Wheelchair toilet (D85 ST100) on the GF at the back on the right,
opposite the bar.

Mash, 19-21 Great Portland Street W1 *Tel:* 020 7637-5555
Near the junction with Margaret Street. A modern bar with a flat
entrance and 80% step free inside. An upstairs restaurant is accessible by a small lift (D80 W90 L90). **Wheelchair toilet (D95 ST70)** on
the GF.

Match Bar, 37-38 Margaret Street W1N 7FA *Tel:* 020 7499-3443
website: www.matchbar.com
Situated 50m from the south-east corner of Cavendish Square, there
is flat access from the street. 70% of bar has flat access, with + 6
steps to mezzanine level and − 2 to small recess at the back. At time
of survey, **wheelchair toilet** was full of cleaning equipment, though
staff claimed it would be cleared soon.

Moon and Sixpence, 185 Wardour Street W1 *Tel:* 020 7734-0037
Near Oxford Street, on the corner of Noel Street. Tiny step at the
entrance, then step free. **Adapted toilet (D80 ST55** blocked by a bin**)**
to the right of the bar. The key is at the bar.

Moon under Water, 28 Leicester Square WC2 *Tel:* 020 7839-2837
Next to the Odeon on the east side of the square. Relatively long thin
pub which can get very crowded. Entrance + 2 steps, then flat
throughout. **Wheelchair toilet (D80 ST80 +)** past the bar and
through the swing doors.

Moon under Water, 105 Charing Cross Road WC2 *Tel:* 020 7287-
6039. Entrances at either end of the pub from Charing Cross Road
and Greek Street. Both have − 7 steps. At the Charing Cross Road
end there is an open lift (D84 W120 L115) to bypass the steps to get to
the lower central section of the pub. This has a large bar, but tables are
either + 2 steps or are at standing-height. At the Greek Street end an
open lift (D84 W128 L86) also bypasses the steps. There is a bar at the
Greek Street end on a level with the entrance and this is the area where
the accessible tables are. **Adapted toilet (D85 ST55 NKS)** directly
opposite the lift at the Charing Cross Road end, on the lower level.

Old Explorer, 23 Great Castle Street W1 *Tel:* 020 7491-0467
At the junction of John Prince's Street. Step-free entrance (with a
slight bump) and step-free inside to 80% of GF: the rest is + 4.
Downstairs bar is − 5 − 13. **Wheelchair toilet (D80 ST70)** in the right-
hand corner at the back, at the far end of the bar. The key is at the bar.

O'Neill's, 166 Shaftesbury Avenue WC2 *Tel:* 020 7379-3735
150m north of Cambridge Circus, just past the junction with Mercer
Street. Entrance + 1 step, and then step free. Most tables have long
benches, or are high up. Three/four tables are of standard height with
movable chairs. **Wheelchair toilet (D80 ST85)** opposite the bar, on
the right.

O'Neill's, 33-7 Wardour Street W1 *Tel:* 020 7479-7941
Located opposite Gerrard Street, the entrance and GF are step free,
but there is also a downstairs bar. **Wheelchair toilet (D80 ST70 NKS)**
towards the back of the GF on the left.

Rupert Street, 50 Rupert Street W1 *Tel:* 020 7292-7141
A gay bar on the corner of Rupert Street and Winnett Street. Step-
free entrance from Winnett Street. About 50% of the bar is step free
and there's a **wheelchair toilet (D80 ST80 NKS)**, but it was being used
for storing cleaning equipment when we visited.

Sound, Swiss Centre, Leicester Square W1D 6QF *Tel:* 020 7863-7330
Basement bar with open-front café on Leicester Street which provides access to bar via an open lift (D80 W90 L110). Some areas in
the basement have a couple of steps but portable ramps are available.
Wheelchair toilet (D70 ST70) to left upon leaving the lift.

Zinc Bar and Grill, 21 Heddon Street W1R 7LF *Tel:* 020 7255-8833
Situated 30m off Regent Street, north of Piccadilly Circus, on a
pedestrianised road. Step-free access using intercom through trades-
man's entrance to right bypasses +3 steps at entrance. **Wheelchair
toilet (D85 ST75)** at back left. Private dining room −15.

**Around Covent Garden and Aldwych, to the east of St Martin's Lane
and Monmouth Street**

All Bar One, 19 Henrietta Street WC2E 9ET *Tel:* 020 7557-7941
Situated at the junction with Bedford Street. Entrance +1 step from
Bedford Street and 50% of the bar is step free. **Adapted toilet (D85
ST66)** on the far right from the entrance.

All Bar One, 58 Kingsway, Holborn WC2B 6DX *Tel:* 020 7629-5171
On the junction with Remnant Street, 90m from High Holborn. There
are +2 small steps at the entrance, which can be bypassed by the fire
exit from Remnant Street if necessary. 100% flat access inside, with a
wheelchair toilet (D85 ST75 NKS) to right at the end of bar.

Aquda, 13 Maiden Lane, Strand WC2 *Tel:* 020 7557-9891
About halfway down the street, which runs parallel to the Strand.
Main entrance +1 step. Step free to the GF bar, stairs to first floor.
Wheelchair toilet (D85 ST100) accessed step free from the other
entrance: key at bar.

Bank Aldwych, 1 Kingsway, Aldwych WC2B 6XF *Tel*: 020 7379-9797 *website:* www.bankrestaurants.com Large bar and restaurant opposite BBC building on corner of Aldwych and Kingsway. Entrance + 1 step, giving access to the bar area at entrance and dining area at rear. The bar area has high stools (100cm +). **Wheelchair toilet (D90 ST100)** next to dining area.

Columbia Bar, 69 Aldwych WC2B 4DX *Tel:* 020 7831-8043
On the junction with Houghton Street, 20m from Kingsway. The entrance has a tiny lip and double doors to the main bar. There are −20 steps to the basement bar (40%) and + 6 to Vault Bar (20%). **Wheelchair toilet (D85 ST70 NKS** though lock was broken**)** on the GF to the right of the main bar.

Fine Line, 77 Kingsway WC2B 6ST *Tel:* 020 7405-5004
Situated 120m from High Holborn, and almost opposite the junction with Remnant Street. The bar has two step-free entrances and is flat within. **Wheelchair toilet (D85 ST70 NKS)** is at the back on the left.

Henry's Bar, 5-6 Henrietta Street, Covent Garden WC2E 8PS *Tel:* 020 7379-1871
Located just off Covent Garden's main square. The entrance and 80% of the GF bar is step free. Basement bar −25 steps. **Adapted toilet (D80 ST67)** to the right just past the bar on the GF.

Knight's Templar, 95 Chancery Lane WC2A 1DT *Tel:* 020 7831-2660
On the junction with Carey Street, the main entrance has + 4 steps which can be bypassed with ramped entrance 20m along Carey Street. Large pub with 15% non-smoking area up + 13 steps. **Wheelchair toilet (D80 ST75 NKS)** on GF at far end of bar from main entrance.

Langley Bar and Restaurant, 5 Langley Street, Covent Garden WC2H 9JA *Tel:* 020 7836-5005
Located halfway down Langley Street, there is a step-free entrance. Then −25 steps are bypassed by an open lift (D80 W80 L145), which gives flat access to the bar, 10% of which is + 1. The restaurant is + 1 but there is a portable ramp available. **Wheelchair toilet (D85 ST80)** requires key from the manager.

Les Sans Culottes Brasserie/Restaurant, 27 Endell Street WC2 *Tel:* 020 7379-8500
Towards the Long Acre end of the road. Flat entrance, and over 50% is step free. **Adapted toilet (D80 ST64)**.

Old Orleans, 31 Wellington Street, Covent Garden WC2 *Tel:* 020 7497-2433
On the corner with Tavistock Street. Main entrance + 3 steps, then step-free access to 50%, with an **adapted toilet (D80 ST55)** to the left. There is an alternative step-free entrance from Tavistock Street, which is normally locked. This can be opened on request.

O'Neill's, 40 Great Queen Street WC2 *Tel:* 020 7269-5911
Opposite the junction with Wild Street, and near the corner with Drury Lane. Through the 'yellow' entrance, there is + 1 step, but there's flat access through the 'blue' entrance. Step free inside, if somewhat cluttered. **Wheelchair toilet (D95 ST85)** around the pub to the left. The key is at the bar.

Porterhouse, 21-22 Maiden Lane, Covent Garden WC2 *Tel:* 020 7379-7917
Situated halfway down Maiden Lane, the main entrance has − 6 steps but there is a gentle slope down to a step-free entrance on the right. 20% of GF is + 2, while the first floor has access via a lift (D80 W95 L150) to the right of the bar. It is then step free, though there is a mezzanine level at + 7. **Wheelchair toilet (D75 ST80)** is to the right of the bar on GF.

Shakespeare's Head, Africa House, 64-68 Kingsway WC2B 6BG *Tel:* 020 7404-8846
Situated 60m from High Holborn, opposite Parker Street, this large pub has + 2 steps at the main entrance but there is ramped access via a side door 30m down Twyford Place. The bar is flat except for + 1 to 10% at back. **Wheelchair toilet (D80 ST70 NKS)** at back left of pub.

WC1

This area is called Bloomsbury and is north of High Holborn. It includes the British Museum and some University of London colleges.

All Bar One, 108 New Oxford Street WC1A 1HB *Tel:* 020 7307-7980
Situated 30m from the junction with Tottenham Court Road. The flat entrance leads to the main bar. There are + 14 steps to an upper level (20%) and − 4 to a lower level. There is an open lift (D75 W85 L115) to the lower level, where the **wheelchair toilet (D95 ST85 NKS)** is situated.

Corts Holborn Bar and Restaurant, 78 High Holborn WC1V 6LS *Tel:* 020 7242-4292
Just west of the junction with Red Lion Street. The entrance, main bar and restaurant are step free. There are − 18 steps to a private function room. **Adapted toilet (D80 ST55)** at the end of the bar in the restaurant area. It contained all manner of junk when we visited.

Goose and Granite, 31 Marchmont Street, Bloomsbury WC1 *Tel:* 020 7923-5961
Opposite the Forte Posthouse Hotel. Step-free entrance and within GF bar. There are + 21 steps to upstairs bar. **Wheelchair toilet (D80 ST70)** around the bar and to the right.

Mybar, Myhotel, 11-13 Bayley Street WC1B 3HD *Tel:* 020 7667-6000 *website:* www.myhotels.co.uk
Located 20m off Tottenham Court Road, the hotel has three entrances. One goes to a sushi restaurant, one to the reception and one to the bar. All three have + 1 step, but inside all link without steps. The bar itself is 100% step free. **Wheelchair toilet (D90 ST85)** situated to the left of Yo Sushi restaurant. From the bar, go through reception and the restaurant.

SW1

Avenue Restaurant and Bar, 7-9 St James's Street SW1A 9LA *Tel:* 020 7321-2111 *website:* www.theavenue.co.uk
Situated 100m uphill from the junction with Pall Mall on the right. It is a spacious bar and restaurant with + 1 step at the entrance. Then flat to 90%. **Wheelchair toilet (D85 ST75)** to the left near the back. On the two occasions we visited, it was being used for storage and on both occasions we were assured this was a one-off.

che Restaurant and Bar, 23 St James's Street SW1A 1HE *Tel:* 020 7747-9380
On the junction with Ryder Street. The front entrance gives flat access to a reception desk and lift (D75 L110 W110) to the restaurant on the first floor. A movable wardrobe (!) blocked the way to the lift when we visited. **Wheelchair toilet (D75 ST80)** to right of the lift on the first floor. A side entrance on Ryder Street gives flat access to the bar, from which there are − 4 steps to the reception and lift. These can be bypassed by going around outside the building.

Lord Moon of the Mall, 18 Whitehall SW1 *Tel:* 020 7839-7701
About 50m from Trafalgar Square and next to the Whitehall Theatre. It is a listed building which presents problems relating to access. A bell is discreetly placed outside if you need help to get in, and we have suggested the provision of portable ramps. Entrance + 3 steps. Step free inside. **Wheelchair toilet (D80 ST120 +)** just past the bar on the left.

Sanctuary House, 33 Tothill Street SW1 9LA *Tel:* 020 7799-4044
A hotel and pub on the junction with Dean Farrar Street. There is step-free access to the hotel reception and to the pub. 80% of the bar is step free. **Adapted toilet (D80 ST50)** near the hotel reception.

Sports Café, 80 Haymarket SW1Y 4TQ *Tel:* 020 7839-8300
Situated between the junctions with Pall Mall and Charles II Street. Step-free entrance with a ramp bypassing − 3 steps to the GF area. Roughly 35% of seating is step free and at a good height. First floor, with pool tables and two more bars, via + 22. **Adapted toilet (D90 ST68)** in the staff area at the back of bar can be reached if you ask member of staff. The door was stuck when we visited, and there was no handle on the inside.

Wetherspoons, Victoria Station Concourse, SW1 *Tel:* 020 7931-0445
Located above the *W.H. Smith* in the centre of the Station. Access is by escalator or stairs (+ 10 + 11). However, there is a lift (D80 W95 L140) in the corner of the building by Platform 8, giving step-free access to the pub/restaurant. **Wheelchair toilet (D85 ST75)**; key from the bar, but a large baby-changing unit needs moving by a staff member.

SE1

All Bar One, 28-30 Fieldan House, London Bridge Street SE1 *Tel:* 020 7940-9981
Opposite the bus terminus, at the end of the street. There is + 1 step at the bar entrance. The non-smoking area (about 30%) is via + 3. **Wheelchair toilet (D80 ST70 NKS)** to the left of the bar.

All Bar One, 34 Shad Thames, Butler's Wharf, Spice Quay SE1 2YG *Tel:* 020 7940-9771
Situated on the waterfront on Butler's Wharf about 150m from Tower Bridge. A ramp to the right bypasses + 1 step/lip to the covered front patio. It is then step free to all of the large bar (some 60m in width). **Wheelchair toilet (D90 ST80 NKS)** in the far left of the bar, next to the Ladies.

Anchor, Bankside SE1 9EF *Tel:* 0870 700-1456
On the riverside by Cannon Street railway bridge, at the junction
with Bank End. The pub dates from the late 17thC, after the
Southwark fire of 1676 and is full of split levels. There is, however,
a new step-free entrance on the corner as you come from the west and
the Millennium Bridge. This leads to a bar where 20% of the GF is
step free. **Adapted toilet (D80 ST65)** on the GF, through the door
marked 'toilets' and just to the right is an open lift (D100 L130) going
to the first-floor terrace bar, bypassing the steps. There is then a ± 1
(10cm) threshold to get to the outside seating.
  The riverside terrace across the road has step-free access from
Bankside and movable chairs and tables. A very pleasant spot in the
summer.

Bar Med, 5 Chicheley Street SE1 7PJ *Tel:* 020 7803-4790
Restaurant and bar across the street from the London Eye, next to
All Bar One. At the entrance, an open lift (D90 W90 L120) with $+1$
step bypasses $+3$. There are -3 to the non-smoking area and
outdoor seating and -18 to a function room. **Wheelchair toilet
(D80 ST80)** to the left of the entrance.

Doggetts Coat and Badge, 1 Blackfriars Bridge SE1 *Tel:* 020 7633-9057
By the river at the southern end of Blackfriars Bridge, on the corner of
Upper Ground. A pub on several floors, with entrances on different
levels. There is access only via a small step (5cm) from the Bridge,
about 25m down Upper Ground via a car ramp. A lift (D80 W110
L120) links all the floors, including the first-floor function room.
Wheelchair toilet (D75 ST100) next to the Ladies directly opposite the
lift on the lower ground floor. From the riverside, you can get in via
$+8+1$ steps. The garden is $-1-8$ from the lower ground floor and
has only pub tables/benches, with similar tables by the river.

The Founders Arms, 52 Hopton Street SE1 *Tel:* 020 7928-1899
An attractive pub on the riverside with ramped access on the Blackfriars Bridge side. It is very close to the Bankside Gallery, and about
300m from Tate Modern. Ramped access as you approach from
Blackfriars Bridge. **Wheelchair toilet (D70 ST70)** to the left of the bar.

The Mulberry Bush, 68 Upper Ground SE1 9PP *Tel:* 020 7928-7940
Upper Ground runs parallel to the river, and the pub is near
Gabriel's Wharf. There is $+1$ step at the open entrance or a step-
free way in to the left. The GF is 90% step free with $+2$ to small area.
First floor restaurant $+17$. **Wheelchair toilet (D85 ST75)** past the bar
on the left; key with staff.

Old Thameside Inn, Pickfords Wharf, Clink Street SE1 *Tel:* 020 7403-4243

Opposite *The Golden Hinde*, a reconstruction of Sir Francis Drake's ship. Main entrance has $+1+3$ steps, which is bypassed with a ramp. 20% of the GF is step free, the rest is $+3$. **Adapted toilet (D85** inward opening, **ST85)** at the end of the bar next to the Gents. The riverside terrace has fixed furniture and can be reached up a ramp outside via -1.

Wine Wharf, Stoney Street, Borough Market SE1 *Tel:* 020 7940-8335 *website:* www.vinopolis.co.uk

Located 30m from the junction of Stoney Street and Winchester Walk. There is a lip at the entrance followed by -2 steps bypassed by a ramp. Open lift (W85 L115) bypasses $+3$ from Vinopolis. Bar and food on the GF. There are $+16$ to a mezzanine level. **Wheelchair toilet (D70 ST75)** on the GF.

NW1 and N1

Albion, 10 Thornhill Road N1 *Tel:* 020 7607-7450

Opposite the junction with Malvern Terrace. Entrance $+1$ step, then step free to 80%, the rest is $+1$. **Wheelchair toilet (D85 ST70)** at the back of the pub to the left, although side transfer can be blocked by the movable handrail which won't stay vertical! Small -1 to beer garden with pub benches/tables. There are also some tables outside at the front.

All Bar One, 1 Liverpool Road, Islington N1 *Tel:* 020 7843-0021

On the corner with Upper Street, almost opposite the Angel Station. Entrance $+1$ step, then step free throughout. **Adapted toilet (D70 + ST55)** en route to the other toilets. Fortunately the cubicle is quite big. The WC was placed in the centre, preventing ST from either side, and the support bars were on the walls, too far away to be useful to anyone! Apart from that, it's a good place.

The Bull, 100 Upper Street, Islington N1 0NP Tel: 020 7354 9174

About halfway down Upper Street, on the corner with Theberton Street. Main entrance on Upper Street is $+1$, but there is a step-free entrance on Theberton Street. GF is step free, and includes the bar and an **adapted toilet (D85 ST75)**, *but D65 to get to the toilet corridor* to the right of the bar. There is also a small first-floor area, accessed only via a spiral staircase.

Crown and Anchor, 137 Drummond Street, Regent's Park NW1 *Tel:* 020 7255-9871
On the corner of North Gower Street. The entrance on the corner has +1+1 steps, the one in North Gower Street is ramped, but is normally locked; the barman will open it on request. **Adapted toilet (D85** inward opening, **ST75**, but obstructed by movable items, making it **ST33)** on the right at the end of the bar.

Engineer, 65 Gloucester Avenue NW1 *Tel:* 020 7722-0950
On the corner of Princess Road. Step-free entrance and inside. **Adapted toilet (D85** inward opening, **ST75)** around the bar and to the right, through the doors and towards the garden. The garden is −1 to some movable chairs and tables, and a further +1 to some pub benches/tables.

The Garden, 179 Upper Street, Islington N1 1RG *Tel:* 020 7226-6276
Opposite Islington Town Hall, 40m south of the junction with Tyndale Lane. Ramped entrance and step free inside. **Wheelchair toilet (D75 ST80)** on the left, near the rear of building. To reach it, go to the right of the bar, turn left and it is the first door on the left.

Kings Head, 115 Upper Street N1 *Tel:*020 7226-0364
Across from St Mary's Church. Step-free entrance and inside to GF. Behind the pub is a theatre. **Adapted toilet (D70** inward opening, **ST90)** behind the bar. The key is at the bar.

Man in the Moon, 40 Chalk Farm Road NW1 *Tel:* 020 7482-2054
30m from the junction with Harmood Street. Ramped entrance on the right, giving 30% step-free access. To reach the **wheelchair toilet (D75 ST80)**, go through the door 3m to left of the bar and it is on your left. This involves going down a ramp that bypasses -3 steps.

Pitcher and Piano, 69 Upper Street, Islington N1 *Tel:* 020 7704-9974
Opposite Islington Green. Step-free entrance and inside to 80%; the rest is +5. **Adapted toilet (D80 ST68)** at the end of the bar on the left-hand side: side transfer was obstructed by movable objects when we visited.

Rat and Parrot, 25 Parkway NW1 *Tel:* 020 7482-2309
At the junction with Arlington Road. Slight hill. Entrance +1 step from both entrances, though the smaller step is at the Arlington Road entrance. Step free to 80% inside; 20% is +1. **Adapted toilet (D90 ST68)** to the right of the bar; key at bar. When we visited, it wasn't working, and the seat was broken. Some movable tables and chairs outside the front of the pub.

City area (EC1, EC2, EC3, EC4 and E1)

All Bar One, 44 Ludgate Hill EC4 *Tel:* 020 7653-9901
On the corner of Old Bailey. Step-free entrance and throughout.
Wheelchair toilet (D80 ST110) on the right as you enter, to the right
of the bar.

Banker, Cousin Lane EC4 *Tel:* 020 7283-5206
On the riverfront, under the arches of Cannon Bridge, carrying the
lines going from Cannon Street Station. Flat access to a bar which
only has high stools and tables. An upper section is $+9$ steps,
overlooking the river, and there's an outside riverside area ($+7$).
Wheelchair toilet (D90 ST70) by the entrance; key from the bar.

Captain Kidd, 108 Wapping High Street E1 *Tel:* 020 7480-5759
About 100m west of Wapping Tube Station, set back from the street
and next to the river. Cobbled street. High kerb, then step-free access
to pub, or $+2+2$ steps to the beer garden. **Wheelchair toilet (D90
ST70)** to the right of the entrance, but -5 steps to get there!

Dickens' Inn, St Katharine's Way E1 *Tel:* 020 7488-2208
This is in the centre of St Katharine's Dock right by Tower Bridge. It
is open most of the day and includes restaurants as well as bars and is
accessible via a ramp (away to the right and bypassing the $+12$
steps). There is a lift (D75 W100 L130) behind the food bar in the
part of the pub near the ramp, leading to a **wheelchair toilet (D75
ST85)** in the basement, and the first-floor restaurant, but you must
ask a staff member to use the lift.

Hamilton Hall, Unit 32, Liverpool Street Station EC2 *Tel:* 020 7247-
3579
In a high and splendidly decorated hall, on the upper level of the
station (which is ground level if you're coming from outside), towards
Bishopsgate. Step-free access from the station side. It is step free from
Bishopsgate, from near the clock tower, and then into the station.
Wheelchair toilet (D80 ST70) but blocked by mop and bucket storage.
'There's nowhere else to put them', according to the manager.

Hogshead, 78 Ludgate Hill, Ludgate Circus EC4M 7LQ *Tel:* 020
7329-8517
On the corner of Ludgate Hill and Ludgate Circus. A ramp bypasses
-6 steps at the main entrance from the Circus. Step free inside.
Wheelchair toilet (D85 ST85) to right of main entrance.

Hung Drawn and Quartered, 26 Great Tower Street EC3 *Tel:* 020 7626-6123
Opposite the junction with Mark Lane. Ramped entrance. The pub is spacious inside, but with very little furniture, and only three tables at chair height. **Wheelchair toilet (D90 ST125** but blocked by movable objects, making it **ST59)** by the stairs; key at bar.

King's Head, 49 Chiswell Street EC1 *Tel:* 020 7606-9158
At the junction with Silk Street. Step free to the pub from either street, but split level inside involves $-2-2$ steps. **Wheelchair toilet (D80 ST80)** by the Silk Street entrance. The key is at the bar, but there is no access to the toilet on Friday or Saturday nights.

King's Stores, 14 Widegate Street E1 *Tel:* 020 7247-4089
At the junction with Sandys Row. Step free only from White Rose Court. **Adapted toilet (D90 ST25**, blocked by fixed handrail) at the end of the bar next to the Gents; key at bar.

Magpie and Stump, 19 Old Bailey EC4 *Tel:* 020 7248-5085
Opposite the Old Bailey, with step-free access throughout via a lift (D80 W100 L140) just inside the entrance (key for lift at GF bar). This bypasses $+9$ steps to the top level, -13 to the lower GF, and another -20 to a basement level. You need staff assistance to use the lift to the lower GF which contains one **wheelchair toilet (D70 ST70)**. There's **another** on the lower lower GF (or basement) **(D70 ST70)**.

Masque Haunt, 168 Old Street EC1 *Tel:* 020 7251-4195
At the junction with Bunhill Row. Most doors have $+1$ step, but the Bunhill Road one is ramped, giving step-free access to 70%. **Adapted toilet (D80 ST70**, but door opens in) behind and to the left of the bar, next to the Gents. Key available from behind the bar.

Melton Mowbray Pie and Ale House, 18 Holborn EC1 *Tel:* 020 7405-7077
About 100m from Chancery Lane Station and opposite Holborn House. Entrance $+1$ step and only part with step-free access, as it is on three levels. Some tables outside in the summer. **Wheelchair toilet (D85 ST130)** on the right, after the entrance.

Mint, East Smithfield E1 *Tel:* 020 7702-0370
Main entrance $+16$ steps, bypassed by a lift (D90 W90 L160) accessed from a side entrance. **Wheelchair toilet (D90 ST90)** to the right of the bar.

Old Tea Warehouse, Creechurch Lane EC3 *Tel:* 020 7621-1913
Just off Leadenhall Street There are separate entrances to two separate
GF bars; both are step free. The Ceylon Cellar Bar downstairs, has −17
steps. **Wheelchair toilet (D80 ST120 NKS)** ahead as you enter the first
bar. Accessible tables and chairs outside at the front.

The Pavilion, 6 Little Britain EC1 *Tel:* 020 7600-8824
At the junction with King Edward Street. Large threshold at entrance,
then step free to the ground-floor bar, which has relatively few chairs
at wheelchair height. A lift (D80 W95 L145) goes to the basement bar
and restaurant, which has a split level bypassed by a ramp; all the
tables and chairs are movable and at wheelchair height. **Wheelchair
toilet (D90 ST80)** to the right of the lift on the basement level.

Red Herring, 49 Gresham Street EC2 *Tel:* 020 7606-0399
Near the Guildhall. Flat access to part of the GF bar. **Adapted toilet
(D85 ST60** obstructed by sink) is unsigned, just to the left of the
entrance; key at the bar.

Sir John Oldcastle, 29-35 Farringdon Road EC1 *Tel:* 020 7242-1013
At the corner of Grenville Street. There is an intercom system outside
to call for assistance. Otherwise the entrance is +2−3, then flat
inside. **Wheelchair toilet (D75 ST75)** to left of bar, next to Gents; key
at bar.

Inner areas

The northern Docklands, and the Isle of Dogs (E14)

All Bar One, 42 MacKenzie Walk, South Colonnade, Canary Wharf
E14 *Tel:* 020 7513-0911
Alongside the middle section of the West India Docks, and a short
downhill walk from Canary Wharf DLR Station by the junction with
Chancellor Passage. Entrance near the footbridge is flat; from all
other entrances there is −1 step. Fairly congested inside. Some tables
at chair height. **Adapted toilet (D85 ST66)** to the left as you enter.
Pub benches/tables and some movable chairs and tables outside.

Cat and Canary, 1 Fishermans Walk, Canary Wharf E14 *Tel:* 020
7512-9187
About 50m from Cabot Square on the waterfront. Flat entrance then
60% is step free. **Wheelchair toilet (D80 ST70)**.

Drummonds, Marsh Wall, Heron Quays E14 *Tel:* 020 7536-0141
Located at the junction with West Ferry Road and opposite the *City Pride*. The small CP becomes a 'garden' in the summer. Step-free entrance, then step free to 60%. **Adapted toilet (D80 ST56)**; key behind bar.

Henry Addington, 20 MacKenzie Walk, Canary Wharf E14 *Tel:* 020 7513-0921
Located some 50m from Cabot Square on the waterfront. Step free to 70% of this spacious pub, including the waterfront patio. **Wheelchair toilet (D80 ST80)**.

Pier Tavern, 299 Manchester Road E14 *Tel:* 020 7515-9528
At the junction with Pier Street. Flat way into both the pub and garden from Pier Street. 80% with step-free access. **Wheelchair toilet (D80 ST70)**.

Slug and Lettuce, 30 South Colonnade, Canary Wharf E14 4QQ *Tel:* 020 7519-1612
Situated on Canada Square to the right from Canary Wharf tube exit. Entrance and bar step free. **Wheelchair toilet (D85 ST120 NKS)** at the back to the right of bar, sometimes used for storage. Seating outside.

Spinnaker, Harbour Island, Isle of Dogs E14 *Tel:* 020 7538-9329
In the Harbour Exchange Square development off Lime Harbour, and on the dockside. Step-free entrance and throughout. **Wheelchair toilet (D95 ST80)** halfway back on the left, opposite the bar.

Waterfront, South Quay Plaza, Marsh Wall E14 *Tel:* 020 7537-3903
The pub is in the middle of the Plaza, next to the river. Entrance + 1 step, then flat to the lift (D80 W100 L120). First floor bar step free, though there's − 1 to the balcony and patio. Restaurant on the second floor. **Wheelchair toilet (D80 ST80)** on the first floor near the patio.

Inner postal districts E

Beckton

Tollgate Tavern, Mary Rose Mall, Beckton E6 *Tel:* 020 7476-3716
At the back of *Asda*, and about 200m from Beckton DLR Station. Supermarket CP outside. Step free to 90% of pub. **Wheelchair toilet (D85 ST80)** by the shopping mall exit.

East Ham

Earl of Wakefield, 72 Katherine Road, East Ham E6 *Tel:* 020 8586-8901
At the junction with Wakefield Street. There is + 1 step to the bars,
flat to garden. **Wheelchair toilet (D85 ST80)** to the right, at the back
of the lounge bar.

Miller's Well, 419 Barking Road, East Ham E6 Tel: 020 8471-8404
Opposite the Town Hall. Ramped entrance, then step free inside,
with ramp bypassing − 1 step to small garden. **Wheelchair toilet (D85
ST75)** past the bar at the back of the pub.

Forest Gate

Holly Tree, 141 Dames Road, Forest Gate E7 *Tel:* 020 8221-9831
Opposite the junction with Sidney Road. Small CP at front on
Dames Road and ramped front entrance. Also CP off Pevensey
Road. Kerb between CP and rear entrance. Steep ramp at the rear
entrance gives 95% step-free access. Raised area + 2 steps. From the
rear entrance level, ledge then − 1 to the garden. **Wheelchair toilet
(D80 ST75)** on the right just after rear entrance.

Railway Tavern, 173 Forest Lane, Forest Gate E7 *Tel:* 020 8555-1177
At junction with Woodgrange Road. Step free. **Wheelchair toilet
(D80 ST90)** at the rear, on the left. Staff said it is normally usable,
but it was blocked by music equipment when we visited.

Manor Park

Golden Fleece, 166 Capel Road, Manor Park E12 *Tel:* 020 8478-0024
On the corner of The Chase. Small CP at front. Entrance on the left-
hand side of the pub on the driveway to the CP has step-free access to
the whole pub. Front entrance has + 1 + 1 steps, the back one + 2.
Wheelchair toilet (D90 ST80) by the other toilets, directly opposite
the step-free entrance, past the left-hand end of the bar.

Stratford

Goldengrove, 148 The Grove, Stratford E15 1TZ *Tel:* 020 8519-0750
Opposite the *Safeway* CP at the junction with Great Eastern Road.
There is a step-free entrance from which you should follow the aisle
round to the left to a ramp which bypasses + 3 steps to the bar.
Wheelchair toilet (D85 ST120) at back of pub on right, immediately
before flat entrance to beer garden.

Goose on the Broadway, 102 The Broadway, Stratford E15 *Tel:* 020 8221-0761
Located 100m to the left of the exit from Stratford Shopping Centre, on The Broadway. Large and spacious inside with step-free entrance and **wheelchair toilet (D80 ST85 NKS)** at far end of pub past the bar.

Swan, 31 Broadway, Stratford E15 4BQ *Tel*: 020 8522-0091
By Tramway Avenue, across busy junction from east entrance to Stratford Shopping Centre. Entrance + 1 step and 80% of the bar is step free. First floor + 21. **Adapted toilet (D85 ST55 NKS)** to the right of the bar behind the stairs.

Walthamstow

Goose and Granite, 264 Hoe Street, Walthamstow E17 *Tel:* 020 8223-9951
On the corner of Selborne Road, about 60m from Walthamstow Central Station. Entrance has + 1 step from Selborne Road; the step-free door on Hoe Street is used as an exit only, and is consequently normally locked on the outside. 60% of the interior is step free, the rest is + 3. **Wheelchair toilet (D90 ST70)** past the left-hand end of the bar and on the right, up a slight ramp.

Wanstead

Cuckfield, 31 High Street, Wanstead E11 *Tel:* 020 8532-2431
On the corner of Wellington Road. The corner entrance gives step-free access to 85% of the pub, but there are + 3 steps from Wellington Road. **Wheelchair cubicle (D90 ST80 NKS)** inside the **Gents (D70)**, at the far end of the pub from the corner entrance, going parallel to the pillars which separate the main body of the pub from the conservatory.

Inner postal districts N

Edmonton

Lamb Inn, 52 Church Street, Edmonton N9 *Tel:* 020 8887-0128
Near the junction with Victoria Road. Flat front entrance, giving 35% step-free access; − 3 steps to rear area. **Wheelchair toilet (D75 ST90)** to the left of the bar.

Highgate

Gate House, 1 North Road, Highgate N6 *Tel:* 020 8340-8054
By the mini-roundabout at the junction with Hampstead Lane. Step free. **Adapted toilet (D85 ST67)** by the Gents; key at the bar.

Red Lion and Sun, 25 North Road, Highgate N6 *Tel:* 020 8340-1780
100m from the junction with Hampstead Lane. Small CP at front. Entrance 1 + 1 + 1 steps. There is a ramped car access bypassing these. Step free inside. **Adapted toilet (D85 ST85** but blocked by furniture, making it **ST35)** to the left, just past the bar. Pub benches/tables outside both back and front.

Holloway

Coronet, 340 Holloway Road, Lower Holloway N7 *Tel:* 020 7609-5014
By the junction with Loraine Road. It is a huge and remarkable pub in a converted 1940s cinema. The entrance has −7 steps, but with a lift bypass (D80 W110 L120). Ask a staff member for the keypad combination. 90% step free inside. **Wheelchair toilet (D85 ST90)** to the right of the bar.

The Holloway, 341 Holloway Road, Holloway N7 *Tel:* 020 7700-2989
At the junction with Camden Road. Ramped entrance and 90% step free inside. **Wheelchair toilet (D80 ST75)** halfway back on the right.

O'Neill's, 456 Upper Holloway Road, Holloway N7 *Tel:* 020 7700-8941
At the junction with Seven Sisters Road. Ramped entrance on Upper Holloway Road, near the *Granada* electrical goods store. 80% step free inside. **Wheelchair toilet (D90 ST95 NKS)** around the bar to the right.

Southgate

New Crown, 80 Chase Side, Southgate N14 *Tel:* 020 8882-8758
In the middle of a shopping parade about 100m from Southgate Circus. Ramped entrance and step free inside. **Wheelchair toilet (D85 ST120 NKS)** straight through, before the Ladies.

Tottenham

Dagmar Arms, 36 Cornwall Road, Tottenham N15 *Tel:* 020 8800-7785
30m from junction with Dagmar Road. On-site CP. Entrance +1 step, then 90% step free. **Wheelchair toilet (D80 ST100)** at the rear through the family room. The garden is −1.

New Moon, 413 Lordship Lane, Tottenham N17 *Tel:* 020 8808-2684
Near the junction with Walpole Road. Step free. **Wheelchair toilet (D85 ST90)** on the left.

Wood Green

Goose and Granite, 203 High Road, Wood Green N22 *Tel:* 020 8888-1624
Opposite Wood Green Underground Station. Entrance +1 step, then step free with ramp inside. **Adapted toilet (D80 ST65)** to the left around the bar, then on your right. Ramped bypass for the −2 to the garden which has pub bench/tables.

Toll Gate, 26 Turnpike Lane, Turnpike Lane N8 *Tel:* 020 8889-9085
Near the junction with Waldegrave Road. Small step, then flat access. **Wheelchair toilet (D95 ST100)** in the back left-hand corner.

Inner postal districts NW

Colindale

Moon under Water, 10 Varley Parade, Colindale NW9 *Tel:* 020 8200-7611
Near the centre of the Parade. Step free. **Wheelchair toilet (D70 ST200)** at the rear, on the left.

Cricklewood

Beaten Docket, 50 Cricklewood Broadway NW2 *Tel:* 020 8450-2972
15m from junction with Skardu Road. Step free via ramped entrance on the right. **Wheelchair toilet (D80 ST80)** at the rear on the left.

Finchley

Old White Lion, 121 Great North Road, Finchley N2 *Tel:* 020 8365-4861
Next to the railway bridge by East Finchley Underground Station.
Small CP at the back, less than 50m away. Step free at entrance and
throughout. **Wheelchair toilet (D85 ST120)** to the right of the bar.
Small threshold to part of the garden with movable chairs, then −2
steps to the rest of the garden. There is also a step-free side gate, the
key to which is at the bar.

Hampstead

Flask, 14 Flask Walk, Hampstead NW3 *Tel:* 020 7435-4580
Step free. **Adapted toilet (D90** opening inwards, **ST115)** off the
saloon bar.

Old Bull and Bush, North End, Hampstead NW3 7HE *Tel:* 020 8905-
5456
At the junction between North End and North End Way. On-site
CP, then ramped access to rear of pub or step free at the front. 90%
of the bar is step free. **Adapted toilet (D85 ST80** partially blocked by
a radiator and a handrail stuck down at the time of visit).

Harlesden

Coliseum, 26A Manor Park Road, Harlesden NW10 *Tel:* 020 8961-
6570
Near the junction with High Street. Step free via ramped entrance on
the left. **Adapted toilet (D70 ST62 NKS)** at the rear on the left; key at
the bar.

Royal Oak, 95 High Street, Harlesden NW10 4TS *Tel:* 020 8965-0228
By the junction with Park Parade. Entrance + 1 step, then step free.
Wheelchair toilet (D85). When we rang, we were told that the toilet
was being retiled.

Hendon

The White Bear, 56 The Burroughs, Hendon NW4 *Tel:* 020 8457-4812
On the corner of Brampton Grove. Small CP in front of the pub with
about six spaces. The right-hand entrance has + 1 steps, the left-hand
one is step free, with 60% of the inside step free. Most of the low

tables have heavy benches or pews. **Wheelchair toilet** to the right of the bar is now apparently in full working order. Pub benches/tables at the front of the pub. Conservatory at back of pub has + 3 entrance but is step free from main bar and there is − 1 from conservatory to back garden.

Kilburn

Goose of Kilburn, 155 Kilburn High Road, Kilburn NW6 *Tel:* 020 7644-9961
On the corner of Priory Park Road. The main entrance on Kilburn High Road has + 1 step, the one on Priory Park Road has + 3. There is a marked 'disabled' entrance to the right of the main entrance, which is step free, but which is normally kept locked, as it goes through a staff area. You'll have to ask. Inside 35% is step free, with five tables at a low level; the rest of the pub is + 2. **Wheelchair toilet (D90 ST80)** immediately to the right as you come in by the disabled entrance. May be locked at times; in this case the key will be at the bar.

Maida Vale

Crockers, 24 Aberdeen Place, Maida Vale NW8 *Tel:* 020 7286-6608
On the corner of Cunningham Place and Aberdeen Place. Entrance with small step, then step free. **Adapted toilet (D80 ST66)** to the right of the entrance in the far corner.

Mill Hill

Indigo Café Bar, 97 The Broadway, Mill Hill NW7 3TG *Tel:* 020 8201-0911
Opposite the junction with Hartley Avenue and Flower Lane and the Roman Catholic Church. Step-free entrance and throughout. **Adapted toilet (D85 ST60)** in the back right-hand corner: turn right behind the partition wall; key at bar.

Three Hammers, The Ridgeway, Hammers Lane, Mill Hill NW7 *Tel:* 020 8959-2346
By junction of Hammers Lane and The Ridgeway. On-site CP. Ramped entrance on the left, then 80% step free. There is − 1 step to a conservatory at the back of the pub. Step-free access to garden via side gate on Hammers Lane. **Wheelchair toilet (D70 ST70)** on the left, just inside ramped entrance.

Muswell Hill

O'Neill's, 291 Broadway, Muswell Hill N10 *Tel:* 020 8883-7382
About 100m north of the big roundabout, near the end of Wood-
berry Crescent. Hilly area. Step free at the entrance and inside.
Wheelchair toilet (D85 ST80) to the right of the bar.

Inner postal districts W

Acton

Red Lion and Pineapple, 281 High Street, Acton W3 9BP *Tel:* 020
8896-2248
Located by the junction with Gunnersbury Lane and the Uxbridge
Road. One entrance with a slight bump. **Wheelchair toilet (D80
ST70)**. There is +1 step to small garden, though step free from
outside.

Chiswick

All Bar One, 197 Chiswick High Road, Chiswick W4 *Tel:* 020 8987-
8211
Approximately 50m from the junction with Linden Gardens. There
are three BB spaces directly outside. Step-free entrance and throughout. **Wheelchair toilet (D90 ST80)** in the back right-hand corner.

The Birdcage, 122 Chiswick High Road, Chiswick W4 *Tel:* 020 8995-
4392
On the corner of Thornton Avenue. Flat entrance and throughout.
Wheelchair toilet (D75 ST70, though the soil pipe slightly obstructs
it, reducing it to **ST62** against the wall) at the back of the pub, past
the bar and on the left just before the garden. This has step-free
access and movable tables and chairs.

Bull's Head, 15 Strand-on-the-Green, W4 3PQ *Tel:* 020 8994-1204
An attractive riverside pub 50m east of Kew Railway Bridge.
Ramped access is from the CP on Thames Road. From here,
70% of the pub is accessible. To get to the pub benches on the
towpath, avoiding the −5 steps at the main entrance, go out of the
rear entrance and use the public footpath down to the river on the
eastern side of the CP. **Wheelchair toilet (D80 ST75)** on the right after
going through the rear entrance; key at bar.

George IV, 185 High Road, Chiswick W4 2DR *Tel:* 020 8994-4624
Opposite the junction with Windmill Road. Three BB spaces directly
in front of *All Bar One* (see separate write-up), 50m away. The right-
hand entrance is step free to 70% of the GF; the left-hand one has
+1 and leads to a split level, which covers about 30% of the GF. The
gallery is +12+5. **Wheelchair toilet (D75 ST85)** directly at the back;
key at bar. The garden is +1 with movable tables and chairs.

Paragon, 80 Chiswick High Road, Chiswick W4 *Tel:* 020 8742-7263
By the junction with Ennismore Avenue. Ramped, but somewhat
bumpy way in to the left of the main entrance, to bypass +1 step.
Adapted toilet (D80 ST42 NKS) en-route to the Ladies at the end of
the bar; key kept at the bar.

Tabard, 2 Bath Road, Chiswick W4 1LN *Tel:* 020 8994-3492
By the junction with Turnham Green Terrace, and 100m from
Turnham Green Station. Entrance +3 steps or a ramp via the
garden. Slightly congested bar. **Wheelchair toilet (D80 ST80)** to
the right of bar. When we visited, the key was at the bar (among
some 50 others, and it took them a little time to find the right one!).

Ealing

Chandlers, 2 Central Chambers, Ealing Broadway W5 2NT *Tel:* 020
8567-4859
Opposite Ealing Broadway Station. CP 200m away off Spring Bridge
Road. Step-free access and **wheelchair toilet (D80 ST80)**.

Drayton Court, 2 The Avenue, West Ealing W13 8PH *Tel:* 020 8997-
1019
By the junction with Argyle Road, and right by West Ealing Station.
Via the entrance under the portal, +1 step followed by a ramp.
Inside it is 70% step free with split levels (±1) to the balcony and to
raised areas. **Adapted toilet (D85 ST65)** with inward opening door,
but a large cubicle with over 100cm clearance from the edge of the
door. Large garden −26, but there's an alternative route via The
Avenue and Gordon Road. This is about 200m long and quite
bumpy in parts. Nice garden once you've got there, and −1 (large)
from there into the theatre downstairs.

Edwards, 28 New Broadway, Ealing W5 2XA *Tel:* 020 8567-9438
Less than 100m from the Town Hall, towards Christ Church. Step
free. **Wheelchair toilet (D70+ ST70+)** just past the other toilets.

Kent, 2 Scotch Common, West Ealing W13 8DL *Tel:* 020 8997-5911
CP. Near the junction with Kent Avenue. Entrance + 1 step, then step
free to about 60% of the bar. **Wheelchair toilet (D70 + ST70 +)**. A
ramp leads down to the large garden, bypassing roughly − 15 steps.

The Green, 10 The Green, Ealing W5 *Tel:* 020 8579-7493
Near the junction with Bond Street, and the mini-roundabout. Flat
entrance and 75% of the pub is step free. + 5 steps to a raised area at
the back. **Wheelchair toilet (D75 ST70 NKS)** at the back of the pub.
Go straight past the bar and turn right.

Mamma Amalfi, 45 The Mall, Ealing W5 3TJ *Tel:* 020 8840-5777
Bar/restaurant about 150m from Ealing Broadway Tube Station
towards Ealing Common, with step-free access and a **wheelchair
toilet (D70 + ST70 +)**.

Old Orleans, 26 Bond Street, Ealing W5 5AA *Tel:* 020 8579-7413
50m from the roundabout where Mattock Lane meets Bond Street.
Ramped entrance gives 80% step-free access. **Wheelchair toilet (D75
ST70)** at the rear by other toilets.

O'Neill's, 23 High Street, Ealing W5 *Tel:* 020 8579-4107
Some 50m north of the junction with Bond Street. Step free to 85%,
via entrance on the right. **Wheelchair toilet (D80 ST90)** to the right of
the bar. Key from the bar.

Town House, The Broadway, Ealing W5 2PH *Tel:* 020 8810-0304
On the corner of The Broadway and The Mall, and about 50m from
Ealing Broadway Station down a gentle slope. Flat entrance (with a
small lip) and 60% step free inside. There are two raised areas, one
with + 1 step, and the other with + 2. Only a couple of tables in the
step free area are at wheelchair height. The others are much higher.
Adapted toilet (D85 ST61) go left at the entrance, past the bar, and
then it's on your right through the door marked 'Gents and disabled'.

Yates Wine Lodge, 5 Mattock Lane, Ealing W5 5BG *Tel:* 020 8840-0988
50m from the junction with Bond Street. Step-free access to about
50%, including the bar but no tables or chairs. These are on upper
levels, with either + 1 or + 2. The + 2 level can be reached by using
an alternative entrance on the left, where there is simply a small ridge
en route. Lift (D77 W100 L135) from the bar level to first floor, then
step free to 60%. **Adapted toilet (D75 ST66)** to the right of the bar on
the GF, at the bar level.

Hammersmith

Hammersmith Ram, 81 King Street, Hammersmith W6 *Tel:* 020 8748-4511
On the corner of Angel Walk, and opposite the King's Mall Shopping Centre. Entrance from the front is a large + 1, with + 1 one third of the way back in the pub, but there is a ramped entrance to the upper (back) level through the small beer garden on Angel Walk. **Wheelchair toilet (D85 ST75)** in the far left corner from this entrance. The garden is congested with immovable benches and tables.

Hop Poles, 17-9 King Street, Hammersmith W6 *Tel:* 020 8748-1411
Opposite the junction with Hammersmith Grove, which normally houses an open-air market. Both entrances on King Street have + 1 step, but there is only a small threshold at the back entrance from Blacks Road, which is through the right-hand set of black, unmarked double doors underneath a 'Willmotts' sign. **Adapted toilet (D85** inward opening, **ST62**) to the left of this entrance, next to the other toilets; key at bar.

Old Suffolk Punch, 80 Fulham Palace Road, Hammersmith W6 *Tel:* 020 8748-6502
On the corner of Distillery Lane. Step-free entrance leads to 40% of the seating area with flat access. The bar itself is surrounded by a platform, reached via either + 1 (large) or + 2 (small), all of which can be bypassed by a ramp. There are other split levels with + 1. **Adapted toilet (D85 ST52 either side)** at the back of the flat area.

Old Trout, Broadway Shopping Centre, Hammersmith W6 9YD *Tel:* 020 8846-9674
Part of the shopping centre which also accommodates the (accessible) Hammersmith District and Piccadilly Lines Underground Station, this pub faces onto Bradmore Square, which is the area behind Smollensky's Restaurant, opposite St Paul's Church. Alternatively, enter the shopping centre through the entrance opposite the flyover and the Apollo. UGCP within the centre, with three BB spaces; the lifts (D90 W105 L135) are opposite the pub, which is step free throughout. **Wheelchair toilet (D80 ST70)** to the right of the Bradmore Square entrance, at the bottom of the stairs and next to the Ladies; key at bar. Pub benches/tables in Bradmore Square.

Plough and Harrow, 120-124 King Street, Hammersmith W6 Tel: 020 8735 6020
On the corner of King Street and Argyle Place, underneath a Holiday

Inn. Main entrance on King Street is step free and gives access to this spacious 60m long pub. **Wheelchair toilet (D80 ST75)** is at the back right next to the other toilets.

William Morris, 2-4 King Street, Hammersmith W6 0QA *Tel:* 020 8741-7175
Situated 50m from the exit of Hammersmith Tube Station, on the right-hand side of King Street. The step-free main entrance gives access to 80% of this large pub; non-smoking area is + 2. Alternative back entrance is + 2. **Wheelchair toilet** to the right of the bar was out of order when we surveyed.

Ladbroke Grove

Duke of Wellington, 179 Portobello Road W11 2ED *Tel:* 020 7727-6727
On the corner of Elgin Crescent. Step-free entrance from Portobello Road; from Elgin Crescent it is + 1 step. Inside is 75% step free. **Wheelchair toilet (D86 ST102)** in the back right-hand corner as you enter from the step-free entrance. A chair was in there when we surveyed.

Shepherd's Bush

Edwards, 170 Uxbridge Street, Shepherd's Bush W12 8AA *Tel:* 020 8743-3010
In the corner of Shepherd's Bush Common, by the junction with Wood Lane. Both entrances + 1 step, then flat throughout. **Wheelchair toilet (D80 ST160 NKS)** in the back corner of the pub, next to the other toilets.

O'Neill's, 2 Goldhawk Road, Shepherd's Bush W12 8QD *Tel:* 020 8746-1288
On the corner of Shepherd's Bush Green. Step free from all entrances to 90% of the pub. **Wheelchair toilet (D85 ST90)** round the bar to the left, and to the left of the other toilets, behind the split level.

Walkabout Inn, Shepherd's Bush Green W12 8QE *Tel:* 020 8740-4339
A huge Australasian 'theme' pub, it's the big green and yellow building between the bingo hall and the Shepherd's Bush Empire (see *Entertainments*). Step-free entrance and throughout the GF. The galleries have + 10 + 8 or + 11 steps. **Wheelchair toilet (D80 ST75)** about halfway back on the left-hand side; key at bar.

Inner postal areas SW

Balham

Moon Under Water, 194 Balham High Road, Balham SW12 *Tel:* 020 8673-0535
Step free with **adapted toilet (D80 ST60)** past the bar and the other toilets.

Brixton

Dog Star, 389 Coldharbour Lane, Brixton SW9 *Tel:* 020 7733-7515
On the corner of Atlantic Road. The main entrance has + 1 step, but the side entrance on Atlantic Road gives step-free access: ring the bell for it to be opened. **Adapted toilet (D61 ST70)** to the left of the bar.

Prince of Wales, 467 Brixton Road, Brixton SW9 *Tel:* 020 7501-9061
On the corner of Coldharbour Lane and opposite Lambeth Town Hall. Small step at entrance; 50% of the interior is step free, the rest is + 2. A slightly congested pub. **Adapted toilet (D85** inward opening, **ST190)** to the left of the bar; key at bar.

Clapham

Falcon, 2 St John's Hill, Clapham Junction SW11 *Tel:* 020 7924-8041
On the corner of Falcon Road. The entrance on the corner has only a small step; two others involve + 1 step, one has + 3. **Wheelchair toilet (D81 ST95** but blocked by a table, making it **ST40)** through the double doors at the back by the far corner of the bar.

Need the Dough, 281 Lavender Hill, Clapham SW11 *Tel:* 020 7924-8021
A pizza/pasta restaurant. On the corner of Lavender Hill and Eccles Road. Hilly area. Entrance involves a small step, then a ramp. 90% step free inside. **Wheelchair toilet (D85 ST90)** to the left of the bar down a short passage; key at bar. Side transfer was only 52 when we visited because of some posters in the way. The garden is + 2 − 1 steps, with + 3 to the second tier. Access via the garden gate only + 1; the manager has the key.

Windmill on the Common, Clapham Common South Side SW4 *Tel:* 020 8673-4578
CP. Flat access through the conservatory entrance. Spacious GF area. **Wheelchair toilet (D85 ST85)** in the corner of the conservatory.

Earl's Court

O'Neill's, 326 Earl's Court Road SW5 *Tel:* 020 7244-5921
On the corner of the Brompton Road. Both entrances with + 1 step, then flat/ramped throughout. **Adapted toilet (D80 ST43)** near the right-hand corner of the pub; key at bar.

Fulham

All Bar One, 587 Fulham Road, Fulham SW6 *Tel:* 020 7471-0611
On Fulham Broadway about 50m from the tube station. Ramped entrance, then flat throughout. **Adapted toilet (D85 ST68)** opposite the bar about two thirds of the way back; key at bar.

Goose and Granite, 248 North End Road, Fulham SW6 *Tel:* 020 7471-0571
On the corner of Lillie Road. Main entrance is + 1; the side one is ramped. Step free inside. **Wheelchair toilet (D80 ST135)** at the back of the pub on the left-hand side of the door to the garden, which has − 1 step to pub benches/tables.

Southern Cross, 65 New King's Road, Fulham SW6 *Tel:* 020 7736-2837
20m from the junction with Wandsworth Bridge Road towards Parson's Green. Entrance with + 1 step, then flat/ramped throughout. **Adapted toilet (D75 ST35 NKS)** on the right as you enter. Some tables and chairs outside the front.

West Brompton

The Fine Line, 236 Fulham Road, West Brompton SW10 *Tel:* 020 7376-5827
On the junction with Hollywood Road, opposite Chelsea and Westminster Hospital. Step free, with **wheelchair toilet (D70 + ST70 +)** on the GF just to the left of the main toilets.

Inner postal districts SE

Greenwich

Gate Clock, Cutty Sark Station, Creek Road, Greenwich SE10 9EJ *Tel*: 020 8269-2000
Opposite Bardsley Lane, next to Cutty Sark DLR Station. The main entrance on Creek Road gives step-free access to Bar and 60% of

seating area. One split level (+3) can be accessed step free from a side entrance. A lift (D80 W110 L140) at the back, left from main entrance goes to the first-floor bar. **Wheelchair toilet (D75 ST70 NKS)** on the first floor.

Gipsy Moth, 60 Greenwich Church Street, Greenwich SE10 *Tel:* 020 8858-0786
Some 80m from *The Cutty Sark*. Step free via a ramp in the garden. **Wheelchair toilet (D85 ST90)**.

Mitre, 291 Greenwich High Road SE10 8NA *Tel:* 020 8355-6760
On the corner of Greenwich High Road and Roan Street. Step-free entrance opposite Stockwell Street. 80% of the bar area is step free. Two beer gardens, one with lip (5cm), the other +1−1 through a door D67. **Wheelchair toilet (D85 ST75)** in the basement, via a lift (D80 W80 L165) behind the bar.

Yacht, 5 Crane Street, Greenwich SE10 *Tel:* 020 8858-0175
Overlooking the river and down a narrow street just off Park Row. Step-free access via the right-hand entrance, the other has −1 step. Inside the split level at the back of the pub is bypassed by an open lift (W72 L144). **Adapted toilet (D75 ST30** blocked by basin**)** on the left-hand side just in front of the split level.

Lewisham

The Broadway, 139 High Street, Lewisham SE13 6AA *Tel:* 020 8297-8645
Located 50m right from the High Street exit from the Lewisham Centre and across the road. Step-free entrance to 50% of pub, with +5+10 steps to first floor. **Adapted toilet (D70 ST62)** on GF past bar on right.

Watch House, 198-204 High Street, Lewisham SE13 6JP *Tel*: 020 8318-3136
Right from the High Street exit of the Lewisham Centre, 50m down the road. Step-free entrance to the bar and 60% of seating. **Wheelchair toilet (D80 ST80 NKS)** at the back.

Camberwell, Catford, Crystal Palace, Grove Park, New Cross, South Norwood, Rotherhithe, Sydenham and Tulse Hill

Amersham Arms, 288 New Cross Road, New Cross SE14 *Tel:* 020 8692-2047

Opposite New Cross Tube Station. Step free via side doors to bar and music. **Wheelchair toilet (D85 ST100)**.

Fox on the Hill, 149 Denmark Hill, Camberwell SE5 *Tel:* 020 7738-4756
Large CP. Step free from CP to bar, but +7 to garden. **Wheelchair toilet (D85 ST75)** at the back of the pub.

Greyhound, 313 Kirkdale Road, Sydenham SE26 *Tel:* 020 8676-9932
On the corner of Spring Hill, and alongside Sydenham NR Station. Large CP on the right of the pub. Entrance is step free from the front or +4 steps from the entrance adjoining the CP. Inside, around 60% of the pub is on the flat, with only one low table, which is surrounded by benches. The rest of the pub is +3. **Adapted/wheelchair cubicles** in the Ladies **(D80 ST66)** and in the Gents **(D85 ST70)** in the back right-hand corner of the pub.

Goat House, 2 Penge Road, South Norwood SE25 *Tel:* 020 8778-5752
On the corner of Sunny Bank. Attached CP. There is flat access at the front entrance and it is step free to about 60%. From the patio entrance there are +1 or +3 steps to the split levels. **Adapted toilet (D80 ST68)** in the back corner to the right of the bar. The patio with pub benches/tables can be reached without steps from the CP or the street, or by +2−1 from the front of the pub.

Green Man, 335 Bromley Road, Catford SE6 *Tel:* 020 8698-3746
Bar/restaurant. At the junction with Beckenham Hill Road. On-site CP. Flat entrance at the front, facing the road. 60% step free inside. **Adapted cubicles (D90 ST60)** in both the Ladies and Gents.

Moby Dick, 6 Russell Place, Rotherhithe SE16 *Tel:* 020 7394-8597
Just off Onega Gate and overlooking Greenland Dock. A small free public CP is outside. The ramp to the right of the main entrance bypasses +6 steps. Inside is step free. **Adapted toilet (D75** inward opening, **ST90)** through the door past the right-hand end of the bar, at the top of the stairs from the main entrance. It is probably large enough for the inward-opening door not to be a problem, but there are no handrails. There is −1 step to the patio overlooking the dock, which has no tables.

Postal Order, 33 Westow Street, Crystal Palace SE19 *Tel:* 020 8771-3003
20m from the junction with Carberry Road. Step-free entrance and

inside. **Adapted toilet (D85 ST60 NKS)** about three quarters of the way back on the left-hand side.

Tiger's Head, 350 Bromley Road, Catford SE6 *Tel:* 020 8460-3768
By the junction with Southend Lane. On-site CP. Step-free access at the front, through the garden (there's a small threshold). Flat to most of the bar. **Wheelchair toilet (D75 ST150)**.

Tulse Hill Tavern, 150 Norwood Road SE24 *Tel:* 020 8674-9754
On the corner of Tulse Hill. CP attached, just off Tulse Hill. Step-free access throughout in a spacious pub. **Wheelchair toilet (D85 ST70)** in the back right-hand corner if you enter from the front, near the other toilets. Pub benches and tables are at the front and back, with flat access.

Outer areas north of the river

Brentford, Greenford, Hayes, Hounslow, Teddington and Whitton

Admiral Nelson, 123 Nelson Road, Whitton, Middlesex TW2 7BB
Tel: 020 8894-9998
By a mini-roundabout at the junction with Hounslow Road and Whitton High Street. From Whitton High Street there is ramped access and then double doors. Nearer the mini-roundabout there is an entrance with +1 step; from Nelson Road there is +1+1. **Wheelchair toilet (D80 ST70)** straight ahead from the easiest entrance, next to the Gents. Outside, the patio has pub benches/tables, and an outside bar in the summer.

Ballot Box, Horsendon Lane North, Greenford, Middlesex UB6 7QL *Tel:* 020 8902-2825
Roughly half way along Horsendon Lane North. On-site CP. Step-free access into the pub, with +1 to 50% inside. **Adapted toilet (D80 ST43)**, through the door marked 'Gents' to the left of the bar, normally unlocked.

Bulstrode, 55 Lampton Road, Hounslow, Middlesex TW13 *Tel:* 020 8572-7845
Next to a tube railway bridge by Hounslow Central Tube Station, and on the corner of Bulstrode Avenue. CP attached. One entrance has step-free access, the other +4 steps. **Wheelchair toilet (D85 ST75)** round the bar to the left. There is no step-free access to

the garden, which has pub benches/tables; there are a few similar tables outside the front, with flat access.

The George Orwell, 10 Broadway Parade, Coldharbour Lane, Hayes, Middlesex UB3 *Tel:* 020 8813-6774
50m west of the junction with Birchway. Two flat central entrances, giving 85% step-free access; −3 steps to rear area. **Adapted toilet (D80 ST67)** on the left.

Harvey's, High Street, Hounslow, Middlesex TW3 *Tel:* 020 8570-0169
By the junction with Gilbert Road, where there are some BB spaces. Entrance step free, then step free to 60%, although there's +1 to the bar. **Wheelchair toilet (D85 ST90)** at the back of the pub on the right.

Moon Under Water, 84 Staines Road, Hounslow, Middlesex TW3 *Tel:* 020 8572-7506
40m east of the junction with Cromwell Street. Step free throughout. **Wheelchair toilet (D80 ST75)** at the rear, on the right; key from the bar.

Myllet Arms, Western Avenue, Perivale, Middlesex UB6 8TE *Tel:* 020 8997-4624
No access from Western Avenue, CP reached from Perivale Lane. Ramped entrance to bar and restaurant. Step free to 40%. **Adapted toilet (D80 ST40)** to the left of the entrance.

Shannon's, 34 High Street, Hounslow, Middlesex TW13 *Tel:* 020 8572-8044
50m from the junction with Kingsley Road. CP behind pub then +1 step to the bar. **Wheelchair toilet (D85 ST100+)** just inside the entrance. Normally locked; key from bar.

Wishing Well, 1250 Uxbridge Road, Hayes End, Middlesex UB4 8JF *Tel:* 020 8561-3541
By the junction with Newport Road. Step free. **Wheelchair toilet (D75 ST100)** at the front, on the right.

Denham, Ickenham, Rickmansworth, Ruislip and Uxbridge

Coach and Horses, High Street, Ickenham, Middlesex UB10 *Tel:* 01895-679335

By junction with Swakeleys Road. On-site CP. **Adapted toilet (D85 ST49)** to the left of the bar.

Good Yarn, 132 High Street, Uxbridge, Middlesex UB8 1JX *Tel:* 01895-239852
100m from roundabout at east end of High Street. Step free to bar area and + 3 steps to dining area. Alternative side entrance to dining area in Johnson's Yard with + 1. **Wheelchair toilet (D80 ST75 NKS)** to the right of the bar; key at the bar.

J J Moon's, 12 Victoria Road, Ruislip Manor, Middlesex HA4 *Tel:* 01895-622373
Opposite Ruislip Manor tube. Entrance + 1 step, then 70% flat. **Wheelchair toilet (D85 ST75)**, left after main entrance.

Middlesex Arms, Long Drive, South Ruislip, Middlesex HA4 0HG *Tel:* 020 8845-0667
50m east of the railway bridge over Long Drive. Rear CP. Step-free entrance. GF has a split level of two steps. **Adapted toilet (D85 ST67)** by the side entrance near the food bar; key at bar.

Old Bill, 45 Windsor Street, Uxbridge, Middlesex UB8 *Tel:* 01895-257932
Pavilions Shopping Centre CP at the back. The front entrance has + 5 steps, but there is a ramped bypass via the garden at the side, followed by a threshold to get into the pub. From here it is 85% step free. **Wheelchair toilet (D70 ST70)** at the back of the pub on the left. Garden has pub benches/tables.

Orchard, Ickenham Road, Ruislip, Middlesex HA4 *Tel:* 01895-633481
By roundabout at the junction with Kingsend CP. Entrance is + 1 step, then step free to 70% of the bar area and 20% of the restaurant. Raised areas are up several steps. **Wheelchair toilet (D80 ST85)** on right side of the building, through the restaurant.

Scotsbridge Mill, Park Road, Rickmansworth, Herts WD3 *Tel:* 01923-778377
Signposted turn-off is about 300m east of roundabout at the junction with the High Street. On-site CP. Ramped entrance on the right, then step free to 15% of the bar and 30% of the restaurant. Several steps to higher or lower levels. **Adapted toilet (D75 ST60)** on the left of bar.

Sylvan Moon, 27 Green Lane, Northwood, Middlesex HA6 *Tel:* 01923-820760

By junction with Dene Road. Step free. **Wheelchair toilet (D75 ST85)** at the rear, on the left.

Vine, 121 Hillingdon Hill, Hillingdon, Middlesex UB10 0JQ *Tel:* 01895-259596
By the junction with Vine Lane. Sloped on-site CP. Entrance +1 step, then 50% with step-free access. **Wheelchair toilet (D70 ST90)** to the right of bar; key at bar. From entrance level, ramped access to outdoor seats.

Borehamwood, Edgware, Harrow, Hatch End, Kenton, Stanmore and Wembley

Apollo, Pinner Road, North Harrow, Middlesex HA1 *Tel:* 020 8427-4462
On the corner of The Gardens. Attached CP has two BB spaces, but it is about a 70m walk round the chain barrier to the front of the pub to bypass +2+4 steps. From the front entrance there is +1 to 50% of the pub, including 3 pool tables but only 2 normal tables! The rest is either +2 or +1 or -4. The terrace, with pub benches/tables is -4-1 from the main body. **Adapted toilet (D90 ST67)** to the right of the main entrance; key at bar.

Blacking Bottle, 122 High Street, Edgware, Middlesex HA8 *Tel:* 020 8381-1485
30m from the junction with Manor Park Crescent. Step free. **Wheelchair toilet (D85 ST200)** at the rear of pub, on the left; key at bar.

Change of Hart, 21 High Street, Edgware, Middlesex HA8 *Tel:* 020 8952-0039
40m from the junction with Spring Villa Road, which has an arch over it. CP at back. All three entrances involve a slight lip, and one has a small step. Inside the pub there is one step, which can be bypassed by going right round the bar. **Wheelchair toilet (D85 ST85)** in the back right-hand corner. Ramp to garden at rear.

Fat Controller, 362 Station Road, Harrow, Middlesex HA1 *Tel:* 020 8426-0161
Just by the junction with College Road. Step free to 80%. **Adapted toilet (D80 ST56)** to the left of the bar.

Hart and Spool, 148 Shenley Road, Borehamwood, Herts WD6 *Tel:* 020 8953-1883

Step free. **Wheelchair toilet (D70 ST75)** at the back of the pub, normally unlocked.

Harvester, Hale Lane, Edgware, Middlesex HA8 *Tel:* 020 8959-6403
By the roundabout where Selvage Lane meets Hale Lane. On-site CP. Step free to 95%. Fixed tables in bar. Small raised section (+ 3) in dining area. **Wheelchair toilet (D80 ST100)** 10m straight ahead from main entrance.

J J Moons, 397 High Road, Wembley, Middlesex HA9 *Tel:* 020 8903-4923
Opposite junction with Park Lane. Entrance + 1 step, then step free via ramp. **Adapted toilet (D75 ST67)** on the right of the pub, by the Ladies.

Leefe Robinson VC, Brockhurst Corner, 76 Uxbridge Road, Harrow Weald, Middlesex HA8 *Tel:* 020 8954-6781
30m from the junction with Elms Road. CP. Ramped central entrance, giving step-free access to 60% of the bar and 45% of the restaurant. Higher levels are + 2 or + 3 steps. **Adapted toilet (D85 ST68)** just inside the main entrance, on the left.

Man in the Moon, 1 Buckingham Parade, Stanmore, Middlesex HA7 *Tel:* 020 8954-6119
Opposite the junction with Church Road. Front entrance + 2 steps, then step free, while side entrance has slight lip. **Wheelchair toilet (D75 ST95)** at the rear, on the left.

Moon on the Hill, 373 Station Road, Harrow, Middlesex HA1 *Tel:* 020 8863-3670
30m from the junction with Gayton Road. Entrance + 1 step, giving 50% flat access. **Wheelchair toilet (D70 ST90)** to the right of bar.

Old Post Office, 397a High Street, Wembley, Middx *Tel:* 020 8795-1768
By the junction with Park Lane. Ramped entrance giving step-free access to 60% of pub. **Wheelchair toilet (D75 ST80)** through the door to the left of the bar.

Preston, 161 Preston Road, Wembley, Middlesex HA9 *Tel:* 020 8908-5744
About 200m north of Preston Road Tube Station. CP in front; from there entrance to the pub is step free. All other entrances have + 1 + 1. **Wheelchair toilet** through the door to the left of the bar and

down the passage. Pub benches/tables are + 1 at front; the garden at the back is + 4 to 80%.

Railway, 375 Uxbridge Road, Hatch End, Middlesex HA5 *Tel:* 020 8428-2184

Next to a petrol station, 70m from the junction with Grimsdyke Avenue and on the opposite side of the road. There are CPs at the front and back, with one BB space at the front, next to the ramped entrance on the left-hand side. The main and back entrances both have + 2 steps. From the front, 60% of the pub is step free: the games area at the back has − 2. There are relatively few tables on the flat in this pub. **Wheelchair toilet (D95)** at the front of the pub on the right-hand side next to the Ladies.

Sarsen Stone, 32 High Street, Wealdstone, Middlesex HA3 7AB *Tel:* 020 8863-8533

25m from junction with Palmerston Road. Flat entrance, giving 100% step-free access. **Wheelchair toilet (D80 ST80)** at the rear, on the right.

Travellers Rest, Kenton Road, Kenton, Middlesex HA3 *Tel:* 020 8907-1671

By junction with Carlton Avenue. Sloping CP. Ramped right-hand entrance giving flat access to 45% of the bar area and 100% of the restaurant area. **Wheelchair toilet (D80 ST110)** on right of building; key from bar.

Village Inn, 402 Rayners Lane, Harrow, Middlesex HA5 *Tel:* 020 8868-8551

20m from the junction with Village Way East. Small CP at the rear. Flat main entrance from Rayners Lane to the bar, from where there are − 6 steps to the dining area. Alternatively, there is + 1 from the CP to the dining area. **Adapted toilet (D80 ST51)** to the right of the bar, not signed.

Barnet, Chingford and Enfield

Duke of York, Ganwick Corner, Barnet Road, Barnet EN5 4SG *Tel:* 020 8449-0297

By the junction with Dancers Hill Road. CP. Step free via ramped side entrance by the CP. After entering, turn right for the **wheelchair toilet (D80 ST70)**.

King's Ford, 250 Chingford Mount Road, Chingford E4 *Tel:* 020 8523-9365

Approximately 30m from the junction with Normanshire Drive. Step-free entrance and flat/ramped throughout. **Wheelchair toilet (D95 ST150)** at the back of the pub on the right-hand side.

Ridgeway, 76 The Ridgeway, Enfield, Middlesex EN2 *Tel:* 020 8363-7537
50m south of roundabout where Lavender Hill meets The Ridgeway. On-site CP. Ramp and + 1 step at main entrance, then 80% step free. **Wheelchair toilet (D80 ST75)** on the left. Seating outside the front of pub.

Royston Arms, 83 Chingford Mount Road, South Chingford E4 *Tel:* 020 8498-2901
By the junction with Westward Road. On-site CP. Step free via ramped entrance on the right. **Wheelchair toilet (D95 ST135)** on the right, by pool tables; key from bar. There is -1 step to the garden, then a ramp down to outdoor seating.

Chigwell and Loughton

Last Post, 227 High Road, Loughton, Essex IG10 *Tel:* 020 8532-0751
About 150m north of the junction with Forest Road. Step free. **Adapted toilet (D80 ST67)** at the rear, to the left of the bar.

Maypole, 171 Lambourne Road, Chigwell Row E11 *Tel:* 020 8500-2050
By the junction with Gravel Lane. On-site CP. Step free to 85% of bar and to seats outside. **Adapted toilet (D75 opens in, ST75)** to the left of the bar.

Plume of Feathers, 123 Churchill, Loughton, Essex IG10 *Tel:* 020 8502-0444
Opposite junction with Sedley Rise. Rear CP, but rear entrance has + 6 steps. It is easier to go round to ramped front entrance. Inside, 55% is step free. **Wheelchair toilet (D90 ST80)** on left of the pub.

White Hart, 692 Chigwell Road, Woodford Bridge, Essex *Tel:* 020 8505-2254
Opposite the junction with Roding Lane North. CP at the back, where the right-hand entrance is ramped; the left-hand one has + 2 steps, while the front entrance has + 4. 70% of the pub is step free; there are + 2 to the pool tables. **Wheelchair toilet (D90 ST145)** in the

back corner of the pub opposite the right-hand end of the bar. Pub benches/tables outside the back.

Barking, Brentwood, Dagenham, Hornchurch, Ilford and Romford

Barking Dog, 61 Station Parade, Wakering Road, Barking, Essex IG11 *Tel:* 020 8507-9109
Right beside Barking Station. CP in Vicarage Field Shopping Centre just opposite. Step free. **Wheelchair toilet (D84 ST70)** at the back of the pub.

Bear, Noak Hill Road, Romford, Essex RM3 *Tel:* 01708-381935
About 100m from the junction with North Hill Drive. On-site CP. Entrance + 10 steps, or a steep ramp to the main door from the CP, and a small step through a side entrance. Step-free access through a door on the extreme left. Flat throughout, and there's a large garden. **Wheelchair toilet (D90 ST85)** near the main entrance. Follow the bar all the way round from the side entrance.

Dick Turpin, Aldborough Hatch, Aldborough Road North, Newbury Hatch, Ilford, Essex IG2 *Tel:* 020 8590-1281
About 150m north of the junction with Applegarth Drive. On-site CP. Step free to the bar and ramp to the dining area. **Adapted toilet (D85 opens in, ST120)** to the right as you enter, then right again, level with bar.

General Havelock, 229 High Road, Ilford, Essex IG1 *Tel:* 020 8478-0512
On the corner of Hainault Street. The Hainault Street entrance gives step-free access to 70% of the pub. The High Road entrance has + 1 step. **Wheelchair toilet (D75 ST70)** to the right of the bar and in the far corner of the room.

Great Spoon of Ilford, 114 Cranbrook Road, Ilford, Essex IG1 *Tel:* 020 8518-0535
30m west of the junction with Wellesley Road. CP off Wellesley Road. Rear entrance by CP has + 1 step. Front entrance on the right is flat. 90% inside is step free; raised area is + 2. **Adapted toilet (D80 ST56)** on the right of the pub near the front (as you face towards rear).

Hinds Head, 2 Burnside Road, Chadwell, Dagenham, Essex RM8 *Tel:* 020 8590-2465

Located on a corner of the roundabout at the junction with Station Road. Nearby pay-and-display CP, free to BB holders. Quite a steep slope from the CP to the pub. Step free. **Adapted toilet (D80** opening in, **ST150)**. Picnic tables outside with step-free access.

J J Moons, Unit 3, 46 High Street, Hornchurch, Essex RM12 *Tel:* 01708-478410
Situated in the middle of the Unit 3 Building including Pizza Hut and McDonald's, by the junction with Abbs Cross Gardens. CP behind, entered via Appleton Way. Step free to 90%. **Wheelchair toilet (D80 ST80)** in the middle of the pub, on the left.

Lord Denman, 270 Heathway, Dagenham, Essex RM10 *Tel:* 020 8984-8590
Located on the High Street about 100m from Dagenham Heathway Tube Station, on the other side of the road. Ramp bypasses $+2$ steps. There are -7 to the food area and toilets, but there's a platform stairlift. **Wheelchair toilet (D85 ST80)** towards the back of the pub at the lower level.

Moon and Stars, 99 South Street, Romford, Essex RM11 *Tel:* 01708-730117
50m from Romford Station, towards Market Place. Step free to 70%. There's a limited number of low tables with movable chairs. **Wheelchair toilet (D85 ST75)** to the right of the main entrance; key at bar.

Three Travellers, Wood Lane, Becontree Heath, Dagenham, Essex RM10 7DS *Tel:* 020 8592-2441
Opposite the Community Centre on a corner, 100m from the junction with Whalebone Lane South. There is a CP with ramped access to the pub; the only impediment is a small lip. **Wheelchair toilet (D75 ST85)** in the far right-hand corner of the pub.

Unicorn, 91 Main Road, Gidea Park, Romford, Essex RM2 *Tel:* 01708-738811
Located about 100m from Balgores Lane, on the left. On-site CP. Step free to 90%. **Adapted toilet (D90** opening in, **ST66)**.

Outer areas south of the river

Chessington, Kingston, Richmond, Surbiton, Walton and Worcester Park

All Bar One, 11 Hill Street, Richmond, Surrey TW9 *Tel:* 020 8332-7141

On the corner of Whittaker Avenue, and opposite the old Town Hall. Open lift (W80 L120) bypasses +3 steps at the entrance. Step free inside. **Wheelchair toilet (D80 ST70)** by the lift.

British Oak, 98 Richmond Road, Kingston, Surrey KT2 5EN *Tel:* 020 8549-0074

On the corner of Richmond Park Road. One entrance has flat access, the other has +2 steps. The inside is step free. **Adapted toilet (D85** inward opening, **NKS ST105)** on the left-hand side of the pub next to the pool tables. There are −4 steps to the garden, which has pub benches/tables – these can be bypassed (somewhat awkwardly) by the gate on Richmond Park Road.

Coronation Hall, St Mark's Hill, Surbiton Surrey KT6 *Tel:* 020 8390-6164

About 30m from the junction with Claremont Road. An open lift (W84 L120) behind the second door round on the right-hand side of the pub gives step-free access to the bar level, bypassing +2 steps at the front and +6 inside. About 50% of the pub is on this level; the rest is −4 or +2. The gallery is +2. There are only about six low tables on the flat. **Wheelchair toilet (D84 ST80 NKS)** by the lift.

Hart's Boatyard, Portsmouth Road, Surbiton KT6 4ES *Tel*: 020 8399-7515

Opposite the junction with St Leonard's Road. On site CP. Ramp at the entrance, bypassing +3 steps giving step-free access to 15% of the bar. There are split levels to the eating areas, but you can arrange to eat in the bar. To get to the balcony overlooking the Thames there is −4. The restaurant is +4+4 above the entrance level. **Wheelchair toilet (D80 ST75)** to the left of the main entrance. Tables and chairs on the riverside behind the pub are step free via the CP and a 10m slope.

Hogsmill, Worcester Park Road, Worcester Park, Surrey KT4 *Tel:* 020 8337-5221

By the junction with Cromwell Road. On-site CP. Flat access from the CP only on the left side of the building. The bar entrance gives step-free access to 20% of the bar. There is a separate door giving step-free access to the lower part of the restaurant which the staff can open if you ask. Other routes to the restaurant involve steps. The **wheelchair toilet (D80 ST100)** is by the restaurant reception desk on the lower level.

King's Tun, 152-3 Clarence Street, Kingston, Surrey KT1 *Tel:* 020 8547-3827

On the left of Clarence Street as you head towards the station. Directly opposite the Options Centre. Three entrances at the front, all step free. A large pub on two floors both of which are 90% step free. The first floor has rather more tables at chair height and is reached by a lift (D80 W100 L147) available on request, bypassing +9+9+8 steps. **Wheelchair toilet (D85 ST90 NKS)** on the GF, on the left-hand wall of the pub as you go in. There's also an **adapted toilet (D85 no ST NKS)** on the first floor by the lift.

Litten Tree, 28-30 Castle Street, Kingston, Surrey KT1 *Tel:* 020 8547-0254
On the corner of Fife Road. Step-free access from Castle Street to 70% of the pub. **Wheelchair toilet (D85 ST80 NKS)** at the back by the other toilets.

The Lot, 1A Duke Street, Richmond, Surrey TW9 *Tel:* 020 8940-6423
Just off Richmond High Street. Ramped entrance, over a few cobbles, then step free to about 70%. **Wheelchair toilet (D80 ST100)** just before the main doors, on the right; key kept at bar.

Maypole, Hook Road, Surbiton KT6 5BH *Tel*: 020 8399-2906
At the junction with Ditton Road. Small CP at rear, but the back entrance has +2−2 steps. Front entrance has +1 small step, and is then 75% step free. **Adapted toilet (D85** opens in, **ST75)** to the left of the bar, where the key is kept.

Monkey Puzzle, Leatherhead Road, Chessington, Surrey KT9 *Tel:* 01372-744060
Situated some 600m north of the junction with Rushett Lane. Flat entrance giving step-free access to 70% of bar area. There are six dining tables at the bar level reached along a corridor to the left of the bar. Most of the restaurant is +20 steps. **Adapted toilet (D80 ST66)** is underneath the staircase which is in front of you as you come in the main entrance.

O'Neill's, Eden Street, Kingston, Surrey *Tel:* 020 8481-0131
On the corner of Apple Market. The entrance from Apple Market through the *Provisions Store* shop-front is flat; from the entrance on Apple Market near the corner there is a slight lip, and from Eden Street there is +1 step. Step free inside. **Wheelchair toilet (D95 ST110 NKS)** on the left of the bar at back. Some movable tables and chairs on uneven paving in Apple Market, but they may only be there in the summer.

Regent, 19 Church Street, Walton-on-Thames, Surrey KT12 *Tel:* 01932-243980

30m from the junction with Bridge Street. Step free to 90%. **Wheelchair toilet (D78 ST80)** to the right of the bar; key at the bar.

Surbiton Flyer, 84 Victoria Road, Surbiton, Surrey KT6 *Tel:* 020 8390-2778
Directly in front of Surbiton Station. Step-free entrance from the corner of the station car park and Victoria Road; from the entrance on Victoria Road there are +3 steps. Inside 90% is step free. **Wheelchair toilet (D80 ST75)** at the back of the pub with the other toilets.

Barnes, Mitcham, Morden, Norbury, Putney, Roehampton, Streatham, Tooting, Wandsworth and Wimbledon

Abbot, 1 Abbotsbury Road, Morden, Surrey SM4 *Tel:* 020 8687-0852
Large pub at the junction with London Road. Step free to 60%. **Wheelchair toilet (D80 ST75)** to the right of bar.

All Bar One, 37 Wimbledon Hill Road, Wimbledon SW19 *Tel:* 020 8971-9871
On the corner with Compton Road. Flat entrance from Compton Road leads to +2 steps bypassed by an open lift (W80 L125). **Wheelchair toilet (D80 ST80)**.

Bar Coast, 50 High Street, Putney SW15 *Tel:* 020 8780-8931
On the corner of Felsham Road. Ramped entrance and step free throughout. A spacious pub, with board games for hire. **Adapted toilet (D85** inward opening, **ST100+** but blocked by furniture, making it **ST68)** to the left of the bar and straight ahead; key at bar.

Brewers Inn, 147 East Hill, Wandsworth SW18 *Tel:* 020 8874-4128
Opposite the Town Hall and on the junction with St Ann's Hill. Small CP. Step free to saloon bar, but −1 step to the other bar. **Wheelchair toilet (D80 ST100)** just inside saloon bar door.

Brown's, 210 Castlenau, Barnes SW13. *Tel:* 020 8563-9003
On the corner of Lonsdale Road, about 100m from Hammersmith Bridge. CP on Lonsdale Road, leading to the garden; from the CP there is ramped access to the main bar BUT via a locked gate (key at bar). The entrance from Castlenau has +2 steps. **Wheelchair toilet (D85 ST70 NKS)** to the right as you come in via the ramped entrance, through the double doors. The garden is large and pleasant, but there are only pub benches/tables.

Castle, 38 High Street, Tooting SW17 *Tel:* 020 8672-7018

50m from the junction with Tooting Broadway Station towards Tooting Bec. Step-free access, and a **wheelchair toilet (D80 ST90)** by the Gents.

Chumley's, 74 The Broadway, Wimbledon SW19 *Tel:* 020 8543-8624
On the corner of King's Road and opposite Wimbledon Theatre. Public CP about 150m away in Gladstone Road. Ramped entrances and 90% step free inside. **Wheelchair toilet (D70 ST100 NKS)** at the back of the pub. Movable tables and chairs outside in the front.

County Arms, 345 Trinity Road, Wandsworth SW18 *Tel:* 020 8874-8532
At the junction with Alma Terrace. CP. Lounge bar entrance has +1 step, then a **wheelchair toilet (D85 ST70)** just inside. Spacious, and garden with a ramped entrance to the pub.

Gordon Bennett, 24 Mitcham Road, Tooting Broadway SW17 *Tel:* 020 8672-5822
Opposite the junction with Longmead Road. Step-free access, but only four low tables available on the flat. 25% of the pub is +3. **Wheelchair toilet (D83 ST70)** towards the exit to the garden. One small step to the garden which has movable tables and chairs.

Grid Inn, 22 Replingham Road, Southfields SW18 *Tel:* 020 8874-8460
At the junction with Heythorpe Street. Step free from Replingham Road. **Wheelchair toilet (D85 ST85)** at the far end of the bar.

Halfway House, 521 Garratt Lane, Earlsfield SW18 *Tel:* 020 8946-2788
On the junction with Magdalen Road. Step-free access and **wheelchair toilet (D85 ST70)**. Small garden, step free from street but −1 step from pub.

Hogshead, 25 Wimbledon Hill Road, Wimbledon SW19 *Tel:* 020 8947-9391
Almost opposite the end of Worple Road and about 200m from Wimbledon Station. Step free to 80% of pub. **Wheelchair toilet (D75 ST75)** at the back.

Hope, 1 Bellevue Road, Upper Tooting SW17 *Tel:* 020 8672-8717
On the corner of St James's Drive. Both entrances have +1 step. The GF is 95% step free, but there are about +5 to get to the bar. A lift to the right of the entrance gives access to the first floor, where there is an **adapted toilet (D95 ST69)** to the right of the bar.

Jack Stamps, 43 London Road, Morden, Surrey SM4 *Tel:* 020 8646-3144

Almost opposite Morden Station. Ramped entrance, but with a central pillar (free width 70) in the doorway. Step free inside. **Wheelchair toilet (D80 ST80)** at the back of the pub.

Jack Stamps, 90 Streatham High Road, Streatham SW16 *Tel:* 020 8677-5600
Near the junction with Leigham Avenue. Entrance +1 step, then 60% step free. **Wheelchair toilet (D70 ST80)** through the door at the back of the pub marked private! Key at the bar.

The Lady St Helier, Aberconway, Morden, Surrey SM4 *Tel:* 020 8540-2818
By the junction with London Road, and next to Iceland supermarket. It is almost opposite Morden Underground Station. Supermarket CP with BB spaces within 100m, and another BB space in Abbotsbury Road. Ramped entrances and step free inside, although a little congested. **Wheelchair toilet (D80 ST90 NKS)** on the left as you enter, opposite the bar.

Mill House, 1 Windmill Road, Mitcham Common, Mitcham, Surrey CR4 *Tel:* 020 8288-0491
80m from the junction with Croydon Road. Large CP. Flat through the bar entrance and for the restaurant area. 30% step free inside. Small garden, and also a children's room and play area with step-free access. **Wheelchair toilet (D85 ST120)** to the right of the bar.

Moon under Water, 1327 London Road, Norbury SW16 *Tel:* 020 8765-1235
At the junction with Northborough Road, opposite *Windsor House* and a petrol station. CP behind the pub off Northborough Road. Ramped entrance to the pub bypassing +3 steps, then step free. **Wheelchair toilet (D85 ST85)** at the back, on the left.

O'Neill's, 66 The Broadway, Wimbledon SW19 *Tel:* 020 8545-9931
Near the junction with King's Road, and almost opposite the Wimbledon Theatre. Public CP about 150m away in Gladstone Road. Ramped entrance and step free inside. About half the chairs and tables are movable. **Wheelchair toilet (D80 ST80 NKS)** at the back on the left.

Railway, 202 Upper Richmond Road, Putney SW15 *Tel:* 020 8788-8190
At the junction with Putney High Street. Step free to 40% of the pub from the High Street. **Wheelchair toilet (D80 ST150+)** past the bar, and turn right. The first door is to the right of the staircase. Then the toilet door is on your left. Not well signed.

Ravensbury Arms, Croydon Road, Mitcham, Surrey CR4 *Tel:* 020 8687-1351
At the junction with Carshalton Road. On-site CP. Step-free access to 80% of pub and half the garden. **Adapted toilet (D80 ST40)** to the left of the entrance.

Spotted Dog, 72 Garrett Lane, Wandsworth SW18 *Tel:* 020 8875-9531
Adjacent to the Wandsworth Shopping Centre with a MSCP. Flat entrance and GF. **Wheelchair toilet (D80 ST80)**.

Whistle and Flute, 46 Putney High Street, Putney SW15 *Tel:* 020 8780-5437
Opposite the end of Putney Bridge Road. Step free to 70%. **Adapted toilet (D80 ST68)** to the right of the bar, and then it's on your left.

Wibbas Down Inn, 6 Gladstone Road, Wimbledon SW19 *Tel:* 020 8540-6788
Just off the Broadway and between Gladstone Road and Russell Road. Very near Wimbledon Theatre. Public CP 100m away in Gladstone Road. Ramped entrance from Gladstone Road, and 90% step free inside. **Adapted toilet (D80 ST58 NKS)** to the left from the Gladstone Road entrance. Patio outside the Gladstone Road entrance with movable chairs and tables.

Croydon

All Bar One, 10 Park Lane, Croydon CR0 1JD *Tel:* 020 8686-1033
On the corner of Park Lane and Park Street. Bar/restaurant. Small threshold at the entrance. GF step free. First floor + 13 + 10 steps (30% of total area). **Wheelchair toilet (D80 ST90)** at far left from main entrance on GF.

Alma Tavern, 129 Lower Addiscombe Road, Croydon, Surrey CR0 *Tel:* 020 8654-5842
At the junction with Grant Road. Entrance + 1 tiny step, then 90% step free. **Wheelchair toilet (D90 ST80)** to the right, behind the bar where the key is kept.

Bar Monaco, 12 High Street, Croydon CR0 1YA *Tel:* 020 8686-4875
Situated opposite Park Street, with step-free access to main entrance and GF bar. Non-smoking area is −8, as is the basement bar. **Wheelchair toilet (D80 ST80** slightly blocked by handrail**)** on right of main entrance.

Cricketers Inn, 36 Addington Village Road, Croydon, Surrey CR0 *Tel:* 01689-842057

Situated at the Addington Village roundabout on the A2022. Take the village exit. Large CP and flat main entrance. There are +2 to a split level; the children's play area in the garden is +3. **Adapted toilet (D85 ST62)** is on the right of the pub from the entrance. Follow the bar round to the right.

Duke's Head, 14 South End, Croydon CR0 1DL *Tel:* 020 8689-9728
Situated on the corner of South End and Parker Road, this small pub has +2 steps at the main entrance which can be bypassed by ramp to left on Parker Road. Step-free access throughout including the beer garden at the back, though this has fixed pub-style benches. **Wheelchair toilet (D80 ST70)** to the right of the ramped entrance.

George, 17-21 George Street, Croydon CR0 1LA *Tel:* 020 8649-9077
By George Street tram station, 80m from High Street. 20% step free, including the bar and **wheelchair toilet (D80 ST70 NKS)** to the left of the entrance. There are +3 steps to the rest of large pub and another bar area.

Hare and Hounds, 325 Purley Way, Croydon, Surrey CR0 *Tel:* 020 8688-0420
Situated at the junction with Mill Lane. Large on-site CP. Step free to 90%. **Adapted toilet (D85 ST60)** is marked 'Ladies' and is opposite the main entrance.

Goose on the Market, 1 Surrey House, Croydon CR0 1RG *Tel:* 020 8688-4798
On the corner of Croydon High Street and Surrey Street, next to Surrey Market. Main entrance +2 steps bypassed by a ramp to the left. 80% of the bar is step free. **Wheelchair toilet (D75 ST75 NKS)** on the right, just past the bar.

Skylark, 34-36 South End, Croydon CR0 0DP *Tel:* 020 8649-9909
Located opposite Spices Street, with step-free entrance to the GF. 90% of the GF is step free. First floor +20. **Wheelchair toilet (D75 ST75)** on the right in the middle of the pub.

Spread Eagle, 39-41 Katherine Street, Croydon Surrey CR0 *Tel:* 020 8781-1134
Next door to the Clock Tower. Step free from the entrance near the Clock Tower, or +3 from Katherine Street. Flat/ramped inside, although somewhat congested. **Adapted toilet (D80 ST64)** directly on the left from the Clock Tower entrance.

Tiger Tiger, 16 High Street, Croydon CR0 1GT *Tel:* 020 8662-4949

Opposite junction with Park Street, this large restaurant and bar has a step-free entrance. Some of GF seating and tables are high. Lift (D90 W105 L150) to the first floor, which has bars and a club. **Wheelchair toilet (D80 ST75 NKS)** on the GF to the right of the lift.

Banstead, Cheam, Purley, Sutton and Wallington

All Bar One, 2 Hill Road, Sutton, Surrey SM1 *Tel:* 020 8652-3521 Off St Nicholas Way, and close to the shopping centre. See chapter on *Shops*. The pub is entirely step free. **Wheelchair toilet (D90 ST75)** at the far end.

Cock and Bull, 26 High Street, Sutton, Surrey SM1 *Tel:* 020 8288-1516 On the corner of Sutton Court Road. Hilly area. BB parking approximately 80m away on the High Street. The main entrance on the corner has + 1. **Wheelchair toilet (D85 ST90 NKS)** to the right of the ramped entrance is + 2 steps.

Foxley Hatch, 8 Russell Hill, Purley, Surrey CR8 *Tel:* 020 8763-9307 South of the junction with Purley Way. Step free to the main bar. **Wheelchair toilet (D85 ST90)** at the back of the pub.

Long Island Iced Tea, 33-5 High Street, Sutton, Surrey SM1 1DJ *Tel:* 020 8642-4930 Next door to *Safeway* and 50m uphill from the junction with Carshalton Road. Hilly area. BB parking 80m away on the High Street. The entrance, and 70% of the GF are step free; + 3 or + 5 steps to split levels. The eating area is upstairs (+ 22) with another + 1 to the front balcony. **Wheelchair toilet (D90 ST75)** halfway back on the right-hand side, opposite the GF bar.

Moon on the Hill, 5 Hill Road, Sutton, Surrey SM1 *Tel:* 020 8643-1202 Opposite the Civic Centre, off St Nicholas Road. Step free to about 25% of the pub. **Wheelchair toilet (D80 ST85)** clearly marked to the right of the entrance.

Wetherspoons, 552-6 London Road, North Cheam, Surrey SM3 *Tel:* 020 8644-1808 Opposite a petrol station, and 150m from *Sainsburys* CP. Step free throughout. **Wheelchair toilet (D90 ST80 NKS)** along the bar and to the right.

Whispering Moon, 25 Ross Parade, Wallington, Surrey SM6 *Tel:* 020 8647-7020

Located on the corner with Woodcote Road. Step free from Ross Parade to the main bar. **Wheelchair toilet (D85 ST85)** on the right as you enter; key at the bar.

Woolpack, High Street, Banstead, Surrey SM7 *Tel:* 01737-354560
Next to junction with Chiltons Close. Attached CP with two BB spaces. Step-free access from side entrance by CP. Front entrance has $+1+1+3$ steps after a gravel path. Step-free access inside, although the pub is somewhat congested. **Adapted toilet (D90 ST65)** to the left of the bar from the side entrance. At the back, $-1+2$ to garden with pub benches/tables, bypassed by gate leading to CP, giving step-free access. Similar tables are at the front of the pub on a patio ($+3$) and on gravel on the flat.

Beckenham, Bickley, Bromley, Orpington and West Wickham

Bird in Hand, 3 Bickley Road, Bickley, Kent BR1 2NF *Tel:* 020 8467-3665
On-site CP. Main entrance -1 step, but bypassed by a ramp on the right side of the building. This leads to the restaurant, and there is $+1$ to the bar. **Wheelchair toilet (D85 ST70)** by the ramped entrance.

Crown, 155 Bromley Common, Bromley, Kent BR2 *Tel:* 020 8460-1472
On the A21, about 4km from Bromley. On-site CP. Lip at the entrance, step-free access inside. **Wheelchair toilet (D75 ST75)** on the far side of the restaurant.

Harvest Moon, 141 High Street, Orpington, Kent BR6 *Tel:* 01689-876931
On the main shopping street. Small lip at the entrance, then step free. **Wheelchair toilet (D80** opens inwards, **ST100)** on the left at the far side of the bar.

O'Neill's, 9 High Street, Beckenham, Kent BR3 *Tel:* 020 8663-1001
By Beckenham Junction Station. The entrance is flat, but $+2$ to a split level inside. **Wheelchair toilet (D100)** to the left of the bar. When we first visited, we didn't see the ST as the staff couldn't find the key! 'It's very big', claimed a helpful barperson. It is, apparently, now more easily accessible.

Pamphilon, 196 Bromley High Street, Bromley, Kent BR1 *Tel:* 020 8313-0795

At the junction with Church Road and Market Square, opposite Allders. Step free to 80% of the pub. **Wheelchair toilet (D80 ST115)** at the end of the bar on the left.

Plough, Croydon Road, Beddington, Surrey CR0 *Tel:* 020 8647-1122 At the junction with Plough Lane. On-site CP. Step free from the garden, or from a side entrance. **Wheelchair toilet (D85 ST75)** on the left side of the pub from the garden entrance.

Railway, Red Lodge Road, West Wickham, Kent BR4 *Tel:* 020 8776-0043 At the junction with Hawes Lane. Very near West Wickham Station. CP alongside with BB spaces. Main entrance is step free, and we were told there is a **wheelchair toilet** to the right of the bar.

Bexley, Dartford and Eltham

Banker's Draft, 80 High Street, Eltham SE9 *Tel:* 020 8294-2578 On the corner with Court Yard. Small threshold at the entrance, then step free. **Wheelchair toilet (D85 ST95)** on the left, past the bar.

Golden Lion, 258 The Broadway, Bexleyheath, Kent DA6 *Tel:* 020 8303-4268 About 450m from the shopping centre, at the junction with West Lane. BB spaces outside. Step free to 95% of the pub. **Wheelchair toilet (D85 ST100)** at the rear, behind a small stage.

Jacobean Barn, Hall Place, Bourne Road, Bexley, Kent DA5 *Tel:* 01322-552748 On the A223 between the intersection of the A220 and A207. On-site CP. The entrance to the restaurant has $+1$ small step, then -5 to bar, but there is an alternative ramped route involving only $+1$. Using both entrances, there is 90% step-free access. **Wheelchair toilets (D85 ST120)** off the bar, and **(D85 ST70)** off the restaurant area.

Old Post Office, 4 Passey Place, Eltham High Street SE9 *Tel:* 020 8850-2942 In the pedestrianised area about 30m from the High Street. Main entrance has $+1+2$ steps, but there is a ramped alternative to the left with 1 small step (unfortunately this door is normally locked). Inside 75% is step free. **Wheelchair toilet (D80 ST75)**. Go right past the bar, then it's on your left.

Paper Moon, 55 High Street, Dartford, Kent DA1 *Tel:* 01322-281127 By the junction with Market Street. CP in Market Street within

100m. Slight lip at the entrance, then step free. **Wheelchair toilet (D85 ST75)**. Key at the bar.

Royal Victoria and Bull, High Street, Dartford, Kent DA1 *Tel:* 01322-224415
By the junction with Hythe Street and near the Priory Shopping Centre. This has a CP on top, but it's a long route from the CP to the pub. Ramped entrance and 80% step free inside. **Wheelchair toilet (D75 ST95)** at the back of the pub. Go past the bar on your left, and down a passageway. Key at bar.

Wrong'un, 234 The Broadway, Bexleyheath, Kent DA6 8AS *Tel:* 020 8298-0439
Some 400m from the shopping centre, just past the Midland Bank. Step free. **Wheelchair toilet (D85 ST75)** at the back of the pub near a fire exit.

Places for afternoon tea

Taking afternoon tea has long been an established British institution. There are, sadly, far fewer teashops these days, and those remaining tend to be small and congested. We are listing here a few central hotels where it is possible to get tea served under generally genteel and upmarket conditions. You may not be able to afford to stay in the hotels mentioned, nor even to have dinner there (they are certainly beyond our budget!), but having a relaxing tea in the middle of the afternoon can be an experience. Even for this the bill will be significant, but it could make a really special treat – those listed were in the £15-£30 bracket. Most need booking in advance, so phoning ahead is advised.

We have surveyed a few of the classic places for tea, like Brown's and the Ritz (which do not have wheelchair toilets), and we've included some of the more expensive central hotels with wheelchair toilet facilities. The intention is to suggest ideas, and not to present a comprehensive listing.

Brown's see Raffles Brown's below.

Claridges, Brook Street W1A 2JQ *Tel:* 020 7629-8860
Entrance has +1 step, and side doors bypass the revolving door. Step free to the tearoom which is straight on from the entrance. **Wheelchair toilet (D90 ST80)** beyond the bar.

Dorchester, Park Lane W1A 2HJ *Tel:* 020 7629-8888 *website:* www.dorchesterhotel.com

Located on Park Lane between South Street and Deanery Street. The main entrance is +3, but there is step-free access from Deanery Street. Tea is served directly behind Reception, which is to the left from the Deanery Street entrance. There is no adapted toilet but we were told that a toilet in one of the bedrooms could be used.

Intercontinental, Hamilton Place W1V 0QY *Tel:* 020 7409-3131
Situated on the corner of Park Lane and Piccadilly. UGCP with lift access. There are −5 steps at the Hamilton Place entrance, but step free through the Coffee House entrance, on the corner of Park Lane and Piccadilly. Afternoon tea is served in the Lobby Lounge (turn right at the Coffee House door). **Wheelchair toilet (D80 ST120)** opposite the Coffee House entrance.

Lanesborough, Hyde Park Corner SW1 *Tel:* 020 7259-5599
Situated just off Grosvenor Place. The UGCP does not have lift access, but it may be possible to park in the forecourt while having tea. Flat entrance. The tearoom is on the GF, with 60% with step-free access and movable chairs. **Wheelchair toilet (D95 ST80)** past Reception on the right.

Meridien, 19-21 Piccadilly W1J 0BH *Tel:* 0870 400-8400
Near Piccadilly Circus. Step-free entrance and tearoom on the GF with movable furniture. **Wheelchair toilet (D85 ST140)** on the lower ground floor accessed by lift (D80 W110 L150).

Raffles Brown's, Albermarle Street and Dover Street W1S 4BP *Tel:* 020 7493-6020 (*hotel Reception*) 020 7518-4125 (*tearooms*)
The easiest entrance is on Albermarle Street via +1 step. Tea is served in the lounge to the right of the entrance. In the basement, reached by the lift (D80 W105 L110) there is an **adapted cubicle (D70 ST0** but with handrails**)** in the Ladies. This is for disabled walkers.

Ritz, 150 Piccadilly W1J 9BR *Tel:* 020 7493-8181
50m from Green Park Station. Entrance from Piccadilly +2 steps, bypassed by a ramp. A side door can be used to avoid the revolving door. Then step-free access to about half the tearoom, with movable chairs. We were told that there is now a disabled persons' toilet but we didn't see it (as we were not smartly enough dressed).

Savoy, Savoy Place WC2R 0EU *Tel:* 020 7836-4343
Halfway along the Strand. Entrance flat, through a side door, but −10−4 steps to get there. These can be bypassed by the use of two lifts (D80 W95 L105) and the kitchen! No adapted toilets.

Shops

One of London's main attractions are the long streets full of shops, many of them famous throughout the world. Our survey teams found that access to shops has improved over recent years, although the greatest improvement has been in the numerous newly built shopping centres around London, particularly with the advent of *Shopmobility*.

In the **Central Shops** section we have concentrated mainly on the Oxford Street and Kensington areas, as well as including famous shops like Harrods, Harvey Nichols and Fortnum & Mason. We have only surveyed a tiny percentage of London's shops, so please do not be limited by listings in this section. Access is generally good, although the majority of big stores have central escalators and less obvious lifts. Most big department stores have a store guide near the main entrance, but these do not normally take account of access issues. Departments are sometimes moved around without the list being amended.

For shop locations, see the map, and note that some of the numbering along Oxford Street (which is very long) is shown. Shops get extremely busy, particularly during sales and throughout the whole Christmas period. Car parking also gets difficult. Near Oxford Street there are CPs attached to Selfridges, one behind Debenhams and an UGCP at Cavendish Square.

There is a Lloyds Bank with step-free access at 32 Oxford Street, W1 (*Tel:* 020 7242-0111). Banking facilities are on the first floor with escalator access, or alternatively a platform stairlift (W70 L74) to the basement, then a lift (D80 W120 L120) to the first floor. Have a look at the *Good Loo Guide* for toilets.

Near Kensington High Street, there's an UGCP on Hornton Street with lift (D90 W125 L140) access to the street. There are **wheelchair cubicles (D85)** in the toilet at the exit. The key is supposedly with the attendant, but when our survey team visited he couldn't find it!

In the suburbs, there are many new and accessible shopping centres. The *Shopmobility* schemes are of considerable importance. Each scheme is independently run and financed, but a central office coordinates information. A list of the schemes in and around London is included in the chapter on *General information*.

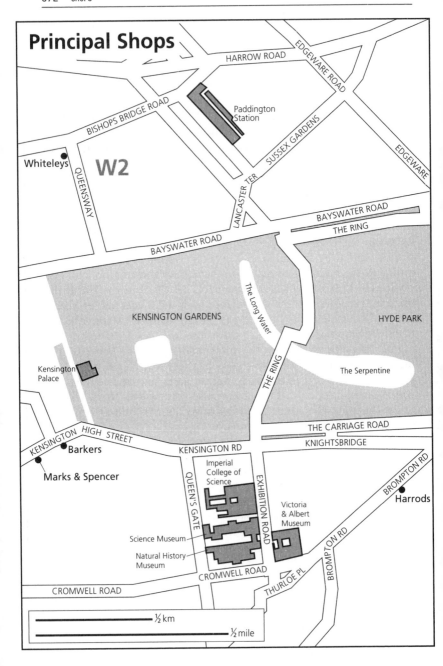

Principal Shops

HARROW ROAD

EDGEWARE ROAD

BISHOPS BRIDGE ROAD

Paddington
Station

SUSSEX GARDENS

EDGEWARE

Whiteleys

W2

QUEENSWAY

LANCASTER TER

BAYSWATER ROAD

THE RING

BAYSWATER ROAD

The Long Water

KENSINGTON GARDENS

HYDE PARK

THE RING

Kensington
Palace

The Serpentine

KENSINGTON HIGH STREET

THE CARRIAGE ROAD

KENSINGTON RD

KNIGHTSBRIDGE

Barkers

Marks & Spencer

QUEEN'S GATE

Imperial
College of
Science

EXHIBITION ROAD

Victoria
&ARodV A

BROMPTON RD

Harrods

Victoria
& Albert
Museum

Science Museum

Natural History
Museum

BROMPTON RD

CROMWELL ROAD

THURLOE PL

CROMWELL ROAD

½ km

½ mile

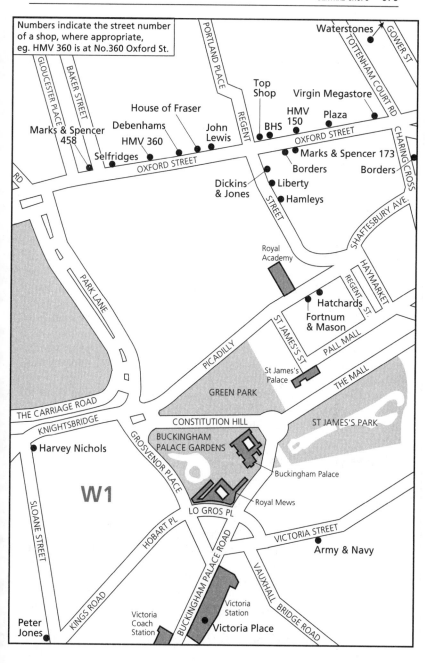

Numbers indicate the street number of a shop, where appropriate, eg. HMV 360 is at No.360 Oxford St.

GLOUCESTER PLACE
BAKER STREET
PORTLAND PLACE
GOWER ST
TOTTENHAM COURT RD
CHARING CROSS

Waterstones

Top Shop

Virgin Megastore

House of Fraser

HMV 150

Plaza

Debenhams

BHS

Marks & Spencer 458

HMV 360

John Lewis

REGENT STREET

OXFORD STREET

Selfridges

OXFORD STREET

Marks & Spencer 173

Borders

Borders

RD

Dickins & Jones

Liberty

Hamleys

SHAFTESBURY AVE.

Royal Academy

PARK LANE

HAYMARKET

REGENT ST.

Hatchards

Fortnum & Mason

ST JAMES'S ST

PALL MALL

PICADILLY

St James's Palace

THE MALL

THE CARRIAGE ROAD

GREEN PARK

ST JAMES'S PARK

KNIGHTSBRIDGE

CONSTITUTION HILL

Harvey Nichols

GROSVENOR PLACE

BUCKINGHAM PALACE GARDENS

W1

Buckingham Palace

Royal Mews

LO GROS PL

SLOANE STREET

HOBART PL

BUCKINGHAM PALACE ROAD

VICTORIA STREET

VICTORIA STREET

Army & Navy

VAUXHALL BRIDGE ROAD

KINGS ROAD

Peter Jones

Victoria Coach Station

Victoria Station

Victoria Place

A scheme usually has an office with adjacent **BB** parking spaces, and offers manual or electric wheelchairs for hire and use. Most have some electric scooters which are particularly useful to elderly people who cannot walk very far, or who find that carrying things is difficult. Some schemes can provide volunteer escorts if necessary, some of whom are trained to guide people with visual impairments. Opening times are variable, and depend both on demand, and on the availability of staff and of finance. Some schemes open every day, others open for perhaps two or three days a week.

Most of the out-of-town shopping centres we have included in the guide have a Shopmobility office. Schemes outside the M25 which we have not included are in Bedford, Bluewater near Dartford, Brentwood, Guildford, Lakeside Thurrock, Watford and Woking.

In the write-ups, we have given the location of Shopmobility offices, and the CP with which it is associated. We have then described the centre starting from this point. Note that the office will almost certainly be centrally situated. Its **BB** spaces may well be in the main MSCP and, on Saturdays and other times, there may even be a queue of cars trying to get in. It means that access is effectively blocked off, and you'll either have to wait in the queue or choose to shop at some other time.

Remember the street and open-air markets for shopping, which have, in principle, good access. They are listed in the chapter on *Open-air activities.*

In the text, shops are listed in alphabetical order. Where there is more than one branch in the same area we have listed them together, but shown them separately on the map.

Central Shops

Army and Navy Stores
105 Victoria Street SW1E 6QX
Tel: 020 7834-1234
A large department store split between two buildings with an upper level link. Two BB spaces on Howick Place. Three flat entrances. The main entrance is on the corner of Victoria Street and Artillery Row. Step-free access throughout the four floors of the main building via two lifts (D135 W190 L160) at the back of the store. There's a restaurant and an **adapted toilet (D90 ST55)** which is behind the lifts, on the second floor.

The second building is across Howick Place and on two floors. Entrance +1 step and then there is escalator/stair access only. The

easiest way to reach the upper floor is probably to use the link
($+4-8$) from the second floor of the main building. Café on the GF.

Barkers of Kensington
63-7 Kensington High Street W8 5SE
Tel: 020 7937-5432
Step-free entrances from the High Street lead to an arcade with a
variety of separate shops. Central escalators serve all four floors, but
there is a well hidden lift (D110 W160 L125) at the very back of the
arcade. There is a restaurant on the second floor and a café in the
basement.

Borders
203 Oxford Street W1D 2LE
Tel: 020 7292-1600
Large bookstore also selling videos and CDs, with flat access everywhere via a lift (D80 W110 L140). Café and **wheelchair toilet (D90 ST
150)** on the second floor.

Borders
120 Charing Cross Road WC2E
Tel: 020 7379-8877
Situated on the corner of Denmark Street and Charing Cross Road.
Entrance + 1 step, but flat throughout once inside. Large branch of
the American chain which sells books, music and videos. A lift (D90
W110 L140) to all four floors is opposite the entrance. Café on the
first floor. **Wheelchair cubicle (D90 ST95)** in men's toilet only on first
floor, left and at the back of the store from the lift. Key from tills.

British Home Stores (BHS)
252/8 Oxford Street W1N 9DC
Tel: 020 7629-2011
Department store with flat entrances and two floors. Lift (D100
W145 L170) at the back of the store on the left. Restaurant on the
first floor with an **adapted toilet (D90 ST120 but door opens in)**
nearby.

Debenhams
334 Oxford Street W1
Tel: 020 7580-3000
Large department store on five floors. Flat entrance on Vere Street
corner but there are 3 steps from Henrietta Place. The GF has a split

level with +5 steps, bypassed by an open lift (W80 L100). There's another split level in the basement (+8), also bypassed by an open lift (W80 L100), but this is potentially obstructed by the café at the top. The main lifts go from the upper GF level. There is a well-hidden lift (D90 W200 L140) before the split level, on the left after the main entrance, signposted 'Exit to Marylebone Lane'. This lift gives access to all floors except the basement. On the upper floors you can cross without steps to the lifts (D80+ W160 L135+) at the back of the store, and get down to the upper level of the GF, and to the basement. If you want to go straight to floors one, two or three, it's simpler to use the hidden lift. Restaurant and café on the second floor, both with flat access. **Wheelchair toilet (D85 ST90)** on the third floor.

Although access has been improved with the provision of the open lifts, the decision of the management not to provide ramps remains disappointing, and it took a lot of pressure to get anything done. They carried out a multi-million pound development only a few years ago, and access issues were clearly not a priority.

Dickins & Jones
224/244 Regent Street W1A 1DB
Tel: 020 7734-7070
Large, spacious and somewhat exclusive clothes store. Step-free access everywhere. Two lifts (D110 W190 L140), on the left of the store from the Regent Street entrance serve all six floors. There are cafés on the second and ground floors. **Wheelchair cubicle (D70 ST105)** in the Ladies on the fourth floor, but no equivalent facility for men.

Fortnum & Mason
181 Piccadilly W1A 1ER
Tel: 020 7734-8040 *Fax:* 020 7437-3278 *website:* www.fortnumand-mason.com
One of London's traditional shops with its own unique style. Flat entrance on Piccadilly, avoiding steps at the other entrances. Three lifts (D75 W160 L70) on the left of the store give step-free access to all six floors. One on the right (D110 W140 L135) goes from the lower GF to the second floor. The lower GF is full of fragile looking items. The upmarket St James Restaurant on the fourth floor has flat access. The Fountain Restaurant is −12 steps from the GF, but only +1 from the entrance on the corner of Duke Street and Jermyn Street. The Patio Restaurant is +10 from the GF but step free via a

staff lift (D80 W120 L160). **Two wheelchair toilets**, one **(D75 ST70)** in the Burlington Room on the fourth floor and one **(D80 ST145)** on the second floor, to the left from the single lift.

Gabriel's Wharf
A small, flat pedestrianised area located on the South Bank between the National Theatre and the Oxo Tower, off Upper Ground. Comprises a number of eateries, bars and shops with step-free access, although there's a slope down from the riverside walk. There are **two adapted toilets (D85 ST95** inward opening door**)** next to the Studio 6 bar/restaurant. Outdoor seating in the summer, but the benches are fixed.

Hamleys
188-196 Regent Street W1R 6BT
Tel: 0870 333-2455 *website:* www.hamleys.co.uk
The world's largest toyshop is on seven floors. The shop is nearly always busy. There is flat access everywhere. It has central escalators. Two lifts (D105 W185 L145) on the left go to all floors. **Wheelchair toilet (D90 ST85)** on the fifth floor by the café.

Harrods
Knightsbridge SW1X 7XL
Tel: 020 7730-1234 *website:* www.harrods.com
A unique institution with a worldwide reputation, where you can buy anything from a horse to a house to a hearse. Despite its address, it is located on the Brompton Road between Hans Crescent and Hans Road. A detailed guide is available at entrances and in store from staff. Flat entrances from the Brompton Road. The store has seven floors and is simply massive, measuring about 200m by 200m. There are numerous sets of large lifts (typically D120 W160 L240) giving step-free access to almost all of the store.
Starting from the bottom and working upwards:
• the lower GF is made up of three separate sections. The main part is step free to all areas, including the (kitsch) memorial to Princess Diana and Dodi Fayed. There is step-free access from the lifts to the wine shop and tapas bar, but the Green Man pub and barber's shop are reached via −11−11−2 steps with no lift access;
• the GF, first and second floors are all step free throughout;
• the third floor has split levels of up to four steps which can be bypassed through the music departments;
• the fourth floor has split levels of up to six steps which can be

bypassed through ramps in the children's underwear department;
* the fifth floor is step-free throughout from the express lift from the GF on the Hans Crescent side of the building near Door Five.

There are twenty-one different eating places, all with flat access except for the Green Man pub (see above) and Caffé Expresso on the GF (+ 8). The remaining seven on the GF have fixed stools and only in the Sushi Bar are these low. The fourth floor restaurants have step-free access from the express lift on the Hans Crescent side of the building or ramped access described above.

There are **wheelchair toilets** on the first floor near the Executive Suite in the Ladieswear department **(D90 ST75)**, on the second floor adjacent to the Ladies **(D85 ST75)** and on the fourth floor adjacent to the Gents **(D85 ST80)**. The wheelchair toilet marked next to the Ladies on the fourth floor does not exist. There is a charge of one pound for the toilets but chair users are exempt from this.

Harvey Nichols
109 Knightsbridge SW1X 7RJ
Tel: 020 7235-5000
Exclusive store known for ladies' outfitting, but with some general departments and a comprehensive food store on the fifth floor. Flat entrances on Knightsbridge. Two central lifts (D70 W110 L110) serve all eight floors. About 25% of GF is + 4 steps. Floors one to five are step free except for − 2 to a small section of the fourth floor. The lower GF is only 20% step free from the lifts: the remainder is either − 1 or − 4. The *Wagamama* restaurant is step free from the lifts, but has fixed tables and benches. The lower basement (level LG2) is 10% step free from the lift; 50% of the floor is − 5 and 40% a further − 5.

An express lift (D90 W160 L135), located to the left of the ramped Sloane Street entrance, serves the GF and the fifth floor. The fifth floor is step free throughout. It contains a *Yo! Sushi*, a food store, restaurant and bar, where the tables are either high or rather low. There are **wheelchair cubicles** in the Gents **(D80 ST80)** by the bar and in the Ladies **(D85 ST120)** to the right of the lift.

There is also an **adapted cubicle (D90 ST62)** on the first floor in a staff area. Ask staff in the ladies' shoe department for assistance.

Hatchards
187 Piccadilly W1J 9LE
Tel: 020 7439-9921 *website:* www.hatchards.co.uk
A smallish but well-stocked bookstore whose customers include the

Queen. Flat entrance, then a lift (D80 W105 L140) at the back of the store goes to all five floors. The second and third floors both have + 1 + 1 steps to a quarter of the area.

HMV
360 Oxford Street W1C 1AB
Tel: 020 7514-3600
Near Bond Street. Flat to the GF, and two lifts (D90 W130 L160) to the LG and first floors.

HMV
150 Oxford Street, W1D 1DJ
Tel: 020 7631-3423
Near Oxford Circus. It has three floors with a lift (D80 W110 L210) to all floors at the back on the right. Step free throughout. On the opposite side of the street is a *McDonald's* (187 Oxford Street) with a **wheelchair toilet (D90 ST70)** although the nappy disposal unit needs to be moved.

House of Fraser
318 Oxford Street W1
Tel: 020 7529-4700
Flat/ramped entrances. Seven floors served by three central lifts (D140 W170 L140). There are eating places on the GF, third and fifth floors, all step free. **Wheelchair toilet (D90 ST110)** on the fifth floor.

John Lewis
278 Oxford Street W1A 1EX
Tel: 020 7629-7711
Between Oxford Circus and New Bond Street. Large department store on seven floors, with flat or ramped entrances. Seven lifts (D115 W155 L180); three at the front on the left, and four at the back on the left, give step-free access almost everywhere. The coffee shop on the third floor is 70% flat but there are + 3 steps to a balcony area. **Wheelchair toilet (D100 ST100 NKS)** on the fourth floor.

Liberty
210/220 Regent Street W1B 5AH
Tel: 020 7734-1234
On the corner of Great Marlborough Street. A store with wonderful character. Liberty designs and patterns are known the world over. It consists of two separate buildings, the Tudor Wing in Great

Marlborough Street, and the Regent Street building. Some departments are congested and displays are often cramped.

On Great Marlborough Street, the entrance on the left is flat, avoiding +3 steps at the right hand entrance and a revolving door at the main entrance. Once inside both the lift (D80 W150 L120) near the entrance on the left, and the lift (D80 W120 L110) to the right of the main entrance, give access to all six floors of the Tudor Wing. Most of the floors in the Tudor Wing have a split level although none take up more than 5% of a floor.

The Regent Street building has three floors, linked by a lift (D80 W105 L200), with step-free access on the GF and first floor. The basement contains a café, but in the menswear department, there are −2 to about 25%.

Access between the two buildings appears to be difficult. There is a step-free route in the basement through a staff only area; otherwise you can use the pavement outside to get around to the other building. There are +8−3 if you use the link on the first floor.

The store contains three eating places, two in the Tudor Wing, one in the Regent Street wing. There is step-free access to all three, in the basement, and on the second and fourth floors. The second floor café has a bar with some high chairs.

There is an **adapted toilet (D70 ST50)** on the first floor of the Regent Street building, opposite the lift.

Marks & Spencer
113 Kensington High Street W8 5SQ
Tel: 020 7938 3711
Alongside High Street Kensington Station. Step-free to all floors via a lift (D130 W205 L245) which is on the left as you enter from the High Street. A second lift (D85 W105 L130) provides access to the basement and first floor only. **Wheelchair toilet (D85 ST105)** on the second floor by the other toilets. A step-free exit on the GF leads to the station and the Kensington Arcade.

Marks & Spencer
173 Oxford Street W1D 2JR
Tel: 020 7440-3400
Some 200m from Oxford Circus towards Tottenham Court Road. Step-free throughout all four floors via a lift (D90 W130 L175). **Wheelchair toilet (D105 ST90)** at the front of the GF on the left. Not signed; in fact it is hidden in a changing area behind a door marked 'Sprinkler Cupboard'.

Marks & Spencer
458 Oxford Street W1C 1AP
Tel: 020 7935-7954
Near Marble Arch. It has five floors with lift (D140 W190 L100) access. The two central lifts go to all floors. The second floor has a split level but there is a ramped bypass. No wheelchair toilet.

Peter Jones
Sloane Square SW1W 8EL
Tel: 020 7730 3434 *website:* www.johnlewis.com
Large department store on eight floors with step-free access everywhere except the fourth floor which is only 20% step free. Flat entrance, then three well-signposted lifts (D110 W150 L140) go to all floors. Café on the sixth floor. **Wheelchair toilet (D70 ST80 NKS)** on the third floor and **adapted toilet (D90 ST90 inward opening door)** on the sixth floor. When we visited, the store was undergoing a comprehensive refurbishment due to be completed in 2004. In the meantime some departments, such as antiques and furniture, have relocated to another store, **PJ2**, on the corner of Denyer Street and Draycott Avenue, about 500m away. This has three floors accessed step free via a lift (D120 W120 L180) and an **adapted toilet (D80 ST62)** on the first floor.

Plaza
120 Oxford Street W1 9DP
Tel: 020 7637-8811 *website:* www.ged59.dial.pipex.com
A shopping centre in the shell of an old department store called Bournes. Flat main entrance, then lift (D80 W80 L150) access to the food court on the first floor. **Wheelchair toilet (D85 ST90 NKS)** on the first floor.

Selfridges
400 Oxford Street W1A 1AB
Tel: 020 7629-1234
One of London's biggest department stores. Each of the five floors measure roughly 200m by 200m. It has its own seven-storey CP (entered from Duke Street), which gives flat or lift (D80 W130 L130) access to the shop. It's not cheap to use.

The entrance on Duke Street and the central one on Oxford Street both have flat access, as does the entrance to the food hall from Orchard Street. From the food hall to the main store there is a minimum of −10 steps, which can be bypassed by an open lift (W80 L100), located by the exit to the Stationery Hall.

The main shop has two lifts (D120 W190 L150) in the centre of the store. The café by the food hall and the restaurant by Duke Street have stepped access. The other seven eating places have flat access. In the toilets on the third floor there is an **adapted cubicle (D90 ST57)** in the Gents and a **wheelchair cubicle (D90 ST110)** in the Ladies.

Immediately opposite Selfridges main entrance on Oxford Street is a 24-hour Tardis-type **wheelchair toilet (D70 + ST70 + NKS)**, at the end of Balderton Street.

Top Shop

36-38 Great Castle Street W1W 8LG
Tel: 020 7636-7700
Located on the corner of Oxford Street and Regent Street. 'London's largest fashion store' has step-free entrances on Oxford Street which lead to four floors of clothes and accessories. A lift (D110 W175 L165) at the back of the shop goes to all floors. The sub-basement level has a café, and a **wheelchair toilet (D80 ST80)** which is left from the lift.

Victoria Place

115 Buckingham Palace Road, Eccleston Bridge SW1 9SJ
Tel: 020 7931-8811
Two floors of shops and eating places built above Victoria Station with ramped access from Eccleston Bridge. From the station there appears to be only escalator access, but there is a lift (D110 W150 L220) to the first floor from halfway down platforms 13/14 (for the Gatwick Express). The platforms are open, so just walk or wheel down.

On the first floor, there's a range of shops, virtually all with flat access. On the second floor there's a whole range of eating places – *McDonald's*, *Garfunkel's* and several other cafés and restaurants. There's also a pub, the *Molly O'Grady's*. All have flat access. On the same level, between *Deep Pan Pizza* and *Benjy's* there's a **wheelchair toilet (D80 ST130 NKS)**. Access to the second level is by escalator or steps, and there is a service lift (D75 W100 L150). *There is no indication anywhere that this exists.* Ask any shopholder to get someone from security to take you there. The lift is accessed from outside by the taxi drop-off point on the first floor (turn left, then left again to find intercom), and from quite near the pub on the second floor.

Virgin Megastore
14 Oxford Street W1D 1AR
Tel: 020 7631-1234
Flat entrances, with escalator or lift (D90 W110 L150) access throughout the four floors. The store is step free throughout and has a coffee
shop and a **wheelchair toilet (D90 ST120)** in the basement. There is
also internet access on the GF and, with low desks, on the first floor.

Waterstone's
82 Gower Street WC1E 6EQ
Tel: 020 7636-1577 *Fax:* 020 7580-7680
Huge specialist in academic books, with an excellent range in general
titles. Flat main entrance, and from Gower Street, although + 1 step
(steep) from Malet Street. Two lifts (D80 W100 L140) give access to
all five floors from either entrance. The odd step on the GF and in
the basement can be easily bypassed by a ramp. The shop is
surprisingly roomy for a bookstore. There is a poorly signed **wheelchair toilet (D80 ST150)** in the middle of the basement.

Whiteleys
151 Queensway W2 4YN
Tel: 020 7229-8844
Shopping and eating centre on three floors built in the shell of a once
famous department store. It contains an eight-screen cinema complex
(see chapter on *Entertainment*). CP is approached from Redan Place
and has three BB spaces near the entrance on the second floor. There
are three flat entrances, and flat/lift (D105 W200 L115) access
throughout. Lifts are near the main central entrance from Queensway.
Shops are on the ground and first floors, the cinemas and restaurants
are on the second floor, and the third floor contains offices. **Wheelchair toilet (D85 ST75)** on the second floor next to *McDonald's*. The
complex covers an area of approximately 150m by 50m.

Out-of-town centres

Most of these have a Shopmobility scheme. All have parking with **BB**
spaces, covered shopping areas and big stores.

Bexleyheath

A compact centre when compared with some others, with an area of
roughly 200m by 70m. The Broadway Shopping Centre is fully

covered, and mainly on one floor. Large CP on two levels, approached from Albion Road, with BB spaces on both levels. On the lower level there are four spaces in the middle and eleven at the eastern end. Lifts (D110 W200 L170) give step-free access to the Centre.

Shopmobility (*Tel:* 020 8301-5237) is based on the first floor by the west side of the CP. It is currently operating with restricted hours. Take lift number eight to Level 1 to get there.

There is flat access at all entrances, and throughout most of the eighty or so stores. *British Home Stores*, *W.H. Smith* and *Marks & Spencer* have two floors, with lift (D90+ W120+ L140+) access. There's a café on the first floor of *BHS*.

There are **two adapted toilets (D80 ST65)** on the GF by the central lifts, and others on the first floor in *BHS* **(D95 ST85)**, and by the café in *Asda*, located separately from the Centre **(D85 ST180)**. Also note the write-ups on the *Wrong'un* and the *Golden Lion* in the *Pubs* chapter.

Bromley

Apart from being on a hill Bromley has good facilities for people with disabilities, particularly in the Glades Shopping Centre (BR1 1DN) *Tel:* 020 8466-8899. The Centre has over a hundred shops on two floors and well-signposted parking on two levels above the shops. The numerous parking areas are named after animals.

The *Shopmobility* office (*Tel:* 020 8313-0031) is in CP level one in Frog Zone, approached from Kentish Way. There are fifteen BB spaces. Lift (D110 W180 L130) access to the middle of the Centre. There is lift access (D75+ W115+ L170+) from all other parking areas to both levels.

All entrances to the Centre have flat access, as do all the shops. On the lower level is an information desk (*Tel:* 020 8466-8899), a food court and various restaurants, the Pavilion Leisure Centre, and **two wheelchair toilets (D90 ST80)** outside *Boots*. On the upper level there are **two adapted toilets (D90 ST60)** opposite *McDonald's*. There is another **wheelchair toilet (D80 ST75)** on the pedestrianised High Street opposite the Churchill Theatre (see section on *Theatres*). The Centre itself is approximately 400m long.

Canary Wharf

Colonnade Shopping Centre, North Colonnade, Canary Wharf E14
Situated under the main tower, the Shopping Centre can be reached
step free from both Canary Wharf JLE exit (which takes you on to
the promenade level, below ground) and the DLR exit (which takes
you on to the GF). There are two CPs (east and west), which each
have six BB spaces, next to the two lifts, on all three levels. The lifts
go to all four floors of the Centre. All shops have step free entrances,
and there are plenty of seats. **Three wheelchair toilets** on the promenade level, one next to the central concourse **(D90 ST120 NKS)**
and two at the far east end of the centre **(D90 ST85 NKS).**

Croydon

Apart from central London, Croydon is the biggest of the shopping
areas we have covered. The town centre has seven major CPs. The
Whitgift Centre (*Tel:* 020 8686-0297) contains about 150 shops on
two main levels. Note that East Croydon station is fully accessible
and only about 200m from the main shopping area,

Shopmobility (*Tel:* 020 8688-7336) is located in the lower level of
the Whitgift CP, clearly signed on Wellesley Road. There are twenty-
nine BB spaces and there is ramped access bypassing −8 steps to the
north end of the Centre. If the BB spaces are full, a lift (D85 W130
L90) links the other floors of the CP. Shopmobility can arrange for
chairs and scooters to be available at a number of the central CPs
including the Drummond Centre, the Surrey Street CP, and also at
East Croydon Station. The CP off Poplar Walk has sixteen BB
spaces. To go to the south end of the Centre, the Allders CP is closer.
This has twenty-two BB spaces on the third floor, with −4 steps
bypassed by a ramp to the first floor of *Allders*, or lift (D80 W125
L150) access to the GF of the **Whitgift Centre**.

The main entrance to the **Whitgift Centre** is flat from the pedestrianised North End High Street. The Centre has three clearly-
signposted sets of lifts (all at least D90 W120 L100). It has a central
café on the first floor.

The Centre contains **three wheelchair toilets/cubicles**:
- on the first floor in both Ladies and Gents **(D85 ST80)**
- on the second floor **(D95 ST85)**. Only the lifts by *Woolworths*
  serve this floor.

If you are coming into Croydon from the south, the Surrey Street
CP on Scarbrook Road is convenient. It has eight BB spaces on Level

1, and flat access to the Surrey Street Market. The CP has lift (D110 W160 L150) access throughout, and from Level 4 there is a step-free footbridge of about 50m which comes out 50m from the Croydon Clocktower (see section on *Arts centres*). Shopmobility vehicles are available.

The Dingwall Road MSCP, entered from Lansdown Road, is some 300m from East Croydon Station. It provides the best parking if you want to use the train. Twenty BB spaces on the GF, and lift (D90 L95 W140) access between floors. **Wheelchair toilet (D80 ST80 NKS)** by the CP entrance.

There are **numerous wheelchair toilets/cubicles** in Croydon town centre (unisex unless stated):

Allders, third floor **(D80 ST180)**. Lift (D105 W200 L155) access at back right of store.

Debenhams in the Drummond Centre, **two toilets (D90 ST100)** on the second floor. Lift (D105 W160 L220) access from central glass lift. Follow signs for toilets, wheelchair toilets not signposted.

Drummond Centre, on the GF, opposite McDonald's, Gents **(D85 ST80)**, Ladies **(D80 ST120)**.

East Croydon Station, Platform 3/4 **(D90 ST110 NKS)** next to the Gents, ask at the office for key.

The George Pub, George Street **(D85 ST100)**, flat from the Whitgift Centre through Allders Mall.

Marks & Spencer in the Whitgift Centre, first floor **(D90 ST85)**.

Mothercare in the Whitgift Centre, GF **(D100 ST110)**, marked 'customer toilet'.

There are wheelchair/adapted toilets in **Fairfield** Arts Complex and in the **Croydon Clocktower** (see section on *Arts centres*).

Hounslow

The pedestrianised High Street is 1km long. There is a large covered shopping mall called the **Treaty Centre** towards one end, measuring about 200m by 80m. The attached MSCP off Grove Road has many BB spaces on Level 6. This gives step-free access to the Centre via lifts (D100 W200 L200). The Centre is mainly on the GF, but Debenhams is on three floors with a lift (D90 W135 L240) inside. There's another lift inside the Paul Robeson Theatre (see chapter on *Theatres*).

Shopmobility (*Tel:* 020 8570-3343) is based on Level 6 of the Treaty Centre CP. Toilets are next to the CP lifts on the GF: one is a **wheelchair toilet (D90 ST70 NKS)**, while the other is an **adapted toilet (D90 ST40 NKS)**.

As described, the High Street is long, with the Treaty Centre near one end. It's about 300m to *Marks & Spencer*, and another 300m to the end of the pedestrian area. There are numerous other CPs with BB spaces along the length of the street, the biggest of which is the Alexandra Road CP with six BB spaces on ground level. There are also three BB spaces in Gilbert Street and a further four in Fair Street, next to *Marks & Spencer*.

Harrow

There are two large malls situated close to each other, St George's and St Anne's, as well as a pedestrianised shopping area some 200m long, on St Anne's Road. Both centres have MSCPs, accessed via the one-way traffic system from Headstone Road. St George's shopping centre has shops on the GF, with restaurants and a Warner Village cinema on the first floor. The main street entrance is step free from St Anne's Road.

The *Shopmobility* office (*Tel:* 020 8427-1200) is on Level 3 of the CP opposite twelve BB spaces. Four lifts (D105 W160 L170) on the north side of the Centre access all floors. There is a **wheelchair toilet (D95 ST90 NKS)** on the second floor beside the lifts.

St Anne's Shopping Centre also has shops on the GF, and restaurants on the Gallery level (first floor). There are step-free entrances halfway down St Anne's Road, and on College Road opposite Harrow-on-the-Hill tube station, although this involves a ramp 20m long. Three lifts (D95 W200 L130) by the College Road entrance access the GF, first, third, fifth and seventh floors. Two lifts in the middle of the 150m long mall access the GF, first, second, fourth and sixth floors. The MSCP has four BB spaces on the second floor. There are **two wheelchair toilets**: one **(D80 ST80 NKS)** on the GF by the central lifts, the other **(D80 ST85 NKS)** directly above on the first floor.

There is a three-storey *Debenhams*, which has step-free access throughout via lifts, 20m to the north of St Anne's Road along Station Road; it has a restaurant and **adapted toilet (D63 ST80)** on the second floor.

Ilford (Redbridge)

The Exchange Shopping Centre (High Street, Ilford IG1 1RS *Tel:* 020 8553-3000 *website:* www.exchange-shopping.co.uk) is about 350m long and on three floors with over 100 stores. The MSCP is entered from Ley Street or Havelock Street and has seven floors;

GF is reserved for BB holders with about fifty spaces. There are six more BB spaces on each floor from two to seven. All the entrances are flat, and the four sets of lifts (all D90+ W100+ L130+) go to all floors. This includes the CP lifts, and the lift inside the department store *Allders*, on three floors. Step-free access throughout. There is a large food court area on the third floor as well as the Centre café.

Shopmobility (*Tel:* 020 8478-6864) is based on Level One (ground level) of the CP. **Two wheelchair toilets (D90 ST80 NKS)** are to the left as you enter from the CP Level 1 (Lower Mall). Level Three (Upper Mall) has a **wheelchair toilet (D90 ST80)** at the back, by *W. H. Smith*.

Kingston

The town centre has a wide variety of shops. The central area is about 500m square, and is largely pedestrianised. There are many peripheral CPs; there is also a river frontage with pubs and restaurants. Helpful maps of the area are available from *Shopmobility* including toilet locations. Their office (*Tel:* 020 8547-1255) is located on level two of the Eden Walk CP, opposite the BB spaces. From here there is lift or ramped access to *Marks & Spencer*; the CP is reached from Eden Street.

The other central CP is by the Bentall centre, reached from Wood Street. Both A and B sections of the CP have BB spaces on Level 8. The Bentall centre has four floors of shops and restaurants, with lift access throughout.

On the other side of Wood Street is a large branch of *John Lewis*, which extends to the riverside. Access is complicated by a split level on the first floor as a road passes underneath. There is step-free access to 95% of the store if you enter from Horse Fair or from the UGCP. There are also large branches of *Marks & Spencer* and *BHS* which have step-free access throughout.

There are numerous **wheelchair toilets**, most of which are shown on the *Shopmobility* map, including ones in:
- **M and S**, second floor by the lifts **(D85 ST80)**;
- **BHS**, first floor by the restaurant **(D90 ST150)**;
- **John Lewis**, first floor on both sides (both **D85 ST75 NKS)**;
- **Bentalls**, one in CP-A Level 8 by the BB spaces **(D85 ST80 NKS)** and in the main shopping centre Level 2, where there are **three (all D85 ST85 NKS)**;
- **Royal Barge**, the riverside pub below *John Lewis* **(D85 ST80)**.

The latest development in Kingston is the **Rotunda** in Clarence Street on the corner opposite Kingston Station. This opened in 2002, and includes a sixteen-screen Odeon cinema (The Odeon, Clarence Street, Kingston KT1 1QP *Tel:* 020 8974-5197). All the screens are accessible step-free via a lift (D90 W100 L130). The cinema foyer is on the first floor, and the escalators can be bypassed by using the lift (D120 W200 L150) which is to the left through some glass doors. It is not entirely obvious, and is not signed. There's a CP about 250m away in Hardman Road. Go through the iron gates towards the 'Bentalls' name on the wall. This CP has 20 BB spaces, and you may be wise to ring in advance to book a place and ensure that the gates are open. In and around the cinema, access to refreshments and to a *Pizza Express* is step free, and there's an open lift (D90 L140) to a lower mezzanine if you fancy a Haagen-Dazs ice cream. There's a **wheelchair toilet (D80+ ST80+)** on each level in the cinema, and one in *Pizza Express*. For hearing-impaired customers, the cinema screens have infrared headphones, and it's probably best to enquire about availability when booking.

In the basement of the development there's a bowling alley while on an upper floor there's a David Lloyd health club, gym and swimming pool. The lift from the GF foyer links to all the facilities. Just 75m from the Rotunda on the opposite side of Clarence Street is *The King's Tun* (153 Clarence Street KT1 1QT *Tel:* 020 8547-3827) which is a Wetherspoons pub with 60% of the GF bar step free, and an **adapted toilet (D75 ST65 NKS)**.

Lewisham

The Lewisham Centre (*Tel:* 020 8852-0094) is situated between Molesworth Street and the pedestrianised High Street, roughly 250m from Lewisham National Rail and DLR stations. It measures about 350m by 150m and contains over 90 shops, cafés, a play area and a leisure centre. Lewisham market operates just outside the main entrance. The five storey CP above the centre is entered from Molesworth Street and is well signed. Levels 1–4 each have seven BB spaces. Six lifts (D100 W110 L200) give step-free access.

Shopmobility (*Tel:* 020 8297-2735) is based in a building under the ramp to the CP on Molesworth Street, and has twelve BB spaces outside, though there is a kerb 14cm high. There are five further BB spaces on nearby Rennell Street.

All the shops are on the GF, have flat access and can be reached by any of the step-free entrances from the street. A customer information desk is located centrally, next to a café (which has fixed tables and chairs). **Wheelchair toilet (D85 ST95 NKS)** by the entrance on Molesworth Street near Endgate Street, and another **(D85 ST80)** which is not signed, in the *BHS* cafeteria. On Rennell Street there are **wheelchair cubicles** which were locked at the time of inspection and there is a 'Tardis' toilet on the High Street outside the Lewisham Centre, which was out of use when we visited.

Romford

A large shopping area spreads out over nearly two km. There are three main shopping precincts, *Liberty, Liberty Two* and *The Brewery*.

The *Libertys* are next to each other and joined by a step-free walkway (passing under Mercury Gardens). Each centre has a CP. The New Liberty CP, is off Western Road to the **west** from Mercury Gardens. It has 31 BB spaces on the GF, ten parent and child spaces on the other three floors, and a pedestrian walkway with a handrail leading to the three lifts (D110 W180 L130). Liberty Two CP, off Western Road to the **east** of Mercury Gardens, has twenty BB spaces on the lower level. The upper level was under refurbishment at the time of survey.

Liberty shopping centre (*Tel:* 01708-746529), on the corner of Western Road and Mercury Gardens, has step-free entrances from all sides. It consists of one level with shops and eateries. There is an open-air market outside, with **two wheelchair toilets (D80 ST90 NKS)** located around the side of the public toilets, which are right then left from the mall. Currently being refurbished, it is due for completion in April 2003.

Liberty Two shopping centre (*Tel:* 01708-733620), on the corner of Mercury Gardens, Western Road and Main Road. There are step-free entrances via *Liberty* and CP. There are three floors of shops, linked by two lifts (D90 W120 L135) in the central atrium, and a café on the GF at the base of the lifts. **Wheelchair toilet (D85 ST160)** on the GF behind lifts. The foyer of the Bingo Hall is on Level Three; step-free access is via a service lift (D180 W250 L150) on Level Two, by the CP entrance. The hall has an **adapted toilet (D80 ST44)**.

The Brewery Retail Park, Waterloo Road, Romford RM1 1AK *Tel:* 01708-742356 is a large retail park covering about 300m by 200m. There is a large outdoor CP as well as a MSCP covering the area between Romford Station and Waterloo Road. A long row of shops, underneath the MSCP, separates the outdoor CP from the

High Street. There is also a large *Sainsbury's*, which includes a restaurant and a **wheelchair toilet (D100 ST135)** at the back by the checkouts. Four lifts (D110 W190 L175) and a travelator (W95) give access to a floor above *Sainsbury's* containing various eateries, as well as a sixteen screen cinema and a 24 lane bowling alley. There is an **adapted toilet (D80 ST60)** in the bowling alley behind the bar. *Shopmobility* (*Tel:* 01708-739431) is just to the south of *Sainsbury's*.

Redbridge see write-up on *Ilford*.

Stratford

Situated 50m from Stratford Station, with other entrances (north) near the Theatre Royal and (west) on the Broadway. Flat and almost entirely on one floor with a MSCP on top of it. The CP has seven BB spaces next to the lifts on each even-numbered level (at time of survey, Levels Six to Eight were closed).

The Centre is set out in a cross shape, measuring some 200m by 100m. There is some cobbled pavement outside the north exit, but otherwise the surfaces are smooth. *Burger King* at the stationside entrance has a lift (D85 W145 L110) to upper seating, and a **wheelchair toilet (D70+ ST70+).** The key is with staff. Two lifts (D110 W170 L155) 50m from stationside entrance go to levels Two, Four, Six and Eight of MSCP. **Wheelchair toilet (D90 ST75 NKS)** 70m from stationside entrance on the left (signed). Three nearby pubs with a disabled persons toilet are listed in the *Pubs and bars* chapter, while the cinema, theatre and Arts Centre are all described in the *Entertainments* section.

Sutton

The town centre has a pedestrianised high street, with two shopping centres, a cinema and numerous pubs and restaurants. St Nicholas Shopping Centre has a seven-floor MSCP, reached by following signs to 'town centre' or for the St Nicholas Centre. There are 27 BB spaces on Level Two and 18 on Level Three. The *Shopmobility* office (*Tel:* 020 8770-0691) is on Level Three of the CP next to the three lifts (D110 W180 L130). The three-floor shopping centre is about 200m long and has step free access throughout via ramps and two lifts (D100 W110+ L230) in the middle. There are **two wheelchair toilets (D80 ST75 one NKS,** the other not) on level three. There is also an **adapted toilet (D80 ST130** inward opening door) on Level One.

Across the High Street is the smaller Times Square Shopping Centre. There is a CP with four split levels and two lifts (D90 W175 L115). There are two footbridges from the CP, one to Marks & Spencer, the other to the Shopping Centre. The Centre has two floors, with a **wheeelchair toilet (D85 ST70)** on the upper GF. There are also **adapted cubicles** on the GF next to the lifts in both the Gents **(D90 ST110)** and the Ladies **(D85 ST110)** both with broken hand-rails restricting ST. Four pubs in Sutton with disabled persons' toilets are listed in the *Pubs and bars* chapter.

Surrey Quays
Redriff Road, SE16 1LL
A retail and leisure park on the corner of Lower Road and Redriff Road. To reach the retail park take the first left on Redriff Road, coming from Lower Road. There is a Tesco superstore, beyond which is the Surrey Quays Shopping Centre. There are thirteen BB spaces outside the main entrance. The GF is about 80m long and includes 40 + shops. To the right from the entrance is a circular lift (D80 radius100) giving access to a first floor with some restaurants. **Two wheelchair toilets**: one **(D90 ST85 NKS)** is straight on from the entrance on the GF. The other **(D80 ST85 NKS)** is on the first floor, to the left, by the Ladies.

The Leisure Park is further round Redriff Road, also on the left. This comprises a nine-screen cinema, bingo hall, bowling alley and several restaurants and bars. There is a large CP, with BB spaces outside the cinema entrance. The bowling alley has four lanes which can be reached by ramp, and a **wheelchair toilet (D80 ST110)** to the right of the information point. For cinema information, see under *Cinemas*.

Sport

Access to the main sports venues is of great importance. Even though the TV coverage of big events may be good, there's nothing quite like being there. You may see less (and you don't get the action replays), but the atmosphere is entirely different, and usually much more interesting.

The emphasis in this chapter is on spectating, but participation is also a vital interest for many. The **London Sports Forum for Disabled People (LSF)**, Ground Floor, Leroy House, 436 Essex Road N1 3QP *Tel:* 020 7354-8666 *Textphone:* 020 7534-9554 *Fax:* 020 7354-8787 *website:* www.londonsportsforum.org.uk *e-mail:* lsf@disabilitysport. freeserve.co.uk is the central co-ordinating body in London. Many new sports centres have provided facilities for disabled people, particularly changing facilities, wheelchair toilets and access to swimming pools. There will be local clubs and events in most sports. The LSF should be able to put you in touch with local disability organisations and clubs, and with community sport providers. Another possible source of information would be GLAD.

Athletics

Crystal Palace National Sports Centre
Ledrington Road, Crystal Palace SE19 2BB
Tel: 020 8778-9876
A large sports complex which, among other events, holds International Athletics meetings in the main stadium. Access is somewhat complicated as the area is hilly. Extensive parking, the easiest of which is by Gate F of the Jubilee Stand (the one furthest from the main entrance). A staff member will show chair users the way through Gate F to the wheelchair area in front of the Jubilee Stand. For the annual international athletics meeting, we were told that temporary platforms for chair users are erected both here and in front of the West Stand. The seats with the fewest steps in this stand are Row A (+ 1 step) of the Jubilee Stand. There is a **wheelchair toilet (D90 ST120)** behind the Jubilee Stand.

The other main building contains the sports hall and swimming pools, with two BB spaces near the main entrance. There is step-free access to all sports activities using two platform stairlifts, and **two wheelchair toilets (D90 ST120)** near the swimming pools.

Cricket

Lord's

St John's Wood Road NW8 8QN

Tel: General enquiries 020 7289-1611 BO 020 7432-1066 *Fax:* 020 7289-9100 *Booking online:* tickets@mcc.org.uk

The home of the MCC (Marylebone Cricket Club), and host to test matches and county games. The office will have details of matches from January each year, and for the big games you need to make early enquiries about chair access and spaces. The ground is large, and has been extensively redeveloped with new stands being built and good new provisions for disabled fans. It measures roughly 100m by 150m, and the nursery ground area is another 100m square.

Parking is difficult on a matchday. There is a drop-off point at Gate 6 at the end of Grove End Road. Entrance is possible through any set of turnstiles. There are three areas for chair users. In the Mound Stand, there are 28 spaces with helpers behind, in the front row. Two other areas can also be made available pitchside in the Allen Stand and the Warner Stand, on either side of the pavilion. The front row in the Tavern Stand is also step free, so recommended for disabled walkers.

There is step-free access to the Tavern Bar in the concourse by the Mound Stand. Bars in the Grandstand can be reached step free by ramps. Lifts (D80 W80 L195) behind the Mound Stand enclosure give access to boxes. Lifts (D70+ W110+ L140+) in the Grandstand give step-free access to the back rows of the Grandstand's lower tier, boxes, and the top-tier debenture seats.

Three wheelchair toilets (all D70+ ST70+ NKS) in concourses: one is by Block QQ sign near the Mound Stand enclosure, the other two are in the Grandstand; one by Block A sign, the other by Block C sign.

Ground tours take place three times daily; lifts give access to all levels, the pavilion and other areas of interest. There is a museum behind the pavilion containing the Ashes and other memorabilia.

The Oval

Kennington SE11 5SS

Tel: 020 7582-6660 *Ticket office:* 020 7820-6650 *Fax:* 020 7735-7769 *website:* www.surreycricket.com

A regular test match venue and home to Surrey County Cricket Club (SCCC). It is situated southeast of Vauxhall Station and northeast of Oval tube station. It is now known as the Amp Oval. Different arrangements apply for ordinary county games and for international games, where the crowds are much larger and no cars are allowed on site.

For county games: parking spaces are available through the Hobbs Gates in the main forecourt and, at the Vauxhall End, behind the Fender Stand. It is a good idea to phone in advance. There are approximately ten chair spaces, with step-free access through the reception area, in front of the Laker Stand and the Bedser Stand at the Pavilion End.

For test matches and one-day internationals: SCCC hires local CPs. On Oval Way, 100m from the Vauxhall Centre Gate, there are 80-100 CP spaces kept for disabled spectators. Ringing in advance is advised. From here, there is step-free access to a large, newly-concreted area in front of the Gover and Fender Stands, with around 100 wheelchair spaces.

There is step-free access to the club shop on the GF of the Laker Stand, by the reception.

The Mound Bar and the Middle Bar, both at the Pavilion end, have +1 step. The Foster's Bar, and a refreshments stand at the Vauxhall End are step free but only open during international games. The only restaurant available to non-members is on the third floor of the Bedser Stand, accessible by lift (D75 W90 L140). **Adapted toilet (D75 ST140 inward opening door)** in the main reception, and a **wheelchair toilet (D75 ST90)** on the first floor of the Bedser Stand, to the right of the lift mentioned above. There is another **wheelchair toilet** (not seen) on the third floor of the Bedser Stand, and an **adapted toilet (D85 ST80 inward opening door)** on the second floor of the members' pavilion, accessed by a lift (D75 W125 L135). The last **wheelchair toilet (D90 ST80)** is at the other side of the ground behind the Fender Stand. If you phone beforehand, they may be able to send you a plan of the ground.

Fishing see write-up on Lee Valley in the chapter on *Days out*, and the Hyde Park write-up in *Parks*.

Rowing

Henley Royal Regatta is the most important event in the rowing calendar and usually takes place in early July. The town gets extremely crowded, as do pubs, restaurants and hotels in the area, and parking is difficult. If you phone in advance you can arrange to drop off a passenger outside the general enclosure. It is possible to hire a boat and moor alongside the course, but book it months in advance and arrive very early in order to get a mooring. Similarly with parking, the trick is to arrive really early, and make a day of it. Bring a picnic to avoid hassles with getting food. Parking concessions to **BB** holders may be suspended locally because of the volume of traffic.

The towpath, which of course gets crowded, is tarmac for about 500m on the side of the river farthest from the town. Thereafter it becomes narrower and rougher. There are two temporary enclosures set aside for watching the race by the bridge on the Berkshire side. Both are grass and get muddy when it is wet. There is a general enclosure with seating, mainly in deckchairs. The stewards' enclosure (basically for members and friends) has a small area set aside for chair users. For membership, or other information, write to the Secretary, Regatta Headquarters, Henley-on-Thames, Oxon RG9 2LY *Tel:* 01491-572153 *Fax:* 01491-575509 *website*: www.hrr.co.uk.

Rugby

Twickenham
Rugby Road, Twickenham, Middx TW1 1DZ
Tel: 020 892-2000 *Fax:* 020 8892-9816 *website:* www.rfu.com
The home of English rugby football. The stadium has been extensively redeveloped, and development of the South Stand continues. Chair users have been extremely well provided for. Tickets for chair spaces are allocated from Twickenham. For international matches, it is advisable to get there really early, as some of the surrounding roads are closed well before the match. There are nearly 300 chair spaces, and a similar number for helpers. Over 200 spaces are at pitch level in the North, South and East Stands, and there are others on Level Three in the South and West Stands, accessed by lift (D120 W150 L170). There are two lifts on either side of the South Stand.

Car parking is provided either within the stadium or at the adjacent *Tesco* supermarket. For details it is best to phone in advance. There is a low bar specifically for chair users on Level Two, reached by the same lifts.

Six wheelchair toilets on ground level on either side of the North Stand, and **four wheelchair toilets** on Level Three. The ones we saw were **D70 + ST70 +**. All Rugby Store shops on the ground level can be reached step free.

Soccer

Following the modernisation of all the Premier League and First Division grounds in the 1990s, the facilities for disabled spectators at most grounds have improved considerably. Wheelchair spaces with step-free access and with a wheelchair toilet nearby are provided at all grounds. Booking procedures vary, and you will need to check with the club over individual matches. Some major games and local derbys will be 'all ticket'. The clubs vary somewhat in their attitude to disabled spectators. Prices also vary, some admitting both chair users and a helper for free, whilst some charge. Whilst a reduced entry cost is a well intended gesture, *what is important is that all potential spectators with disabilities can get in.*

At the main grounds there are no longer any terraces, where spectators were able to stand to watch a match. As a result a group of disabled people who may have a problem are those with arthritis. This is because most seats are small, with cramped legroom, stopping you from stretching your legs! Access to most seats is via steps.

A much more detailed guidebook called *Access to Football Grounds* is available, which was published early in 2003 by PHSP. To get a copy contact Access Project, 39 Bradley Gardens, West Ealing W13 8HE or look at our *website:* www.accessproject-phsp.org.

Some grounds have an area nearby where chair users and other disabled people can use their BB. These arrangements are usually somewhat ad hoc, and can vary from match to match. Check when you book. Many grounds are situated in residential areas and were built long before most of us had cars. As a result, the approaches can get blocked up long before kick off and opportunities for parking are zilch. Be warned! In the *Football Grounds* guidebook we suggest the best ways of using accessible transport to get to and from grounds.

Arsenal FC
Highbury Stadium, Avenell Road N5 1BU
Tel: 020 7704-4000 (club) 020 7704-4040 (ticket office)
website: www.arsenal.co.uk
Disabled persons' contact: Angela Alefounder at the club
Spaces for wheelchair users: 102 in total; 10 away
Highbury is a ground with recent developments at the North Bank and Clock Ends. All the stands have two tiers. It is situated in a residential area and houses back on to the ground on two sides. It is a long walk to go all the way round the ground. The area is slightly

hilly. Chair spaces are pitchside, with home supporters having a slightly raised platform.

Charlton Athletic FC
The Valley, Floyd Road, Charlton SE7 8BL
Tel: 020 8333-4000 (club) 020 8333-4010 (ticket office) *Textphone:* 020 8333-4094
website: www.cafc.co.uk
Disabled persons' contact: Alan Milner (Mon + Fri only) *e-mail*: disability@cafc.co.uk
Disabled Supporters Association: *Tel:* 020 8302-6509
Spaces for wheelchair users: 104 in total; 7 away
The Valley is in a residential area of east London quite close to the Millennium Dome. Development in recent years has resulted in new West and North stands. The area around the ground is somewhat hilly. Street parking is difficult. There are spaces for wheelchair users at pitchside, mid-tier and at the top of stands.

Chelsea FC
Stamford Bridge, Fulham Road SW6 1HS
Tel: 020 7385-5545 (club) 020 7386-7799 (ticket office)
website: www.chelsea.co.uk
Disabled persons' contact: Jill Dawson
Spaces for wheelchair users: 106 in total; 30 away
Stamford Bridge's development is now complete. The club own a large site in exclusive southwest London called *Chelsea Village* which houses hotels, night clubs and penthouse flats. The only way into the site is off the Fulham Road. A railway runs behind the West Stand and *Chelsea Village* buildings surround the remaining stands. The area around the ground is fairly flat. The spaces for wheelchair users are nearly all pitchside with more or less flat access. Parking is very difficult.

Crystal Palace FC
Selhurst Park, Whitehorse Lane SE25 6PU
Tel: 020 8768-6000 (club) 020 8771-8841 (ticket office)
website: www.cpfc.co.uk
Disabled persons' contact: Cheryl Smith (ticket office)
Roger Dixon (visually-impaired supporters)
Spaces for wheelchair users: 54 in total; 12 away
Selhurst Park is in a residential area in south London. Houses more or less surround the ground. There is a small CP outside a *Sains-*

bury's store by the ground and street parking is difficult. There are some quite heavy slopes around the ground, especially by the Holmesdale Road end. There are two areas for disabled fans, a separate platform at one corner and a mid-tier area.

Fulham FC
Stadium: Rangers Stadium, South Africa Road W12 7PA
Correspondence address: FFC Training Ground, Motspur Park, Surrey, KT3 6PT
Tel: 0870 4421-222 (club) 0870 4421-234 (ticket office)
website: www.fulhamfc.co.uk
At the time of writing, where Fulham will be playing in the future is unclear. They are currently playing at the QPR ground, and there are discussions about ground-sharing with Chelsea next season (2003/4). Both grounds are described here.

Millwall FC
The New Den, Bolina Road SE16 3LN
Tel: 0207 7232-1222 (club) 020 7231-9999 (ticket office)
website: www.millwallfc.co.uk
Spaces for wheelchair users: 78 in total
The New Den has four identical two-tier stands in an enclosed site in south London. Railway lines run past two sides of the ground, with access only being from Zampa Road. As with most London grounds, parking is difficult. There is one pitch-length mid-tier area for chair users.

Queens Park Rangers FC
Rangers Stadium, South Africa Road W12 7PA
Tel: 020 8743-0262 (club) 020 8740-2575 (ticket office)
website: www.qpr.co.uk
Disabled persons' contact: Jenny Elliot c/o ticket office
Spaces for wheelchair users: 19 in total; 5 away
Rangers Stadium, is home (at the time of print) to both QPR and Fulham. The enclosed tight-fitting ground, with four more or less even-sized stands, is in a flat residential area near Shepherd's Bush. The Uxbridge Road (A4020) runs nearby. Parking is difficult. There are two small areas for chair users, one on each side.

Tottenham Hotspur FC
White Hart Lane, 748 High Road, Tottenham N17 0AP
Tel: 020 8365-5000 (club) 0870 011-2222 (ticket office)
website: www.spurs.co.uk

Disabled persons' contact: *Tel:* at club: 020 8365-5161
Spaces for wheelchair users: 48 in total; 7 away
White Hart Lane is a smart enclosed ground in north London. Recent developments leave only the West stand with support columns partially blocking the view. The area around is flat and the site is surrounded by a school and a residential area. There is talk of extending capacity or of relocation, but this is difficult. There are limited provisions for disabled fans at present.

West Ham United FC
Upton Park, Boleyn Ground, Green Street E13 9AZ
Tel: 020 8548-2748 (club) 020 8548-2700 (ticket office)
website: www.westhamunited.co.uk
Disabled persons' contact: Gina Allen in ticket office *Tel:* 020 8548-2725
A Disabled Supporters Association is in the process of formation
Spaces for wheelchair users: 98 in total; 6 away
Upton Park is in a fairly dense residential area deep in east London. It has a large new stand, the Dr Martens with two castle turrets outside marking the entrance. Developments of the last decade have extended capacity to nearly 40,000. West Ham tube station is within two miles and is fully accessible. There are several areas for chair users.

Wimbledon FC
Contact Details for 2002-3
Selhurst Park SE25 6PY
Tel: 020 8771-2233 (club) 020 8771-8841 (ticket office)
website: www.wimbledon-fc.co.uk
Disabled persons' contact: Cheryl Smith in ticket office
The current situation for Wimbledon is somewhat confused. They have a shared ground with Crystal Palace at Selhurst Park for the last decade. The club have since announced a move to a new stadium in Milton Keynes.

New Wembley Stadium
Enquiries: 11th Floor, York House, Empire Way, HA9 OWS
Tel: 020 8795-9000 *Fax*: 020 8795-5050
website: www.wembleynationalstadium.com
The information below is modified from details we were given by the New Wembley Stadium Group. The stadium will have the capacity to hold over 90,000 spectators. A key feature is that it will consist of a

single bowl rather than four separate stands. There will be a spacious external concourse. It is planned that access for disabled supporters will be available to all levels and facilities. Parking for up to 250 **BB** holders is included in the plans, and there will be up to 580 spaces for chair users and 400 for ambulant disabled supporters, spread throughout the stadium and at all price levels. We hope that earlier mistakes in other new grounds and stands about sightlines and an obstructed view when people in front stand up will be avoided.

Tennis

The All England Lawn Tennis and Croquet Club
Church Road, Wimbledon SW19 5AE
Tel: 020 8946-2244 for ticket information, 020 8971-2473 for ticket enquiries and 020 8944-1066 for other business
website: www.wimbledon.org
This is where the world's most famous tennis tournament takes place, for two weeks towards the end of June. The site is triangular in shape, and is effectively over 600m down two of the sides and some 200m across the base, so it's quite large. Along the Church Road side, the ground is only gently sloping, but there's a considerable hill by No 1 Court up towards the Aorangi picnic area currently better known as Henman Hill. During the tournament, the whole area gets very busy with tens of thousands of fans watching matches and generating huge amounts of traffic. Site development is ongoing, and a new No 2 Court is due to be completed by 2005.

There are just a few show courts which will host the most prestigious matches. On all of these you have to book in advance to get a place. Early on in the tournament, many of the matches are played on Courts 4 to 19, and it's possible to get really quite close to the action, although you'll almost certainly have to be patient waiting for a slot or a spot from which you can get a good view. The site is very 'open' so roaming around and taking in the atmosphere and stopping to have some strawberries and cream can be as much a part of the day out as watching tennis.

There's an excellent plan/map available which shows the step-free routes around the site, and you would do well to get hold of one of these in advance. The standard *Wheelchair Users' Guide* has a small plan, but a double size one (which is much clearer) is available if you ask. Although the site is quite large and confusing, particularly when there are literally thousands of people there, there is a small army of well-trained people wandering around with a sign over their heads saying 'information'. We found that they were both helpful and knowledgeable.

The provisions for disabled spectators are fairly minimal. The number of chair users who can get tickets is tiny. Even on the brand new No 1 Court there are only forty spaces for disabled people amongst some 10,000 spectators. As there is little or no provision for disabled walkers (for example to enable them to book the more easily accessible seats) the 40 seems fairly minimal especially as there are only ten spaces on the (much older) Centre Court. We understand that there are some difficult compromises to be made, and that there are commercial considerations affecting policy. However the official guidelines for new stadia being built suggest a minimum of 100 spaces for chair users in a 10,000 seater stadium – and **there seem to be NO proper guidelines yet covering provisions for disabled walkers.** Nearly all the seats involve stepped access, and generally there are quite a lot of steps. Little thought has been given to allocating those seats which do not involve many steps to disabled walkers.

If you do manage to come, you'll be well looked after.

Getting hold of tickets is a somewhat chancy process. Many go to corporate entertainers, others are distributed through tennis clubs, and additionally, there is an annual ballot for seats on the show courts. There is a separate ballot for the chair spaces. To apply, write to the Ticket Department, POB 98, Church Road, Wimbledon SW19 5AE by the previous December marking both the letter and envelope 'Wheelchair'. The closing date for applications is December 31st. Even if you don't have a ticket, chair users and other disabled people can join the queue 'on the day'. There are some ground entry tickets, and there are unreserved chair spaces on Courts 6, 13, 14, 15, 16, 17, 18 and 19, but most of these courts will not feature the 'big name' players, though you may well get to see some interesting tennis, including veterans' matches and mixed doubles. Be warned that you may have to queue for several hours – but you'll catch something of the atmosphere, even if you only go and watch the big video screen on Henman Hill, and have some strawberries!

There is a reduced entry charge after 5pm.

It is impossible to prebook tickets since almost all show court tickets are issued by ballot. If it were possible, best seats would be: Centre: Row Z step free, back row B – use lift by Gate 5 for chair users' area (see earlier); Court One: 4 to Row J at SW corner (if chair users' access is used), +10 to Row R (public staircases).

There is no on-site parking but BB spaces are available in Car Park 8 opposite Gate 4 on Church Road. You almost certainly need to reserve a space in advance. Car parking in the area around the club is inevitably very difficult and is strictly controlled. Many local people rent out their front gardens during the tournament fortnight. There is a drop-off point by Gate 19 next to Car Park 4 behind Court One. Note that the nearest accessible station is Wimbledon for both main-line trains and the Underground. If you have a problem walking long distances, it's probably worth taking a taxi to the club, and getting dropped off outside one of the gates – and getting a cab back afterwards. A good pickup point is the rank just to the left of Gate 13 as you come out. There are nine parking bays for electric scooters by the debenture lounge at Centre Court, and scooters must enter the grounds through Gate 4 off Church Road.

Centre Court has four spaces for chair users at court level (North East corner), which are accessed from under the debenture holders' lounge. Another six spaces at the very back of the South East corner are accessed by a lift (D100 W110 L110) opposite Gate 5. There is a steep ramp from the lift to the viewing area, but stewards are usually on hand to help. **Two wheelchair toilets (D70 + ST70 +)** in the North West corner and South East corners of the court.

Court Number One has 20 spaces for chair users on each side of the court with adjacent seating for helpers. Access is through Gangways 8, 12, 26 and 30. There's a **wheelchair toilet** at each corner of the court.

There are unreserved viewing areas on Courts 6 (grass sloped area), 13, 14, 15, 16, 17, 18 and 19. All are courtside and are accessed step-free. There is also a step-free route to Courts 3, 4, 5, 6, 7, 8, 9 and 10. The main area of the **Aorangi Picnic Hill** has steep ramped access at its north end near to Gate 19.

There is a wide variety of catering facilities all around the site which as far as we could see were all sensibly accessible. At certain times, they can become very crowded which presents its own difficulty. There are a good number of **wheelchair toilets and cubicles** around the site. All are clearly marked on maps and operate with RADAR keys, and several are around Court Number One. Those that we saw were all **D70 + ST70 + .**

There is also a museum and tearoom, see the chapter on *Museums and galleries.*

Annual events

We include simply a fraction of the events that take place every year. In general, provision for disabled spectators is now made at most events, and certainly things have improved. Sometimes you have to make enquiries and arrangements in advance. Currently, chair users are better provided for than disabled walkers, in the sense that there are sometimes special arrangements made and enclosures at viewing points provided. A practical suggestion is for disabled people who can walk a bit but who find crowds and steps and distances a problem to use a wheelchair just occasionally, in order to go to the Proms, Beating the Retreat or even to Wimbledon tennis championships. It's not cheating and it might open up possibilities of getting around that you just hadn't thought of as being practical.

There's a more comprehensive list in the *Eyewitness Guide*, or the *Rough Guide*, but we mention most of the principal ones here. You can also get information from the LTB. We have included many venues for major shows and sporting events in the guide text. Some of the events are open-air, and therefore accessible.

The Chinese New Year is celebrated in the streets of Soho with paper dragons, processions and a mini-carnival. Can be very crowded. *Jan/Feb*

Pancake races are held at Lincoln's Inn Fields on Shrove Tuesday, six weeks before Easter. *Feb/Mar*

Richmond Festival Amateur and professional performances in venues around Richmond, including the Orange Tree and Richmond theatres. For information *Tel:* 020 8979-3848 or 020 8994-0934 *website:* www.richmondfestival.org.uk *Feb/Mar*

Spring Equinox celebration, Tower Hill. An ancient ritual involving Druids wearing white hooded gowns to mark the coming of Spring *Tel:* 020 8659-4879. *Mar 21*

The Oxford and Cambridge Boat Race is rowed from Putney to Mortlake. To get a view, get there early (Hammersmith Bridge is often a good spot) but remember that you'll only get a brief view of the crews and the pursuing launches and there'll be a lot of people around, crowding the local pubs and making parking awkward. It's a good idea to bring a small radio to keep yourself informed about the race. *Late Mar/Apr*

The London Harness Horse Parade is held on Easter Monday with brewers' vans, drays and other horse-drawn vehicles on show. The parade goes twice round the Inner Circle in Battersea Park at about midday. *Mar/Apr*

The London Marathon run from Greenwich to Westminster is a mixture of serious athletics and a fun event with the runners going past one street party after another. Disabled participants play a prominent role. *Apr*

The Chelsea Flower Show is organised by the Royal Horticultural Society and is held in the grounds of the Royal Hospital, Chelsea. Parking in the area is difficult and entrance is not cheap. It may be possible for BB holders to negotiate parking with the organisers (RHS, 80 Vincent Square SW1P 2PB *Tel:* 020 7834-4333; Flower Show Information *Tel*: 020 7649-1885; *website*: www.rhs.org.uk/chelsea). The show gets extremely crowded. A good time to go, to avoid the crowds, is early in the morning; or you could become a member of the Society and go to the preview day. It's a glorious show and access is generally good. Main entrance on the Embankment, with flat access. Paths are either tarmac or grass but there are some kerbs and gentle slopes. There are two well-signposted portable adapted toilets, not quite big enough for sideways transfer but very adequate. If you can cope with the crowds and want to see a fantastic flower show, this is the place to go. There are picnic areas, plenty of shade and bands playing. Note that guide dogs are not allowed to go round, but the organisers can normally provide an escort if needed. Contact them in advance. **A special evening for disabled people is arranged every year**. Call the organisers for details. *Late May*

Trooping the Colour is the best known of the several events held during the summer in Horse Guards Parade. Temporary stands built on scaffolding are erected around the square. Access is up steps and there are bench-type seats and few handrails. A procession also goes to and from the Palace along the Mall. *Saturday nearest Jun 11.*

The other events include **Beating the Retreat** by various regiments, and the Major General's Review which is a rehearsal for the Queen's

Birthday Parade. Disabled spectators for the military events should contact the Brigade Major, HQ Household Division, Horse Guards, Whitehall SW1A 2AX. Write in as early as Jan/Feb, especially for Trooping the Colour, as a ballot is held for places. *Tel*: 020 7414-2479 for Trooping the Colour and the Review, and *Tel*: 020 7414-2271 for Beating the Retreat. There are 50 chair spaces for Trooping the Colour, up to 100 for the Review and about 40 for Beating the Retreat.

City of London Festival, 230 Bishopsgate EC2M 4HW *Tel:* 020 7377-0540 *website*: www.colf.org. The festival consists mainly of concerts and exhibitions in various churches and halls, some of which aren't otherwise open to the public. The main box office is situated in the Barbican Centre *Tel:* 020 7638-8891 *Textphone:* 020 7382-7297. Although most of the concerts and events take place in old buildings where there are steps (at one or two venues there are quite a lot of steps), the organisers say that they can help any disabled person to get in, provided they know about it. The organiser we spoke to was very clued up and knew how many steps there were at most of the halls and where there was a lift to bypass them. If he didn't know precisely, he would find out. As they use different places each year, there is little point in giving too much detail. Many of the venues used are described elsewhere in the guide. *June/July*

Hampton Court Flower Show. Slightly easier to get into than Chelsea. *July*

Open Air Theatre Regent's Park and **open air concerts** at Kenwood House take place throughout the summer. Both the Open Air Theatre and Kenwood House are described elsewhere in the guide. *May/Sep*

Promenade Concerts take place at the Albert Hall during *August and September*. The famous Last Night of the Proms is on the *Saturday nearest 15 Sept*. A parallel concert for the last night is held in Hyde Park, with separate live music as well as linkup to the Hall. (See Royal Albert Hall under *Music venues – classical*)

Notting Hill Carnival A huge event in the Ladbroke Grove and Notting Hill area, W11. There are carnival processions with colourful floats and participants, and much street-dancing and partying. It is primarily a celebration of the local West Indian community and its traditions, but it has grown from being a purely local event into something that attracts tens of thousands of people. Can be great fun, though local parking is a nightmare! *August Bank Holiday weekend*

Fair on Hampstead Heath NW3 (near North End Way). This is held on August Bank Holiday and there are likely to be other fairs at other places on spring and summer bank holidays. See the local press and *Time Out* or *What's On.*

London Open House Weekend when many interesting buildings are opened up for just one or two days in the year. Information from London Open House, Unit C1, 39-51 Highgate Road NW5 1RS *Tel:* 020 7267-7644 *website:* www.londonopenhouse.org. They publish a listing which includes basic access information. You can download it as a .pdf file, get it directly from the address above, or it is included free with the *Evening Standard* one day early in September. The organisation also organises architectural tours throughout the year. *Sep*

The State Opening of Parliament, usually at the end of *October*, provides an uncrowded opportunity to see pageantry and the Queen. We recommend viewing from the south side of the Mall.

Guy Fawkes' Night commemorates the attempt in 1605 to blow up monarch, Lords and Commons when assembled in Westminster. There are both private and public firework displays. All generally accessible. *November 5th and over the adjacent weekend/s*

The London to Brighton Veteran Car Rally starts at Hyde Park Corner. It commemorates the Anniversary of Emancipation and is an opportunity to see period costumes as well as cars. *First Sunday in November*

The Lord Mayor's Show is a large carnival-style procession through the City. The City Information Centre can advise about the precise route. *Second Saturday in November*

Christmas Decorations There are usually spectacular lights in Oxford Street and Regent Street, and traditionally there is a Norwegian pine tree in Trafalgar Square during *December.*

408

Open-air activities

Open-air events and venues have the dual attraction of being generally accessible and surprisingly varied. There's music, politics, art and shopping, in addition to the parks, historical statues and architecture. Doing things in the open can enable you to get a real feel for London – and to see and experience many things that the visitor intent on the standard tourist circuit will miss. We have mentioned elsewhere the potential interest and variety of London's statues, and if you follow this up you will find out a great deal more than most people who either visit or even live in London.

Boating and river trips

Around London there are numerous rivers, canals and waterways which, with planning and organisation, can be used to provide an enjoyable way of touring some scenic, out-of-the-way parts of London. The Thames passes through the centre of London and boats can be taken from Westminster, Millennium, Embankment, Tower and Greenwich piers among others. All these have step-free ramped access down on to the pontoon, though this is usually rather steep, and there is often a small step on and off the boats.

The piers are operated through TfL's London Riverboat Services (*Tel:* 020 7941-2400 *website:* www.tfl-river.co.uk), who can give details of different operators and can provide some access information. A map showing all the piers can be downloaded from the TfL website. TFL publish a *River Thames Boat Service Guide* which is regularly updated. More of the boats are becoming wheelchair accessible, but it's still a bit of a lottery as to whether the boat you want to take will be one of them. The TfL Call Centre (*Tel:* 020 7222-1234) can give full timetable information.

The Main Piers

Westminster Millennium Pier About 50m along the Victoria Embankment from Westminster Bridge. There is step-free access from Westminster Tube Station. The $+5-5$ steps over the flood barrier can be bypassed by a ramp. Portakabin contains **wheelchair toilet (D85 ST180 NKS)** with ramped entrance, located on Victoria Embankment, 50m east of the entrance to the pier. On exiting the pier, wheelchair users should take the ramp to the right as signposted.

Millennium Pier On the south bank of the Thames, just by the London Eye. It provides step-free access to boats.

Charing Cross Pier Not used as much as in the past, it is situated just to the north of Hungerford Bridge, and there is a step-free route down from the Embankment.

Tower Pier Situated off Lower Thames Street, just to the west of the Tower of London, it provides steep ramped access down to the boats.

Greenwich Millennium Pier Located next to the Cutty Sark, it provides ramped access to riverboats, with a slight hump at the top of the ramp. There is a **wheelchair toilet** next to the entrance.

Riverboat Services

There are a number of operating companies. Some specialise in scheduled services, others in chartered trips. We have concentrated on the scheduled services. Of these, we found that *City Cruises* and *Catamaran Cruisers* were the most accessible. However, wheelchair users are welcome with other operators and although access to the boats is not necessarily step free there are generally staff available to help.

City Cruises, Cherry Garden Pier, Cherry Garden Street, Rotherhithe SE16 4TU *Tel:* 020 7740-0400 *e-mail:* info@citycruises.com. This operator runs five boats which it claims are accessible. The service runs from Westminster and Millennium Piers to Greenwich, stopping en route at Tower; a variety of different tickets is available. A disabled person and those travelling with them travel half price. Trips are at least every hour throughout the day.

One boat we travelled on, *Millennium Dawn*, had a small lip from Westminster Pier and a lip into the covered seating area on the lower deck, where there is a bar, tables, fixed seats and a large space for wheelchairs. There are + 12 steps to the open top deck, where there is more fixed seating. Staff will help chair users up and down. **Adapted toilet (D70 ST66)** on the lower deck. Another boat, *Spirit of the Millennium*, was the same except for + 1 and then a lip to the lower deck, + 14 to the upper deck, **adapted toilet (D75 ST100 partially obstructed by the basin, inward opening door)**.

Catamaran Cruisers, Embankment Pier, Victoria Embankment WC2N 6NU *Tel:* 020 7987-1185 *e-mail:* info@bateauxlondon.com *website:* www.catamarancruisers.co.uk

Operating a hop-on/hop-off service which stops at many piers, and a circular cruise which starts and ends at Westminster pier. This is a popular service which advertises itself as being 'accessible'. Only the circular cruise can guarantee step-free access, as the hop-on/hop-off service only uses one suitable boat per day, usually the 11.15 from Greenwich and 16.00 from Westminster. Phone in advance for details. We took the circular cruise, which operates in the summer months hourly from 14.30. There is a threshold/lip at the entrance. The boat has one level, with fixed seating and a space for wheelchairs. Food and drink is available. **Wheelchair toilet (D90 ST75)** contained movable cleaning equipment.

In the future, more boats should become accessible. For example, *Crown River Cruises* (*Tel:* 020 7936-2033 *website:* www.crownriver.com) have five boats, of which they claim at least two are already accessible, while they hope to modify the whole fleet within the next few years.

Markets

Street markets tend to be crowded but the stalls are all basically accessible and they are lively and interesting places. If you're selective you can often pick up a bargain. It's advisable to arrive early to avoid the worst of the crush. Around the big markets there will be parking restrictions, even on a Sunday. A useful book is *The London Market Guide* by Andrew Kershman, published by Metro Publications, PO Box 6636, N1 6PY. Bear in mind that, even for chair users, crowds can be a pickpocket's delight.

There are numerous small markets scattered around the city, but the main ones are:

Brick Lane E1 and E2, operates on Sunday mornings, covering a substantial area. It is off the Bethnal Green Road just north of Shoreditch station. It includes Sclater Street and Cheshire Street. Some of the market is in the street and some in covered areas. It is a general market with a strong East End flavour. Included are electrical goods, hardware, fruit and veg, clothes, cameras, books and old furniture etc.

Brixton SW9. Mainly around Brixton station off Atlantic Road, Electric Avenue and Coldharbour Lane. Dominated now by the local black community, with all kinds of food stalls, African fabrics and clothes and stalls where soul, rap and reggae are played and sold.

Camden N1. A group of markets running the length of Camden High Street into the southern part of Chalk Farm Road. Some are on derelict land off the road with roughish surfaces. It's a haven for hipsters and wannabe hipsters, and gives you a high chance of spotting drummers from struggling indie bands.

Covent Garden WC2 see chapter on *Places of interest* under Holborn and the Strand areas.

Greenwich SE10, has a Flea Market in Thames Street open on Sundays, an Antiques market in Greenwich High Road open Saturdays and Sundays, and an indoor Crafts Market in Bosun's Yard, Greenwich Church Street, also open on Saturdays and Sundays. There's also the Central Market in Stockwell Street.

Petticoat Lane, Middlesex Street E1, and surrounding streets. Usually crowded, and parking nearby can be a problem. Something of a tourist trap, but very varied stalls and quite an atmosphere. Main market on Sunday, some stalls during the week as well.

Portobello Road W11. This spills over into the surrounding streets. Like Camden it is really a group of markets with different things to sell and different opening times. Antiques and bric-a-brac on Saturday is the really big event, but also clothes, fruit and vegetables, hardware, etc. Monday to Saturday.

Other markets include: Atlantic Rd SW9; Chapel Market, White Conduit Street N1; Columbia Road E2; The Cut SE1; East Street SE17; High Street Walthamstow E17; Kingsland Waste E8; Leather Lane EC1; Ridley Road E8; Vallance Road E1; Whitecross Street EC2.

Parks

London has several large and delightful parks. Even near the centre you can get right away from the traffic and bustle. The main parks were all parts of royal estates and books published specifically on the Royal Parks are available from The Old Police House, Hyde Park W2 2UH. More information can be found on the *website:* www.royalparks.gov.uk.

Battersea Park SW11
A lovely spot with a lake, zoo and river frontage on the south side of the Thames. Ample parking. Good for picnics and relaxing. Most of

the paths are paved, and odd steps can be bypassed. There are just a few slopes.

On the riverfront is the **London Peace Pagoda**, a magnificent structure with gold tableaux depicting the birth, enlightenment, preaching and death of the Buddha. It's +14 steps to the walkway around it, but you can see perfectly well from ground level.

There's a small zoo for children south of Parade, and east of the pagoda. A ramp bypasses the −10 at the entrance. In the zoo itself there is ramped access everywhere, bypassing the odd step, and it is step free to the animal contact area and the reptile house.

The restaurant to the east of the boating lake has step-free access, but fixed seating inside. **Wheelchair toilet (D85 ST90)** 400m west of the Chelsea Bridge entrance, near to the zoo. **Wheelchair cubicles (D75 ST70)** in men's and women's toilets in the southwest corner of the park, 30m west along Carriage Drive from the all-weather sports pitches.

Greenwich Park see chapter on *Places of interest*, outer London.

Hampstead Heath see chapter on *Places of interest*, outer London.

Holland Park W8 and W14.
Access from Kensington High Street or the CP with four BB spaces in Abbotsbury Road. Pleasant area with tarmac paths. Café with flat access from the side, near Holland House. Open-air theatre nearby, +15 at the entrance or a 30m slope on the left. **Wheelchair toilet (D80 ST125 NKS)** 100m from the entrance on Ilchester Place.

Hyde Park and Kensington Gardens W2 and W8.
Tel: 020 7298-2100 (Park Manager)
This vast stretch of parkland covering over 240 hectares was a hunting ground for Henry VIII. It measures some 2km by 0.75km and includes a large artificial lake. The whole area is fairly flat, and there are tarmac paths throughout. Limited parking on West Carriage Drive which runs between the two parks, with small CPs either side of the Serpentine Bridge. There is also a large UGCP with entrances off Park Lane and North Carriage Drive; but note that there's a longish walk of approaching 500m to get out.

There are benches scattered around the parks, and in the summer it is possible to hire deck chairs from the north side of the Serpentine, or from the round pond in Kensington Gardens. There are tracks for cycling and horse riding.

Liberty Drives *Tel:* 020 8960-3722 or 07767-498-096 provide free five-seater electric carts which take disabled people around the park. Ring to check when they are operating; when we visited they were available four days a week during the summer. There are pickup points at most of the main gates, and at the CP north of the Serpentine Bridge. You can arrange to be dropped off anywhere in the park, and be picked up later. The carts are primarily designed for disabled walkers, but there are plans afoot to provide wheelchair-accessible carts in the near future.

These parks are a lovely place to come and sit outside on the grass in the summertime – it's easy to forget that you're in the middle of a big city!

You can take a 'green' route right the way through central London by going through Kensington Gardens, Hyde Park, Green Park and St James's Park.

Some of the Parks' principal features
- the **Serpentine Gallery** (see chapter on *Museums and Galleries*);
- **fishing** is allowed at the eastern end of the Serpentine;
- an **open-air market** on Sundays by the park railings right down the Bayswater Road as far as Queensway;
- the **Rose Garden** by Hyde Park Corner;
- the **Orangery Gardens**, between Kensington Palace and the Orangery;
- the **Round Pond** for model boats, ducks and swimming dogs is towards Kensington on high ground, approached by a broad tarmac path;
- **Speakers' Corner** is near Marble Arch with easy access. Here you can listen to people talking about anything and everything – particularly on a Sunday afternoon.

Refreshments are available from:
- the Dell, a self-service restaurant on the eastern end of the Serpentine, which has flat access to chairs and tables inside and out;
- the Lido Café, next to the Lido. To get inside, use the ramp at the eastern end of the building;
- the Orangery in Kensington Gardens.

There are several kiosks near Marble Arch and by the Black Lion Gate, Queensway.

The Lido *Tel:* 020 7706-3422 *website:* www.serpentinelido.com is located on the southern side of the Serpentine. The Lido incorporates a children's playground and paddling pool, grass and deckchairs for sunbathing, and changing rooms and access to a part of the Serpentine which is cordoned off for swimming (max. depth 2m). A lift (D75 W105 L130) gives access from the GF to the paddling pool. On this level there is a raised section with + 2 steps where there are some pub benches. The playground is − 3 − 4 − 3 but these can be bypassed by going down on the grass. For swimming, a concrete 'beach' can be accessed by crossing the bridge over the public footpath and going down − 8 − 12 steps. Flat access to the beach is on the GF opposite the main entrance; the gate needs unlocking by a staff member. There's a **wheelchair toilet (D85 ST100)** behind the stairs on the GF. **Boating on the Serpentine** is from the northern side of the lake. There are wheelchair-accessible motor boats which provide a half-hour trip around the Serpentine; run by Bluebird Boats, The Boathouse, Serpentine Road, Hyde Park W2 2UH, *Tel:* 020 7262-1330, *Fax:* 020 7262-1440. Staff members will also help transfer people into rowing boats if necessary.

There are several **wheelchair/adapted toilets** as follows:
- at the Dell Café, **adapted toilet (D90 ST50)** when the baby changer is retracted;
- **wheelchair cubicles (D80 ST85 NKS)** in both the Ladies and Gents about 100m east of the Dell;
- **adapted cubicles** in both Ladies and Gents some 200m northwest of the Dell (Both **NKS**, Ladies **D80 ST59**, Gents **D90 ST75**). There is a tiny step en route to each;
- by the Lido, as mentioned above;
- in the southwest corner of Kensington Gardens by Palace Gate. Flat access from Kensington Gore, but − 5 from the park. Both Ladies and Gents have quite large cubicles, but with inward opening doors **(D75)**;
- at the **Serpentine Gallery** (see chapter on *Museums and Galleries*).

Regent's Park NW1 see chapter on *Places of interest* under Regent's Park.

Richmond Park, **Surrey** see chapter on *Days out* under Richmond and Kingston.

St James's Park and Green Park SW1 see chapter on *Places of interest* under Westminster and St James's.

Bandstands

Details of performances are available from the various parks super-intendents, and also from the LTB. To get details of all the events in all the royal parks, send a stamped addressed envelope to Old Police House, Hyde Park W2 2UH *Tel:* 020 7298-2000, and ask for a list of summer entertainment programmes.

Some of the performances are of very high quality and to stop and listen to an open-air concert can provide a welcome contrast and rest. Bandstands are to be found in many places in central London, including the following:

Hyde Park W2, just north of Dell restaurant.

St James's Park SW1, near the north side of the bridge over the lake.

Tower Place EC3, opposite the Tower of London.

Victoria Embankment Gardens WC2, near Embankment Station.
Further out, stands are to be found in a number of parks, including Battersea Park SW1, Regent's Park, Victoria Park E9 and on Parliament Hill NW3.

Street art displays

There are several large displays of painting, sculpture and handiwork to be seen in London, mainly on Sunday. All are easily accessible. It's fun to wander along to look even if you don't intend to buy. The main ones are:

- in the Bayswater Road along the railings of Hyde Park, stretching sometimes almost the entire length from Marble Arch to Queensway;
- in Piccadilly along the Green Park railings from Hyde Park Corner;
- in summer only in Heath Street, Hampstead, starting at Whitestone Road.

Exhibition halls

Exhibitions and special events are held at various places in London throughout the year. Some of the main ones are listed below. Access provisions have improved considerably during the past few years, but for some exhibitions the problem is simply the number of people who want to go and therefore the parking problem outside and the difficulty of seeing inside. Exhibitors at an exhibition often build special temporary stands inside the hall, and sometimes build in steps rather than a ramp. This is something we cannot guide you round, as it is highly variable.

Obviously, an off-peak visit (such as on a weekday morning) has its attractions, but not all disabled people and their friends can avoid the crowded peak periods, and organisers need to take note of this. The responsibility for the use of the building lies with the exhibition or event organiser and not primarily with the building manager or owner. The user hires the hall lock, stock and barrel and decides how it shall be organised and used – and that includes the use of lifts, catering facilities and so on. The number of chair users admitted is at the discretion of the hall management and the event organiser.

Alexandra Palace, Alexandra Palace Way, Wood Green N22 7AY *Tel:* 020 8365-2121 *Fax:* 020 8883-3999 *website:* www.alexandrapalace.com *e-mail:* info@alexandrapalace.com. At the top of a steep hill. As you go up through the CP to the entrance there's a fairly severe slope for about 20m. There are not only several BB spaces near both the main west entrance and the east entrance, but there are also drop-off points near the Palace for those with disabled passengers. There are +4 steps to the Palm Gallery where exhibitions are held, but with a ramped bypass. Inside the distances are quite considerable and if you find walking difficult you may well want to use one of the wheelchairs available. The Ice Rink similarly has +4 with a ramped bypass.

Near the entrance there is flat access to a **wheelchair toilet (D85 ST130)** the pub and café, both with movable chairs and tables. The exhibition space is simply vast, but flat everywhere, with bars and snack bars all round the side of the hall. There are four other **wheelchair toilets** on the GF and a lift (D110 W135 L190) to the lower GF where there is another **wheelchair toilet (D90 ST100)**. To the north of the main building, there is also a lake with wheelchair access to fishing areas.

Barbican Exhibition Halls, Golden Lane EC1 *Tel:* 020 7382-7058 (or via the Barbican administration), have step-free/lift access everywhere and wheelchair toilets on all levels. For a general write-up on the Barbican area and the Barbican Centre see chapters on *Places of interest*, and on *Arts centres*.

Central Hall, Westminster SW1, is quite often used for exhibitions and meetings, and has much improved access. See chapter on *Places of worship*.

ExCeL, London Docklands E16 1XL *Tel:* 020 7069-4000 *Fax:* 020 7069-4747 *website:* www.excel-london.co.uk *e-mail:* info@excel-london.co.uk A massive new exhibition and conference centre in Docklands. Situated just north of Royal Victoria Dock, to the west of London City Airport, it is served by the accessible Custom House station on the DLR. There are two vast on-site CPs which claim to have '315 bays suitable for disabled drivers'.

From here, the entrance is step-free, as is the whole site. There are lifts to all four levels and **twenty seven wheelchair toilets**. There are also a number of eating areas with step free access. The site is huge, measuring over 400m by 200m giving a total area of some 90,000 sq metres.

Earl's Court, Warwick Road, SW5 9TA *Tel:* 020 7385-1200 BO 0870 903-9033 *website:* www.eco.co.uk This is one of London's major exhibition centres, and includes a cavernous hall where various events are staged. It is in a residential area, so parking is limited. There are twenty-two BB spaces next to the building, approached from the Warwick Road entrance, and these are allocated on a 'first come first served' basis. There are also spaces reserved for disabled drivers in both the Seagrave Road CP and in the Red CP. You can ring in advance to book these on 0800 056-8444. Earl's Court Piccadilly line platforms have step-free access to street level via a lift and the District Line will become fully accessible during 2003. An access leaflet is available with good floor plans.

There are three venues; Earl's Court 1, where most of the big exhibitions and concerts are held, Earl's Court 2 and Earl's Court Conference Centre. The main entrance is on Warwick Road. From the foyer/reception area, two ramps bypass + 3 + 3 steps. The turnstiles can be bypassed by going through a gate (W76). A platform stairlift (W66 L85) followed by a ramp bypasses + 8 + 2 into the main inner foyer. From here it is step free to Earl's Court 1. Two large lifts (D100 W150 + L150 +) serve all floors of the building, though, for safety reasons, wheelchair access is prohibited to Level Four.

Earl's Court 2 can be reached step free from the entrance off Old Brompton Road, while the Conference Centre, on Level Three, can be reached step free via the lifts.

There are **wheelchair toilets and wheelchair cubicles** in several parts of the building. The one we saw was **D80+ ST80+ NKS**. These include two unisex on the west side of Earl's Court 1, and cubicles in the toilets on the south side of the hall near the Brompton entrance. On level Two in Earl's Court 1 there are unisex toilets on the east side of the hall and on the west side by the first aid post. In Earl's Court 2, there are **adapted toilets** at each end of the GF on the west side. In the Conference Centre there is one unisex toilet to the right of the lifts.

Overall, facilities have improved here enormously over the years. The number of chair users allowed in at any one time is at the discretion of the organisers of particular events, and as these vary widely, it may be best to check.

Olympia Hammersmith Road, West Kensington W14 8UX
Tel: 020 7603-3344 *website:* www.eco.co.uk
This is the larger of the two exhibition and event halls in west London. Both Earl's Court and Olympia are under the same management. Olympia has three separate halls, which may be linked for some of the biggest events like the annual showjumping competition, as well as a conference centre. There is an access leaflet available with good floor plans.

The hall is in a residential area, so parking is a problem. There is a CP at the end of Olympia Way called Olympia Parking. This has six BB spaces allocated. There are more potential spaces on Olympia Way, if the allocated spaces are taken. There is an advanced booking line (0800 056-8444) for the CP.

The **Grand Hall** in Olympia Way (alongside the railway line) has step-free access to the foyer. From here there are several steps to the main GF level, but you can be taken through Gate B where a ramp gives step-free access. The Grand Hall is used, among other things, for showjumping and for computer exhibitions. There are various eateries with step-free access. **Four wheelchair/adapted cubicles**, situated within each Gents and Ladies toilet, on the GF. The one we saw was **D80 ST140**. There is both a passenger lift (D80), which was switched off when we visited, and, if needed, a huge service lift. Either gives step-free access to the upper galleries. There is also a smaller hall, the Pillar Hall, adjacent, with +2 steps bypassed by removable ramps.

The **National Hall** off Hammersmith Road has step-free access to the foyer. From here, an open lift (W75 L110) bypasses −4 steps to the hall. **Adapted toilet (D85 ST67)** on the GF, and a larger **wheelchair toilet (D80 ST100 +)** on the first floor and reached via a lift (D80).

Olympia 2, also off Hammersmith Road, has step-free access to the foyer. As with the National Hall, an open lift (W75 L115) bypasses the steps into the hall. The hall has three floor levels, step free via two lifts (D100 W100 + L100 +). **Wheelchair toilets (D85 ST70)** on all levels, generally well signed.

Olympia Conference Centre is reached from Hammersmith Road. A ramp bypasses −4 at the entrance, which takes you to two lifts (D100 W100 + L100 +). The Conference Centre is on Levels Two and Three, though Level Two is now used by Sotheby's, the auctioneer. Level Three has 100% flat access from the lift, including an auditorium, from which seats can be removed if you phone in advance, and a **wheelchair toilet (D80 ST70).**

Wembley Conference Centre, Elvin House, Stadium Way, Wembley HA9 0DW *Tel:* 020 8902-8833 *website:* www.wembley.co.uk\venues The Centre was built in the 1970s when access was not really considered. Consequently there are some split levels and steps. For some events, there may be temporary ramping in places. There is a small dedicated CP outside. Ramped front entrance. Inside there are three floors, and four lifts (D150 W300 L200).

Access to the Grand Hall from the GF is via + 16 steps. There are up to 16 chair spaces in the hall reached with step-free access from the lift on the second floor. They are, however, right at the back of the hall. The hall is fitted with an induction loop.

Access to most other conference suites involves steps, except the Thames Suite which has step-free access. There are **three wheelchair toilets (D70 ST80)**. From the foyer, follow the red side corridor (to the left), and they are just past the main toilets on the right. There is also an **adapted cubicle** in all Ladies and Gents.

Wembley Exhibition Halls, Elvin House, Stadium Way, Wembley HA9 0DW *Tel:* 020 8902-8833 *website:* www.wembley.co.uk\venues. There are a limited number of BB spaces outside each hall. There are three halls, all with step-free access to the main facilities. Ramped entrance to Hall 1 from Stadium Way, near the Conference Centre. With different exhibitions, some of the stands may involve steps or other access barriers. There are lifts in each hall (D80 W150 L110 in Halls 1 and 2) and (D80 W250 L110 in Hall 3). **Wheelchair toilets (D75 ST75)** in each hall. The restaurant facilities are accessed by lift and are on the first floor in each case.

Recommended itineraries

We have tried to identify and suggest smallish areas where there are a number of varied sights, where you will find wheelchair toilets *en route*, and where the majority of the places to be seen are described in this guide. Obviously you must study your map, because only you know what sort of distance you can cope with. Both the Collins, and the A-Z Super Scale maps are particularly good for detail. We have in mind the visitor who has only two or three days in which to see London. It's difficult to represent everyone's interests, and you'll have your own ideas about what you want to see. We hope that with the judicious use of other guides, you can plan your visit to make the most of your time and resources, doing the things of most interest to you.

The Barbican and St Paul's

One varied group of sights is centred on the Barbican area. Parking is possible at the Barbican Centre. Alternatively you might be able to reserve a parking space at the Museum of London. Around the Barbican Centre are St Bartholomew-the-Great and St Giles Cripplegate churches and the Museum of London. There are wheelchair toilets in the Barbican Arts Centre and in the Museum of London. Postman's Park offers a possible shady picnic spot, although a good number of office workers will probably have the same idea. A little further afield are the Guildhall, the Clock Museum and St Paul's Cathedral. There's also the new step-free link from St Paul's across the river using the Millennium Bridge which joins up with the next itinerary.

The Riverside Walk along the South Bank

This now stretches from County Hall and the London Eye under Waterloo, Blackfriars, Southwark and London Bridges right along to Tower Bridge. Relatively nearby is the JLE with accessible stations at Waterloo, Southwark and London Bridge. This means that you can, for example, park near the Festival Hall, visit various sights such as the Aquarium (in County Hall), go on the London Eye, visit Vinopolis, Shakespeare's Globe Exhibition, Southwark Cathedral, the London Dungeon and HMS Belfast, and then take the tube back to near your parking spot. There's a whole range of interesting places en route, including the Festival Hall and National

Theatre, Gabriel's Wharf, the Oxo Tower, the Bankside Gallery and Tate Modern, the Golden Hind, and Hays Galleria. There are also some excellent accessible pubs, including *Studio Six* in Gabriel's Wharf, *The Founders' Arms* near the Bankside Gallery, *the Anchor*, and *The Old Thameside Inn* near the Golden Hind. There are wheelchair toilets in the Festival Hall and National Theatre, Gabriel's Wharf, The Founders Arms, Southwark Cathedral and at London Bridge Station. The construction of the new pedestrian bridges at Hungerford Bridge and the Millennium Bridge has made access to and from the north and south banks of the Thames much, much easier. While the Millennium Bridge is ramped, the Hungerford crossings are currently dependent on somewhat unreliable lifts.

Around Tower Bridge

At the east end of the City there's a compact area to see including the Tower (where access is very limited inside), the Tower Bridge walkway, St Katharine's Dock and All-Hallows-by-the-Tower church. A possible extension to this visit could take in HMS *Belfast*, the London Dungeon, City Hall and Hays Galleria. Parking is possible in the UGCP at the Tower Thistle Hotel, or the Minories MSCP. The area can be accessed by the new DLR to Tower Gateway or from the JLE to London Bridge. There are wheelchair toilets at the Tower, in the Tower Thistle Hotel, Dickens' Inn, City Hall, Hay's Galleria, and in the Tower Bridge Museum.

Westminster to Piccadilly

Westminster to Piccadilly is a somewhat larger area containing, again, a wide variety of sights. Parking is possible on the South Bank, see under *Arts centres*. It's a very congested area during the week and CPs are used mainly by season ticket holders and are often full by 09.30. One way of getting quite close is to use the JLE to Westminster.

If you decide to take in the whole area, St James's Park provides a good place for a rest or a picnic. Interesting places en route could include the Westminster sights, the Cabinet War Rooms, Horse Guards Parade with its guard, and the galleries on Trafalgar Square. Whitehall itself is interesting with the Cenotaph, which is the national war memorial, government offices and numerous statues to famous people. Alternatively, you may prefer to concentrate on the Westminster area. The Abbey is largely accessible, although somewhat congested. Down Victoria Street, to the west, are the Army and Navy Stores and Westminster Cathedral. Wheelchair toilets are detailed in the *Good loo guide*, and there are also toilets in the Cabinet War Rooms.

A river trip to Greenwich

Again it is possible to park on the South Bank, or to take the train to Charing Cross. Alternatively you might park at Greenwich and do the boat trip the other way round, possibly visiting either Trafalgar Square or Covent Garden. A river trip is an ideal way to see London, provided the weather is OK. At Charing Cross and Westminster Piers there is (steep) ramped access. Some of the boats operating are accessible. See the write-up on river trips. The trip itself enables you to see much of central London in a really relaxed way, and Greenwich has some amazing buildings, as well as the park and National Maritime Museum. Don't miss seeing the pedestrian tunnel under the Thames, with its Victorian lift. Wheelchair toilets en route are detailed in the Greenwich write-up. The ones around Charing Cross are in the *Good loo guide*.

Canary Wharf and the Museum in Docklands

A surprisingly different and varied day out can be had in the newly-developed Docklands area. There is ample parking in the MSCP on Hertsmere road to the north of Canary Wharf, as well as in the large UGCP underneath Canada Square. There are step-free train connections via JLE and DLR to Canary Wharf. Obvious sights to see include the interesting Museum in Docklands, and Number 1 Canada Square – Britain's tallest building. There is a multiplex cinema in Hertsmere Road, and a vast shopping complex in the centre of Canary Wharf. Development work in the area has not quite finished, but there are already several pleasant walks past gardens and water features along the north and south banks of West India Dock. Pubs and restaurants run the length of these banks, but, as with the shops, are only open during the week. There are wheelchair toilets in the Canary Wharf JLE Station, the Canada Square shopping complex, and in most of the pubs along MacKenzie Walk and Fisherman's Walk.

A walk through the parks

If you want a relaxing walk or wheel, then a route starting somewhere in Hyde Park, going past the Serpentine to Hyde Park Corner, and then on through Green Park and St James's (past Buckingham Palace) will keep you in the 'countryside' for quite a long time. En route you can visit the Wellington Arch, and at the end you can go and visit places round Trafalgar Square, or around Westminster.

The good loo guide

This section brings together the information on accessible toilets in central London, which is scattered through the guide, and there are a few more that did not justify a mention anywhere else. To be accessible, there are two major criteria. The first is that the cubicle is large enough for a chair user or other disabled person. It should have support rails and lever taps and various other equipment, but we do not have enough space to give full details of every one. The second criteria is that it should be open, or use the NKS lock.

We strongly recommend that you get an NKS key, as this will open a large percentage of wheelchair toilets in both in London and elsewhere. A key can be obtained from RADAR and costs less than £5, including postage. RADAR publishes the *National Key Scheme Guide* listing over 4000 NKS toilets around the country, saying where they are.

We have highlighted public wheelchair toilets that are available 24 hours of the day, such as the 'Tardis' toilets found on some pavements **by putting them in bold** in the listing. Tardis toilets are large freestanding unisex cubicles which can either be opened using a RADAR key, or you can pay 20p. They are automatically cleaned after use.

We have also put **in bold** other toilets that can be accessed for most of the day such as those in shops, museums and rail stations. Those in pubs and hotels are slightly less 'public', and you may feel obliged to buy a drink if you want to use one, but if your need is urgent, they can be really useful. Note that some pubs get extremely crowded at certain times, as do fast food outlets such as *Burger King* and *McDonald's*. On Friday and Saturday nights they may even have bouncers to control the number of people allowed in. Where we have mentioned a hotel toilet, we have tried to give the precise directions of where to find it. This will enable you to go straight to it without asking, as if you were staying there (or, of course, if you were planning to meet someone in the lobby).

The *Good loo guide* covers the central London area, and is split up according to postal districts. If you don't happen to know which postal district you are in, then it is normally written on street name signs, for example, Oxford Street W1. Note that pub names are set in italic.

Good Loos - West

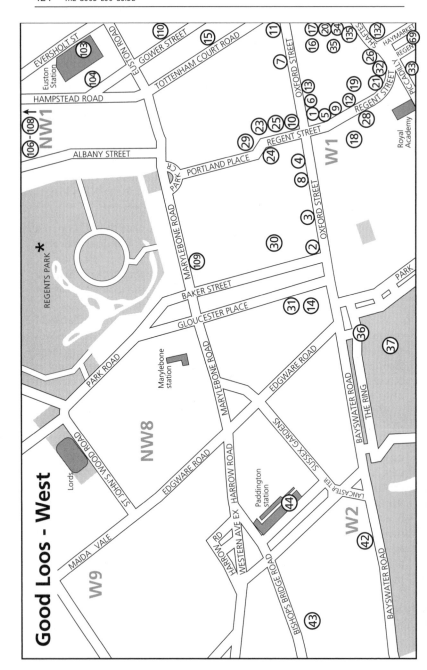

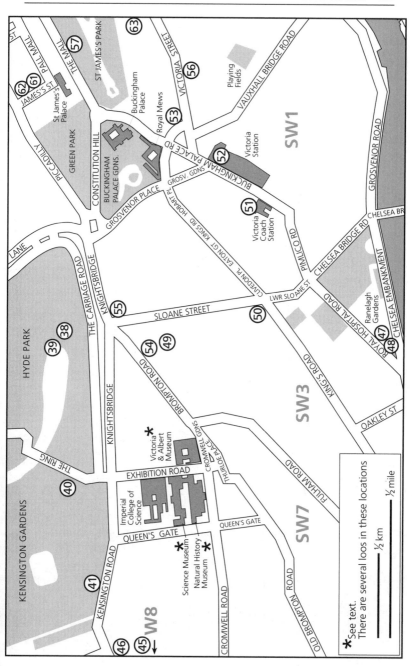

*See text.
There are several loos in these locations

½ km
½ mile

Good Loos - East

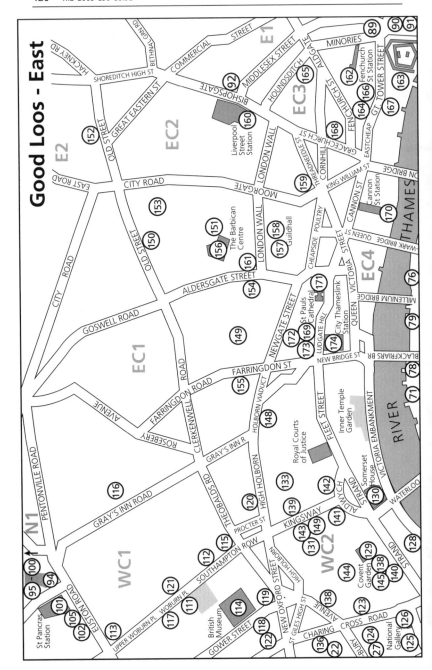

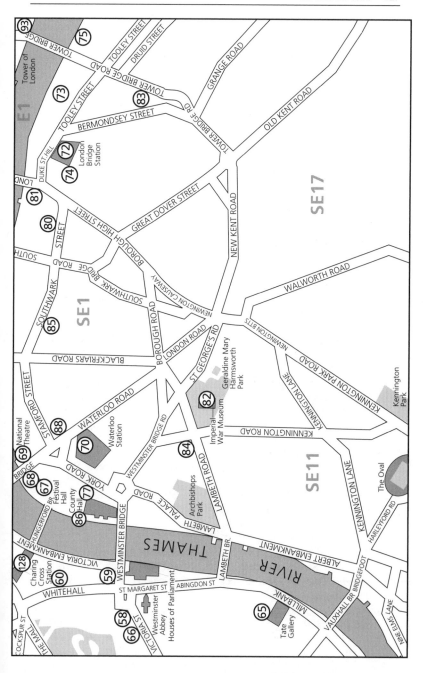

W1

1 **Borders**, 203 Oxford Street see page 375

2 **Selfridges**, Oxford Street see page 381
   Opposite Selfridges there's a Tardis toilet (NKS, 24 hrs) at the end of Balderton Street.

3 **Debenhams**, 334 Oxford Street see page 375

4 **John Lewis**, 278 Oxford Street see page 379 and BHS, 252 Oxford Street see page 375

5 **Dickins & Jones**, 224/244 Regent Street see page 376

6 **Marks & Spencer**, 173 Oxford Street see page 380

7 **Plaza**, 120 Oxford Street see page 381

8 **House of Fraser**, 318 Oxford Street see page 379

9 **Liberty**, 210/220 Regent Street see page 379

10 **Top Shop**, 36/38 Great Castle Street see page 382

11 **Virgin Megastore**, 14 Oxford Street see page 383

12 **Hamleys**, 188 Regent Street see page 377

13 *McDonald's*, 187 Oxford Street, opposite HMV see page 379

14 Thistle Hotel Marble Arch, Bryanston Street see page 91

15 *Jack Horner*, 236 Tottenham Court Road see page 321

16 *Moon and Sixpence*, 185 Wardour Street see page 322

17 *All Bar One*, 36 Dean Street see page 320

18 *All Bar One*, 3 Hanover Street see page 320

19 *Bar Red*, 5 Kingly Street see page 321

20 *Blues Bistro and Bar*, 42-43 Dean Street see page 321

21 *Cheers*, 72 Regent Street see page 321

22 *Manto*, 30 Old Compton Street see page 321

23 *Mash*, 19-21 Great Portland Street see page 321

24 *Match*, 37-38 Margaret Street see page 322

25 *Old Explorer*, 23 Great Castle Street see page 322

26 *Rupert Street*, 50 Rupert Street see page 323

27 **Trocadero** see page 147 and *Sound*, Swiss Centre see page 323

28 *Zinc*, 21 Heddon Street see page 323

29 **All Souls**, Langham Place see page 178

30 **Wallace Collection**, Manchester Square see page 212

31 Marriott Hotel, 134 George Street see page 96

32 **Piccadilly Circus** see page 143

33 **Fortnum & Mason**, 181 Piccadilly see page 376

34 *O'Neill's*, 34 Wardour Street see page 323

35 **Broadwick Street**, 50m west of the junction with Wardour Street. **Tardis toilet NKS**.

W2

36 **Marble Arch**, in the ramped subway which runs from Speakers' Corner (by the park), under the roundabout to the west side of Edgware Road. **Wheelchair cubicles (D85 ST75) in both Ladies and Gents**.

37 **Hyde Park**, 200m northwest of the Dell café see page 414

38 **Hyde Park,** 100m east of the Dell café see page 414

39 **Hyde Park,** at the Dell café see page 414

40 **Kensington Gardens**, by the Serpentine Gallery see page 205

41 **Kensington Gardens**, by Palace Gate see page 414

42 Columbia Hotel, 95-99 Lancaster Gate see page 96

43 **Whiteleys**, 151 Queensway see page 383

44 **Paddington Station**, on Platform 1 inside the first aid room.

W8

(Both are just off the map)

45 Copthorne Tara Hotel see page 106.

46 **Marks & Spencers**, 113 Kensington High Street see page 380.

SW3

47 **National Army Museum**, Royal Hospital Road see page 198

48 **Chelsea Physic Garden**, 66 Royal Hospital Road see page 156

49 **St Saviours**, Walton Place see page 184

SW1

50 **Peter Jones**, Sloane Square see page 381

51 **Victoria Coach Station** see page 41

52 **Victoria Station** and *Wetherspoon* pub see pages 48, and 327. And **Victoria Place** see page 382

53 The end of **Bressenden Place**, at the junction with Victoria Street. **Tardis toilet NKS**

54 **Harrods**, Brompton Road, Knightsbridge see page 377

55 **Harvey Nichols**, 109 Knightsbridge see page 378

56 **Army and Navy Stores**, 101 Victoria Street see page 374

57 **St James's Park** see page 153

58 **Outside QE2 Conference Centre**, opposite Westminster Abbey see page 178

59 By Westminster Pier see page 408.

60 Banqueting House, Whitehall see page 155

61 *Avenue*, 7-9 St James's Street see page 326

62 *che*, 23 St James's Street see page 326

63 *Sanctuary House*, 35 Tothill Street see page 327

64 *Sports Café*, 80 Haymarket see page 327

65 **Tate Britain**, Millbank see page 206

66 **Central Hall**, Storey's Gate see page 179

SE1

67 **Royal Festival Hall**, see page 253

68 **NFT1** see page 251

69 **National Theatre** see page 252

70 **Waterloo station** see page 49

71 **Gabriel's Wharf**, next to the *Studio Six* see page 377

72 **London Bridge station** see
page 48

73 **Hay's Galleria**, Tooley Street
see page 134

74 *All Bar One*, London Bridge
Street see page 327

75 **Design Museum**, Shad
Thames see page 193 and *All
Bar One*, 34 Shad Thames see
page 327

76 **Shakespeare's** Globe, 21 New
Globe Walk see page 205 and
Anchor, Bankside see page
328

77 *Bar Med*, 5 Chicheley Street
see page 328

78 *Doggetts Coat and Badge*, 1
Blackfriars Bridge see page
328

79 **Tate Modern**, Bankside see
page 207 and *Founders Arms*,
52 Hopton Street see page
328

80 **Bramah Museum of Tea and
Coffee**, 40 Southwark Street
see page 189

81 **Southwark Cathedral**,
Borough High Street see page
177 and *Old Thameside Inn*,
Pickfords Wharf see page 329

82 **Imperial War Museum**,
Lambeth Road see page 194

83 Travel Inn, 159 Tower Bridge
Road see page 101

84 Days Inn, 54 Kennington
Road see page 101

85 Express by Holiday Inn, 103
Southwark Street see page
101

86 **London Eye**, Jubilee Gardens
see page 137

87 **Oxo Tower**, Barge House
Street see page 137

88 **St Johns**, Waterloo Road see
page 181

E1

89 **Shorter Street** at pedestrian
entrance to Minories CP.
Tardis toilet NKS

90 *Dickens Inn*, St Katherine's
Way see page 331

91 **Cloister Walk**, near St
Katherine's Dock. **Tardis
toilet NKS** see page 129

92 *Kings Stores*, 14 Widegate
Street see page 332

93 Tower Thistle Hotel, St
Katharine's Way see page 102

N1

(95-100 are just off the map)

94 **King's Cross station**, York
Way. By platform 8

95 *Albion*, 10 Thornhill Road
see page 329

96 *All Bar One*, 1 Liverpool
Road see page 329

97 *Garden*, 179 Upper Street see
page 330

98 *King's Head*, 115 Upper
Street see page 330

99 *Pitcher and Piano*, 69 Upper
Street see page 330

100 **N1 shopping centre**, Upper
Street see page 273

NW1

(106-108 are just off the map)

101 **St Pancras station** see page
46.

102 **Euston Road** by the corner
with Chalton Street. **Tardis
toilet NKS**

103 **Euston station** see page 45.

104 *Crown and Anchor*, 137
Drummond Street see page
330 and Ibis Hotel, Euston
see page 99.

105 **British Library**, 96 Euston Road see page 189

106 *Engineer*, 65 Gloucester Avenue see page 330

107 *Man in the Moon*, 40 Chalk Farm Road see page 330

108 *Rat and Parrot*, 25 Parkway see page 330

109 **Marylebone Road**, 50m west of the Planetarium. **Tardis toilet NKS**

WC1

110 **Waterstones**, 82 Gower Street see page 383

111 **Russell Square**, by the corner of Bernard Street and Southampton Row. **Tardis toilet NKS**

112 Bonnington Hotel, 92 Southampton Row see page 98.

113 Travel Inn Euston, 1 Duke's Road see page 96

114 **British Museum**, Great Russell Street see page 190

115 Grange Holborn, 50-60 Southampton Row see page 98

116 Holiday Inn, 1 Kings Cross Road see page 97

117 Royal National Hotel, Bedford Way see page 97

118 Radisson Edwardian Marlborough, 9-13 Blooms-bury Street see page 98

119 *All Bar One*, 108 New Oxford Street see page 325

120 *Corts*, 78 High Holborn see page 326

121 *Goose and Granite*, 31 March-mont Street see page 326

122 *Myhotel*, 11-13 Bayley Street see page 326

WC2

123 **Photographers Gallery**, 5 and 8 Great Newport Street see page 202

124 Leicester Square see page 142

125 **National Gallery** see page 198

126 **National Portrait Gallery** see page 201

127 **Charing Cross station** see page 48

128 **Victoria Embankment**, 50m east of Embankment station (**D80 ST80 NKS**)

129 **Covent Garden** see page 141. Also the **Theatre Museum** nearby where the toilet is before you get to the pay desk see page 208

130 **Somerset House**, Strand see page 145

131 *Henry's Bar*, 27 Endell Street see page 324

132 The junction of **Shaftesbury Avenue** with Great Windmill Street. **Tardis toilet NKS** see page 143

133 *Knight's Templar*, 95 Chancery Lane see page 324

134 Thistle Hotel Charing Cross, Strand see page 99

135 *Bar Monaco*, 39 Shaftesbury Avenue see page 321

136 *Moon under Water*, 105 Char-ing Cross Road see page 322

137 *O'Neill's*, 166 Shaftesbury Avenue see page 322

138 *All Bar One*, 19 Henrietta Street see page 323

139 *All Bar One*, 58 Kingsway see page 323

140 *Aquda*, 13 Maiden Lane see page 323

141 *Bank Aldwych*, 1 Kingsway see page 324

142 *Columbia Bar*, 69 Aldwych see page 324

143 *Fine Line*, 77 Kingsway see page 324

144 *Langley*, 5 Langley Street see page 324

145 *Porterhouse*, 21-22 Maiden Lane see page 325

146 *Shakespeare's Head*, 64-68 Kingsway see page 325

147 *O'Neill's*, 40 Great Queen Street see page 325

EC1

148 *Melton Mowbray Pie and Ale House*, 18 Holborn see page 332.

149 **West Smithfield**, roundabout. On the east side of the roundabout near St Bartholomews Church and the junction with Little Britain. **Tardis toilet NKS**

150 *Masque Haunt*, 168 Old Street see page 332

151 *Kings Head*, 49 Chiswell Street see page 332

152 Express by Holiday Inn, 275 Old Street see page 102

153 London City YMCA, 8 Errol Street see page 121

154 *Pavilion*, 6 Little Britain see page 333

155 *Sir John Oldcastle*, 29-35 Farringdon Road see page 333

EC2

156 The **Barbican Centre** see page 255

157 *Red Herring*, 49 Gresham Street see page 333

158 Guildhall, Gresham Street see page 126

159 **Bank of England Museum** see page 188

160 **Liverpool Street station** see page 47 and *Hamilton Hall*, see page 331

161 **Museum of London**, London Wall see page 197

EC3

162 **Fenchurch Street station**, upper level concourse, lift access. NKS see page 47

163 **Tower Hill**, almost opposite the ticket office for the Tower, see page 130

164 *Hung, Drawn and Quartered*, 26 Great Tower Street see page 332

165 *Old Tea Warehouse*, Creechurch Lane see page 333

166 Novotel Tower Bridge, 11 Pepys Street see page 103

167 **All-Hallows-by-the-Tower**, Byward Street see page 125

168 *New Moon*, Leadenhall Market see page 128

EC4

169 *All Bar One*, 44 Ludgate Hill see page 331

170 *Banker*, Cousin Lane see page 331

171 By **St Paul's Cathedral**, on the corner of the churchyard and New Change. **Tardis toilet NKS**

172 *Magpie and Stump*, 19 Old Bailey Road see page 332

173 *Hogshead*, 78 Ludgate Hill see page 331

174 **City Thameslink** Station see page 46

Index